D1452926

For a complete lit of books in the series, see pages 343–345.

HATRED AND FORGIVENESS

JULIA KRISTEVA

TRANSLATED BY JEANINE HERMAN

COLUMBIA UNIVERSITY PRESS   NEW YORK

COLUMBIA UNIVERSITY PRESS

Publishers Since 1893

NEW YORK   CHICHESTER, WEST SUSSEX

La Haine et le pardon: Pouvoirs et limites de la psychanalyse III © 2005 Librairie Arthème Fayard

English translation © 2010 Columbia University Press

Library of Congress Cataloging-in-Publication Data
Kristeva, Julia, 1941–
[Haine et le pardon. English]
Hatred and forgiveness / Julia Kristeva ; translated by Jeanine Herman.
p.   cm.—(European perspectives)
Includes bibliographical references (p.   ) and index.
ISBN 978-0-231-14324-0 (cloth: alk. paper)—ISBN 978-0-231-51278-7 (e-book)
1. Psychoanalysis and literature.   2. Psychoanalysis in literature.   3. Literature—Psychology.
I. Title.   II. Series.
✓ PN56.P92K7313   2010
809'.93353—dc22   2010024645

CONTENTS

FOREWORD

PIERRE-LOUIS FORT

"Kristeva's work constitutes this admonition: that we are still going too slowly, that we are wasting time in 'believing,' i.e., in repeating and humoring ourselves, that often a supplement of freedom in a new thought would suffice to gain years of work," Roland Barthes wrote in 1970, speaking of the originality and innovative power of this body of work.[1]

Thirty years later, the qualities underscored by Roland Barthes were recognized by the Holberg Prize awarded to Julia Kristeva—the first person to be given this honor—by his Royal Highness of Norway, Crown Prince Haakon, on December 3, 2004, at the University of Bergen, for her "exceptional work" and its "capital importance" in "many disciplines in the human and social sciences."[2] It is worth noting that on this occasion psychoanalysis was recognized for the first time in an international interdisciplinary forum.

At the award ceremony Julia Kristeva gave a talk entitled "Thinking About Liberty in Dark Times."[3] The title of this speech resonates with her engagement as a vigilant intellectual in a political and cultural context that is both shifting and destabilizing, not only because the idea of "thinking about liberty in dark times" is remarkably current but also, above all, because it is the main theme of many of the lectures the author has given over the past ten years, which have accompanied her publications, her analytical practice, and her university teaching: a presence, a necessity, and a gift. A presence in the sense of the political and ethical challenges Julia Kristeva enjoys taking again and again, because nothing is more stimulating to her than what seems impossible. A necessity, too, as a positive counterpoint to crisis situations, a way of going back to the essential, an attempt at rebirth, successful each time. And a gift, because thought, as Julia Kristeva understands and practices it, is a sharing, a generosity, a promise, and a proposal of human, spiritual, and intellectual opening.

Hatred and Forgiveness is composed of six parts and concludes with an interview as a kind of overture rather than a finale. Certain texts appear here for the first time; others are based on earlier reflections.[4] The reader will not be surprised to find fragments that, while published elsewhere in part, have become topical again in light of specific social and cultural situations, making this collection an illumination open to other perspectives. Nor will it be surprising to read a few prescient texts that echo the current state of things. Indeed, Julia Kristeva is capable of being a "public intellectual" as *Le Monde* recently wrote: parallel to her research, she willingly participates in public debates with various social actors, attempting to share with them her psychoanalytical interpretation of current political events.[5]

The volume begins with "World(s)": the world as it is, as it was, as it might be; the world as it gets by or doesn't; the world, or rather *worlds*, because Julia Kristeva is particularly attentive to singularities, especially when the threat of a generalized Santa Varvara looms.[6] Worlds in the plural, then, to reflect on the rustle of people, individuals, and souls—those to whom the author listens with endless curiosity. To begin *Hatred and Forgiveness*, Julia Kristeva gives us a section on Europe, freedom, secularism, and vulnerability, inviting us to examine the fundamental questions of identity and religion and bringing us back to what is sometimes forgotten when not sacrificed: the speaking subject, our inalienable singularity.

The second part is called "Women," as women have long been central to her research. Among her most famous essays, we could cite "Unes femmes" published in 1975 and "Le temps des femmes" published in 1979.[7] When the last volume of her *Female Genius* trilogy was published, Julia Kristeva went back to a woman who was one of the leading lights of feminists in the twentieth century: Simone de Beauvoir.[8] In this series of texts, Julia Kristeva explores aesthetic and political territories in relation with the feminine. And she ventures over one of the continents dear to her, that of motherhood, examining its meaning and issues, without neglecting mother-daughter relations.

A psychoanalyst since the mid-seventies, Julia Kristeva revisits desire and law, hysteria and time, and hatred and love in the third part of this volume, aptly entitled "Psychoanalyzing." She examines the analytical practice, questions the soul, renders homage to Freud, rereads Paul Ricoeur and André Green, takes a look at St. Teresa of Avila, and does not hesitate to invoke literary texts by Proust and Colette alongside clinical cases. One essay, in particular, which gives this volume its title, is worthy of note: "Hatred and Forgiveness" retraces the clinical meanderings of the destruction of connection to others as well as the reconstruction of psychical space through transference/countertransference. It may be read as an example of the crisis-and-reconstruction of identity and meaning, which is this book's main preoccupation.

Religions are the red thread of the fourth part of the collection. Not that they do not appear in other parts; in this book as a whole, religion is at the forefront. Julia Kristeva goes behind the scenes of faith, examining the notions of atheism and belief, connection and rejection, tolerance and peace, and, of course, love. While at times the religious ramifications of certain texts fade in favor of more humanist or political considerations, they remain latent and emerge clearly when the author writes about the fate of Israel.

In the fifth section, Julia Kristeva discusses Roland Barthes, whose thought she has not ceased to explore, and renders a lovely homage to him.[9] There is an essay on Marguerite Duras, in which she examines her kinship with the writer and studies her poetics, and one on Georgia O'Keeffe, in which she retraces her life to illuminate the sources of her painting—human subjects and aesthetic subjects united and marked by their diversity.

In "Writing," the last section devoted more specifically to writers, we find some of Julia Kristeva's favorite authors: Proust, the subject of her *Time and Sense: Proust and the Experience of Literature*, and Aragon, analyzed in *The Sense and Non-sense of Revolt* and *Intimate Revolt*.[10] This auscultation of the major writings of the twentieth century, parallel to her own vital experience, was bound to lead Julia Kristeva to the novel, which she defines as being "the unbearable elevated to the savor of language."[11] As the author of four novels, *The Samurai*, *The Old Man and the Wolves*, *Possessions*, and *Murder in Byzantium*, she explains in the interview at the end of the book her predilection for the "metaphysical detective novel," which led her to the "novel of the Subject" as opposed to the "novel of the Ego," revealing the dynamics of her polyphonic fiction and her critical writing.

Six dense and varied sections make up *Hatred and Forgiveness*. Six sections in the image of their author: daring, inventive, kaleidoscopic, iridescent. Six sections in which we find a psychoanalyst and a philosopher who "ships herself on a voyage,"[12] a novelist and an intellectual who provokes and incites thought, now as ever.

TRANSLATOR'S ACKNOWLEDGMENTS

To Julia Kristeva, for graciously elucidating certain points, and to the Corporation of Yaddo, for time and space.

PART 1

WORLD(S)

THINKING ABOUT LIBERTY IN DARK TIMES

First of all I would like to thank the Holberg Prize Jury for their generosity in awarding me this first Holberg prize for research in the field of the human and social sciences, law, and theology. I would also like to thank you for your presence at this conference, for the interest you have shown in my work, and for your participation in detailed and gracious discussions of my ideas, which I regard as both an honor and highly stimulating. Finally, I would like to thank you for giving me this opportunity to talk about the intellectual quest which has brought me here today, and how I relate it to the present moment in history.

You have in front of you today a European citizen, of Bulgarian origin and French nationality, who considers herself a cosmopolitan intellectual; this last quality alone would have been enough to merit persecution in the Bulgaria of my childhood. Much has changed since then, and although my country of origin is still struggling with various economic and political problems, the way is now open, not only for Bulgaria to become a member of NATO, but also for her to join the European Union as a full member. All of this would have been impossible to imagine thirty-nine years ago, in 1965. That was the year I left Bulgaria to continue my studies in

Paris, thanks to a grant furnished under the policy of that visionary leader, Charles de Gaulle, who had already foreseen a Europe stretching from the Atlantic to the Urals.

Now, in 2004, I still think of that time, in the not-so-distant past, and of all the efforts, sometimes discreet, but sometimes quite risky, made by many intellectuals and others during the communist era. Thanks to such courageous individuals, Bulgaria is today a member of the community of democratic countries. This fact may seem miraculous, until one remembers the suffering, the never-failing hopes and the constant underground work of so many members of the thinking professions, which slowly ate away at the foundations of totalitarianism.

It is customary on occasions such as this to evoke the memory of one's parents, and indeed I think of my father, Stoyan Kristev. This educated member of the Orthodox Church wanted me to learn French from an early age and duly registered me at a primary school run by French nuns, so that I could absorb some of the critical spirit and taste for freedom for which France is rightly famous. I also think of my mother, Christine Kristeva, who combined a sharp scientific mind and a strong sense of duty with a gentle nature and passed on to me the kind of rigor that is such a necessary part of one's development, especially for a woman, and even more so for a woman in exile. This is my family background, which was reinforced by the respect for culture and education that had developed in Bulgaria during the course of its turbulent history; it is the foundation on which I subsequently placed what French civilization had to offer me. I have a strong sense of indebtedness to France, and feel proud, in the globalized world in which we live today, to bear the colors of the French Republic in the various countries and continents which I have occasion to visit.

There is a line in my book *Strangers to Ourselves* that I hope you won't mind me taking the liberty to repeat here. I wrote that "one may feel more of a foreigner in France than in any other country, but at the same time one is better as a foreigner in France than in any other country." The reason is that, although its universalism may be ambiguous, the French tradition of critical questioning, the importance given to political debate, and the role of intellectuals—exemplified by the Enlightenment philosophers who are so emblematic of French culture—are factors that continually revivify public debate, and maintain it at a very high level. This is a real antidote to national depression, and to its manic manifestation in nationalism. I would therefore like to pay tribute to my adoptive culture, which is never more

French than when it is engaged in self-criticism. To the degree that it is able to laugh about itself—and what vitality there is in this laughter!—it is able to forge links with other cultures. I have absorbed this French language and this French culture so thoroughly that I am almost taken in by those Americans who welcome me as a French writer and intellectual.

The Holberg Prize rewards my work, which it calls "innovative, and devoted to exploring themes at the frontiers of language, culture and literature," and which you consider to be "of capital importance" in the "numerous disciplines of the human and social sciences," as well as in "feminist theory." Indeed, since I first arrived in France at Christmas 1965, just when the feminist movement was gaining new momentum, I have never stopped thinking about the contribution that women have made to contemporary thought, and this work has crystallized in my recent trilogy on Feminine Genius: Hannah Arendt, Melanie Klein, and Colette. You might wonder what the connection is between this trilogy and my origins.

Well, I could speak to you at length about the intelligence and the endurance of the women of my country of origin, many of whom have distinguished themselves in literature, and many others in various struggles for liberation. Nevertheless, I did not devote my work on female genius to them, because I wanted to use examples that were known and accepted everywhere. My aim was to address the following question: "Is there a specifically feminine form of genius?" This question is not a new one, but it still retains much of its mystery. I will return to Hannah Arendt, Melanie Klein, and Colette. But first I would like to reveal to you something that is not in these books.

My research on this topic led me to the discovery that the first female intellectual—and as such, necessarily a European—was neither a saint like Hildegarde of Bingen (1098–1179) or Angela of Foligno (1248–1309), nor even a writer (the writers came later) such as Mme de Sévigné (1626–1696) or Mme de Staël (1766–1817) who, as a theoretician, writer, and political thinker, has always been considered the first female intellectual in the strict sense of the word. I discovered that the first female intellectual was in fact a Byzantine, a woman from my native region. Her name was Anne Comnena, and she was the author of a superb history of the crusades and of the reign of her father, the Emperor Alexis I. This was the monumental Alexiade, in fifteen volumes. Born in 1083, Anne Comnena began writing this work in 1138 at the age of fifty-five, and completed it ten years later; as the first female historian, she offers us an interpretation of this period that is very different from those of western chroniclers such as William of Tyre or Foucher de Chartres. This devotee of what would later be called orthodox Christianity was nevertheless raised on the Greek classics and was a fervent reader of Homer and Plato. She was sensitive, melancholy, and indeed romantic, a girl who was proud of her father; she was a philosopher and a politician, and her writing shows an awareness of the need for European unity, which was such an important issue at that time.

Since I am convinced that a wider Europe will only really come into being if there is a genuine dialogue between the eastern and western churches, and if a bridge can be built across the abyss which still, unfortunately, separates the Orthodox and Catholic churches in particular, I strongly believe that the exceptional work of Anne Comnena, among others, will be essential for thinking about our future Europe. That is why I made her one of the main characters in the novel that I have just published in France! I didn't do this for chauvinistic reasons, since Anne Comnena wasn't Bulgarian, but a Byzantine princess, although her grandmother was a member of the Bulgarian nobility, and there were many marriages between Bulgarian sovereigns and the royal families of the new states that were constantly testing the borders of the Empire. In this region, wars and peace treaties followed each other in rapid succession, making this part of the world famous for its conflicts, but also for the ability of its inhabitants to find ways of coexisting. All of this was present, and prescient, in the work of Anne Comnena, a female genius whom the future Europe would do well to rediscover. Coming as I do from the Balkans, I am pleased to have contributed to this rediscovery. I would therefore like to invite you to read Anne Comnena, in addition to Arendt, Klein, and Colette. Europe still has many surprises in store for us.

Nevertheless, without isolating women's experience as a separate "object" of study, I would like to place this experience in the context of the various political, philosophical, and literary debates which have nourished women's—and men's—liberation in recent times. In other words, I only accept the "feminist" label on the condition that my thinking on the themes of writing and feminine sexuality is seen within the general framework indicated by the title of my presentation today: "Thinking about liberty in dark times." With hindsight, I think that this title could apply more generally to what, outside France, is often referred to as "French Theory." This expression was coined in American universities, and my name is often associated with it. If I emphasize the American reception of my work today, here in Norway, it is because I believe that without the English translations of my books, and without the recognition that I have received in the United States, my work would not have been accessible to readers in your country and all over the world, and it is in this context that my work has been recognized and honored by the Holberg Prize. I hope, in what follows, to be able to place my own work in the context of this "French Theory" movement, and further, to shed light on the difficult, and sometimes conflictual, dialogue between two different conceptions of liberty at work today.

When I arrived in Paris, the war in Vietnam was at its climax, and we often protested against the American bombing. It was then that René Girard, having attended one of my first presentations of Bakhtine in Roland Barthes' seminar, invited me to teach at the University of Baltimore. I could not see myself collaborating with the "world's policeman," as we used to say at that time and, in spite of the dialectical advice that I was given by my professor, Lucien Goldmann, who used to say, "My dear, American imperialism has to be conquered from the inside," I honestly did not feel that I had the strength for such a challenge. So I remained in France. It was 1966. Several years later, in 1972, I met Professor Leon Roudiez from the University of Columbia, at the Cérisy conference on Artaud and Bataille. That is how I made my first trip to New York in 1973, and ever since I have been a Visiting Professor at the Department of French at Columbia, which, without improving the quality of my English, has at least helped me make many friends and find accomplices in the very unique context of American Academia. At present, I have the honor of teaching in the Graduate Faculty of the New School for Social Research—the university that welcomed Levi-Strauss, Roman Jakobson, and Hannah Arendt during and after the Second World War.

Of all these experiences, which I cannot summarize here tonight, and which I wrote about in my first book, *Les Samouraïs* (Fayard, 1990), I would simply like to mention two symbolic images that have become inseparable from my psyche and which, I hope, may give you a sense of what my attachment to the United States means.

The first one is a tiny amateur photograph, in black and white, that Leon Roudiez took of me, and which shows me with my long student hair, on the ferry that took me to the skyscrapers of Manhattan. Since I do not have a picture of my arrival in Paris, this one is the only and best proof of my renaissance in the "free world." You can see this picture in *Kristeva Interviews,* a book published by Columbia University Press. I would like once again to take this opportunity to express my gratitude to my collaborators at Columbia University Press for their loyalty and friendship. It is thanks to their efforts that my work has become accessible to an English-speaking public all over the world, as I have already said.

The second image that I have in mind is that of my apartment on Morningside Drive, which overlooks Harlem Park, close to Edward Said's apartment and to the flat where Arendt used to live. It is where I usually stay when I teach at Columbia, a place flooded with that unusual American light, dazzling and inviting at the same time. Here I wrote pages that are dear to me from *Histoires d'amour/Tales of Love* (1983) and *Soleil Noir/Black Sun* (1987) as well as the books on Female Genius, a place that remains, in my personal mythology, a space of happy solitude.

Many people were surprised when Philippe Sollers and I decided to devote a whole issue of *Tel Quel* (71/73, Fall 1977) to New York. What came across in that issue was praise of American democracy, as opposed to French centralization, which seems so hierarchical and Jacobin by contrast. It was actually an acknowledgment of what seems to me to be the most important quality of American civilization, and which also explains my attachment to American academia, namely, its hospitality. To be precise, in the designation "American," I should include the USA's neighbors to the North: Canada and Canadian universities.

By hospitality I mean the ability that some people have to offer a home to those who do not have one or temporarily lack one. Fleeing communism to go to France, I did not encounter that kind of hospitality, although France has given me my French nationality, for which I will always be grateful. My adoptive country is grounded in its administrative and cultural history, although it is also famous for the radically innovative spirit of many of its citizens, such as the artistic, philosophical, and theoretical avant-gardes that have seduced me, and have ensured its glory abroad. Such innovations often engender violent rejection, if not active hatred. America, on the other hand, seems to me to be a country that welcomes grafts and even encourages them.

It is, however, a profoundly French woman that you are welcoming today, whether you consider me a Gallicized European or the very "essence" of Frenchness. This often comes as a surprise to the French themselves who obviously do not see me as one of them. Sometimes, after returning from New York, while passionately discussing my work as part of "French theory," I am even tempted to take myself for a French intellectual. At other times I actively consider settling abroad for good, all the more so when I feel hurt by the xenophobia of that old country that France is.

In this modern world of ours, in this "New World Order," we seem to lack a positive definition of humanity (not in the sense of the "human species" but rather the quality of being human). We sometimes have to ask ourselves what "humanity" or "humanism" is all about when we confront "crimes against humanity." My own experience, though, makes me think that the minimal definition of humanity, the zero degree of humanity, to borrow an expression from Barthes, is precisely hospitality. The Greeks were right when they chose the word "ethos" to designate the most radically human capacity, which from then on is referred to as the ethical capacity and which consists of the ability to make choices, the choice between good and evil—and all the other possible "choices." It is interesting to note that the word "ethos" originally meant a "regular sleeping place or animal shelter." By derivation it came to mean "habit" and "character" and what is characteristic of an individual and a social group.

I found this sense of hospitality in the United States, which, despite the numerous faults of the "American way of life," for many still represents a future in which we will live in a globalized society, where foreigners share their lives with other foreigners.

This hospitality, which I am so happy to experience again today, here in Norway, was first and foremost hospitality toward my ideas and my work. When I travel I take with me a French and European cultural heritage, in which there is a mixture of German, Russian and French traditions: Hegel and Freud, Russian formalism, French structuralism, the avant-gardes of the "nouveau roman," and *Tel Quel*. I hope that Americans, and now you here in Bergen, will feel that my "migrant personality" is less "French" in the sense of being somewhat arrogant and haughty. As a foreigner, I have managed to appropriate this culture and I hope that the elements of this French and "old" European culture, so often inaccessible and jealous of its own purity, which I will present to you today, will be accessible to you as English-speaking foreigners. Certainly part of my work has resonated in a special way in American universities and has further developed in a direction that I am most pleased with, and which encouraged me to continue. Sometimes, however, I am surprised by the images of myself and my work that are reflected back to me, and I have difficulty recognizing myself. I have never had and will never acquire a taste for polemics, partly because I am convinced of at least one thing: either these interpretations go against me in a useless way, and consequently exhaust themselves in the process (for example, certain militant and "politically correct" comments), or they are part of a more personal quest of original and innovative American men and women who assimilate my work into theirs at their own risk, which may well be, after all, a wonderful way of practicing this hospitality that I have been talking about. Isn't the whole idea of a "transplant" or "graft" meant to generate unexpected consequences, the very opposite of cloning? However, as regards the politically correct interpretations, I have never had the impression that they were widespread in European universities, whether of Latin, Germanic, English, or Scandinavian language, no doubt because these institutions are more attuned to the European sensibility which underlies my work, and to which I will return in a moment.

Some Themes of Our Interface

I will now revisit some of the main themes of my work that have given rise to much discussion. They are: intertextuality, the distinction between the semiotic and the symbolic, the concepts of the abject and abjection, and my emphasis on the themes of the foreigner and foreignness.

1. The concept of intertextuality has enjoyed a certain degree of success internationally. This idea, which I developed from Bakhtine, invites the reader to interpret a text as a crossing of texts. Very often, in formalist or structuralist approaches this has been perceived as a return to "quotations" or to "sources." For me it is principally a way of introducing history into structuralism: the texts that Mallarmé and Proust read, and which nourish the *Coup de Dés* and *A la Recherche du temps perdu* allow us to introduce history into the laboratory of writing. Mallarmé's interest in anarchism, for example, and Proust's interest in Zohar's Jewish mysticism and the Dreyfus Affair are useful materials in this kind of approach. Also, by showing the extent to which the internal dimension of the text is connected to the external context, such interpretations can reveal the inauthenticity of the writing subject. The writer becomes "le sujet en procès": this French expression means both a "subject in process" and a "subject on trial." As such, the speaking subject is a carnival, a polyphony, forever contradictory and rebellious. The post-structuralist theme of intertextuality also gave birth to an idea that I have been trying to work on ever since, especially in my

books from 1996 and 1997, namely that of the connection between "culture" and "revolt."

2. The distinction that I have established between the semiotic and the symbolic has no political or feminist connotation. It is simply an attempt to think of "meaning" not only as "structure" but also as "process" or "trial" in the sense I have already mentioned, by looking at the same time at syntax, logic, and what transgresses them, or the trans-verbal. I refer to this other side of "meaning" as trans-verbal because calling it pre-verbal could give rise to certain difficulties. The semiotic is not independent of language, but underpins language and, under the control of language, it articulates other aspects of "meaning" which are more than mere "significations," such as rhythmical and melodic inflections. Under the influence of Freudian distinctions between the representations of things and the representations of words, I try to take into consideration this dual nature of the human mind, and especially the constraints of biology and the instinctual drives that sustain and influence meaning and signification. This is because we may indeed affirm that in the beginning was the word, but before the beginning there was the unconscious with its repressed content.

I am personally convinced that the future of psychoanalysis lies in this direction, that is, between the translinguistic logic of the unconscious, and biological and neurobiological constraints. At the Institute for Contemporary Thought at the University of Paris 7, we try to bring biologists and psychoanalysts together in their work. Our basic preoccupation is the opening up of psychoanalysis to biology as well as to a more active involvement in social politics. In this connection I fully support and indeed am actively involved in President Chirac's campaign for the integration of handicapped citizens into French society. We hope that this approach, along with a close rereading of Freud's texts, will revitalize contemporary psychoanalysis in the long run.

This "semiotic" trans-verbal aspect of our research is connected to the archaic relation between mother and child and allows me to investigate certain aspects of the feminine and the maternal in language, what Freud used to call "the black continent" or Minoan-Mycenaean (after the name of the Greek civilization that preceded the civilization of classical Greece). This "other logic" of the feminine and the maternal that works against normative representation and opposes phallic representation, both masculine and feminine, is perhaps my own contribution to the endeavor to understand the feminine as connected to the political via the sacred.

I am convinced that this new twenty-first century, which seems to be in such need of religion, is actually in need of the sacred. I understand the sacred as the desire of human beings to think, not in the sense of calculation, but rather in the sense of a need for fundamental questioning, which distinguishes us from other species and, a contrario, brings us closer to them. As a writer, psychoanalyst and semiotician, I believe that the human characteristic that we call the sense of the divine and the sacred arises at the very point of the emergence of language. "The semiotic" with its maternal ties seems to be the farthest we can reach when we try to imagine and understand the frontiers between nature or "physis" and meaning. By understanding the "semiotic" as the "emergence of meaning" we can overcome the dichotomies of metaphysics (soul/body, physical/psychical). My preoccupation with the sacred is, in fact, anti-metaphysical, and only feminist in a derivative sense. If I am indeed passionately attached to the recognition of women in social, intellectual, and political life, this is only to the extent that women can bring a different attitude to the ideas of "power" and "meaning." This would be an attitude that takes into consideration the need for the survival of our species, and our need for the sacred. Women are positioned at the intersection of these two demands.

3. The abject and abjection are concepts I developed on the basis of my clinical experience when facing the symptoms which I also call *New Maladies of the Soul* (Columbia University Press), in which the distinction between "subject" and "object" is not clear, and in which these two pseudo-entities exhaust themselves in a dialectic of attraction and repulsion. Borderline personalities, as well as some depressive personalities, can be described from this psychical basis, which is also reminiscent of an archaic state, of the communion which exists in the act of maternal holding. The mother object is the first result of the process of expulsion of what is disagreeable in this archaic state. In this process, which I have called abjection, the mother becomes the first "abject" rather than object. Artists such as Picasso and de Kooning clearly understood something of this process.

Using the concepts of "abject" and "abjection," I first tried to understand the complex universe of the French writer Céline, master of popular fiction, and of Parisian slang, argot, a carrier of exceptional emotion. Instead of taking the cathartic road of abjection as religions do (and I believe any religion is in fact a way of purifying the abject), Céline insists on following imaginary abjections, which he then transfers to political realities. His anti-Semitism and his despicable compromises with Nazi ideology are expressed in his pamphlets, which I attempted to read objectively, as an analyst, without giving in to the feelings that they inevitably arouse.

My adventures in the very dangerous territory of abjection have nevertheless resulted in many alliances. Many artists from all over the world have recognized themselves in the experience of the abject, which is close to the psychotic states that they encounter in the process of artistic creation. But my research has also given rise to a sharp reaction in some academic circles and certain journals, which affirmed that if I chose to analyze Céline, it was only to excuse him, as if trying to understand necessarily means trying to forgive. That was one of the most radical rejections of my work, due to a misreading. I personally perceived it as a form of partisan excommunication that amounted to an attack on thinking itself.

That "excommunication" now seems to me to be the tragic precursor of a more recent event, more comic than tragic, in which two ambitious academics set out to unmask French "impostors" (this was the name they gave to French Theorists), by rejecting our "pseudo-scientific models," when in fact we never tried to create scientific models, only metaphorical transfers.

4. The concept of strangeness or foreignness, is also, as you may know, close to my heart. Writing my book *Strangers to Ourselves*, for which I received the Hertz prize from the Academy of Paris, gave me an opportunity to outline a history of foreigners, their actual destiny, and the way in which they are perceived in the West, and also to state my own position in this debate, a position which again seems to be accepted with some difficulty. First of all, I believe that in order to fight the state of national depression that we are experiencing in France (but not only in France) as a result of globalization and the influx of immigrants, and also in order to oppose maniacal reactions to this depression (such as that of the Front National), it is important to restore national confidence. This has to be done in the same way we sometimes have to restore the narcissism or the ideal "ego" in a depressed patient, before proceeding to the actual "analysis," i.e., to the dissolution of his system of defense and resistance.

I am convinced that, in the next century, the cosmopolitan society that we have been dreaming of ever since the Stoics and throughout the

Enlightenment, will not be possible in the utopian shape of the "melting pot," universalized and standardized by the market, the media and the internet. At most, this will lead to a more or less conflictual cohabitation of nations and of various "social groups" that will live with and against each other. Combining a certain amount of respect for "national identity" and support for the idea of the "common good" (*l'intérêt général* as Montesquieu called it), this approach will have to replace the excesses of contemporary globalization.

Two Types of Civilization

You will no doubt have identified, as I have outlined these four themes—and I could have chosen others—areas of agreement and disagreement between us. Without going deeper into this research, I would like to take the opportunity that you have granted me to distance myself from this personal research in order to consider the wider cultural and political context in which we work, and in which this collective research has been elaborated.

The collapse of the Berlin Wall in 1989 brought to light the difference between two types of culture, a European culture and a North American culture. In order to avoid any misunderstanding, I want to make it clear from the start that I am referring to two visions of freedom or liberty that all democratic societies without exception have elaborated and of which, unfortunately, we are not sufficiently proud. I am speaking of two visions of freedom, which both rely on the Greek, Jewish, and Christian traditions, and which, in spite of shameful as well as glorious episodes, remain our most important achievement. These two visions of freedom are nevertheless both essential. They are sometimes, as is now the case, opposed. Fundamentally, however, these two versions of freedom are complementary, and indeed I believe they are both present in each of us, whichever side of the Atlantic we find ourselves on. If I continue to oppose them in what follows, this is only for the sake of the clarity of my exposition.

Immanuel Kant, in his *Critique of Pure Reason* (1781) and his *Critique of Practical Reason* (1789), defined for the first time something that other people also must have experienced but were unable to articulate, namely the fact that freedom is not, negatively speaking, an "absence of constraint," but positively speaking, the possibility of "self-beginning," *Selbstanfang.* Thus, by identifying "freedom" with the capacity for spontaneously beginning, Kant opens the way for praise of the enterprising individual, for the initiative of

the "self," if I may transfer his cosmological considerations to a more personal level. At the same time, he subordinates the freedom of Reason, be it
pure or practical, to a cause, divine or moral.

I will extrapolate by saying that, in a world increasingly dominated by
technology, freedom becomes the capacity to adapt to a "cause" always outside the "self," and which is less and less a moral cause, and more and more
an economic one. In an ideal situation the two operate at the same time. In
this line of thought, which is favored by Protestantism (I'm referring here
to Max Weber's work on the connection between capitalism and Protestantism), freedom becomes the freedom to adapt to the logic of cause and
effect, Hannah Arendt would say "to the calculus of consequences," i.e., the
logic of production, of science, and of the economy. To be free in this sense
would be to profit from adaptations to this logic of causes and effects and
to the economic market.

This kind of freedom culminates in the logic of globalization and the
unrestrained free-market. The Supreme Cause (God) and the Technical
Cause (the Dollar) are its two coexisting variants, which guarantee the
functioning of our freedom within this logic of "instrumentalization." I
am not denying here the benefits of this kind of freedom. It has the advantage of being able to adapt to the logic of "causes and effects" that culminates in a specific way of thinking, which is "thinking-as-calculus" and
scientific thinking. I believe this vision to be crucial for our access to technology and automation. American society seems to be better adapted to
this kind of freedom. I am merely saying that this is not the only kind of
freedom.

There is also another vision of freedom that emerged in the Greek
world, at the very heart of its philosophy, with the pre-Socratics, and developed in the Socratic dialogue. This fundamental variety of freedom is not
subordinate to a cause, which means that it is prior to the concatenation
of Aristotelian "categories" that are a premise for scientific and technical
thinking. This fundamental variety of freedom is in Being and, moreover,
in the Being of Language Which is Being Delivered/l'Etre de la Parole Qui
se Livre, a Being which delivers, gives, or presents itself to itself and to the
other, and liberates itself in the process. This liberation of the Language-
Being that occurs in the encounter between the Self and the Other, was
emphasized in Heidegger's discussion of Kant (in a 1930 seminar "The Essence of Human Freedom," published in 1982). This approach inscribes
freedom into the very essence of philosophy, as eternal questioning, before

allowing it to become fixed—only subsequently to this original freedom—in the succession of causes and effects and the ability to master them.

Don't worry, I would like to assure you that I will not go any further in this debate. I have already oversimplified the two conceptions of freedom in Kant and Heidegger. What I am interested in discussing, in the context of the modern world, is this second conception of freedom. This second kind of freedom is very different from the kind of calculating logic that leads to unbridled consumerism; it is a conception that is evident in the Speech-Being, in the Presenting of the Self to the Other.

I hope you understand that it is the psychological and social connotations of this kind of freedom that constitute the essential themes of French Theory. The poet is its main custodian, together with the libertine who defies the conventions of social causes and effects in order to bring out and formulate a desire for dissidence. Not to mention the analyst in the experience of transference and counter-transference. But we mustn't forget the revolutionary who put the privileges of the individual above all other conventions; this is the foundation of Human Rights, and the slogan of the French Revolution, Liberty-Equality-Fraternity, which at the time reinforced the ideas of English Habeas Corpus. If we are able to hear and interpret these various figures, we will be better equipped to liberate ourselves from a certain vision of the 18th century which has become dominant, and which mistakenly takes the legacy of the Enlightenment to be a kind of abstract universalism.

But I would like to return to our present reality. In spite of all the difficulties, we are on our way toward building a European Community that cannot be ignored. In this often chaotic European assembly, the voice of France, which sometimes has difficulty making itself heard when it calls for the construction of a "social Europe," still finds allies in other governments and in the public opinion of various countries. While all of them are deeply attached to their particular cultural traditions, they all implicitly or explicitly share our notion of freedom. We are trying to promote a "social model" which is not exclusively that of laissez-faire capitalism, often identified as "the American model." Our emphasis on this cultural difference is not only due to the fact that we belong to a tradition and possess a memory which may be older, "more refined" and "more sophisticated" and so on, because it originates in the "Old World." Rather, it is due to the fact that we have a different vision of freedom, namely one that ranks the uniqueness of the individual over economic and scientific factors. When the French government, whether on the left or the Gaullist right, insists on our "solidarity" in opposition to "liberalism" in the classic sense of unregulated economic and social competition, this should be understood as nothing other than a defense of this conception of freedom.

We are fully aware, of course, of the risks that may come with such an attitude: those of ignoring contemporary economic realities, submitting to excessive corporatist demands, an inability to take part in international competition, idleness, backwardness. This is why we need to be alert and always remember the new constraints of our technological world, of the domain of "causes and effects." At the same time, however, it is not difficult to see the advantages of this other type of freedom, which is supported in many European countries. This is an aspiration rather than a fixed project, driven by a real concern for the uniqueness and fragility of each and every human life, including those of the poor, the disabled, the retired, and those who rely on social benefits. It also requires special attention to gender and ethnic differences, to men and women considered in their unique intimacy rather than as simple groups of consumers.

The basis for this convergence at the European level, then, is that there is another kind of freedom, which needs to be defended; that, in the post-modern era, it is not the best economic and technical performance which is most important from the point of view of human liberation—although this was indeed the case in the previous period of capitalism. From this perspective what matters is the particular, the art of living, taste, leisure, the so-called "idle" pleasures, grace, pure chance, playfulness, wastefulness, our "darker side" even, or, to put it in a nutshell, freedom as the essence of "Being-in-the-World" prior to any "Cause." These are the elements that characterize European culture, and, one may hope, offer an alternative to the globalized world in which we live.

I recently tried to describe this aspect of human uniqueness when I discussed "Feminine Genius" in a trilogy on the life and work of Arendt, Klein, and Colette. The notion of individual feminine genius can take us beyond mass feminism, in which the uniqueness of each woman risks being submerged, although clearly this notion of genius can be extended to both sexes.

Can we preserve this understanding of freedom as a general human value? This is by no means certain, since all indications are that we are being carried away by the maelstrom of our calculus thinking and by our consumerism. The only counterpoint to this seems to be the rebirth of religious sects for which the sacred is no longer "a permanent questioning," as the very concept of human dignity would require, but a subordination to exactly the same logic of causes and effects, only taken to extremes—in this case under the authority of sects and fundamentalist groups. This means that today's religious alternative, to the extent that it degenerates into a clash between fundamentalisms, is not only an unreliable counterpoint to technological mastery, but actually mirrors its logic of competition and conflict, which it only serves to reinforce.

We cannot, of course, be sure that this alternative vision of freedom that I am trying to rehabilitate today can become more than an aspiration, but the future remains open.

Of course, Europe is far from being homogeneous and united. In the context of the crisis in Iraq and faced with the terrorist threat, some people have claimed that a rift has opened up between the countries of the "Old Europe" (to use their terminology) and those of the "New Europe." Without going too deeply into this complex set of problems, I would like to express two, highly personal, opinions on this issue. Firstly, I believe that it is important that the "Old Europe," and France in particular, take very seriously the economic difficulties encountered by the "New Europe," which result in these countries depending to a large degree on the United States. But we must also recognize the cultural, and in particular, religious differences that separate us from these countries, and we must respect these differences. Our famous "French arrogance" does not equip us very well for this task, and the Orthodox Christian countries in particular feel somewhat bitter about this. My second point is this: the knowledge that we in Europe have of the Arab world, after so many years of colonialism, has made us very sensitive to Islamic culture and rendered us capable of softening, if not entirely avoiding, the "clash of civilizations" to which I have referred. In this situation, what is at stake is our ability to offer our active support to those in the Muslim world who are now seeking to modernize Islam. At the same time, however, the insidious anti-Semitism in our countries should make us vigilant in the face of the rise of new forms of anti-Semitism today.

Let me return now to academic life, and in particular to the question of French Theory with which my work is often associated. I have spoken at length, although too briefly for such important questions, about the political implications of this European vision of freedom. This vision is deeply ingrained in our social experience as well as in our way of thinking. This might explain the enthusiastic welcome that my work has received in some

American universities, here in Norway, and elsewhere in the world. You will have observed that this "French" research, in confronting the American economic, political and academic establishment, in its demand for liberty, often takes the form of political contestation. Nevertheless it is fundamentally concerned with a way of being, which reveals itself in the act of re-volt, in other words, in turning back on itself, in accomplishing its anamnesis, in renewing itself continually through a process of self-questioning. Those who forget this mode of thinking and being limit themselves to the activity of politics in the strict sense of the word, which then becomes a betrayal of the freedom of thought. This is why, in my last two books on the culture of revolt (*The Sense and Non-Sense of Revolt* and *Intimate Revolt*), I discuss the idea that "political revolution" (the French Terror of 1793 and the Russian Revolution of 1917) can be seen as the stifling of re-volt in the sense of free questioning and permanent restlessness. Totalitarianism, in all its horror, appropriated the idea of revolt only to transform it into a deadly dogma. Nevertheless, the attitude of vigilance we now display in the face of various nihilistic political demands, which are marginalized by the "society of the spectacle," does not rule out forever the possibility of the kind of liberty of revolt of which I have been speaking from establishing itself in the political domain, provided that it first develops in the domain of thought. This, at least, is the hypothesis I would like to submit to you today.

As a way of protesting against the limitations of consumerism and positivist reasoning, many of you have based your reflection on our research, and have paid attention to the ethical, as well as theoretical dimension: "French Theory" and "continental philosophy" have become forms of protest in many countries all around the world. However, some interpretations of our thought, influenced by the ideology of political correctness, have radicalized its political implications. This is not to say that our research does not have a political content, because of course it does, but this political position is implicit: it underlies and informs a particular way of thinking. In the final analysis, a fundamental characteristic of our approach has been forgotten. This is that, as I see it from my own experience, our research cannot be reduced to the production of "theory"; it is more than this, and it is something else besides. I would say that it is a process of "thinking through" or "working through" in the sense that Freud used to speak of dreamwork. It is thinking as "disclosure," in a way which Heidegger, and in another way Arendt, expressed it, opposing it to thought-as-calculation. It involves a replenishing of thought in fiction, and for this reason in the sensitive body, which evokes Spinoza's "third kind of knowledge," but also the sort of rationality that belongs to "free association" and "transference" as they are manifested in the psychoanalytic experience.

I could observe that this thought and this liberty continue to develop in France, that intellectual life is neither in decline nor stagnating in that country, as is sometimes claimed. The proof can be seen if we look at some recent trends, which I will now outline briefly.

First of all, the insistence on the speaking subject in research in the human sciences—history, anthropology, sociology, and so on—is becoming more and more pronounced; this does not mean that objective facts are underestimated or ignored, but that, by taking them into consideration, the researcher is much more subjectively involved in their interpretation. In France, we will soon initiate a national debate on the role of the human sciences organized around this general theme of "fact and interpretation." It goes without saying that the part played by psychoanalysis in this is crucial.

Also, and this is undoubtedly the result of the psychoanalytical perspective on human beings, the imaginary is increasingly perceived as an essential component of our psyche, but also and primarily as the realm of the kind of freedom which I am defending here today. We are alive precisely because we have a psychical life. This is the intimate dimension of our existence (what in French we call our *for intérieur*), which allows us to shield ourselves from internal and external attacks on our being, i.e., psychological and biological traumas, as well as external social and political aggression. The imaginary metabolizes them, transforms them, sublimates them, works-through them and in this way keeps us alive. What am I referring to when I speak of the imaginary? Well, for example, the fantasies that psychoanalysis works with. Literature, for its part, offers a refuge for our loves and insomnia, our states of grace and crisis. Religion opposes laissez-faire capitalism and its logic of causes and effects by bringing something more to the "human soul." The human sciences and human thought are now ready for a fruitful and critical encounter with this religious imaginary, an encounter which neither condemns nor ignores it. The religious experience also becomes analyzable under this approach; it is possible to unveil its logic, and its benefits as well as its failings. Here, too, I believe, French Theory can make an important contribution. Along with colleagues in Paris, I recently created the Institute for Contemporary Thought, the core of which is the Roland Barthes Interdisciplinary Centre, which deals with themes situated at the interface between literature, philosophy, psychoanalysis, ethics, and religion. We are trying to develop the exercise of liberty-as-thinking on a larger scale, with the aim of re-thinking the traditional boundaries between disciplines, and this in spite of the differences between the various researchers involved in this project.

I would like to conclude these thoughts—which, given the gratitude I feel on this occasion, have perhaps been a little too centered on myself and my own research—with some wider considerations.

I have deliberately emphasized the European origin of this type of freedom, which, in my opinion, underpins what has been called French Theory. I must emphasize that nobody has a monopoly on this conception, and that the Catholic and Protestant worlds have rich potential in terms of this variety of liberty. Of course, the idea of "being chosen" in Judaism, though different from the idea of freedom I have tried to outline here, makes a person coming from this tradition particularly capable of restoring what we so lack, i.e., an interaction of these two versions of freedom: economic neo-liberalism and fraternal and poetic freedom, causal and "disclosing" versions of freedom.

Earlier, when criticizing the resurgence of French nationalism, I pointed out the fact that this intimate and fraternal type of freedom is indeed a difficult and perhaps an impossible choice. Still, this is the challenge that France is ready to face, and, in the long run, the challenge that Europe as a whole must be willing to take. Personally, I am strongly committed to this vision, and I am doing what I can to contribute to its realization.

In this context, America, the America that I love, an America which no longer has any enemies and which would like to silence its opponents, risks becoming a fourth Rome, after Byzantium and Moscow. In this New World Order, America has imposed a financial, economic, and cultural oligarchy that is liberal in its inspiration but risks excluding an important dimension of human liberty. Other civilizations have other visions of human freedom. They also need to be heard in this globalized world and to be allowed to add their own corrections, through diversity, to this new global vision of human destiny. The diversity of cultural models is the only guarantee for the respect of the "humanity" I referred to earlier in my lecture, a humanity we described in terms of "hospitality" for lack of a better definition. At present, instead of this liberty, humanity is betraying itself in a process of increasing technical and robotic uniformization. Hospitality is not just the simple juxtaposition of differences, with one model dominating all the others, and feigning respect for others while in reality being indifferent toward them. On the contrary, hospitality is a genuine attempt to understand other kinds of freedom in order to make every "way of being" more multiple, more complex. The definition of humanity I was looking for is perhaps just this process of complexification.

In this sense, understanding (or lack of understanding) on the part of Americans for a European alternative could turn out to be a decisive step. The old saying of the French moralists is well known: if God did not exist, we would have to invent Him. I would paraphrase this by saying: if Europe did not exist, the world would have to invent her. This is in the interest of our plural world, and also in America's interest. Whatever the economic and diplomatic competition between the Old and New parts of Europe, our "old" Europe needs to make her voice heard in the "new" countries. European intellectuals have a particular responsibility here.

At the end of the day, my own intellectual journey could have no higher ambition than to draw attention to the diversity of the human experience of freedom. I dare say that this vocation is not so far from that of Ludvig Holberg, in whose name we are gathered here today. At the frontiers of "old" Europe and the new world, Norway has the political and cultural advantage of being in a position to work for the extension of these various freedoms in these dark times. Far from being a foregone conclusion, this project is an ongoing struggle.

Holberg Today

I would naturally be pleased if our work together, and in particular the exchanges which will result from this conference, organized in connection with the awarding of the Holberg Prize, were to lead to a better balance between these two kinds of freedom. I believe that Ludvig Holberg's work was not so far removed from such considerations. To conclude, I would like at least to try to persuade you that this is indeed the case.

As an author of comedies, a historian, and a novelist, Ludvig Holberg was an incisive writer whose humor did not spare his own person: "when my illness attains the region of the heart," he writes in his Second Autobiographical Letter,

I am usually gripped by an irrational desire to start reforming, and I begin launching vehement attacks on depraved humanity. But the pain only needs to move to a different part of the body, and at once there is nobody more indulgent than I of human weaknesses. That is why, as soon as I feel the desire to reform, experience has shown me that, rather than launching attacks upon humanity, I would do better to launch an offensive upon my intestines, as I generally find that my enthusiasm subsides after taking a few laxative pills: as soon as they have taken their effect, the world seems perfectly bearable. . . . Often I have found myself obliged to leave my companions in disgust and to seek remedy in solitude. I admire nothing more than brevity, as a result of which I despise above all else these incorrigible poseurs who assassinate their victims with interminable story-telling.

In order to avoid "assassinating" you with my interminable story-telling, I would only like to remind you that this "Nordic Molière," who was a reader of Voltaire and of Montesquieu, was a moderate man, but radical in his way, scathing about all kinds of excessive enthusiasm, and preferred laughter to religious fanaticism, writing several comedies as well as a history of the Kingdom of Denmark and Norway, a history of religion, a history of the Jews, a history of women (indeed, he is considered "the first Scandinavian feminist"). This constant movement between genres and disciplines nevertheless attained its polyphonic, intertextual unity—the kind of unity brought about by Diderot's *homme orchestre*—only in his works of fiction. How could I fail to identify with such a figure! Holberg's philosophical novel, Niels Klim's subterranean journey, mixes political satire and utopianism in such a way that the satire dissolves into the fantasy, and the facetious remarks triumph over the moral message, with the result that, today, we read this novel as a defense of the pure imaginary.

Although Baron Holberg described himself as an ascetic, and something of a hypochondriac, while managing to remain a comical figure, the first to acknowledge his importance after his death was none other than the libertine philosopher Giovanni Giacomo Casanova, in the preface to his own subterranean utopia, *The Icosameron* of 1788. He writes: "Plato, Erasmus, the Chancellor Bacon, Thomas More, Campanella and Niels Klim are those who have given me the desire to write this story, or this novel."

More than two centuries later, I would like to thank Ludvig Holberg for having given the jury that takes his name the desire to bring us together this evening. Thank you for your patience and for your friendship.

2

SECULARISM

"VALUES" AT THE LIMITS OF LIFE

The passionate debate we having now prompts me to begin with a question often asked in 1968: "Where are you coming from?" I will begin by answering it myself. I will try to address a few aspects of the debate on secularism as a woman and as a psychoanalyst, while limiting myself to three points:

1. The ravages of totalitarianism and notably the tragedy of the Shoah led to *revising* the heritage of the Enlightenment that had taken the form of a critique, indeed, a rejection, of religion. At best, we inherited from the eighteenth century and the French Revolution the attempt to contain religion by throwing light on it: that is secularism. At worst, some have pushed it as far as persecution: Stalinist atheism is one example. The return of the repressed was produced; many politicians took advantage of this for a new geopolitical division. To restrict myself to philosophy, some of the greatest thinkers seized on Mallarmé's words—"Nothing is exclusively secular, because the word has precisely no meaning"—to open the doors of complacency with religious discourse and religious practices.[1] Atheism, even more than the secularism that concerned Mallarmé, "has precisely no meaning." As for me, I think—as I believe I demonstrated in *Revolution in Poetic*

Language—that Mallarmé, this "stealer of fire," was expressing a concern not to eradicate the sacred but to rediscover it in the very depths of language, to the point of the nothingness in which the everyday as well as the absolute are mired. On the other hand, some have wanted to reintroduce religion to address the "loss of values."

But it is Hannah Arendt's vigilant position that seems most pertinent in this difficult debate. When, after the war, Arendt was among the first to diagnose that a denial of faith led to a new, abject form of anti-Semitism that allowed itself to declare the "superfluity of human life," the American Transcendentalist school led by Waldemar Gurian, which included Eric Voegelin (at the University of Notre Dame in Indiana), saw this as saying that totalitarianism was less the product of a sociohistorical process than the consequence of secularism and the atheism concealed within it. Today Arendt's response can be taken as is. Without rejecting the fact that secularism, confused with atheism, managed to contribute to the end of ethics, Arendt maintained that the totalitarian phenomenon was unique and that none of the earlier elements, whether they belonged to the Middle Ages or the eighteenth century, could be considered its source. Arendt is careful to distinguish her own philosophical inquiry from some sort of religious position, but also to relegate the *political use* of the "divine" to the pernicious nihilism she fought with all her might: "Those who conclude from the frightening events of our times that we have got to go back to religion and faith for political reasons seem to me to show just as much lack of faith in God as their opponents."[2] In these remarks we can make out an echo of the opposition Nietzsche and Heidegger formulated regarding the utilitarianism inherent in what some considered the "value" God. "God" is not a political, social, media-friendly value, but an investigation of meaning and language. This is what I would like to say to those in favor of religion in schoolbut who forget that it is just as urgent to accompany that project with the analysis allowed by philosophy, psychoanalysis, art history, and anthropology.

2. It has probably not escaped you that secularism, which has preoccupied the French Republic for more than a century, has to do with women. Where does this sudden discovery come from? Have some women, under the influence of their fathers and brothers, claimed a passion for the veil and called on government leaders to help? Do women in *chadors* constitute a considerable part of the electoral body? In any case, the question has been raised: would young women who wear the veil be better served if they were

allowed to wear the veil in school (failing which they might no longer go to "our" school)? Or is it preferable to forbid wearing the veil in schools of the Republic?

What I hear on the couch compels me to note that a young girl pushed by her father and brothers to wear the veil, and who has also understood and integrated the education of the national school system, often experiences a dramatic conflict between these two incompatible universes. Some have the strength to renounce the veil, but family pressures create an intolerable anxiety that drives them to analysis. Others, who are not in analysis but whose friends tell me of their dramas, form dual personalities or "as if" personalities. They pretend to belong to both sides: they circumvent family prohibitions, while at the same time having trouble taking their studies seriously when these (history, biology, anthropology, literature, psychology) question the status of the "protected"—in fact, walled-up—woman, as wearing the veil implies. Between two incompatible discourses, they "choose," so to speak, academic failure, if not depression.

More dramatically, you have no doubt heard of the book by the American journalist Barbara Victor, *Army of Roses: Inside the World of Palestinian Women Suicide Bombers.* Most of these women are "dual personalities," like the patients I just mentioned: young women who are often brilliant students, who have integrated modern knowledge and modern mores. Hostile to this aspect of their personality, those around them begin rejecting them before then reintegrating them into the family network, then the fundamentalist network, blaming them for their difference and promising them recognition only in the paradise of the martyr. There is not such a wide gulf between these Palestinian girls and our young girls in veils. What unites them is the psychical split from which they suffer, which makes them politically vulnerable and able to be manipulated. This psychical split—which we fuel precisely by authenticating the ideology of the "walled-up woman" de facto, by authorizing the wearing of the veil while at the same time maintaining a critical discourse on the topic of fundamentalism—is fraught with consequences.

A ban on wearing the veil might be a necessary clarification, provided it is accompanied by the introduction in school curriculums of the teaching of comparative religions, relying on acquired knowledge of the human sciences and doing justice to the diversities of Islam itself as well as to women and the veil. On the other hand, the so-called tolerance that cloaks itself in the "rights of man," so as to avoid taking a position, not only makes the task of the teacher more difficult, but ignores the intrapsychical necessity of limits, prohibitions, and laws that signify that "everything is not in everything, and vice versa," and that allow a person to be educated in the face of the complexity of reality, gain access to personal knowledge and make personal decisions.

3. Secularism as I understand it would be meaningless if we did not recognize the *shortcomings of the humanist discourse* in which fundamentalist faith is engulfed. The lovely republican motto "Liberté, Égalité, Fraternité" is not sufficient, as we know, but "social measures" against various forms of exclusion are also insufficient and cannot reduce the ill-being of those who turn to religious solutions. We are forced to note that we do not have a secular discourse on the fundamental experiences of human fate and that the need to create a rigorous, and, I would say, *fate-based,* humanism is making itself felt more and more painfully. Here are some examples.

With the lack of a secular discourse on motherhood, mothers are left with the consumerism of disposable diapers or at best child psychiatry, the latter declaring itself "barren" at a psychiatry conference held in Montpellier, where it was proclaimed loudly and clearly that French psychiatry is in bad shape.

Disability is another "problem area," as noted by the president of the Republic (see the following chapter "Liberty, Equality, Fraternity and . . . Vulnerability"), which demonstrates how French attitudes and national policy are behind compared to other democracies, despite considerable advances made since the law of 1975. I have taken on this problem area as a cause. And so I am in the process of verifying that the discourse of Christian compassion, however infantilizing and *miserabilist* it may be, is the most frequent and effective basis of the still-too-rare solidarity I am looking for in France along with disabled citizens. This "not like the others" exclusion, which confronts us with the anxieties of disability, narcissistic injury, and the fear of physical or psychical death well beyond the anxieties of castration, still causes fear and is met with much ignorance. Could this be a result of the absence of religious sentiment as some suppose? Or, on the contrary, is it due to a poor interpretation of the religious discourse that sees disability as a consequence of predestination, of original sin, indeed, as a hindrance to the French ideology that calls for instant and earthly *beate vivere* (happiness), through jouissance, high-performance, and ease? The fact is that we encounter many obstacles and a good deal of indifference outside religious or community medias, and I am more and more convinced that a true cultural revolution is necessary to realize the objectives of the National Council on Disability, which I head, "to sensitize, inform, and train." I am taking the liberty of inviting you to join us. Because we need a new secular discourse, capable of speaking honestly about ill-being or lack of being, moving not toward *integration* (a term that involves a denial of suffering and a rush toward normalization) but toward *interaction* between citizens who are disabled and those who are not. This is about a democracy of sharing, a very concrete and urgent necessity in France, a democracy of sharing that, as far as this particular area is concerned, consists of

- providing personal assistance to disabled persons,
- deinsulating disability,
- changing the attitudes of the French.

A new historic period is beginning; we all sense it. Will it be a new division of international sovereignty or unilateral influence? Will we be faced with unprecedented political and genetic manipulation? Or will advances in science and technology allow us more suitable responses, in solidarity with the lives of every person? Another human destiny is taking shape on the threshold of this third millennium, which demands a more complex humanism to avoid a new barbarity supported by technology—to recognize concretely the suffering of those who are different, to interact with this suffering in a project of life. Secularism will not withstand the impact of religions without this more complex humanism, capable of recognizing suffering and giving people the chance for a better life, a life plan, a direction. Support for the disabled is part of this and perhaps offers a new, unprecedented opportunity itself. The sciences augment knowledge, but will we let them respond in a suitably ethical way? This, it seems to me, is the main concern of the secularism in place, well beyond political battles and the vagaries of geopolitics.

3

LIBERTY, EQUALITY, FRATERNITY AND . . . VULNERABILITY

Disabilities are *multiple*—motor, sensory, psychical, mental—and *singular*. Each disabled person is a singular person experiencing his or her situation in a specific, different, unique way. Yet, whatever the disabilities, they confront us with incomparable exclusion, different from others: the disabled person opens a *narcissistic identity wound* in the person who is not disabled; he inflicts a threat of *physical or psychical death*, fear of collapse, and, beyond that, the anxiety of seeing the very *borders of the human species* explode. And so *the disabled person is inevitably exposed to a discrimination that cannot be shared.*

If I attempt to share this situation, however, it is not only because of my son's neurological difficulties, which led to an atypical education for him and exposed me to the singularity of each disabled person. Nor is it because, as a psychoanalyst, I have treated psychical disabilities (depression, psychosis, borderline states, and other disorders). But because my frequent visits outside the Hexagon have convinced me that, compared to countries like Sweden, Norway, Belgium, Canada, the United States, and many others, France has been slow to establish a true solidarity with disabled people and to provide personalized support for each of them.[1] In fact, at the dawn of this millennium, while biology, anthropology, and astrophysics explore human frontiers and the most advanced democracies refuse discrimination against people whose bodies and minds test our notions of human identity, trying to incorporate them into every level of society, France, in this difficult, provocative, and promising moment, is still a long way from creating what one would be right to expect from the country of the rights of man.

More fundamentally still, faced with the rather cynical pragmatism of some and the religious clashes of others, I am convinced that humanism— which has always been in search of itself, from its emergence in the past to its crises or revitalizations today and in times to come—can find a chance to revitalize itself in the battle for the dignity of the disabled by constructing what is still sorely lacking: respect for a vulnerability that cannot be shared. My ambition, my utopia, consists of believing that this vulnerability reflected in the disabled person forms us deeply, or, if you prefer, unconsciously, and that as a result, it can be *shared*. Could this humanism be the "cultural revolution" with which to construct the democracy of proximity that the postmodern age needs?

The outsize nature of this ambition is actually built on ordinary, painful, everyday experiences. Here are three, among many others:

John, Claire, and the Woman on Television

People Say I'm Crazy was the title of a documentary shown on TV in the United States that I saw during a recent visit. The film aims to show how a schizophrenic person can be "cured" and "integrated" into society. The hero, stuffed full of medications that make him "obese" (his complaint), might be saved by his sister, a filmmaker who comes up with the idea of filming poor John, who likes to draw and make woodcuts. Thanks to the film, his works are soon made public; he has an exhibition; he is showered with grants. The madman has become "a disabled artist." He can leave the appalling shelter he shares with a few others of his kind, even find a certain serenity, because social services now pays for a home worthy of being called one. Now he is cured. The only thing left to do is to award the film a prize, which happens shortly thereafter.

From time to time, the artist protests against the camera that is trained on him and, to some extent, against those who are making his illness a work of art. But he ends up going along with it and participates, so to speak, in the filming. Isn't the camera a third party that recognizes him, a bit of space between his ill-being and his family? John is not crazy enough to deprive himself of that. More than the charming, "very American" therapist who encourages him with her kind, "social workery" advice, his filmmaker sister's loving recording promotes the artist's "works," which no one appears to understand but in which John seems to have enclosed his life. Then something apparently happens, but that is for another film. This movie will not reveal it.

No words or interpretations accompany his creations: dramatic representations of brains and the seething viscera of abject flora and fauna. No one seems to contemplate letting the disabled artist speak of his anxieties and desires or the exclusion in which "people" wall him up, which is nevertheless referred to in the title of the documentary, *People Say I'm Crazy*. Perhaps he was unable to speak? Perhaps no one thought of trying to let him speak? Perhaps he tried to speak after filming? Who knows?

Today, the patient has disappeared; he is the object of a film and, we might say, a coauthor, and it is true that this venture compelled him to produce and exhibit objects that might even, with some luck, be sold. What success! Clearly, he has been cured. What else could a good disabled person hope for in a cheerful society of all-pervasive spectacle? All the patient has to do is become a producer and/or an object of the *show*.

An immense sadness keeps me from applauding with both hands. Something seems to be missing from this lovely "integration" represented by the art opening and the film. Since the *question of the subject* is not raised, there is no *sharing*. I witnessed a *process*, perhaps even a practice, but not a *personal rebirth*; I saw an exhibition, and commerce, but no *interaction* between the disabled and the able. The disabled person was certainly helped, but it was in order to help him include the objects he made in a circuit of consumption, success measured by access to the screen. The person, the subject, is absorbed by his objects, and his psychical life seems cured, because it has quite simply disappeared.

The malaise that pervaded me on seeing this spectacle has only reinforced my engagement in the National Council on Disability,[2] whose motto is to "sensitize, inform, and train," and which proposes nothing more or less than a revolution of mentalities: "changing outlooks," shaking up hypocrisy and productivist righteousness by attentive support of the *subject* beneath the *producer of images* (which, for example, is what John became), the *subject* in the limited body or mind (which might awaken and develop if given personalized treatment). *What is the subject?* That which in a man or woman remains open to a search for meaning and sharing. Despite the limitation, and sometimes even in cases of great dependency brought on by multiple disabilities, this opening, this evolution, this sharing are possible: that is my experience; that is my conviction.

I also met Claire, Mother Courage. Since the birth of her daughter, Marie, "people" noticed a few indefinable motor difficulties, before "people" told her that Marie, age three, was autistic. Marie's father withdrew into his work: "With a disability, nothing can be done," he seemed to say, without saying it and sometimes saying it. It was a way of disappearing to protect himself from depression. This man's pain had cemented the opening. Sharing had turned into flight. Claire was left to handle everything, and Mother Courage became a militant member of an organization. In response to Marie's father, her own personal slogan was "We have to face it, as if nothing were the matter." Salvation through the Band-Aid of denial, refusal. Claire tried to convince herself that all was not lost (that her daughter would not be lacking), if they "both" could just get something: any available help, financial aid, a place in a daycare center or a little school, a CAT scan . . . the list was endless. The courage, rage, and despair of community work. Mothers soldiering on with steely resolve. Claire's struggle kept her going. She directed all her energy toward pleading her case to public authorities, which she found, rightly, to be indifferent, hostile, and arrogant. Oh, the malaise of the isolated world of disability, its outbursts and bitterness! Ceaseless demands reiterated without satisfaction, suffering in silence for being unable to share the wound, the intolerable, the unshareable! Since Marie's birth, Claire lived in another world, an antiworld, the world of disability cut off from the world. She couldn't bear it any longer and had come to see me for analysis. I referred her to a colleague. It so happened I met her three years later. In the course of her analysis, Claire had taken the time to lose herself in a third party: to cry and share her anguish, first with her analyst, then with her coworkers—work she had taken up again thanks to her therapy. "I deinsulated myself," she told me. "Marie and I were no longer two people with a single body. And Marie found a job; she makes photocopies at a law office where everyone respects her as she is. She even has a boyfriend now."

I knew, as Claire did, that nothing had really been resolved, and yet I shared her joy, wondering: will it always take psychoanalysis and the help of a kindly attorney to "deinsulate" disability? Might disability, paradoxically, become an opportunity to bring us closer to the most vulnerable, and lead us to reconsider the political link itself? To spread *charity* thanks to a democracy of proximity and solidarity, so often discussed but slow in coming, in which the disabled would not expect a kind of generous compassion but quite simply the respect of their rights? To do this, everyone must be convinced that they *have* a right to these rights: "All human beings are born free and equal in dignity and rights." A true "cultural revolution" that perhaps is not impossible today.

Still, no one would deny that disability often provokes fear, when not shame. This shame was recently admitted to on television: a mother who had failed her child, who was unable to make her healthy, still felt guilty (as did the father). In the face of this sort of trouble, you want to hide. It's easy to understand her! And yet, the pride, the unconscious desire for parental power in these maternal tears! This tragic and courageous admission touched the parents of disabled children, ultimately revealing the archaic weight of a culture from which we have trouble detaching ourselves: a culture that posits human beings as creatures capable of excellence, pleasure, and achievement in the image of an all-mighty Creator; a culture of absolute parental power; a culture that blames vulnerability when it does not exclude it; a culture of the "perfect child" who is able to repair parental malaise. Because guilt is the daughter of omnipotence, while the Man-God(issued from the marriage of the Renaissance and Thomist rationalism)responds perfectly to our narcissistic fantasies;it continues to inhabit us, unbeknownst to us, by continuing to deny the *lack of being* essential to the human condition.

A human, too human, reaction. Perhaps stronger in France than elsewhere, since here the Greek worship of natural beauty was joyfully wed to the goddess of Reason; since a prevailing Catholicism—or what remains of it in people's unconscious—prefers to glorify the Resurrected without lingering on kenosis, sparing themselves Protestant melancholy in order to cohabit with absolute power, whether that of the monarch or of centralizing and in fact elitist republican Jacobinism; and, finally, since globalization, which one would think would put our hexagonal importance in perspective, has not prevented us from claiming that we are the best, worthy of the best, deserving of the best, etc.

In this context, to inscribe the disabled within the republican pact—not as a marginal group that merits compassion but as people with the same rights as others—constitutes an ambitious challenge.

Why Today?

We all sense a new historic period beginning: Good has lost its bearings in the globalization of the spectacular and is contrasted with Evil, or rather the axis of Evil, against which terrified humanity has been asked to mobilize. Others are seeking a new foundational myth, when not trying to reconstruct or deconstruct the divine. And yet, "fundamentally," as we say, in the everyday experience of the excluded in their incommensurable diversity, a new humanism is being sought. I would even say that humanity has never had such a rebellious, free, and human ambition. It is not a matter of a new mythology of love. I see it rather as a challenge to nature and to the tragic: the acceptance and support of vulnerability expresses the desire of men and women to overcome the most insurmountable of fears—one that confronts us with our limitations as living beings. I am wary of the term *integration* of the disabled: it has a whiff of charity about it toward those without the same rights as others. I prefer *interaction,* which expresses a politics that has become an ethics, broadening the political pact to the frontiers of life. And it is not surprising that we find a majority of women on this new political front: would that be because after years of feminism and expanding its best ambitions, they are able to revitalize the age-old feminine capacity to care for psychical and physical life, making it a political act, a political philosophy? Do not see in this praise of female caretaking any attempt to reduce woman to the infirmary of the Good Samaritan! As an exile of the communist regime, I am convinced that if the political link is not implicitly one that allows us to care for our most singular, most unshareable vulnerabilities and creativities, it is doomed to run aground in new forms of totalitarianism. On the contrary, inscribing vulnerability at the center of the political pact (understood as taking care of others) seems to me to be the best antidote to barbarity and thus an excellent opportunity to produce, through politics, the *feminine* in women as well as men.

Three projects undertaken by the president of the Republic allow us to consider these preoccupations with a bit of optimism.[3] "A whole man, composed of all men and as good as all of them and no better than any"—Sartre's words could be the motto for the national "Disability" project.[4]

Yet, as those concerned know, this project, no doubt the most difficult of the three for the reasons I have just mentioned, seems, if not broken, than at least unmonitored by the public and not yet on par with other advanced democracies.

Charity; or, The "Political Subject"

Contrary to a widespread notion, charitable organizations are never directly or specifically interested in the disabled. "The work of charity" (which comes from Matthew 25: "For I was hungry and you gave Me food; I was thirsty and you gave Me drink; I was a stranger and you took Me in; I was naked and you clothed Me; I was sick and you visited Me; I was in prison and you came to Me . . . Assuredly, I say to you, inasmuch as you did it to one of the least of these My brethren, you did it to me") is addressed indistinctly to all those who need help—the poor, the sick, the leprous, the rootless, and the invalid. From the start of these works of charity, the Byzantine martyr Zotikos shocked the ancient world by caring for "crippled" lepers: he no longer left the infirm to divinity by "exposing" them, but welcomed them as a gift from God with the power to "sanctify" us. St. Augustine integrates the anomaly into the normal, and with him the infirm become lovable, helpful. However, "houses of God" in the Middle Ages excluded lepers and, sometimes, the paralyzed and the incurable. Where were the disabled? medievalists wonder today. The Franciscans did the most to help the poor and infirm, because, like St. Francis, they glorified them. Starting with the epidemics of the fourteenth and fifteenth centuries and the mystical resurgence, society begins to treat the marginal, but it is still difficult to find the disabled within these blurred categories.[5]

The only exception was the foundation of the Quinze-Vingts Hospital for the blind by Saint Louis: a royal initiative rather than that of the Church, though inspired by the Dominicans and Franciscans. Moreover, the various Catholic or Protestant communities or establishments caring for the disabled today do not necessarily claim confessional ties and offer civil support that, ostensibly, does not rely on a specific notion of disability within the faith. Personally, I feel great admiration and unswerving gratitude toward associations whose often discreet charitable motives effectively supplement the shortcomings of the state. I will note, however, that their actions are based on a generous philosophy of caring and support, rather than on "interaction," and thus take the risk of infantilizing the disabled person.

In sum, in the spirit of the Old and New Testaments, the ecclesiastical attitude toward the "poor" interprets the mission of the Church as a "community of the suffering servant" and *blends* all disabled people *together* without taking into consideration the *specificity* of their sufferings and exclusions. Now these differ radically from racial, ethnic, religious, and economic exclusions, because disability confronts the able-bodied person with the limits of life, with the fear of deficiency and physical or psychic death: disability therefore awakens a catastrophic anxiety that in turn leads to defensive reactions of rejection, indifference, or arrogance, when not the will to eradicate by euthanasia. A scientific approach a century or two old and yet still in its infancy allows us to identify various forms of disability and ways to anticipate and support them for the disabled person's improved development, but it must be surrounded, indeed preceded, by a specific philosophy of disabled life, and a fraternity suited to the singularity of disabled men and women: a philosophy and a fraternity based on a *right to compensation*, which theology seems to leave aside.

Indeed, whether we talk about the *Lumen Gentium* of November 21, 1964, the theological response to Pope John XXIII's wish to make the Church a "Church for all and particularly the poor"; the four texts by John Paul II from 1979 to 2001 concerning his vision of mankind, the poor in the Church, and the meaning of suffering; or Jean-Marie Lustiger's support of the activities of Jean Vanier's L'Arche ("to recognize the disabled person as a brother equal in dignity is to understand our true condition and consequently how our society should function and live"), the believer is always called on to "suffer along."[6] The personalized support of those who suffer from a disability undeniably starts with empathy with the disabled person, but this modern support cannot do without the specific knowledge of the ill-being or the fight for the recognition and compensation of rights within the social pact that aims to remove this person from the compassionate margins, where we tend to isolate him, with love.

The recognition of people with disabilities as political subjects is the work of the Enlightenment. Written by Diderot, *Lettre sur les aveugles à l'usage de ceux qui voient* (1749) (Letter on the blind for the use of those who see) marks the first phase in a social awareness of disability, after its being handled by the religious orders. In the eighteenth century France was at the forefront of this domain, as it was of others. The philosophy of the Enlightenment demonstrates the capacities of the "infirm" and rehabilitates the limited person as a political subject. These positions open the way to education and to the development

of educational techniques based on the disability. The French Encyclope-
dist was struck by his meeting with a geometry professor at Cambridge,
who, though blind at birth, and never having seen the slightest object,
was capable of doing very sophisticated calculations with volume. He had
concluded that if a genius like this could be struck by infirmity, it was because something was not working properly in the "divine order," which was
supposed to identify "beautiful nature" with "divine reason." This revolt
against Christian rationalism led Diderot the deist to become an atheist,
which resulted in his imprisonment at Vincennes.

In the following centuries, there is a clear increase in the number of
people with disabilities (injured in work accidents or wounded in the two
world wars). The state then takes responsibility, the disabled person re-
quests more and more solidarity from the national community, and the law
of 1975 crowns this *second phase*. Inspired by François Block-Lainé, Simone
Veil, and Jacques Chirac, this law took an important step: asserting national responsibility, pledging resources to the condition of the disabled,
and leading the way for therapies tailored to specific needs (notably with
the creation of Cotorep).

Since then this law, made unreadable by numerous amendments and de-
crees, has fallen out of synch with the new approach to disability, which, in
international texts, associates individual parameters (limitations) and social parameters (disadvantages) and does not consider disabled people "objects under treatment" but *emerging subjects*. That, moreover, is why certain
people involved in aid to the disabled continue to refer to them as *personnes
en situation de handicap* (people in a situation of handicap)—terminology that,
far from being politically correct, has the advantage of indicating that the
handicap is the result of a limitation *and* a social response, in other words,
a "situation" created for the disabled person by society's reception of them.
In short, the law of 1975 has become obsolete. For example, the obligation
to send disabled children to school was indicated so vaguely that it has always managed to be avoided. There are still tens of thousands of children
who are not in school because of their disability; they could be, with support. Another example: benefit payments, access to jobs, accessible public
transportation and public places; none of this is addressed.

The shortcomings are enormous, and the state has largely passed responsibility on to volunteer organizations, which assume a large number of the
tasks. Yet organizations do not always follow the most useful advances; they
often get caught up in competition and internal conflict. Better evaluation

is necessary as well as state services taking on some of the burden. Not that we have to centralize everything, but how can such colossal work be left to individual initiative?

· Of course, many institutions in France support the disabled with maximum attention and exemplary care. Yet structures of admission are often relegated to isolated executives, cut off from the social flux. To break with this phenomenon of ghettoization, the *training* of those capable of interacting with the disabled must be improved: from psychiatrists to instructors, special ed teachers to teacher's aides, from home caregivers to personal attendants, all should feel valued and able to provide optimal care.

Today, we are in the *third phase* of the history of disability, which we are trying to establish in France, notably by relying on the "law for the equal opportunity of people with disabilities," which has just been voted on by the two chambers of Parliament.

What Will the New Law Bring?

It's going in the right direction. Its intentions and propositions are bringing radical innovations that may enable us to catch up, provided amendments follow and an effective national solidarity is established. Among the contributions of the new law: the extension of the general principle of nondiscrimination toward people with disabilities; the simplification of care and support by the creation of a one-stop service or a "commission on rights and integration" involving regional disability centers; "personalized compensation" or support through local agencies of technical and human aid; physical and functional "accessibility" in all places, school, work, transportation, buildings, culture, leisure, for all disabilities and not motor disabilities alone; the full responsibility of the Ministry of Education to enroll children with disabilities in schools closest to home; the recognition of various forms of psychic disabilities; priority given to work in an ordinary workplace; the creation of a national support fund (Caisse nationale de solidarité), notably by eliminating one holiday, with a part of the revenues allocated to people with disabilities and the rest to the dependent elderly.

Under the pressure of organizations, joined by the National Council on Disability ("to sensitize, inform, and train"), and after several amendments brought by deputies from both the right and the left, the text of the law has been considerably improved. And, although it still leaves a lot to be desired, so considerable are the needs and delays, it represents an advancement on which a new politics of disability can finally be built in France.

It is here that the National Council takes on all its meaning.

From the National Council on Disability to General Assemblies

Charged by the president of the Republic with the mission of reflecting on disability in France, resulting in a report published as *Lettre ouverte au président de la Republique sur les citoyens en situation de handicap, à l'usage de ceux qui le sont et de ceux qui ne le sont pas* (Open letter to the president of the Republic on citizens with disabilities, for the use of those who are disabled and those who are not),[7] I made several concrete proposals concerning schools, businesses, culture, accessibility, old age, and multiple disability. Among these proposals, I envisioned the need to start a true "cultural revolution" to change the way the disabled are viewed—based on real interaction between the able and the disabled—to allow for political interventions that would finally be effective. Because my inquiry convinced me that, whatever the reasons for the French delay and the shortcomings of measures taken or neglected, the core of the difficulties lies in *the abyss that separates the world of disability from the world of the able*. And it is urgent to create *messengers* between these "two merciless worlds": one of disability, with its sufferings and its protective but also aggravating isolation; the other, a society of performance, success, competition, pleasure, and spectacle that "doesn't want to know." That is why the National Council was created, to sensitize, inform, and train, its goal being to work toward interaction between the able and disabled.

Difficult tasks, you would be right to assume, but ones we have tried to accomplish by

- gathering over a hundred personalities from the worlds of science, arts and letters, sports, and the media, to *change the discourse and outlook on people with disabilities*, with scholars contributing new and specific information to lift the veil of ignorance, and the fears linked to it, and artists, athletes, and media personalities adding their sensibilities and resources as eloquent examples of possible interaction;
- publishing a series of articles in the national and local press to enrich the debate on the law being prepared;
- public service announcements on public television channels devoted to the theme of "encountering" a person with disability;

- organizing a Tour de France of disability: disability and the comic book in Angoulême; disability and citizenship in Lille; psychical disability in Nice and Vannes.

These initiatives, which do not duplicate the activities of other organizations but amplify them and address them to people without disabilities, acting in concert with these organizations, led to an assembly on disability on May 20, 2005 at UNESCO.

We called this assembly "Disability: Time for Engagement." It encouraged a taking into account of people with disabilities by everyone and was held at the UNESCO headquarters in Paris, a symbol of universal brotherhood. It was not another colloquium that gathered specialists and experts around scholarly reflections or generous denouncements. The National Council was concerned instead with rallying around the question of disability those who would normally turn away from it. We invited figures from the world of academia, business, local authorities, and central administrations.

What was the philosophy of this initiative?

To answer this, we have to go back to an earlier question: where does the French lateness in the domain of disability come from? From a Catholicism that is certainly compassionate but that infantilizes the person and moreover does not develop the basic solidarity of the Protestant experience—seeking "grace" through effort and mutual aid here on earth? From an excessively centralizing Jacobinism that neglects community ties? From a secularization that exalted the Man-God and, in battling rightly against the *miserabilism* and masochistic latencies of the Christian religion, nevertheless leans toward a triumphal humanism that creates humanity in the image of an all-mighty God, where there is no place for vulnerability? If these hypotheses are true, with secularization supplanting the compassion of our world, don't we risk getting stuck in this impasse in France as well—an impasse that threatens all countries, but France even more dramatically—reducing the disabled to either patients or workers? John's story, which I mentioned at the beginning, is an example of this: Americans manage this "process" more efficiently than we do, and consumerism triumphs in the most insidious of good consciences.

I would prefer to try to rehabilitate the *subject* in the imperfect body, to remove him from the exclusion in which in which he has commonly been enclosed. I prefer to believe that real and necessary cultural change will help us improve laws and material compensation.

Twenty-five years of analytic practice have convinced me that listening to the unconscious reveals the *vulnerability of the speaking being*: at the borders of biology and meaning, a permanent imbalance, a source of anxiety but also creativity. Since psychoanalysis is the quintessential intimate experience, there can be no politics of psychoanalysis. On the other hand, listening to the *speaking being* is a Copernican revolution of values and norms, opening new possibilities of connection to others, which constitutes the very essence of politics. If listening to the unconscious reveals the vulnerability of the speaking being, psychoanalysis must inevitably encounter the central preoccupation of the third millennium: what meaning to give the limits of life—birth, death, deficiencies? Transferring the religious and philosophical ambitions of an Occident concerned with human singularity to the very core of scientific rationality, the Freudian discovery of the unconscious is probably the only approach to the human that is likely to avoid euthanasia in the name of science as well as the pseudo-humanism of armoring the patient in the carapace of a worker. We all know about bodybuilding; we have come to the point of *producer-building*. Will advanced democracies have the means to support life with its limits and shortcomings, soliciting and favoring the subject within them? That is the issue for which the Freudian discovery of the unconscious prepares us, if we admit that it is a discovery of *the essential vulnerability of the speaking body*.

To sum up analytical listening this way requires some explanation:

Eros and Thanatos, which Freud unveiled in the unconscious of twentieth-century men and women, did not reveal a desiring superman (as certain acolytes of Lacan would have it) or result in feeling sorry for suffering humanity (as post-Freudian orthodoxy suggested). In fact, the duel between the hedonists and the nihilists is one of those French exceptions that do well in the media, but that cannot withstand the complexity of psychic life as revealed on the couch of the contemporary psychoanalyst.

It is *the delicacy of the speaking being* that the analyst listens for today, the analyst who knows his Freud and has read Lacan, Melanie Klein and Bion, Winnicott and Frances Tustin. The Freudian journey into the *night of desire* was followed by attention to the *capacity to think*: never one without the other. The result? Modern psychoanalysis, as I understand it, seems to be the bringing to light of this vulnerability that arises at the intersection of biology and language and a perpetual rebirth of the subject, if and only if this vulnerability is recognized. Situated in this untenable place, psychoanalysts have the (unique?) privilege today of accompanying the emergence of new capacities of thinking/representing/thinking, beyond the frequent and increasingly noticeable disasters of psychosomatic space—capacities that are so many new bodies and new lives.

As for biology, it has been observed that "cellular death" is "programmed" in the gene pool of living beings, so that it assumes the role of a sculptor, gradually "removing" or "canceling out" inherited elements of both parents, chance and error being the fate of this creative destructivity, of this cohabitation of death in life.[8]

From another perspective, we need only observe how people all over the world, who brood over politics when they don't reject it, will mobilize for causes considered "humanitarian" (though not without discrediting them at times). In reality, these are modern experiences of *the tragic* that ask humanity to give meaning to its very *being*—to birth, death, reproduction, ecological catastrophes, health emergencies (the tragedies of tsunamis, "mad cow" disease, "bird flu," deadly heat waves, not to mention AIDS), and, with even more anxiety, to give meaning to the limits of humankind itself, revealed by personal "deficiencies" inseparable from social "disadvantages": I have named the obstacles.

Sharing Vulnerability

Contrary to the propaganda with which globalized technology assaults us, the global age that has followed the modern age is not one of the high-performance, pleasure-filled Man, bisexual master of his desires and/or their debacles. The vulnerability that is revealed today on the couch is precisely that which is determined to deny the manic invasion of hyperproductivity, all-pervasive spectacle, and suicidal religious warfare.

Coming from different horizons, a question is emerging: how do we inscribe in the concept of the human itself—and therefore in philosophy and political practice—the constitutive part of the destructivity, vulnerability, and imbalance that are integral parts of the identity of the human race and, singularly, of the speaking subject?

By adding a fourth term (vulnerability) to the humanism inherited from the Enlightenment (liberty, equality, and fraternity), analytic listening inflects these three toward a concern for sharing, in which, and thanks to which, desire and its twin, suffering, make their way toward a constant renewal of the self, the other, and connection. It is because I have been sounding out the delicacy and vulnerability of men and women who have put their trust in me for more than two decades that, in the plans of the president of the Republic to catch up in terms of personalized support of citizens with disabilities in France, I believe I have heard an appeal . . . to psychoanalysis! Because no other discourse, no other inquiry or therapy, is better able to recognize lack of being and to inscribe it in a project of continual rebirth, whether subtle or startling.

I am not speaking only of the psychoanalytic approach to *psychic disability* (psychosis or autism), which, in the best of cases, causes the subject to come about where he was barred. Without denying pharmacological help or other approaches that facilitate social behaviors, I also want to discuss an approach whose goal is the protection and optimization of psychic life, insofar as it is an infinite quest for meaning, *bíos* transversal to *zoe*, a biography with and for others. What John, in the documentary, did not manage to say or think, although the film (almost in spite of its producers) allowed one to imagine the possibilities. Because other disabilities—*mental* (trisomy), *sensory* (deafness, blindness), or *motor* disabilities—lead those affected by them to situations of deficiency that expel them from the social link in different ways. Because those not afflicted with these incapacities are faced with the anxiety of castration, the horror of narcissistic injury, and, beyond that, the intolerableness of psychic or physical death: thus deepening the most untreatable of exclusions.

Having come to terms with their vulnerability, analysands and all those trying to open their speech to the unconscious can offer disabled subjects the best chance for the desires, anxieties, and creativities of excluded people, those not like others, to be expressed and worked out. Finding our limits gives us the ability to share those of the disabled subject, failings and flashes of brilliance alike, in the full sense of the word *share,* which is not fusion, osmosis, or identification. To share: to take part in a distinctiveness beyond the separation imposed on us by our fates; to participate, without erasing the fact that each is "apart" and recognizing the part that cannot be shared, that is irremediable.

Those rejected because of race, social origins, or religious difference have given rise to political struggles that, for at least two centuries, have taken up the baton of charity and have managed, against all odds, through law and mindsets, to reestablish the well-named "rights of man": a horizon that is still unsatisfying but now a part of "good sense," so that it seems obvious to us to resist racism as well as religious persecution or disparagement based on class. The same does not go for the exclusion from which people with disabilities suffer. The voluntarism of the beautiful humanist soul that sustains a fairly generous solidarity, followed (not always) by legal and social measures, has revealed itself incapable of traversing the fears and anxieties that control the unconscious—and often conscious—rejection of the disabled by those who are not.

It is precisely here that *psychoanalytic listening to vulnerability* could take on political meaning, addressing not only those affected by a disability but the society of others, who, instead of integrating them, might have real interaction with them. Rest assured, I am not suggesting "psychoanalyzing" anyone (unless they seek it out, which does happen), nor am I saying "we are all disabled," as we were able to say "we are all German Jews," New Yorkers in the Twin Towers, gays, or women! I am simply saying this: by lending a psychoanalytical ear to the incomparable singularity of *this exclusion that is not like others* from which people with disabilities suffer, it becomes clear that it concerns us. Not necessarily because "it could happen to anyone," but because *it* is already in me/us: in our dreams, our anxieties, our romantic and existential crises, in this *lack of being* that invades us when our resistances crumble and our "interior castle" cracks. Because to recognize it in me will help me to discover the incomparable subject in the limited body, to construct a common life project. A project in which my fear of castration, narcissistic injury, defect, and death, repressed until now, is transformed into attention, patience, and solidarity capable of refining my being in the world. In this encounter could the disabled subject become not my analyst but my *analyzer*?

I am not claiming that this social contract supported by *psychoanalytic listening* might dissolve disability in vulnerability. If every speaking being is constructed around a central deficiency, disability inflicts a very different trial: the disabled subject is confronted with the *irremediable*, lacks or insufficiencies that evolve within certain limits, when they don't stagnate or worsen. Yet the analysand who has not confronted the irremediable in himself has not completed his journey to the end of the night. And how many unfulfilled desires, aptitudes in a state of vigilance, and possibilities for an amazing life there are in this cohabitation with the irremediable!

Aren't we very far away from psychoanalysis in this dream of citizenship shared with the most fragile? In a way. But not really, if we admit that far from being a world away, a coded language, or a cult of initiates, psychoanalysis is another way of being in the world.

As I write these lines—here as in my *Open Letter to the President of the Republic*—I catch myself hoping that our efforts to "sensitize, inform, and train" can really change people's mentalities. That each of us can slip into our own dreams, the most bizarre or most repetitive, and rise to the surface, listening to those who speak, walk, hear, see, or move about bizarrely, crazily, or scarily. New worlds then open to our listening, difficult or enchained, neither normal nor disabled, a flowering of surprise, worlds becoming polyphonies, resonances, different yet compatible, worlds finally returned to their plurality. Don't tell me I'm dreaming or that this is poetry. What if this were the private face of the politics of disability?

PART 2

WOMEN

4

ON PARITY, AGAIN; OR, WOMEN AND THE SACRED

The adoption by the Senate—finally—of the proposal for male-female parity runs counter to the fears of defenders of universalism. We should revisit the presuppositions of these fears and contrast them with another vision of the symbolic pact on which our society now relies, since parity now appears in article 3 of the Constitution.

Power and Politics

Today we associate "power" with "politics," so much so that when men or women of *power* speak, many decipher it as the expression of *political* thought. Let's consider politics, on the contrary, as the experience of a debate in which free individuals appear and take stock of each other in their plurality so as to better reflect on the public interest. Hannah Arendt already urged us to consider the Greek city as the model of such an ideal as well as favored moments for social rupture and cultural change—before new power or new tyranny comes to stifle such aspirations. And what if France today—which is bordering on "moldy"—engaged in the discussion on parity (and Europe), outlined a politics understood as a vibrant questioning, a lively polemics, a life of the mind that would not be an archaism but a sort of prospecting, capable of shedding light on other people as well?

Women and men of power—as distinguished, despite the inevitable similarities, with those who have tried to make a life of politics—have opposed parity. Whatever their personal talents, the path to power was likely facilitated by the support of a family, husband, lover, or clan, so that these women (or men) did not cruelly experience—unless they conveniently forgot—the ostracism of a political struggle, whose bitterness, though general, was exerted with particular virulence toward the female sex. These women (or men) hoped that the "good will" of political parties, stimulated by a few incentives, would be enough to change such negative discrimination. The first divergence that separated adversaries of parity from its partisans is worth underscoring: it highlights two different conceptions of politics. Certain men and women, amalgamating politics and power, have wanted to conserve the privilege of this power by confining it within the enclosure of the parties or legislation that concern them: the same vision would be angelically optimistic if it did not reveal less admissible ambitions and privileges.

A Metaphysics of the Universal

This divergence is doubled by another discordance with more metaphysical trappings. Opponents of parity have maintained that it would be inadmissible to touch the universal principle of the Republic, which states that the citizenry is one and indivisible: its foundations should be untouchable, at the risk of seeing democracy sink into communalism, after smiling at the "second sex."

In the very French (or Parisian) way, we were quick to be ironic about this debate: what difference does it make if the universal is sexed or not, people said. It would interest no one outside the sixth arrondissement and a few purists of republican Jacobinism. But the question is more serious, because it touches on what is most fundamental about the Republic, insofar as republican universalism is in fact the *foundation* of public jurisdiction and public morale. Shielded since the Revolution from religious authority, liberated from divine right and having managed to inscribe the separation of Church and State into its laws, the Republic has no other function than to ensure the universality of the citizen. That is to say, Universality is our God; that is what guarantees each citizen—regardless of sex, origin, belief, and so on—equal access to rights, all rights. To touch this universality amounts to touching the republican sacred: the issue at hand is a basic one—it is nothing other than the question of women's relationship to the foundation, which is to say, the sacred.

Now we mustn't forget that the universalist principle—a sacred principle whose generosity, with its feats and limitations, has been proven—descends directly from the One unity of Intellect and Being, which, since Plato's metaphysics by way of the autarchy of late Hellenism, constituted the foundation of Roman citizenship. Two thousand years of politics have been inspired by this universality (though all its multiple, more or less felicitous variants cannot be enumerated here) at the basis of religious as well as partisan institutions (from the Vatican to the Élysée, not to mention the Kremlin). The founders of the Republic, among other descendents of the universal, managed to translate it in the boldest, most appropriate way for the history in progress, by molding it in the shape of a universal citizenry. The sacred introduced into political legislation this way would consecrate democracy and make the French Republic one of the most egalitarian regimes in the world, along with the one that was issued from the American Revolution. This sacred excluded foreigners, as we soon found out: but the prosperity of the United States over the past two centuries and its dynamism, still alive today, do not raise the question of the citizenship of migrants and other "undocumented" people, except with prudence and parsimony. The metaphysical universal, like its republican variant, excluded women in a similar way: do we need to be reminded of the numerous studies on discrimination against women in postrevolutionary society, notably in parties and labor unions on the left? The regression in relation to the spirit of the Enlightenment is due not only to a wariness in regard to women, thought to be easy victims of the Church, but also to much deeper philosophical and sexist prejudices. We have often criticized the occidentalist, European limits of this universalism that ignores other cultures.

More profoundly, and beyond regional ideology, metaphysics itself, subjacent to universalism, is made this way: the body, and sex along with it, being effaced or rather becoming homologous to the One—the unity of Intellect and Being caught in the quest for Truth and Beauty. The worship of the One celebrates unity of thought as an invisible activity, capable of mastering the universe as well as the human beings unified and globalized by it; and it is expressed in monotheism as the worship of *one* God. Whether it is explicitly a matter of *one* paternal God or *one* abstract principle, the universal is sacrificial: in the sense that all mental representation (sign, idea, thought) abandons, loses, or sacrifices matter, the thing or object to which representation refers. That is why the philosophers of Antiquity were able to think of this universalizing One as turned toward death, the "color of death": in Indo-European languages the sacred is a unifying "sacrifice" (from the Latin *sacer*) that separates, forbids, and pacifies the social pact. Yet a second type of sacred is suggested in the same societies, signifying "overflowing life" and "growth" (from the Avestan *spenta*) that refers to fertility and force of spirit. The phallic rites of veiling and unveiling, in the Mediterranean mysteries, and the celebration of paternal power, finally, in the monotheist religions, complete the panoply of universalist metaphysics for our civilization. And even when a tradition like Taoism recognizes two universals, the *yin* and the *yang*, the feminine and the masculine, the rational governing of subjects and affairs under the aegis of authority imposes recourse to a certain universalism with Confucius, source of domination and distributor of hierarchies. It would take the slow development of technology and the mutations it induced in social links for this founding universality to be inflected toward plurality: notably in the form of protestant communalism, among other scissions, whose libertarian aspirations were not exempt, as we know, from dogmatic, sectarian, and repressive deviations. If it is true that metaphysics is a complex and cumbersome heritage, its dismantlement is no less risky or problematic. Inscribing sexual difference in the universal is one decisive gesture in this process of endless dismantling: an experience that has nothing to do with rejection but everything to do with redefinition.

It is here that the female aspiration to parity in republican universalism has emerged today. As speaking, thinking beings, women participate in this sacrificial universality, this "being-for-death" on the metaphysical level and, on the level of human affairs, in citizenship that is equally constricting and equally protective for everyone. However, insofar as political life is not contemplation or government founded on domination, even the perspicacious domination of the wise, and if, instead, it is a collective activity involving singular and different actors, women as potential and increasingly real actors in this collective life ask to be recognized in their difference.

Indeed, a political life is not based on submission to equality alone, however beneficial. A political life, which is not political power, is founded (or, in any case, may be founded) without renouncing the universal principle, by including the recognition of different actors. "God created man and woman," the Bible tells us. Jesus, quintessential Man of action, emphasized the conjunction "and," the indication of difference: the Christian innovator needed different human beings so that the religious and political activity he was inaugurating could be oriented toward freedom through debate. Conversely, St. Paul, who was a man of salvation, favored the alternative "or," "man or woman" being the indistinct ensemble of all the faithful saved in the universality of faith. Starting with this first difference between the sexes posited by the biblical text and accentuated by the mystery of Christ's incarnation (and despite the often repressive dogmatism), the singularity and respect of every individual was demanded vigorously first by Scotism, then by the rights of man in the secular mutation of Christianity. So that it is *singularity* that remains the goal—now more than ever, beyond *parity* and along with it—of an advanced democracy, that is, one based on consent in negotiating conflicts.

As soon as the One is incarnated and metaphysics timidly concerns itself with humanity (vibrant because plural), it makes its way toward the recognition of differences, sexual difference primary among them yet irreducible to the others, because it establishes the life of the species, which is inevitably political. That this difference is *also* natural does not in any way reduce it to biology: social factors and the specific relationships of the two sexes to meaning (which expresses their relationship to the Universal) structure the female "gender" based on the female "sex" and the male "gender" based on the male "sex." But it is based on this sexual difference that culture is built; and one need only take a glance at the elementary structures of kinship, from so-called savage societies to our own, to see that the recognition of sexual difference gives human culture its specificity, which, against the grain and definitively, gives it its meaning. So that the history of civilizations is a long variation on and slow evolution of the thought and rules concerning this foundational difference, thereby creating the multiple combinations of human groupings.

Is female difference pure biology or at best a subtle sensibility without significant impact on the thought and behavior of women? Opponents of parity have seemed to suggest this by referring . . . to Freud. When, on the contrary, the founder of psychoanalysis never ceased to assert the symbolic differences associated with biological destiny, giving way perhaps to a misogyny that at times discredited women but never underestimated their differences! Does psychic difference have any influence on thought and citizenship? To be continued . . . In any case, if over half of humanity—namely, women—contributed nothing different to thought and citizenship, it would appear urgent to accord this half the means to make themselves heard, notably in politics—especially in politics!—so that other areas could also be transformed, within their own logic. In the hypothesis of the symbolic, professional, or political identity of women and men, the universalist principle could only be expanded by taking into account this half of humankind, which up until now has found itself cast aside.

Even if it is to be feared that the domination of technology may confirm the metaphysical tendency toward standardization that is consecutive to universality, and that women, good girls and good students, may only enter political space in order to manage the power of the city and business as well as men—perhaps even better than men—but not in other ways than men. That is not the only hypothesis, but nothing says that, in the future, political women will be anything other than the brilliant daughters of their fathers, who, we have seen over the past few decades, govern states as if they were men, "real" men!

As for women's *difference* (differences of sexuality, bisexuality, mentality, thought, relationships to meaning and to political power), it would not be fair to pretend that this is a new claim. After Simone de Beauvoir, the French feminist movement since 1968 has clearly expressed these positions and, whatever its mistakes or excesses, it marked the struggle of women on the planet by the psychoanalytic and political affirmation of this difference.

The New Motherhood

Motherhood itself, through the voice of a few women, if not the entire movement, was also claimed at the time as the free realization of each and an invaluable contribution to civilization. Motherhood is certainly not the only thing that differentiates women from men, but it remains essential. Religions and various fundamentalisms have so brutally assigned women to reproduction alone, and, in counterpoint, female liberation movements have so ferociously opposed this "repression" that—against all evidence—it seems difficult to speak of motherhood today without being accused of normative thinking. Now it is precisely in this experience that the specific relationship of women to meaning and to the other is completed, refined, and differentiated: another who is the child, neither the object of erotic desire nor the object of physiological need, but another subject. The beginning of this otherness, of this enigmatic love of the different, which the Scriptures encourage: "Love thy neighbor as thyself." If this precept seems impossible to us, isn't it because beyond exceptional mystical love it conveys the optimal—but very difficult—connection between a mother and her child and vice versa? It may be that by deepening this link, by becoming conscious of its risks and glories, women may shift it from private life or aesthetics, to which tradition has confined it, toward the city, so as to adapt their speech to the level of this connection. This would not be the least of their contributions to a politics that has yet to be constructed, not as a regime of authority and domination but as a harmonization of differences, which is precisely where modern democracies are heading now.

For economic reasons, women devoted to female emancipation and particularly to the debate on parity tend to be women without children or women who share masculine identification to such an extent that motherhood seems oppressive, inopportune, or, at the very least, secondary. In contrast, when supporters of parity place the valorization of the maternal vocation at the forefront, they promise a political destiny to the large majority of women, mothers of families. Which is enough to threaten the more or less virile militants managing "their" private domain of female emancipation. Don't let them tell you the change in the Constitution won't help the average housewife become a woman of politics! On the contrary, the law, and particularly the highest law of the Republic, has a symbolic and educational value that escapes no one and whose effects are major because they bring with them a cascade of concrete measures; as a source of more public debate than any other legal measure, it is profoundly modifying mental attitudes.

Finally, since parity also addresses so-called ordinary women, which is to say, mothers, a new way of thinking about the species is being inaugurated. Are we destined to have "artificial" or "assisted" reproduction, "cloning," increasingly "modern" and "blended" families? Perhaps, but then another humanity is taking shape, very different from the current Homo sapiens, with its sexual differences, prohibitions, codes of meaning, and moral codes. Unless mothers stop giving birth to children in order to be seen as "having parity" with men and participate fully in the construction of meaning in the political arena . . . which they will leave to their descendents . . . ?

The control of procreation has not made women superfluous nor has it identified them with men, as some claimed to believe or fear. Paradoxically, by liberating themselves from natural risks, women have become the deciders of procreation as well as human fate on every level. As a result, their importance in social life and political life, now and in times to come, goes beyond the value they might have had in matrilineal societies and, without any relationship with a new type matriarchy, this importance brings with it a necessary symbolic and political recognition. It is a matter, let us gravely intone, of nothing more or less than the future of mankind.

Clearly, sexual difference seen this way cannot be confused with the identity politics of various groups formed according to biology, history, or behavior. If by chance the threat of that existed, a legislator could certainly prevent it with a restrictive clause reserving positive discrimination for women, leaving out any other social, religious, or political category—which they are not doing. And though this positive discrimination might seem humiliating to many of us, it is not only a necessary remedial measure but a logical necessity. It must be said that, on the eve of the third millennium, we have no "values" other than life; we expect politics to go beyond the management to which it condemns itself, to open to the meaning of our human lives, and if this is the objective of the redefinition taking root in the republican pact, its universality is realized for two.

Parity ultimately reflects a humanity brought back to its constitutive and increasing supreme duality. A humanity that has not forgotten the meaning of the sacred, sacrifice, or procreation, but that associates it explicitly, equally, with women, and consequently modifies the foundations of the social contract by inviting men, through reciprocity, to find a new balance for themselves in a universality that has long been dual, without admitting it. The shifting meanings of feminine and masculine, as well as their concrete realizations, can only be developed and supported this way: psychoanalysis, ahead of other approaches in the domain of psychic sexuality, will also have an opportunity to counter its current relative discredit.

As for France, which has dealt with metaphysics in the political arena for two centuries, inscribing parity in its Constitution gives it the advantage of formulating this consciousness for the entire world, possibly changing civilization.

5

FROM MADONNAS TO NUDES

A REPRESENTATION OF FEMALE BEAUTY

The reflections here are not intended to be an inventory of images of women in Western art over the past two thousand years. Rather, I will try to explore how the idea of "femininity," specific to Christianity, led to the crystallization of a certain notion of "beauty" and how this conception of beauty in turn influenced the notion of "sexual difference," and the way we think of women, well beyond aesthetics.

I would like to place this brief voyage through beauty and the feminine under the sign of Ronsard, "Votre oeil me fait un été dans mon âme," which I read as: Beauty is the soul made fully visible, like a flower in summer light. Nothing intimate is hidden; everything can be unveiled by the viewer's eye. The infiniteness of the mind, and the technology that manifests it, wards off death through the infiniteness of representation, which is pleasure. The pleasure of seeing and revealing my soul is called beauty.

A Smile: Seeing, Mirror, Miracle

Beauty and, in particular, female beauty, is the most surprising and paradoxical invention of Christianity—its miracle, in the true sense of the term, and the direct consequence of the initial miracle, the Incarnation.

What is a miracle? In Latin, *mirus, -a, -um*, "astonishing," "strange," "marvelous," goes back to the Sanskrit root *smayate*: "to laugh." In the memory of this word, there is an invitation to admire with pleasure—the pleasure of seeing and revealing (oneself). The smile, which is the most spiritual of the physical manifestations, is at the source of the identity the mirror reflects back to us (a baby becomes a child when he smiles at his image in the mirror). All marvels have their source in this jubilatory alchemy of a demonstrable spirituality. The miracle of female beauty is inscribed in this visibility of the smile, which presents the intimate while allowing it to remain enigmatic. So, along with the *mirror*, Mona Lisa's *smile* summed up female beauty in our civilization, before Leonardo's famous painting underwent the sacrilege Marcel Duchamp would perpetrate against it but that Rimbaud had already written about in *A Season in Hell*: "One evening I seated Beauty on my knees. / And I found her bitter. / And I cursed her." It took almost two thousand years to get to this point. And today I would like to retrace the major phases of this focus on the beautiful in femininity.

First, a few reminders:

1. This beauty—which might be called a miracle, mirror, or smile—is preceded by Greek Being, which is revealed in appearance and phenomena and by the worship (also Greek) of the harmonious body, preferably male, but also female: the reemergence of Greek and Roman antiquity in Christian art fertilizes and modifies it, to which I will return.

This beauty coiled in the feminine is also preceded by the invisible Jewish God, whose traces can be found in the elusive Love that sets the Shulamite aflame—precisely because it is elusive—in the Song of Songs. The modern will find this ode to the invisible even in Freud, who recommends "we close our eyes" in order to know ourselves, and in Levinas, who asserts, "The best way of encountering the other is not even to notice the color of his eyes!"[1]

2. In the negotiation that occurs between the invisible truth of the Bible and the Greek worship of appearance, the Christian miracle was nothing other than a manifestation of infinity as the infiniteness of the *amorous soul* in a body devoted to the *other*.

Today we think we know that the pleasure of seeing is specific to the man and even more to the male—the phallic subject with the penetrating gaze. As for the woman—is it because of her body, hollow, vaginal, and uterine, her jouissance, which is not visible (except in the smile, which might be feigned!) or because of her removal from public space, her confinement to private space?—she allows herself to be seen, asks to be seen, calls for the connection of the gaze, adorns herself for it, needs the eyes of the other in order to be. In the dialectic of seeing/being seen, the female occupies the place of being seen. But if the female beauty that follows from this is not only a fetish—an object of exchange and constant embellishment, as a certain militant feminism feared—it is because the pleasure of seeing is immediately caught in the net of the Christian logic that maintains two principles of faith: the *Incarnation* and *Love*.

It is indeed through woman that Incarnation occurs: Mary's body is indispensable to the visible coming into the world of the invisible God-Father. Yet what is being made to appear is not a body as such but an amorous body, love being this assumption of the self and this devotion to the other whose highest degree, as Hegel would say, is the "subject's identification with another person of another sex." Based on desire, love would be this "spiritualized physical relationship" that brings everything into its orbit and only values objects in terms of their link to love. As Hegel's *Aesthetics* concludes, love is revealed in all its beauty in the character of women. We cannot overemphasize the genius of a Christianity that has linked the fate of love to woman.

If love can be represented thanks to the Nativity, which is its proof, invisibility no longer exists, and everything is beautiful, if everything is love. In other words: *it is not the thing or the act or the Greek exploit or Pompeian or tantric sexual prowess that are admirable but the amorous psychical interiority* that underlies them. Stendhal was mistaken when he wrote that beauty is a "promise of happiness." The opposite is true: love is a promise of beauty.

Narcissus's face-to-face encounter with his own image was catastrophic, as we know from Ovid. But this encounter was transformed with Plotinus and Christianity in the first years of our era in a gesture—hands joined in prayer—signaling an amorous introspection of the Self with the self, possible if and only if a third party observes and loves us, the Plotinian νοῦς, or the Christians' God the Father. To modulate desire-pleasure in an idealization of the other: that is what reconciles narcissism and love, the mirror and the link, pleasure with others and concern for others. Female sexuality, turned more toward the interior and the invisible—for economic and historical reasons as well as biological ones, no doubt too numerous to address here—could only be recognized, received, and favored in the logic of this love, traced this way. And which would become that of conjugality and fidelity, in the image of the link that unites Christ to his Church, for better or worse.

3. The history of this beauty, which merged with Western art history, would constitute a series of what must be called *the* representations of women, historic versions of femininity in our civilization, examples of which follow. If there is not an "essence of the feminine," it is because we find successive forms for it, a modifiable and historically constructed figurability. *The history of femininity is the history of the feminine as Western artists have depicted it, notably painters.* Literature espouses the canons of this history and sometimes precedes them but never contradicts them; it is the immediacy of the visible that imposes them as canons for all of civilization on the psychological, economic, and political levels. Dante (1263–1321) and his Beatrice are contemporaries of Giotto (1266–1337) and precede Fra Angelico (1400–1455) and Bellini (1432–1516); Proust (1871–1922), who defines "style" as a "vision," exists alongside the Impressionists; Georges Bataille (1897–1962) and Joyce (1882–1941) live in the time of Picasso (1881–1973).

4. The love of the Father and of the Son can first be seen in the modality of *iconic reserve* manifested by Byzantine icons, the first permitted Christian representations. The icons' modesty, a sparseness, indeed a sort of frugality of the visible, closer to etching than figuration, is meant to contemplate what theology calls kenosis, which is a confrontation with nothingness, the ordeal of death, the violence of hell, and martyrdom. This stumbling block of nothingness touched on by the icon is nevertheless made observable, so that by being manifested and enduring under the gaze, death or kenosis predict or prescribe resurrection. Nevertheless—starting with this period, which could certainly be called "economical" in terms of representation— the central role of the Virgin in orthodoxy and its iconography signals the extent to which the mystery of loving man acceding to the visible relies on Mary, mother of God, who allows him to become incarnate, become "flesh."

Figuration softens the Byzantine canon even more: we see it already in the Macedonian icons of the twelfth century whose expansion was mysteriously suspended, no doubt by the Turkish invasion, for one thing. Then, on the tympanum of the Bourges Cathedral in the thirteenth century, female bodies delivered from sin appeared for the first time: gracious figures rising from the dead, happily leaving their tombs. Finally, fifty years later, Giotto's frescoes on the walls of the Arena Chapel in Padua offered the first nudes in European painting.

We can follow this passage from madonnas to nudes in the work of a single, and in this case exemplary, painter—Giovanni Bellini—though the process develops during the entire Renaissance and the periods that follow. We find that the nuances of love are reserved, not exclusively but with particular insistence, for femininity. Motherhood, seduction, cruelty: the palette of psychical beauty becomes an economy of the feminine.

In other words, love—to the point of death, for Christ—is also a love through and for life: it is through the intermediary of the woman-mother that man-God can show this vibrant, lively side of amorous passion. Provided the mother-woman assumes her share of *sacrifice* under the aspect of *purity*. Once the negotiation between vivid/visible pleasure and victimized suffering is settled, love affects us as beauty.

5. The feminine as viewed by men: the imaginary of the feminine is a masculine imaginary, as Georges Duby says. This presents us with an enormous problem that calls for psychoanalysis, which I will touch on briefly, before discussing a few masterpieces in the world of madonnas and nudes.

Phallic eroticism connotes as "beautiful" the manifestations of weakness or failure that Freud referred to with the formidable term of *castration*. A sense of delicacy, grace, cunning, frailty, fatigue, or sadness comes to dress it, confess it, or camouflage it, so that it can live, survive. Nuances of love: it is up to women to bear these sins of power and self-control; it is on women's faces and bodies that "one" is authorized to see and show them: women thus admit castration, while consoling it, constructing it, and sublimating it. If the sublime, as Kant says, is a beauty beyond ugliness, it is precisely because, in Freudian terms, the sublime rebuilds an image beyond the collapse of identity, passionate crisis, or melancholic breakdown produced particularly in the amorous experience. When man takes on these same attributes, he is admitting "his" femininity.

The feminine of man—which we have seen so often in the passion of Christ for his Father and in the innumerable crucifixions and descents from the cross—is not a simple reprise of female beauty or of these failings— suffering, weakness, sadness, grace, modesty, ecstasy, joy—already explored on the bodies of the madonnas (first veiled, then in various states of undress, and finally nude). If Christ offering himself in the Passion for the Father is sublime, this beauty remains serious, rarely allowing a hint of seduction or pleasure to filter through. It is up to the feminine body to make explicit the joys of eroticism—the smile—caught in the trap of love; the male body of Christ and the martyrs, however naked, are careful not to reveal it, and only proclaim the anxiety of nothingness. The Baroque Bernini needed Saint Teresa in order to sculpt a naked ecstasy able to consume the borders between "eros" and "agape": but if the sculptor was indeed reconstructing a woman's passion, how could he touch on it so closely if not by pouring his own into it?

Wasn't this feminine beauty of the amorous space—from seduction to suffering—nothing other than a projection of the man's feminine from the start? The transfer of male fantasies onto female bodies, simple supports, passive objects of male desire, objects of exchange of male desire, destined only to support this desire as it concentrates in the always slightly sadistic gaze of the voyeur? If every artist were a potential Picasso, female beauty would be a variant of bullfighting, on canvas and in color. Yet how can we not see that the gesture of the painter is not only the thrust of a skillful torero into his victim's flesh, but a veritable embrace of the woman by this other woman that the painter becomes in his amorous identification with his model?

We do not know much about the femininity that would be the product of the feminine imaginary alone. Female painters seem to take up the canon of female beauty established by their brothers or fathers and are content to add another smile, another act of cruelty, without changing the logic. There is a National Museum of Women in the Arts in Washington, D.C., established in 1987. The idea is interesting and laudable, but the results are somewhat disappointing, not only because the great works already belong to other famous museums. Yet a hypothesis emerges: if the issue is seeing the invisible (and this is the wager of Christian beauty), a single economy is in order. The eye is phallic, and, whether a man or a woman, a viewer must sort out their psychic bisexuality to make the splendid secrets of the invisible visible. Art created by women under these conditions can only be a variant of this economy: a modulation, not a radical departure. Artemisia Gentileschi cuts off heads with a suave coldness, while Caravaggio devotes himself to his sadomasochistic jubilation to the point of the grotesque; Georgia O'Keeffe's flowers are saturated with the brazenness of female genitalia, while Cézanne's trees reveal the sovereignty of the human gesture blended with the vibrations of Being. These differences signal different points of view, but the economy of visible beauty, the attempt to manifest the infiniteness of the soul in the infiniteness of the body are not at all questioned by the second sex.

There is another hypothesis, however, internal to this history of beauty centered on the feminine. In fact, the negotiation of the feminine as beauty, in the sense I mention here, has engendered a history of representation that is far from closed. Its deconstruction, specific to modern or postmodern art, opens new possibilities: abstraction, minimalism, psychosis. From what appeared to us as beauty, these possibilities only retain the initial ambition to manifest infinite love. But today this project has come to the point of abolishing not only the figure but the contours of all identity, sexual difference, and the conscious Ego itself, in these (always risky) journeys "to the end of the night." At the very least, women are not absent from these explorations; they are among its most intrepid pioneers. Perhaps because, from madonnas to nudes, they have nothing to lose by pursuing this beauty in their own way, which now appears to be a risk: beauty exploding in the unveiling of the invisible, in the most secret, most scandalous margins.

The Virgin

I have led you to the "end of the night" (the temptation of modern art, when not its threat) to return, in celebration of this second millennium, to its dawn.

Early in our era, around the Mediterranean, a few artists had already acquired an exceptional mastery of the individual portrait, as well as the representation of couples in love. The large, anxious eyes of Fayoum's portraits seem much more expressive than those of the first Byzantine icons. And the frescoes of Pompeii, depicting satyrs and nymphs, or simply patrician nobles, already excelled in the art of the nude. Yet placed in the perspective of the long development of beauty in Christian art, these exploits, which infuse certain epochs and make them fertile, seem to be lacking the refinement of the *amorous soul* that would become artists' quintessential subject for two thousand years.

Love was certainly Greek, and Plato's *The Banquet* reproduces the impulse toward the Good and the Beautiful, as well as the violent dramas opposing body and soul, but these are played out among men, and Diotima is only an external inspiration. In Homer love remains discreet when it takes on the domestic aspect of conjugal fidelity that unites Ulysses and Penelope (from afar), while the "affair," as we would say today, between Paris and Helen is still judged immoral. For Aeschylus and Sophocles, love has to do with *hybris*, subject to divine and political design, and only Euripides comes close to passion with Phaedra, provided guilty straying is seen there. To get to the troubadours and Petrarch, we had to go through the *psychic space* that the invisible and no doubt most prestigious cathedral in Christendom was, built on the principles of the Incarnation and Love. The role of Mary is clearly essential in the construction of this architecture of Christian sub-jectivity and its art. Moreover, artists and lovers of art were not wrong to place themselves under its protection: Scrovegni, the patron of Giotto de-picted in the famous frescoes of Padua's Cappella degli Scrovegni, was a member of the order of the Cavalieri Godendi, known for their wealth and extravagance, without that contradicting their defense of the existence and dignity of the Virgin.

Mary, mother of God, is the centerpiece in this crystallization of Chris-tian beauty around Love and the Incarnation, as I have said. This inevitably leads to a defense and illustration of her logical role in the formation of Christian and post-Christian subjectivity and its aesthetics. Because how-ever absent she is from the Trinity constituted by the Father, Son, and Holy Spirit, however reduced to an axial void around which this Trinity revolves (Philippe Sollers speaks bluntly of the "Virgin's hole"), Mary is indeed the patron saint of painters.[2]

Her virginity constitutes the major scandal: our sensibility and simple reason can only denounce the dreadful inequity this virginity imposes, women's exclusion from sexuality, a punitive chastity that seems to be the price women must pay for admission to the sacred—and to representation! Once we denounce the male chauvinist manipulation, as I think we should, let's take a look at the ruses of this perhaps not so insipid virginity.

The adjective *virgin* that characterizes Mary might have been a transla-tion error: the Semitic term that refers to the social and legal status of a young, unmarried girl may have been replaced by the Greek term *parthe-nos*, which refers to a physiological and psychological situation. Of course, I protest this mutilation, this archaic, to say the least, way of reining in women and controlling the birthrate. I would like to imagine, however, that, with the figure of Mary, human beings were able to conceive of a be-ginning before the beginning. I would like to understand in their divaga-tions on virginity a proto-space, a timelessness, where a "chora" existed prior to the Word according to Democritus and before Plato mentioned it in *Timaeus*—a space before space, a prototype of the Kantian "schema." It was a matter of thinking of a preliminary to the Beginning: a nonimprint, a nonplace removed from the control of the original *technè*, the primordial furrow. "That place from whence come my sleep and my slightest movements," as Rimbaud says.[3] When Meister Eckhart asks God to "free" him of God (or perhaps to make him "a virgin" of God?), isn't he too envisioning this nonplace, this unthinkable outside? I would like to imagine that the Virgin would urge us to dream to this point: before time, before the subject, before the beginning, which is the beginning of desire. That this nonplace before the beginning of desire, at the limits of the psychic, is referred to as feminine and maternal when it concerns a certain experience of retreat—*to the point of melancholy, an autistic, speechless sensibility*, a gaping cavern in everyone—makes us envision the "feminine" in a very different way than as a symmetrical double of the masculine: didn't Freud say that the feminine is what is most inaccessible to both sexes? The most inaccessible because "before the beginning" and in this sense "virgin"? Who among us is still listening to this "virginity" in one's self? To this unthinkable, unimaginable aspect of the untouchable femininity of both sexes? To a subjectivity that would not only be desire, which Eastern religions explore in their own way in their praise of the "void"?

Virginity is not the only scandal raised by the mother of God. It is only the first in a series of traps set for femininity by the sacred figure of Mary over two thousand years: the body reduced to the ear and tears (hide this sexuality from me, which I am not supposed to see, under all the draping possible, as imagined by the best painters and everyone else!); the sanctification of suffering and pain and, only after that, the recognition of an unequaled power: our Queen of Heaven may dominate the mystical abysses but barely frequents the pathways of ecclesiastical power . . . And so on. In my tradition, that of Orthodox Christianity, the role of the Virgin as the power of intercession between the Son and the Father is heavily emphasized: her immortality is even suggested, since she is the only one in the evangelical saga to not die; she is content to pass from life via the "Dormition" (Theophane the Greek's superb fourteenth-century icon at the Tretiakov Gallery could be added to the well-known masterpieces by Andrei Rublev). None of this would be possible, however, without *The Pilgrimage of the Mother of God Among the Torments*—an apocryphal text from the twelfth or thirteenth century that recounts how Mary was spared none of the torments afflicting us poor sinners, so as to better defend her Son, and us, before a Father whose pity can seem rather difficult to obtain. This Marian role is certainly enviable, but it demands a boundless immersion in suffering: cynics would say that Mary shows signs of exceptional masochistic tendencies. I would say that the suffering is for Mary, while the smile is reserved . . . for the painter! Who by painting the depression of the mother of God dominates his own Marian suffering—his own identification as a man with a melancholic woman (I will come back to this with Giovanni Bellini).

Mary's presence, discreet in the Gospels, is increasingly amplified throughout the centuries under the pressure of a popular paganism, eager to consolidate the role of a goddess-mother at the heart of triumphant monotheism. And thanks to the painters who are revealed in their biographies to be sensitive to the maternal and the feminine, in a homosexual or heterosexual mode, and who long to sublimate this maternal and this feminine. Theologians themselves get in on the act, seeing Mary as a pretext for logical and dogmatic debates and refinements. Since the birth of Jesus is free from sin, shouldn't his mother's be free from sin as well? Logical coherence requires it, and this will be very beneficial to painting: because how can one present a woman freely, unless she is unsullied by sin? St. Bernard is still reluctant to celebrate the conception of Mary by St. Anne and St. Joachim, thereby trying to slow the comparison of Mary to Christ. But Duns Scotus (1266–1308), a subtle logician, invents *praeredemptio* as an argument: if Christ saves us through redemption, the Virgin who bears him "must" be included retroactively in what makes this redemption possible, starting with her own conception; in other words, she has "preredemption," and hence . . . an "Immaculate Conception" that washes away original sin. And this, among other things, makes the representation of Mary possible, more alive than ever in her body free from sin, on the walls of Italian churches. Dante and Giotto emerge in the wake of Duns Scotus; beauty seems discretely prepared by the religious vision of the Virgin's sinless body.

The theological quibbling to which Mary will be subjected, however, will be very slow to emerge as dogma, that is to say, as law for believers: the dogma of the Immaculate Conception only dates from 1854, the Assumption of the Blessed Virgin from 1950: which, of course, did not prevent Titian and so many others from painting Mary ascending into heaven. Similarly, the one who wore her royal crown in painting for so many centuries without batting an eye was not proclaimed queen until 1954 by Pius

XII; and she has only been Mother of the Church since 1964! A way of reconciling—some would say "rehabilitating"—women by "relying" on the image of the Virgin. Official code could then catch up with what had happened, or was imposed, outside of official authorities, and this was very useful in the eyes of these authorities. Why?

Far be it from me to respond in the place of authorities, albeit indirectly. What does Mary represent? In her beautiful book on the Virgin, Marina Warner cites verses by Caelius Sedulius, who sums up the uniqueness of this figure marvelously: "She . . . had no peer / Either in the first mother [Eve] or in all women / Who were to come. But alone of all her sex / She pleased the Lord." Mary, a woman? Not so sure. Rather, "alone of all her sex." A certain femininity needed to consolidate everybody's sexual identity?

In other words, Mary is a *clever construction*, to begin with, that calms social anxiety on the topic of birth: she fulfills a male being that femininity disquiets, since she only has eyes for her son, no other man; and also satisfies women, no less disquieted by desire. So that a certain community between the sexes can be established beyond their flagrant incompatibility and their permanent war, and in spite of them. What if this were a version of the sacred, the version of the sacred that women obviously cherish, namely, the possibility of stable coexistence between the two sexes? We call this the "sacrament of marriage," we make the family sacred, and many take offense at such conformism—though the vogue for marriage and other civil unions show no signs of slowing. Out of concern for security? Or as another version of feminine beauty?

Question: who is it in this Marian alchemy that allows or at least facilitates "a certain understanding" between the sexes? Because, as I mentioned, the idea of the "couple," including the emancipation of the individual and notably the woman, developed in Judaism and Christianity, however imperfect in terms of our modern expectations.

First, from the Nativity to the *Pietà* by way of the *Mater dolorosa* and the *Regina Caeli*, the Virgin has nothing of the lover about her: she is a devoted mother, exclusively. The "good mother," in whom Melanie Klein believes so little that she speaks of a preference for the "bad" one: Winnicott's "good-enough" mother, who gives herself to her son, body and soul, to the extent that without her the beloved son would have no body, because (let's remember) this god has only become a man by the grace of his transit through the body of Mary, "full of grace." This grace is ultimately an extraordinary defense of secular motherhood, on the threshold of primary narcissism: the origin of love that every being needs to go on. And the lack of which is the sinister source of all depression, if not psychosis. In sum, Mary rehabilitates the primary base of our identities and future images. No images without what modern psychoanalysts call "mother-baby co-excitation" and what Winnicott identifies with the serenity of "being"—in opposition to the phallic "action" or "doing" of the drive and desire, which will be developed later and will punctuate the evolution of the speaking subject. Before the current crisis of individuals and families, an attempt was made, quite rightly, to rehabilitate the role of the father. Our modern interest in beauty, this recourse to the sublime to dress the wounds of our original repressions, would indicate that we now need a more archaic compassion than the protection of the father, more radical care than that offered by the father: nothing other than what Catholicism offers its faithful through the image of Mary. In addition, and in the same sense, it is often suggested that the success of feminism in Protestant countries might be due, among other things, to the greater initiative the reformed have accorded women on a social and ritual level. On the other hand, we might wonder if this militant and somewhat agitated expansion of Anglo-Saxon feminism is not the result of a lack in the Protestant religious edifice of a place for the maternal. This maternal noted by the Orthodox and around which Catholics constructed the Virgin, with every possible ambiguity—still under scrutiny— makes Catholicism difficult to analyze, or "difficultly analyzable," as Lacan would say. Of course, the more difficult it is, the more agreeable it is to analyze endlessly.

On top of this, the preoedipal symbiosis of the son with his mother, that is, the not desirable but charitable mother, the mythic "good mother" of Klein and Winnicott, allow man's feminine traits to be sublimated. We will see this with Giovanni Bellini, the magnificent painter of madonnas who put himself in his mother's place (a mother absent, in fact, from his biography: dead? A teenage mother?) in order to paint *himself* in gentleness and Marian melancholy. As for the girl, whose case is not anticipated in the Christian family, she can also find something to appease her desire by identifying with both protagonists of the duo: "I am the suffering male child of this mother who loves only me," she says to herself, satisfying her latent homosexuality, but I am also the mother, the one who needs to devote herself to the other. Nevertheless, this appeasement can only result in creativity if the daughter assumes her bisexuality and, like the son, allows herself to take the risk of defying the law, *seeing* her objects of desire and not being satisfied with being seen.

The second advantage of the Virgin, which goes hand in hand with this sacrificial motherhood, is to *favor the imaginary*. Because deployed around this archaic link of the child and mother is the entire continent that extends just this side of and beyond language: a profusion of sensorial and drive-related traces that connect Word to flesh, precisely. Without the recognition of this pre- or translinguistic treasure that occurred through the extraordinary promotion of the imaginary in Christianity, the Christian Word could not have transformed the Greek Logos into Christian and divine Speech. The Word in which the amorous trajectory of the Son toward the Father will develop, on the one hand, and the rationality of Christianity will develop, on the other, allowing it to join Aristotle and clear itself in the *cogito* of Descartes before opening the way to modern philosophy—and so the Christian Word in fact revolves around Mary! Because Mary, in the solemn adventure of the Word, assembles *figures outside language: silence, music, and painting*. The Virgin is at once the patron and privileged object of art. Around the thirteenth century, with St. Francis of Assisi (1181–1226), the tendency is affirmed to represent a terrestrial, human, very human Mary and thus poor, modest, and humble: to encourage both the humanist sensibility and the glorious representation of nature and the everyday—birds, animals, bodies of every sort. It is not only a matter of allowing the representation of cosmic misery and feminine masochism. It is everyday experience, natural life, *haecceitas* according to Duns Scotus, and the concrete singular that become the object of a figuration freed from the Byzantine canon. Through the Counter-Reformation, the Jesuits will once again revive the splendors of representation, Baroque this time, still with the help of Mary: after Titian and Tintoretto, Bernini, Rubens, Monteverdi. And all of humanity can sing with Palestrina: "Eia mater, fons amoris . . ."

Again, why do artists rush to Mary? Let's be blunt: the censorship of Mary's sexuality (this is a mother with no desire, no eroticism beyond her son) protects the artist from the anxiety specific to the oedipal drama and allows him to appropriate in the brilliance of his art the mother's supposed jouissance, while the representation of Mary gives it a halo of cool self-restraint. The artist incorporates the denied feminine jouissance with which he identifies, restoring it to us in the visible form he has engendered himself by displacing it in a deluge of forms of which he is properly the father and mother, the hermaphrodite creator. These beautiful invented forms are at once an infralanguage and a supralanguage, when they emerge in the *verbal art* as well: Isn't literary "style" a vision, a melody, and also a silence that infiltrates everyday language? Isn't painting—unlike photocopies and television—a vision of transformed forms? Forms whose author is now the sole creator: at once subject and object?

Finally, the sorrowful Mary consoles the always somewhat depressive solitude of women, while at the same time encouraging their regal fantasies of omnipotence. On the one hand, Botticelli: young madonnas, languid or dejected from pleasure or frustration, we do not know; on the other, the implacable Virgin, paradoxically called the Virgin of Mercy by Piero della Francesca, shielding the powerful and powerless of this world with her cloak. Before undressing her, painters used the Virgin to denude the secrets folds of the feminine soul.

Mary's consecration is the intrapsychical condition that favors the flowering of Western art. Once this flowering occurs, it bears within it the source of the second miracle, nothing other than the pleasure of its own deconstruction. Once Mary's love life was made visible, once beauty coiled around that femininity, nothing could prevent the freeing of themes and forms of various representations inspired by other cultures, economies, or politics. Tying representation to the amorous experience that included women, beginning with the Virgin, should have led—with the help of the evolution of science and technology—to the deconstruction of the initial dogmas themselves, such as sin or virginity. Having unleashed the subjective, varied, innovative representations of romantic life, *Christianity opened the way for a surpassing of religion itself:* a surpassing that does not necessarily take place in an aesthetic religion (though there is that temptation) but in the endless search for multiple representations, which from now on constitute our minds—not a dead letter but a life of the mind: an infinite imaginary genesis, constant rebirth through the imaginary. This is not the least of the discoveries of the Christian imaginary and its post-Christian evolution: namely, that beauty is our therapy.

Certainly, in all civilizations aesthetic experiences rely unconsciously on the narcissistic mother/child link, and they require the worship of the mother as well as her absorption by the artist—which may take the form of blasphemy, indeed, matricide—in order to modulate the ordinary signs of social exchange into new, appealing, regenerative signs. But making this dependence explicit in a preconscious, if not conscious, way, makes the subject of Catholicism in this archaic link freer, more playful, more insolent, in short, more artistic, for better or worse. "Literature and Evil," Georges Bataille warned: indeed, the promotion of the imaginary to the rank of guardian of the life of the mind in our civilization has often gotten mired in the limits of perversity and immorality.

Giovanni Bellini

Bellini's work will allow us to see, in the trajectory of a single painter, the slippage that is a feature of the representation of the feminine in the West from madonnas to nudes.

Giovanni Bellini, son of Jacopo, leaves his commentators perplexed. Dead at ninety in 1516, according to Vasari, he must have been born in 1426. Yet it was in 1429 (three years later) that Anna Rinversi, Jacopo's wife, registers the birth of her first-born child. If Giovanni were born earlier, he could only have been an illegitimate child, Jacopo's son, or Anna's from a previous marriage. Other biographers maintain that Vasari was mistaken and that Giovanni was the youngest in the family, after Nicolosia (who would become Mantegna's wife) and Gentile, another illustrious painter of his time. This hypothesis is corroborated especially by Giovanni's social situation in relation to Gentile: the latter was the official painter of the Venetian aristocracy at Ducal Palace before Giovanni; in certain paintings, we see Giovanni represented third, after Jacopo and Gentile. It does not explain why in 1459 Giovanni lives alone, in San Lio, in Venice, away from the paternal family (which does not seem to be the case for the other two children). Nor does it explain why Anna Rinversi's last testament of November 25, 1471, does not mention him among her heirs (who are Nicolosia and Gentile). Anna Rinversi does recognize herself as Giovanni's mother, which invites the hypothesis of an illegitimate birth or another hidden marriage.

This is the biographical framework that greets the viewer of canvases by this quintessential painter of motherhood. He is the son of his father: he takes Jacopo's name, works in his studio, and continues his pictorial tradition. He is also a brother: Gentile cedes his position at Ducal Palace when he leaves for Constantinople, and Giovanni completes certain of his paintings. But his mother is absent: a lost mother. Early separation from an illegitimate genetrix, abandoned, dead, or kept in the shadows? Denial of a "sin" outside the law, the sin of Jacopo or Anna, of which Giovanni was the product? Whatever the truth, Anna does not seem to have replaced the "real mother," the way Signore da Vinci's wife replaced Leonardo's real mother. We may recall that Leonardo (1452–1519, Bellini's contemporary, twenty-six years his junior) would depict Jesus with two mothers: St. Anne and St. Mary form the figure called "Santa Maria Meterza," a saturation of motherhood, split in two if not intrusive, in Leonardo's famous painting, in which Freud thought he saw the tail of a vulture, a fantastical sign of maternal power.[4] With Bellini, we are at the antipodes of this: is it because Anna ignores Giovanni to begin with that he will become the melancholic painter of beautiful madonnas, themselves romantically melancholic?

Even if we can only remain circumspect before this biographical gap and commentators' confusion, let's take a look at the paintings, and the distance, if not the hostility, that separates the child's body from the mother's. The maternal place is nevertheless there: fascinating, attractive, enigmatic, privileged, *ergasterion*, a vibrant place. But direct access to this place—none. The painter is its melancholic exile, *desdichado avant la lettre,* the reject of an inaccessible mother, inaccessible because abandoned and melancholic herself. In Bellini's eyes, it seems there does exist a maternal *function*; however, far from being the mother's solicitude for the baby-object of all her desires painted by Leonardo, she is, in the Venetian's work, only an ineffable, impersonal jouissance, outside discourse, outside narrative, all in all resistant to the figure. The painter/son paints to mark this jouissance that allows itself to be seen not in the mother/child scene but solely in the painter's art: folds of colored surfaces, the juxtaposition of full tones and unrestrained volume resolved in a contrast between "warm" and "cool" colors, in an architecture made of color alone, a sudden brightness that opens onto color, curbing vision, beyond its thickness, toward bedazzlement. Bellini depicts a mother with no trace of love, but his art imagines and produces in color the vibrations of a passion that is all the more intense because it is imaginary.

To gain access to this art, Giovanni is inspired by his father's technique but modifies it. While Jacopo remains fixed within the Byzantine canon and passionate about the architectural innovations of his son-in-law Mantegna, Giovanni innovates. The pleasure that springs from his paintings, beyond the canonic theme of the *sacra conversazione*, seems indeed to be the pleasure of an uninhibited body able to integrate, before the primal scene, the maternal as well as paternal jouissance, which belongs to both sexes: the draping that covers the madonnas, the trees surrounding them, the hands brushing lightly against the child's body, the child's fingers strangling the mother, and the landscape, finally, that disengages from the maternal figure and extends, more and more autonomous—as if the theme of Mary were only a screen to pierce through to free the way to the world's variety and to allow the painter to drown in it. This liberated subject is not yet the woman; perhaps it is the secret that bursts forth in the chromatic range of the painting: it is the painter who serves as the feminine of the Madonna so as to assert his own polyphony, his own polymorphism.

The series of madonnas between 1485 and 1499 is significant in this evolution. What we see here is the experience of the painter's marriage and fatherhood and the subsequent death of his wife and son, which drastically alters, or induces, the representation of motherhood according to Giovanni Bellini. The Byzantine and sweetly seductive mother of the 1440s–1480s (see *Virgin and Child*, 1470, Pinacoteca dell'Accademia, Bergamo; fig. 5.1) is replaced, from 1480 to 1500, by the hostility and subtle disappointment of *Madonna with Two Trees* (1487, Galleria dell'Accademia, Venice; fig. 5.2), or by the separative vengeance of the small strangler in the Museum of Art in São Paulo (*Virgin with Standing Child*, 1487, São Paulo Museum of Art; fig. 5.3); before arriving at the jouissance of St. Francis (*St. Francis in Ecstasy*, Frick Collection, New York), without maternal mediation this time, against the ecstatic green of a craggy desert background.

Personal life, as well as the history of Venice, seeped into these two series of feminine representations, which soon became three. New customs: the impoverished patrician class engenders so many lawbreakers, seducers of nuns and the young, that courtesans complain of being neglected. Patrician women rise in turn and ask the pope for the right to wear frothy dresses and sumptuous finery. Carnival replaces the Feast of the Assumption. New ideas, too: Pietro Bembo, a Petrarchist and neo-Platonist, acts as a go-between for Isabelle d'Este and Bellini, so that the painter is able to execute paintings with pagan subjects and spread the Florentine doctrine, which holds that the point of departure for a spiritual ascent toward God is not virgin motherhood but carnal love. But the apotheosis of this slide from the sacred toward sensual pleasure is unquestionably *The Dream of Poliphilus* (1467), attributed to the Dominican monk Francesco Colonna, who abandons Reason and Will for the glory of female nudity and unheard-of eroticism.

In this context Bellini's interests turn toward the representation of figures other than the mother and sacred subjects (he completes a series of portraits)—and especially toward the placement of the body, now minimized, in a landscape whose skillfully traced folds replace the Marian draping, as in *St. Francis in Ecstasy*. What is to be done, at the end of this life, when Venice discovers Antiquity, humanism, the female body, carnal passion, the theories of Bembo, and *The Dream of Poliphilus*? While accepting secular or pagan commissions, Bellini drags his feet, complying reluctantly. Until the astonishing Venus that is *Young Woman Holding a Mirror* (1515, Kunsthistorisches Museum, Vienna; fig. 5.4), in which he seems to have reconciled the figure of the naked woman with an architectonics of pleasure—subdued when he painted the madonnas—and his palette. Here the painter's jouissance and the woman's do not oppose each other or flee each other: they converge.

The division of pictorial space is the same as in the last paintings of the Virgins: one-third landscape, two-thirds panel. Except in the foreground, the body of the traditionally dressed mother is replaced by the nakedness of a curvaceous young woman against a luminous landscape in the background. If the manner is that of Giorgione (1477–1510, another younger contemporary; fig. 5.5),[5] and if the female body radiates no less sensuality than the one painted by the young disciple, it is not so much the iridescence of the flesh that captures the gaze as this specifically Bellinian light. It does not come from the juxtaposition of volumes or from the isolation of forms, as in Leonardo, but from the luminous working of the color itself, sparkling in its substance and at play with its counterpart, nothing other than a shaded complementary color. The colored light thus builds a curved and open space and is clearly distinguished from the masses of light that divide bodies and volumes in the work of other painters of the same period. This process, unique to Bellini and to this painting in particular, is all the more radiant through the play of light around the body of the nude, showing her face and neck indirectly. Thanks to two perpendicular mirrors, the shaded front portion of the canvas is fractured, bending and beginning a third space—neither background nor foreground but a corner of the painting opened to the public. An inversion of perspective, a reversal of the point of view of seeing/being seen: enough to make cubists dream! A reflected, circular gaze, concerned with fracturing space as much as possible, by following the refraction of rays of light, of vision itself. Who is looking at the nude? *She* is looking at herself. The painter is also looking at her. We, the viewers, contemplate her as well. What difference, what interference is there between the nude, the painter, and the viewer? Who is who? A vortex of gazes.

The face is that of *Madonna with Blessing Child* (1509, Detroit), *Madonna with Two Saints* (1409, Galleria dell'Accademia, Venice), and *Madonna with John the Baptist and a Saint* (1500–1504, Galleria dell'Accademia, Venice). But the averted, modest, ecstatic, melancholic, or reticent gaze of the Virgins sees itself: the one offered to the painter's gaze is offered to herself, subject and object of vision. She encounters herself not in the child, this object-for-others, or in the eye of the painter or viewer—as the angle of the two mirrors opening out would lead one to believe. She encounters herself in this pseudo object that is the mirror itself. Which reflects her own gaze, now inseparable from that of the painter, who sees all: the naked body that exhibits itself and the solitary contemplation of introspection. Face to face: the model and her painter, but also their crossed interior spaces. An erotic object: a naked woman viewed by a man; a narcissistic object: a woman looking at herself in a mirror that reflects the awareness of an unsurpassable limit in her eyes: "This is how it is." And the circular space of the painting that situates the painter's pleasure at all the reversible points of these interferences. The Virgin has extracted herself from her exile, draped as she was in an invisible elsewhere, torn between here and the beyond. But the woman finally found nevertheless remains split: on the one hand, the naked body, already erotic; on the other, the uncertain search for the image itself, her own, no doubt. Her relaxed, motherly stomach reminds us that her appearance is only a point of view, a play of light, an always elusive appearance, perhaps impossible to depict, that will always need the painter's penetration. Added to the unsatisfied gaze of the Madonna is the erotic encounter of two gazes—that of the model and that of the artist. The osmosis between "seeing" and "being seen," masculine and feminine, is underway more than ever. Osmosis or chase? Old Bellini is not really appeased; isn't he ready to topple over into the vertigo of the Baroque?

At ninety, with this *Young Woman Holding a Mirror*, Bellini easily enters the sex shop of his era. And, starting from the madonnas, he surveys it with the same connoisseur's mastery as Giorgione and Titian (1490–1576) whose *Assumption* (Basilica di Santa Maria Gloriosa dei Frari, Venice) signals the triumph and achievement of Marian art in Baroque art. As if he had only been waiting for the go-ahead provided by the change in politics and mores in order to manifest, through a representation of nakedness, this jouissance of the feminine already coded in his discreet projection into the very place of virginal motherhood, apparently restrained but in fact restored by his own painterly passion for color. The sex shop allowed the old master to make explicit, to the secular world, what had always been at work through the veils of the madonnas: female jouissance, at the borders of autoeroticism, desire, and the ideal, at the threshold of the otherness that the child represents. What Freud calls "original repression," which the painter visits by appropriating the sexual identities he needs, whatever they happen to be. But the sublimity of this last painting resides less in the audacity of the nakedness (into which Bellini projects himself this time, leaving the madonnas behind) than in the movement and light of color. This mark of Bellinian participation in the pleasure of what he is seeing, in the pleasure of the mother and the woman, is now detached from the madonnas who, as we have seen, facilitated the painter's identification with the feminine as well as the expression of his psychical polymorphism and the plasticity of his language. From the Renaissance to the present day, the search for new forms has always favored the female body and its parts (breasts, hands, legs, knees, buttocks, etc.) to charge them with the intensity of the artist's amorous desire. Yet what creates the beauty of these fetishes is precisely the way they are revealed: here Bellini's light went far beyond the thematics of the nude in which the following period would excel—a light that could only truly be seen after Poussin, Cézanne, and Rothko.

Resistance and Provocation

Bellini's exceptional destiny allows us to present, in shortened form, a history of beauty that lasted several centuries. The representation of naked beauty that follows will, as we know, have a richness and variety it is impossible to address here. I will only point out a few types:

After the Baroque period of the Counter-Reformation, French art of the eighteenth century places the female body at the heart of the quest for beauty in its own way: this time, according to the rhetoric of transgression and mischief that will make the female nude an outpouring of humor. The interplay of flesh and draping, the lively rhythm of trips to the country, blind man's bluff, and swings are the narrative background against which is displayed a beauty that blends the feminine with witticism and the sensuality of gardens. They announce the Impressionists and Colette. I could have reminded you of Watteau's graceful drawings of nudes. I chose the opulence of Fragonard's volumes, which, along with his sense of movement, never let us forget that these are women. While letting us see that this femininity is no less surprising for being feigned and is coextensive with the life of the social being—of being, quite simply, since it is the voluptuous truth of the painter himself (see Fragonard's *The Useless Resistance* or *The Surprise*; fig. 5.6). The smile of seeing everything, beyond sin and virginity, is finally unlocked, and we are amused by it: it is called *The Bolt*, with a wink.

The nineteenth century is more social: Goya's *Maya desnuda* (The Nude Maja) has Spanish local color; Manet's *Olympia* provokes less with her legs than with her dark glower, no doubt revealing dark desire, in counterpoint to her flowery black servant; Courbet's *Sleep* (1866, Musée d'Orsay, Paris; fig. 5.7), meanwhile, appeals to the mores of the Belle Époque and the new splendors of Gomorrah. The beauty of this femininity accompanies social liberation and is part of the new image of the emancipated woman. But nudity can also serve as a warning against a culture of attorneys and professors who overload their conference halls to the ceilings with naked nymphs, according to the best conventions of the institute—the Liard Room at the Sorbonne is one example—so as not to see either the misery of the street or the revolutions revitalizing contemporary painting.

With Rodin and Picasso, however, the intensity of form prevails over the theme of the nude. Rodin's *Iris, Messenger of the Gods* (Musée Rodin, Paris; fig. 5.8) is more than a provocation that presents obscene female genitals to the viewer's face. The violence of the movement that cuts the body in two, the stiff right arm stuck to the leg in spasms, the left arm cut off like the head, and the raised left foot, which seems to serve as a support for climax—or flight—possess a grace dissolving the borders between heaven and hell. And *Woman with Pillow* (1969; fig. 5.9) by the older Picasso (he was eighty-eight) weds the fixed terror of madonnas to the castrating power of African mother-goddesses and the insolence of the new nudes of our time that do not follow women's magazines standards of female beauty and stubbornly refuse our compassion for their loveless bodies. Loveless except for the love of the painter, who, decidedly, would be among the first—and no doubt among the last—of the lovers of this strange femininity. "I am a woman. Every artist is a woman and should be butch," Picasso (always causing a stir) says to his friend Geneviève Laporte. "Homosexual artists cannot be real artists, because they love men," he goes on.[6] Picasso is exaggerating, because he is defending himself against the woman he could be with a man, against his male homosexuality. But let's take the first part of his confession: the artist paints a woman as if he were a woman loving his double. And we should add that there could be a thousand and one ways to be a woman and to make the invisible feminine visible.

I have taken you from madonnas to nudes without having come full circle. On the contrary, the circle is more open than ever. The miracle continues: passion persists, and its most intimate secrets can be seen. Perhaps not at the movies, much less on television, which is antipainting. The miracle continues in the new temples that are museums, in spite of the fact that they are archives: they remind us where what we think we see comes from. And constantly invite us to look with new eyes. When the speed or brusqueness on the streets of New York, Paris, or Florence have gotten to you, and you have nothing else to do, or no longer know what to do, do what I do: go into a museum or a gallery and refashion your psychical life. You should also read *Women* by Philippe Sollers. Then you will see that in addition to beauty in the feminine there is a grimacing femininity that reflects and oversees the malaise of the civilization. This is only a station on the long march that tied love to the visible, and the infiniteness of the soul to representation, two thousand years ago, using the female body as an object, the bosom of the human body. Beauty is its name; freedom is another. And the only possible protection against these impasses and risks, which freedom knows all too well, is to keep the memory of what has brought us where we are, two thousand years later, alive. The path that leads from madonnas to nudes is one of its capital stages, and one of the most beautiful.

6

THE PASSION ACCORDING TO MOTHERHOOD

I have known Jean-Didier Vincent for a long time, and we have referred to each other's work in our writings. Which is to say, I read him attentively. And his role in initiating this debate on the passions from the perspective of biology strikes me as central and indispensable.

I will not address the complex problem of the possible or impossible encounter of biology and psychoanalysis, though it remains at the heart of this exchange. To leave it in the shadows is surely not the way to clarify the debate, but we would need more time. Moreover, this epistemological question has been addressed in other forums in our society, notably by André Green, around cognitivism.[1]

I will start the dialogue with some free association and the state of my passions today—which is to say, what impassions me today. I am like you: the further I advance in my analytical practice, the more I find conferences boring. But because the issue here is the passions, and because a colloquium of psychoanalysts should involve risk, I have decided to risk presenting before you a few of my current inquiries, as yet incomplete and in this sense passionate, and thank you in advance for having the benevolence to listen to them as such. Nevertheless, as a guide to the following free associations, I will sum up the main points:

- Is maternal passion the prototype of passion?
- Can one defuse passion?
- What happens to passion and the removal of passion in the analytical experience?

I remember the distinction between the *emotions* and the *passions* from Jean-Didier Vincent's book, *Qu'est-ce que l'homme?* (What is man?) in the chapter "Man, Passionate Interpreter of the World."[2] Emotions belong to all vertebrates; they express their fluctuating relationship to their body and environment and have the function of adaptation and communication, a consequence of natural selection. The *passions*, on the other hand, are specific to man, because they suppose the existence of reflexive consciousness. Reflexive consciousness—which you call "impassioned consciousness"—is a particular activity of the "subject" (you use the terms *subject* and *brain* interchangeably and say that "every animal is a subject"). If every animal is a subject, we will speak of "reflexive consciousness" only when the fluctuating central state of the subject's (or animal's) brain integrates the fluctuating central state of the other into its extracorporeal space. That is, with reflexive consciousness, we are in another realm of the animal's or subject's brain. It is a matter of the capacity for an encounter (or sharing) of the same with the other and, simultaneously, of the same with oneself as another. "Man, unlike an animal, knows that he knows, and reflects on the experience of his body in consciousness in the form of feelings." Examples: *attachment* and *aggressiveness* are *emotions* proper to animals (as well as to men when they behave like animals); they are used to communicate, but they are wordless. Love and hate, on the other hand, are passions expressed in the language of feelings, in words of hatred or in a lover's discourse: "Passions are recounted and make man a hero in a novel"; "Because of passions, man is not an animal."

I remember the role of *reflexive consciousness*, insofar as it is coextensive to *language*, the constituent factor of the passions (to be distinguished from the emotions).

I also recall that there are three primordial emotions: *desire*—which leads the way, is tied to lack, and expresses the body's needs (water, minerals, energy to stay alive)—is an impulse toward the other; it brings *pleasure* and its cohort, *suffering*. All affective states function, therefore, on the basis of these *oppositional pairs* (pleasure/suffering brought about by desire), and as a biologist you locate the responsible chemical substances and implicated cerebral regions, the "paths of reward" and "pathways to punishment." These oppositional processes take place in the profound structures of the brain and are projected onto the cortex where cognitive maps, supports for representations, are put together. Under certain circumstances, or during certain periods in the life of a human subject (adolescence, motherhood, a particular encounter, a romantic state, mourning, etc.), these can be "vandalized" or can "snowball" under the pressure of the oppositional processes to which the brain was exposed during epigenesis.

These concepts speak to the analyst, of course. I would see in these *oppositional processes* of pleasure/suffering, supports for what we call the "opposed pairs" of *drives*, as well as the biological foundation of their transmission, which is transgenerational and indeed inscribed in the memory of the species and in epigenesis. Nevertheless, and you point this out as well, the development of the prefrontal cortex allows the apprehension of *time* thanks to *language* and *categorization*, of which man alone is capable. The unconscious processes, notably those Freud calls "primary processes," seem to be the result of an interaction (an application in the sense of a bi-univocal operation) between what you call "oppositional processes," on the one hand, and the elements of language, on the other. Is the unconscious a taking into account of oppositional processes by the linguistic reflexive consciousness: of the biological real by the symbolic?

First proposition: Is the language of the unconscious—with its "work," its "displacements," and its "condensations," which dreams reveal to us— the first language of passion, in your sense of the word? If we use the term *symbolic* to refer to the language of consciousness (with its linear temporality and its categorizations), I have proposed the term *semiotic* to refer to a different language, the unconscious "language" found in children's echolalia before the appearance of signs and syntax, and especially in the discourse we receive as aesthetic (poetry, literature, painting, music, which redistribute logical categories under the pressure of oppositional processes).

From this perspective, the passion that results from the interaction between desire/pleasure/suffering, on the one hand, and linguistic reflexive consciousness, on the other, would be an *imaginary* formation, a being on the frontier.

Second proposition: Passion is an imaginary state; the imaginary is the organ of passion, its chosen terrain for action and even its very being. I am not saying the imaginary is the "expression" of passion (which would suggest that there could be passion without expression, speechless passion, deprived of reflexive construction). This is not the case, since reflexive construction, or language, is immanent to passion. All passion is already self-reflective, which is to say, takes into account the otherness of the other and the self. The moment it is experienced as passion, and not as emotion, it is a border state between the real and the symbolic, biology and reflexive consciousness. *The imaginary and passion are two inseparable sides of the same human experience.* One can "store away" the imaginary expression of passion, repress it, isolate it, foreclose it, or simply suspend it for a time. But passion is different from emotion in that it is also the consequence of a symbolic impact; it results from its transformation by oppositional processes.

"Freudian dualism," the unconscious at the crossroads of drive and meaning, from your perspective would also be a theory of the various regimes of passion. By listening to dream narratives and other phantasmatic narrations, Freud's object is nothing other than passion, since it is this interface where reflexive consciousness modulates emotions with their neuronal and hormonal map, and since, vice versa, emotions are included in language, otherness, and time. By intervening in the imaginary discourse, which is the very being of passion, analysis can have access to passion itself, insofar as it has two sides, psychical *and* somatic.

What's more, by listening to unconscious passions, Freud is starting another revolution: not only does reflexive consciousness inform our emotions, he says, but there are also emotions informed by the reflexive consciousness of which this consciousness is not aware. These other passions—deeper or more archaic, repressed or censored—are unconscious passions; they change the very regime of language, because they speak the language of the primary processes and can only be understood in the link, itself passionate, between subjects: the link of transference-countertransference.

This is a capital moment in the history of thought, establishing *the discourse of passion* as the central object of observation, of listening, with the therapeutic and philosophical intention to act on both the psychical space dominated by reflexive consciousness and the corporeal space ruled by the brain or the subject. I emphasize this architecture of the human, which takes shape starting with a comprehension of the passions at the crossroads of the oppositional processes and reflexive consciousness, to highlight the inevitable place psychoanalysis occupies there. Dialogue among the life sciences (of which psychoanalysis is a part) has barely begun; and, far from being marginalized in this context, as one might fear, perspectives such as yours allow psychoanalysis a crucial place.

After these general remarks, I would like to take a moment to consider what we might call a core passion: maternal love. You have given me occasion for it because you use maternal love as an example of the meaning you give *passion* as distinct from *emotion*. But it is also a theme that is personal for both of us.

Significantly, symptomatically, to show—and understand—passion, you invoke two representations of motherhood based on codes of Christianity: the *Annuciata* by Antonello da Messina (1474) and the *Annonciation* by Simone Martini (fourteenth century). I wanted to look at these paintings and the divided representation of the mother they exhibit (the advance and retreat before the Angel Gabriel's speech, who represents the Word, the body's placement to the right and the gaze turning to the left, the orientation of the gaze inward and the hand outward), so many signs that you point out and I would like to explore further . . . another time! Today, to this pleasure and disturbance that maternal passion depicted evokes in the art lover, I will simply add a few more strictly clinical observations.

I believe that a two-sided oedipal phase exists for the woman: first, the little girl's attachment to her mother, a period Freud considers most obscure and that he compares to the Minoan-Mycenaean civilization before classical Greece.[3] Then there is a change of objects and an attachment to the father as the new object of desire in the heterosexual evolution. I have noted that this change of object is accompanied in the girl as in the boy by a phallic phase in which the subject (girl or boy) identifies not with the penis but with the phallus of the father (symbolic authority, the order of language and thought): so many psychosexual shifts that favor intellectual development. This complex path (attachment to the mother, attachment to the father, phallic identification) not only prepares for what Freud calls the "psychical bisexuality" of the woman, which would be more accentuated in her than in the man, but also prepares for what appears to be an *extraneousness* to, or estrangement from, the phallic or symbolic order on the part of the woman-subject. I prefer to use the term *extraneousness* because it is more than a *repression* and less than a *foreclosure* or *isolation*.

This *extraneousness* presents itself in various ways. Extraneousness is the hysterical complaint against the order of language that does not express emotions (what cognitive scientists call "noncongruence" between the affective and cognitive registers in the hysteric). Extraneousness, also, the greater academic ability of little girls that nevertheless takes on the aspect of a defensive construction, if not a "false self" dissociated from the affective register, and in puberty, on the contrary, under the impulse of new romantic attachments, recedes before better results by boys. Extraneousness, again, a feminine distance in terms of political agitation, if not the political order itself, which led Hegel to refer to women as "the eternal irony of the community" (it remains to be seen whether the phenomenon of female politicians confirms or invalidates this hypothesis). Extraneousness, finally, the hysterical depressiveness in the sense of an eternal disappointment regarding the erotic link and a retreat, also disappointed, toward an object of a narcissistic type; a more frequent depressiveness in women but one that appears to be less radical, less suicidal, for them than for men.

Question: could this extraneousness orestrangement be based on neurobiological data, notably, on the particularities of the two hemispheres of the brain that, according to some hypotheses, are not the same in men and in women? It is no doubt fascinating, but does not modify the analyst's listening.

Clinically speaking, the extraneousness to the phallic-symbolic order that I outline here is manifested in a specific way during pregnancy and in the experience of motherhood (particularly, but not only, in the beginning). Whatever the hormonal changes may be, and they are unquestionable (though studied less than rats pressing levers to obtain light or cheese), the pregnant woman, your *Annunciata*, is caught up at once in external familial and social preoccupations, control over her environment and the well-being of her child, and suspended in a passionate reverie that the painter represents in the form of a body receding or turning away as well as a gaze turned inward or absent. She listens to the speech of the archangel, but above all she is listening to her body and this not-yet-*other* germinating within her who will be a new *object* and then, with a bit of luck, a *subject* and from now on, a target of love, sometimes of hate, and often both at once. You yourself write that this reception of the child on the part of the mother is an "education" that instructs her "brain" (or subject). "The inaugural object is a face, the mother's. Even a blind baby 'sees' the maternal figure—a purely affective vision, without lines, without colors, and without movements—a sort of blind vision, the look of love in the nascent stage."[4] The mother's face instructs/modulates the baby's brain, you say. I would say: within certain limits, maternal passion modulates the future subject.

Question: what is this maternal passion? We have psychoanalytical theories on the baby's supposed precociousness; on the hysterical woman's or female lover's unconscious; fewer, perhaps, on the mother as subject. Placing her alongside the baby, Bion envisions the existence of an "innate preconception of the breast," an a priori knowledge of the breast that evokes the Kantian notion of an "a priori pure concept." You would say that in the baby there is an "empty thought" of the breast as object, perhaps a motion or an emotion that formed during epigenesis in the triad of desire/pleasure/suffering aimed at a missing pole of satisfaction. Starting with this a priori of the "already there breast," starting therefore with this transcendental given of a drive originally endowed with a "thing in itself," and which, according to you, is the motion of the desire/pleasure/suffering triad, the child later experiences the mother's "real breast" or her face as a frustration, negatively. The union of the preconception (for you, emotion in the sense of oppositional processes) and nonrealization engenders the proto-thought of the child (Bion speaks of "beta elements," "sense impressions," and "bizarre objects" that the child uses in projective identification and that we find again in psychotic thought).

Allow me to take the mother's side: I note that her passionate state is characterized by an afflux of three fundamental emotions (desire, pleasure, aversion) that do not destroy reflexive consciousness, but that inflect it, when they do not, as you say, "vandalize" it. The uncertainties of the desiring link with the father, its inevitable fluctuations and frustrations, regardless of the success of the amorous couple, are replaced by the promise, in a future time, of a link, unknown and risky, certainly, but whose "object" already inhabits the "subject" and for nine months is inseparable from her. The extraneousness of the pregnant woman, the strangeness of this "interior" faced with the external world, is accentuated: the future mother becomes an object of desire, pleasure, and aversion for herself. We call this shift a "narcissistic withdrawal" and wonder about the exact status of the object in this maternal adventure. Is it an "object" in the sense of logical categories, a "subject" separated from the "object," an "object" to know, to respect in its otherness? No pregnant woman or mother has this altruism, this obsessional, that is to say, philosophical, distance. Is it, on the contrary, a simple denial of the other, a quasi-maniacal self-stimulation of the female subject, who, in a state not unlike "possession," would be incapable of taking into account an existence separate from her own, and who would only be able to absorb it, monopolize it, dominate it? Here we recognize the crazy mother, the witch, the psychosis-inducing mother, or more commonly, dare I say, the phallic mother.

Miraculously ("miraculously," because even though it seems impossible, this alchemy manages to take place, and consequently, humanity exists, thinks, speaks, lives), motherhood is a passion in the sense that the emotions of narcissistic attachment and aggressiveness, filtered through reflexive consciousness and through the unconscious that speaks of Eros and Thanatos, are transformed into love (with its more or less attenuated correlate of hate). I would even say, in this experience of motherhood, passion takes on its most human aspect, that is to say, the furthest from its biological foundation, which nevertheless accompanies it (the famous drives of attachment and aggressiveness), and that it takes the path of sublimation without ceasing to be a passion. This begins by the passion of the pregnant woman for herself: her destabilized "self," a loss of identity, because divided by the intervention of the lover-father, and, through this intervention of the other, inhabited by an unknown third party—an embryo, a fetus, then a baby, a child, though for the moment an indiscernible double, an a priori object, if you will, but in fact a formless *pre-object*, the empty content of a self-stimulated container in and against the link to the father-genitor and the environment. Though dominated by narcissism, this initial maternal passion is no less triangulated: the absent or inward-looking face of the one who is pregnant "looks" without "seeing" the father and the external world or the feelings of motion and emotion taking place in her body.

This first stage of the passion turned within is followed by the mother's passion for the new subject that will be her child, provided he/she ceases to be her double, but from whom the mother *detaches herself* to allow the child to become an autonomous being. This motion of *expulsion*, of *detachment*, is essential. Thus the negative immediately inhabits maternal passion;[5] and I have noted that the Freudian idea of negativity in the psyche was taken up by Melanie Klein and her disciples, Susan Isaacs and Paula Heimann—well before Lacan and Hippolyte—in the famous *Controversies* in London during the Second World War (a school whose contribution to the analysis of mother/child relations is well known). In this apprenticeship of the relationship to the other, the mother realizes both *the greatest intensity of the drive*, provided it remains in the register of narcissism and self-stimulation (at this point, I would say Melanie Klein's "projective identification" is the mother's with the baby as much as the baby's with the mother), and *an inhibition of the drive in terms of the goal* that allows affect to be transformed (as Catherine Parat has shown) into tenderness, care, and benevolence.

Taking into account the feminine extraneousness to the symbolic order, I think, without *an optimal experience of motherhood*, the female subject has difficulty attaining—and perhaps never attains—a relationship to the other sex, or a relationship to the other, whatever it is, that is not pure emotion (attachment/adversity) or pure indifference. I said: *without a relationship to maternal passion*, it being understood that motherhood is a biological and symbolic process and analytical, self-analytical, or sublimatory work can arrive at the same structural modifications. I am emphasizing the structural experience of motherhood: I am not fundamentally "pro-birth."

It is in motherhood that the link to the other can become love—but it is neither obligatory nor standard and, when it happens, it is at the price of multiple failures coupled with modest successes!—in the sense of an emotion filtered through reflexive consciousness and the unconscious, a drive that is held back in terms of the goal and thus capable of renouncing its own satisfaction, and that is realized by an attention to the real presence of the other, which is always frustrating. As you know, Freud thought that "to love one's neighbor as oneself" was an illusion, the wishful thinking of the Gospels. As always, Freud was right: love of this sort is only possible for St. Francis and a few mystics like him. But I would say it is also possible for the mother, for this enigma that a "good mother" is—a horizon never reached by anyone, of course, but that brushes against us intermittently, indispensable in allowing the *infans* to find the transitional space that will allow it to think. It is in motherhood that a woman can find a chance to remedy the hysterical drive/meaning, emotion/cognition noncongruence and to experience the amorous passion that is the condition of life for her and her child.

Female psychoanalysts and feminists (notably, Nancy Chodorow, Jessica Benjamin, and Dorothy Dinnerstein) have emphasized the relationship of the "precocious object" that is constructed in the female subject well before the oedipal phase, in the mother-daughter relationship, and the transmission of maternal desire between mother and daughter. As for me, I am attentive to *the instability of the relationship of the precocious object* in the experience of motherhood. It is true that we may speak of the link of the precocious object in the little girl and the woman: as if there were always already an *object* for a *woman*, and her eroticism always implicated an external pole, while in the man eroticism may more easily be a tension internal to the subject himself.

On the cultural level, and not the psychoanalytical one, and contrary to the most widespread schemas, I have been able to note that what seems common to "female genius" in experiences as diverse as those of Hannah Arendt, Melanie Klein, and Colette is precisely the attention paid to the *link* and the *object* rather than the solitude or solipsistic incantation and dramas of subjectivity per se. I would say that if this quest for the object, which is rooted in the daughter-mother dyad, leads in the postoedipal, heterosexual experience of the woman to eternal disillusion, to "extraneousness," motherhood provides a laboratory for working through. First a narcissistic double, then a target of projective identification, then a separate and autonomous other, the link of the mother to her child is a veritable analysis in action. A link to the other is constructed; it emerges from narcissism and establishes the possibility itself of an other who would no longer be pure strangeness, a product of phallic identification and repression, but would set in motion both the autoerotic satisfaction of drives *and* their inflection toward another, becoming fully and thus solely a *subject* of sharing and reflexivity.

All amorous passion, provided it is not just erotic exaltation, participates in this experience of love I am attempting to capture in the passionate link, in a constant working through, between mother and child. If we are capable of love in our erotic ties as adults, it is because we keep and reconduct this inaugural passion that allowed the narcissistic states of our mothers to blossom in conflicting links with the pseudo objects that we were at first, by way of score settling and reparations vis-à-vis themselves through us, then by outlining spaces of thought with the beloved other that we finally become in order to think and live by ourselves.

I would not want to leave you with the image of an idyllic maternal love: the word passion that I apply to maternal love should not be confused with the warriorlike passions we see pouring forth from our television screens, for example, expressed by so many religious, ethnic, or national combatants. I do not share Winnicott's idea of an initial serenity of maternal love that would be coextensive to pure "being" and would only later develop into a drive-related "doing." As far back as I go in my experience of analysis or self-analysis, the drive-related "doing" of the mother and the child are already there, and the "oppositional processes" filtered through consciousness and the unconscious vandalize the link.

I think *motherhood is* (perhaps) *a constructive analysis of a possible link* to the other, when it resembles an analysis of borderline states and perversions. I think that in motherhood, as in these analyses, what is constructed is what was not constructed during the oedipal evolution, that is to say, a veritable dual relationship that implies an equilibrium of drive-related satisfactions *and* ideals, the real *and* the symbolic (you see the meaning I give the word *passion*: to me *passion,* in the sense of "maternal love," means "authentic experience," the "truth of the subject" in the link to the other—and isn't this what analysis is aiming for?). But along this path, whether that of motherhood or of the difficult analyses of *borderline states* or "false selves," we encounter a hysteric inflected toward psychosis and perversion; and I share the opinion of authors as different as François Perrier and André Green for whom female sexuality takes shelter in motherhood so as to live out its perversion and madness, which could also be a chance to work them through. Seduction, part objects, fetishistic elations, emotional disturbances, decompensation, manic states—the very possibility of "psychical representation," indeed, of "psychical space" is threatened. Passion then becomes a sort of ethnic war, the most ferocious being those that involve the smallest differences, the ones we wage on ourselves through the intermediary of those closest to us (the trial of the mother who committed infanticide that was all over the news testifies to this).

Yet in most cases a certain *detachment* is produced (if not optimal than at least relative). And it is from this defusing of passion that maternal love ultimately becomes a force of psychical and vital support. Since most mothers are not in analysis, and therefore do not benefit from our supposedly competent assistance, we have to admit that something in the very structure of maternal experience favors this metabolism of passion into dispassion. I invite you to consider three factors: *the place of the father*, *time*, and the acquisition of language.

I will not linger over the essential role of the father or his representative, which leads to a reappropriation of the triangular oedipal structure, as the mother remakes, repairs, or analyzes her oedipal phase after the little girl failed at it in what I call extraneousness. This aspect has been addressed at length in the analytical literature. I will say a few words about the two others.

We often say the *acquisition of language* by the child is a reacquisition of language by the mother. In the projective identification of the mother with the child, the genetrix inhabits the mouth, lungs, and digestive tube of her offspring and, by accompanying the child's echolalia, leads the child to signs, sentences, and stories. She unconsciously relearns her mother tongue, that of the Minoan-Mycenaean period which she repressed while becoming "extraneous," and, for that very reason, very capable in the phallic country of fathers. This reconciliation with the mother tongue, for the mother, is not only a reconciliation with her own childhood or with her own mother but also a disinhibition of her imaginary, the socially acceptable creation of a personal sensorial language: the "baby talk" the mother shares with her child is every mother's "search for lost time." Every mother retraces Marcel Proust's path in her own way when she assists her child in acquiring language. By speaking the language of her child, a woman remedies the noncongruence between affect and cognition that the hysteric complains of, and her emotions cease to be exiles of the social world of reflexive consciousness and become passions, in the sense of a psyche experienced as authentic, at the interface of emotion/consciousness and the unconscious.

As for *temporality*, it has always seemed paradoxical to me that the Western philosophy of time should refer exclusively to that of death. The parameter of death, which is certainly crucial, is only one of the aspects of temporality. Motherhood is clearly preoccupied with it but favors another caesura: that of *beginning*. That conception and labor are the initiatory acts that scan the chain of duration, renewing it, affects the temporal experience of both parents, but the mother more so, through her body's implication. Philosophy teaches us now that the logic of freedom does not reside in a transgression, as it was easy to think, but precisely in the capacity of beginning. Winnicott himself suggested that the infant only begins to leave the uterus when he is sufficiently free in his movements, when he has reached a certain biopsychological completion, a certain autonomy: for him a beginning and autonomy are two sides of the same state.[6] The mother's time is confronted with this opening, this beginning or these beginnings, in the plural, if she has several children or grandchildren. The ephemeral that awakens concern in us is then covered in wonder before the ephemeral as a new beginning. And biological destiny becomes a risk and chance for freedom, since it allows itself to be absorbed in the transgenerational continuation, in that of the living, where the mother is inscribed by giving birth. One could interpret this experience of temporality as duration through a new beginning, as a phallic elation to which the desire for the child can be compared in a Freudian way: it seems clinically indisputable, acting as a counterweight to this "extraneousness to the phallus" specific to the woman that I have pointed out. The time of beginning and the duration it imposes on consciousness, and even more on the unconscious, contribute forcefully to compensation for phallic castration. Moreover, by containing hysterical depressiveness, this experience of temporality can bring up feelings of elation (Christianity is a religion of triumph and glory, a religion of heaven, beyond infernal passion, because it is based on this temporality of beginning—a religion of birth and its repetition through the resurrection). But this experience of temporality can be frozen in a formidable paranoid horizon in which the maternal unconscious is engulfed, caught in the vertigo of manic omnipotence: the figure of the Virgin, after being *Mater dolorosa*, is a regal figure, Queen of Heaven and the Church, who, for two thousand years, has encouraged female paranoia. Still, by recouping the time of death and that of beginning and new beginning in duration, the unconscious temporality of the mother can *also* have an analytical value of detachment vis-à-vis the unique object, the invitation to plurality, becoming a source of dispassion and freedom.

All of which to say that if maternal love seems to Jean-Didier Vincent and myself to be *the prototype of human passion* (in the sense of an interface between emotion and reflexive consciousness/the unconscious), it also seems to me to be *the prototype of this* unshackling *of passion* that allows the human being to establish some distance vis-à-vis his two torturers—*drives and the object*—which are also his two passionate supports. Since the mother is there for me to leave her, and since there is no good mother except the one who lends herself to matricide, the good mother would be "orestian" rather than "oedipal"—that is what Klein the *mother* certainly saw, and went along with, more than one might like to admit! Perhaps one had to be a woman and a mother (never perfect, that goes without saying) and maintain this extravagant relationship with sublimation, like Colette (but a mother is always in sublimation, through her immersion in the mother tongue), to write what I have not found in the writings of men—this detachment, this defusing of the amorous link that is nevertheless maintained: "Love, one of the great commonplaces of existence, is slowly leaving mine. The maternal instinct is another great commonplace. Once we've left these behind, we find that all the rest is gay and varied, and that there is plenty of it. But one doesn't leave all that behind when or as one pleases."[7]

At the risk of scandal, I would even say that the "good-enough mother" loves no one: her passion is eclipsed in a detachment that, without necessarily becoming monstrous (which happens, but not fatally), is called serenity. No other link and every link. Colette, again, on the ideal mother, her own, Sido, who refuses to visit her daughter, whom she adores, because "her pink cactus is probably going to flower."[8] A mother loves nothing and no one if not "flowering": "waiting for the possible bursting into bloom of a tropical flower held everything up and silenced even her heart, made for love."⁹ I translate this as the framework of a passion, of love, like the framework of society, seems restrictive to her; her framework is that of cosmic beginning. In other words, in a paraphrase of Freud in the feminine, the good-enough mother can say: "I have succeeded where the *female* paranoiac fails."

I would like to add an observation to these aspects of amorous passion regarding the mother and the biological foundations of the passions pointed out by Jean-Didier Vincent, to suggest how the *interface* between "oppositional processes" prepares for the emotions, on the one hand, and variants of reflexive consciousness/the unconscious, on the other; and to underscore that this interface of passion can be modulated in terms of the unconscious experience of the protagonists. The subjective experience and more particularly the unconscious experience of the mother does not "instruct" the biological data that remain essential; and yet in the narrow way in which the mother, the "inaugural object," as you say, interacts with her own emotions and that of the child, it instructs them nonetheless. It is through the maternal conscious and unconscious experience (in close relationship with that of the father, on whom I have chosen not to focus today) that the modulations of our passion pass—perhaps, in the long term, to the point of modifying the neuronal and hormonal map itself.

Now to conclude, since as you see what interests me is dispassion, which I am trying to understand in order to find out how a mother arrives at the impossible, I wonder where we can find the flowering of it outside of optimal motherhood. Two responses come to mind: in sublimation and on the couch.

Unlike repression, which deflects it, sublimation establishes passion in the subject and, for this very reason, without ignoring drives, does not give free rein to desire, as Lacan suggests. More maliciously, sublimation disinhibits perversion but uses it as a path of access to the infantile, to make passion a discourse of passion. The artist is a pervert who has recaptured the polymorphous pervert within, the child, and uses perverse experiences not as an end in themselves, but to arrive at a new passion, one that is true for him, more satisfying than real passions, though never sufficient—namely, the communication of his passion through the signs of reflexive consciousness (poetry, painting, novels, cinema).

We belong to a divided civilization. On the one hand, the civilization of technology feeds the passion for calculation, increasingly disconnected from primary affects and unconscious pleasures (twenty-first-century glo-balization hopes passions will be reduced under the twofold effect of Nas-daq's economic well-being and Prozac's biological well-being; meanwhile, crises of passion are having direct impact, in the form of religious wars, for example). On the other hand, we are becoming a society of the image with two valences: the stereotyped, lulling image would be the new opium of the passions of the people and the cathartic image, a sublimatory activ-ity, whose complex panoply goes from brilliant performances to auxiliary activities in art studios or art therapy, allow passion to rejoin its specifi-cally human, favored terrain, which is the imaginary. It is there that passion can be defused without denying itself; because it remains in contact with drives, oppositional processes, and, in seeking new languages, calls on the secret drives of the other, the art lover, the recipient, the public.

But it is on the couch—through the invention of the "talking cure" that Freud bequeathed to us, which consists of letting passion speak—that hu-man passions are called to a new regime. Oh, I'm not hallucinating. I know, as you do, that psychoanalysis does not always reach its objectives. But these objectives are implicit in its setup, and why not articulate them in the passion for truth that analytical passion (and even this conference) should be? By placing passionate discourse on the couch, implicated in a passion-ate discourse through countertransference (in the sense of the interface of the drive *versus* reflexive consciousness), Freud makes psychoanalysis a treatment of the passions by way of the passions: *he impassions in order to disim-passion.* As a result of being immersed in his own passions and those of his analysands, the analyst may become disimpassioned almost to the point of melancholy and lost in the wilderness. I am not referring only to repression, but to an excess of analysis, when the analyst begins to consider that passion is just a psychosomatic malady he should get rid of through analysis—like an illusion, like a religion? Freud was not far from thinking such a release possible. Which suggests a certain obsessionalization of the cure, indeed, a no less common tendency toward normalization through the cure. If this specter of normalization/obsessionalization lies in wait for us, this to me is the most antianalytical impediment of the Freudian invention.

Freud came across it and avoided it; in his life, as in his clinic, he re-mained passionate. Since we no longer know what it means to be Freudian, I encourage you to consider that analysis is interminable insofar as passion is the truth of man, and passion itself is interminable. Provided we add—and this is where Freud integrates the aesthetic sublimatory experience, just as he integrates the maternal experience (without saying so and often without recognizing it)—passion is the imaginary: an unconscious experience, an act, a language. This is also what biologists suggest: passion is not the emotion it depends on, but an emotion put into signs. I would add that the more we work out/work through our signs (instead of throwing stones, as in guerrilla warfare, one would throw paint, as in a Pollock drip painting, or throw words out to one's analyst who would reconstruct their meaning), the more passion will be clarified without being extinguished. The powers and limits of psychoanalysis are to develop—as the "good mother" does—as many representations as possible to accompany the explosions of narcissistic self-stimulation, to the point of making them necessarily conflicting object relations in order to finally liberate them in a plurality of connections. That is the end of the cure, which I would compare to motherhood in connections of detachment. The end of the cure neither represses nor abandons passion for a man or a woman; it does not drown the poison of passion. Transference and countertransference are passions that include unconscious experience as well as words and acting out. The end of the cure defuses passion, but by increasing the objects and discourses of passion; by doing away with a link (notably, that of transference) so as to make others possible. Not necessarily to allow the patient to find the right object, the right passion, but to allow him to repeat his passion, to establish links that can be signified and thought, at the interface of drives and meaning, in a free community. In short, and it is to this question that Jean-Didier Vincent's book has led me, is psychoanalysis alone in thinking that between a humanity without passion (because technology has stamped it out) and a humanity whose most passionate passion is one for death there remains another regime of passion, namely, one that works through its imaginary substance indefinitely, and that this regime of passion is the future of mankind, since it is the truth of women?

7

THE WAR OF THE SEXES SINCE ANTIQUITY

Citizens of the third millennium will not understand (our children already do not understand) that for millennia, half of humanity—the female half—was mistreated in culture and excluded from politics. At the rate things are going, with the help of female politicians and parity, we are starting to minimize this age-old discrimination that has no problem ostracizing from humanity those who are nevertheless the mothers of the species. We have a tendency to forget that awareness of this exclusion has only been expressed for barely a century, first by various feminist currents, then by certain observers looking at culture in a new, stunned, politely scandalized way, so as to try to propose a history of mentalities attentive to this exclusion. François Charpin is among them. An engaged historian? A Latinist seduced by Simone de Beauvoir and bitten by the psychoanalysis bug? Not really.

This man—whose tentative smile and affably stooped posture I can see now, whose voice I can hear with its reverential gentleness, the gentleness of a scholar filled with fraternal respect for the texts—cast his anxious blue gaze on tradition, wanting to analyze the past with the critical demands of our era, without forgetting their specific meanings and the constraints of time. The work that his colleagues have chosen to publish is a preliminary draft of the research he was engaged in, alongside work of much more technical precision, which his demanding mind would certainly have found to be imperfect.[1] Nevertheless, to my mind, this outline bears witness to a deeply ethical, modern inspiration, which, as a result of knowing ancient history to the letter, attempts to open it up again to the minds of readers today.

We could also read these pages as François Charpin's novel: a sort of personal selection, no doubt inspired by his own history and dreams, that presents a bouquet gathered at leisure in the gardens of Greek and Roman Antiquity. We knew that the Greeks, though very complacent toward virile beauty and control, disdained neither the goddesses nor the hetaera. Nevertheless, in his own way, François Charpin emphasizes the active role of the Greek woman as she appeared to him in *The Odyssey*: a true actor, particularly in the reconstruction of the character of Ulysses. The young and beautiful Nausicaa washes the hero and allows him to be reborn; while the faithful Penelope seems less a subservient wife than a rather clever political leader. She does not merely wait; she governs after her husband's departure, with the support of the people and the gods, while also sustaining the hope of suitors; then, having gotten a taste of freedom, she refuses to identify Ulysses upon his return, which is in fact a very insolent independence! The couple finally reunited will be free of illusions, and, if their union lasts, it is because it is devoted to this strange power involving the management of memory. We are a long way from the Song of Songs, *Tristan and Iseult*, and *Romeo and Juliet*!

It is thus to Rome that François Charpin will attribute the true casting aside of the second sex that our modernity will condemn and combat. Indeed, the historian sees a static and grievous universe in *The Aeneid* that establishes the durability of Being, contrary to its Greek flow. The women of this static time are no longer actors but mere extras of history: no Circe, no Calypso, no Nausicaa. Savage virgins and Amazon warriors replace them, or else absent, forgotten women. Such as Creusa, who follows her husband Aeneas from afar, as they flee into exile, and who disappears without anyone noticing: a wife who effaces herself without reproach, with the most obliging discretion. The subsequent marriage of Aeneas and Lavinia will essentially be a political matter, from which affective and physical motives will be entirely absent.

In fact, this eviction of feminine subjectivity is not without consequence for the male ego itself. Fashioned according to the canons of virtue and the demands of paternal authority, Aeneas's Ego is not really developed, our historian-analyst observes, after counting the use of the pronoun *ego* in the text. In a more complex way (Freud would say *perverse*), the power of the *patres* that neglects women when it does not culpabilize their desire (aren't they the only inspiring ones, thereby threatening the solidity of male political control?), leaves the man to his drives and so transforms the supposed absolute master into a slave of his own desires. So a leader like Caesar may indeed appear to be "the husband of all wives and the wife of all husbands," as Suetonius said, and the tyrant's homosexuality may be passionately praised; in François Charpin's lucid observations, men with unbridled desires are revealed to be unhappy children, abandoned by their mothers or else hated by them. The monstrosities of Nero, Caligula, and Tiberius reveal these "personality disorders" that cannot conceal the distress of the unloved little boys they once were, which their abject behaviors attempt to abreact. Yet, as the logic of perversion requires, even in their most immoral fantasies they are not free but demand these fantasies be ordered by law and dictated by supreme power.

It is the incompatibility between men and women that stands out in this sober research, and a tragic impression emerges, which, as we may suspect, has diagnosed the war of the sexes since the dawn of time as well as its aggravation in Roman Antiquity. The exclusion of women in the life of the city will be the major symptom, and François Charpin deciphers it in the three figures of Roman femininity he brings to the fore: the *forgotten* woman, the *effaced* woman, and the woman *slave*.

Who remembers the mother of Romulus and Remus? Her name was Rhea Silvia; she was a Vestal Virgin who was raped (by the god Mars or by her uncle Amulius?). After giving birth, Rhea Silvia simply disappears from history—the now famous Roman female wolf replaces her in the imaginary. In a somewhat similar way, the Sabines are kidnapped by Roman men and hauled away as loot. Deprived of all subjectivity, they must surrender their hearts after surrendering their bodies, so that the Stoic ideology of power can gradually be established: "ego, parentes, patria." Not without opposing the war and later bringing peace to the two states! For the feminine *can* change its spots, blending in and bringing peace, provided we know how to read.

But it is the passage from the monarchic regime to the Republic in 509 that most incurs the historian's wrath, reading Livy. An impeccable revolution, the ancient writer claims. Perhaps, Charpin replies, provided we exclude Lucretia's suicide. But it's over for free women, those princesses devoted to literature, languages, divination. The Republic now relies on the housewife; it takes away speech, and politics is reserved for men more than ever. Lucretia's last words imply that the adulterous and violated woman must die: the sacrifice of the heroine is necessary to republican virtue.

There are other analyses, sketched out, cast aside, that resonate with other revolutions, the French Revolution, to begin with. Didn't the Tennis Court Oath, the fraternity of men proclaimed by the republican motto—Liberté, Égalité, Fraternité—erase half of humanity, too, in their own way?

Finally, Monica, St. Augustine's mother, provides material for the portrait of the woman slave. No less than the Republic, the Christian Church is called on to answer for its own exclusion of women before the court of reading. Denounced as extravagant, unfaithful, arrogant, the women in *City of God* prolong the fate of Roman women, already considered the "flawed sex." Commonly beaten as a result, and without protest. Not even Monica protests, she who is so beloved by her son: doesn't he owe her everything, particularly his conversion, and even his ecstasies? But he only describes her as a "holy woman" insofar as she is "in service to her husband as a slave is in service to his master." Because to be married, up to and including the Christian code, is to be a servant. The historian's perspective and his unfinished work oblige him to neglect the material and spiritual benefits the Christian family contributed to women and children. Among other things. And it ends with Augustine's (all in all intellectual) rehabilitation of Monica, who was not so slavish as all that. Charpin's commentaries here are far from being an exhaustive opus, as we have said: it is a draft that raises thorny problems and opens the possibility for research.

Because, in the end, can we be certain that these Roman or Christian archaisms have been left in the past, have been surpassed and overcome in our world, which is proud of its female politicians and its parity? Reading the anxieties of our colleague and consulting our own, we are convinced that he is speaking of us, he is speaking to us—through Lucretia, Monica, the Sabines, and Rhea Silvia. Not to reassure us—or discourage us!—by showing us the extent to which the current exclusion of women is rooted in a past that hasn't really passed, but to find the logic of this mythic thought of the excluded feminine, and the historical context of its elaboration, so as to allow us to keep our distance from it within ourselves and in the society around us. Charpin's Roman men and women are, alas, our contemporaries. Alas and so much the better! This writing, halfway between the vigilant study of texts and the anxieties of a man in modern life, takes hold of us in our most secret depths and appeals to our everyday struggles.

8

BEAUVOIR, PRESENTLY

I thank you for your invitation to be here today, but I wonder what I can add to the remarks of Sartre's brilliant biographer, Bernard-Henri Lévy, and his contributions to the topic of this colloquium, "De Beauvoir à Sartre et de Sartre à Beauvoir" (From Beauvoir to Sartre and from Sartre to Beauvoir).

As a woman, a citizen, a psychoanalyst, and a writer (but certainly not as a specialist), and with an interest that has never waned, I have followed and continue to follow the path of these two literary giants, who provoked scandal and influenced many of our fates. I will limit myself to reformulating the theme of this conference, taking into consideration my limits and current experience, which I will articulate as follows: What presence does Beauvoir have today? How is Beauvoir present to me and perhaps to you, here and now? The following remarks will be personal, since the *present* has never been so plural, perhaps never more so in history. Never has the present been so pulverized into a multitude of fragments, crystallizing singularities that are as varied as they are explosive in the clearly globalized world that is our own.

I will follow three lines of inquiry to try to zero in on Beauvoir's presence today: first, the equality of the sexes and the myth of universalism, according to Simone de Beauvoir; then, the male/female relationship, as revised and corrected by her; and, finally, what good is the novel?

The Equality of the Sexes and the Myth of Universalism

Women's struggle for their emancipation in modern times has seen three stages:

- the suffragettes' demand for *political rights*;
- the affirmation of ontological *equality* with men (versus "equality in difference"), which led Simone de Beauvoir in *The Second Sex* (1949) to demonstrate and prophesy a "fraternity" between men and women beyond their natural specificities;
- the search for the *difference* between the sexes, in the wake of May '68 and psychoanalysis, that would encourage original creativity on the part of women, in terms of sexuality as well as a range of social practices, from politics to writing.

At each of these stages, the aim was the liberation of women as a whole: in that, feminists did not depart from the all-encompassing ambitions of the progressive movements that ensued from the philosophy of the Enlightenment and, going further back, from the dissolution of the religious continent, whose heavenly teleology these movements aspired to on earth, with negativity in revolt. Today we are all too familiar with these total and totalitarian impasses and promises. Feminism itself, whatever its variants in Europe and the United States, has not escaped these limits, and the tendency has ended up hardening into a militancy with no future that thinks it can include all women, like all proletarians, or the entire third world, without regard to the singularity of each subject, in a call to arms as fierce as it is hopeless.

Yet we should recognize that the most illustrious of these inspirations, Simone de Beauvoir, never underestimated the "subject" in a woman or the "individual" who felt "a vague need to transcend herself." Faithful to this perspective, which followed from existentialist ethics, and appropriating Marxism in her own way, the philosopher sought to free women from the inferior status compelling them to be man's Other with neither the right nor the opportunity to constitute herself as Other in turn.

Indeed, this is the message of *The Second Sex*.

Deprived of the possibility of projects and transcendence, the woman formed by the history of a society dominated by men is fated to immanence, frozen into an object, "since her transcendence is itself perpetually transcended by another, essential and sovereign consciousness."[1] While struggling against the reduction of woman to biology alone—"One is not born, but rather becomes, a woman" (SS 267)—Simone de Beauvoir did not shrink before metaphysics, since it was metaphysics that enclosed the woman in the other so as to posit her as facticity and as immanence and to refuse her access to true humanity: that of autonomy and liberty.

Yet, while pushing aside the problem of difference in favor of that of equality, Beauvoir kept herself from pushing the existentialist project very far, though she articulated it nonetheless, which would have led her to contemplate, through the condition of women in the plural, the chance for freedom for each as a singular human being: "The drama of woman lies in this *conflict* between the fundamental aspirations of every *subject* (ego)—who always regards the self as the essential—and the compulsions of a *situation* in which she is the inessential. How can a *human being in woman's situation* attain fulfillment? . . . I am interested in the fortunes of the individual as defined not in terms of happiness, but in terms of liberty" (SS xxxiv).[2]

Indeed, though Beauvoir's reflection drew largely on the accomplishments of female "subjects" or "individuals," all as exemplary in their genius as Saint Teresa or Colette by way of Mademoiselle de Gournay or Théroigne de Méricourt, it is less to the "human being" and the "fortunes of the individual" that *The Second Sex* is devoted than to the "feminine condition" as a whole. Because it was from the transformation of this condition that the author expected possible individual autonomy and feminine creativity, these "fortunes" of the singular being whose liberation, according to her, should have been history's primary objective.

The author of *The Second Sex* no doubt came too early to defend female singularity, when so many sexual and economic "conditions" still hindered the emancipation of women. Her philosophical journalism, presented in a tone of intense engagement, coupled with vast pedagogical erudition and tinged with irony as clear-sighted as it was elegant, would assure her book's unsurpassed success: while its issues remain topical, the *global era* that has

followed *Les temps modernes* is proving too steeped in conservatisms and archaisms, and it is not certain that the "conflict" between the condition of
all women and the free fulfillment of each—a conflict that is at the basis of
female suffering, according to this philosophy—can be resolved, if we are
only concerned with the "condition" while underestimating the "subject." In
her reflections, by favoring the transformation of the feminine "condition,"
Beauvoir herself contributes to pushing aside the essential issue, that of the
singular initiative, and to obscuring the vague chance of the *haecceitas* dear
to Duns Scotus, vigorously defended and fulfilled by a female philosopher,
a female psychoanalyst, and a female writer. Arendt, Klein, and Colette—
and countless others—did not wait for the feminine condition to bear fruit
in order to realize their freedom. Isn't "genius" precisely this breakthrough
through and beyond the "situation"?

Calling on the genius of every woman, and every man, is not a way to
underestimate the weight of History—more than anyone else, these three
women confronted it and overturned it with courage and realism—but an
attempt to free the feminine condition, like the human condition in general,
from biological, social, or fateful constraints, emphasizing the conscious or
unconscious initiative of the subject over the burden of an agenda, dictated
by these various determinisms.

Isn't the singular initiative, in short, this minimal but ultimate inner
strength on which the deconstruction of every "condition" depends? By
examining the irreducible subjectivity of these three women and their creative singularity, it is their "individual fortunes" "in terms of liberty"—to
use Beauvoir's words—that was of interest in my own inquiry. And so, beyond our divergences, I wanted to take up and develop an essential idea in
The Second Sex. Under the constraint of History, on the one hand, and her
own existentialist option, on the other, Beauvoir had to leave the following
question unanswered: how can a woman achieve fulfillment, her individual
fortune in terms of liberty, the modern sense of happiness, through the
feminine condition? By formulating my inquiry this way, I wish to express
my debt to Simone de Beauvoir—a pioneer too often and unfairly criticized or underestimated—and to dedicate my *Female Genius* triptych to her
memory.

Equality of the sexes according to Beauvoir, who aspired to "fraternity"
(note the masculine) between men and women socially, is inscribed philo-
sophically under the regime of the universal, the genealogy of which goes
back to the Platonic Ideal, to Plotinus's νοῦζ, and to republican ideals of

universal man dear to the French Enlightenment: it would be impossible to list the many historical variants of the metaphysics of the universal, which remains the touchstone of the rights of man and modern culture. Listening to psychoanalysis, we know that it is sustained by the *denial of the female body*, the denial of *female homosexuality*, and the denial of *maternity*. And by the worship of the phallus and the great man (Sartre), who has his own ambivalence, aggressiveness, and dependencies.

We are all too familiar with the violent lashing out, which I would describe as phobic, studded throughout Simone de Beauvoir's *The Second Sex*, against the degradation of the menstruating body, the slavery of pregnancy, the horrors of the sexual abuses women have undergone, and the pain of giving birth. I will quote a few:

"Gestation is a fatiguing task of no individual benefit to the woman but on the contrary demanding heavy sacrifices. It is often associated . . . with . . . vomiting . . . which signalize[s] the revolt of the organism against the invading species" (*SS* 29–30).

"Childbirth itself is painful and dangerous. . . . Nursing is also a tiring service. . . . It has been well said that women have 'infirmity in the abdomen'; and it is true that they have within them a hostile element—it is the species gnawing at their vitals" (*SS* 30).

"Woman is of all mammalian females the one who is most profoundly alienated . . . and the one who most violently resists this alienation" (*SS* 32).

Or this: "The body of a woman—particularly that of a young girl—is a 'hysterical' body, in the sense that there is, so to speak, no distance between the psychic life and its physiological realization. The disorders of puberty are made worse. . . . The organic disorder is itself brought on by a psychic state. . . . It is in great part the anxiety of being a woman that devastates the feminine body" (*SS* 332–333).

"The self-control," imposed on "well-bred" young girls by their upbringing, "kills spontaneity." For girls at school, "this ennui is catching," because desire for boys takes over : "Boys are better," and "This is a debilitating conviction" (*SS* 335).

Other quotes are not necessary; you have heard them. While stipulating—for the first time and with exemplary courage—that "one is not born, but rather, becomes a woman" and thus denouncing the sociohistorical manipulations that ultimately produce female slavery, the author of *The Second Sex* does not fail to reveal her refusal—which is more than unconscious, often conscious, indeed, militant—of sexual difference as manifested by menstruation, menopause, motherhood, and lesbianism, among other things. She also asserts her admiration, if not her fascination, for the phallic power of the muscular male body and man's "infinitely privileged" destiny.

Do we need extra proof of this denial of the feminine that I am advancing, which is the private side of Beauvoir's universalism and, implicitly, of all universalism?

While Sartre himself defined desire, and especially man's desire, as "troubled"—"If the desiring consciousness is troubled, it is because it is analogous to troubled water"—since the sexual is neither "distinct" nor "clear,"[3] Beauvoir imagines the erect male sex organ as "simple and neat as a finger" (SS 386), and compares vaginal lubrication to carnivorous plants and to swamps that swallow up children. As Toril Moi notes, where Sartre considers the penis an instrument, Beauvoir—already Lacanian without knowing it?—*deifies* the male organ by seeing it as an instrument of transcendence.[4] Let's consider a hypothesis. A fairly phallic Beauvoir, faced with a rather feminine Sartre, goes beyond the homeliness of the man to share the intellectual superiority of the philosopher in a fraternal way. This revolving door allows the future author of *The Second Sex* not only to assume her partner's castration and/or femininity "naturally" and to enjoy, in his place and as a woman, the femininity of the master's mistresses, but also to dominate them as if she were not only a man but the thinker himself! Each of them fully mobilizing his/her psychic bisexuality to form a *ménage à quatre* with each other? Would this explain why Sartre was one of the few men, perhaps the only one, who did not fear castration when faced with an assertive woman like Beauvoir, so respectful of the symbolic phallus and the master of thought? So many (all in all, amusing) hypotheses to be asserted or invalidated considering the feminist's surprising suppleness, who, contrary to appearances, and in the end and in hindsight, seems to free herself from her contradictions.

One example: in a 1945 review of Merleau-Ponty's *The Phenomenology of Perception*, which highlights the corporeal embodiment of consciousness and the constitutive ambiguity of perception and sexuality, Beauvoir appreciates the "richness" of the analysis, which in fact contrasts sharply with Sartre's thesis of existence as pure in-itself. And while her own conception of female sexuality in *The Second Sex* and in her novels is striking in its ambiguity and closer to Merleau-Ponty overall, the philosopher does not hesitate to proclaim her preference for *Being and Nothingness* over *The Phenomenology of Perception*.

In a more empirical if not existential way, we may recall that Beauvoir, inclined to female friendships beginning in adolescence, never got over losing Zaza, the great love of her youth, who died prematurely. "There is something virile in the young professor's manner," Inspector Davy noted, a member of the *agrégation* jury in February 1935, regarding the applicant's teaching. We are familiar with the different versions of the privileged relationship Beauvoir maintained with some of her students: Olga, who became Xavière in *L'Invitée* (*She Came to Stay*) and Ivitch in Sartre's *L'Age de raison* (*The Age of Reason*); Nathalie Sorokine, Lise Oblanoff in *Mémoires d'une jeune fille rangée* (*Memoirs of a Dutiful Daughter*), some of whose character traits can be found in Hélène in *Le Sang des autres* (*The Blood of Others*); or Bianca Bienenfeld, called Louise Védrine in *Memoirs*. The publication of *Lettres à Sartre* (Letters to Sartre) and *Journal de guerre* (War Journal) in 1990, the book by Bianca Lamblin, *Mémoires d'une jeune fille dérangée* (*A Disgraceful Affair*) in 1993, and the "Sorokine affair" uncovered by Gilbert Joseph, among others, in 1991, in *Une si douce Occupation: Simone de Beauvoir et Jean-Paul Sartre, 1940–1941*— which mentions the complaint, filed by Nathalie Sorokine's mother, accusing Beauvoir of corrupting a minor, which would result in the instructor's exclusion from the National Ministry of Education[5]—all have elements that provoke debate. But they leave no doubt as to Beauvoir's lesbian tendencies, a dominatrix and predator both of her own girlfriends and Sartre's. Tendencies she concealed in the grid of Hegelian logic, borrowing a rationalization for her passionate dramas from the universal figure of master and slave, so as to justify, repress, or sublimate them. Starting with *She Came to Stay* (1941)—this "frivolous story" about a love triangle that shines a spotlight on the love affairs in the Sartre-Beauvoir relationship—the Hegelian motto "Every consciousness pursues the death of the other" doesn't serve to justify a crime story or detective novel but introduces a universalist metaphysics capable of justifying the implacable passion, admitted and denied, between Françoise and Xavière, also known as Beauvoir and Olga Kosakiewicz. We would have to wait for *The Mandarins* (1954) for psychoanalysis to appear in the guise of a character, not as a clinical approach to Beauvoirian passions. Much more than Freud, it was Heidegger and Kierkegaard—the concern for presence and Ego—who were Beauvoir's chosen companions throughout her career, so that existentialism will never truly cross the border that separates metaphysics from the Freudian discovery.

Yet we must recognize that in this veritable alchemist's crucible where Beauvoir struggles between her passionate truth, which is her bisexuality, and the defenses that metaphysics offers her, between overwhelming sexuality/bisexuality, the juvenile exaltation of freedom, and the intellectual concern for truth (so many kinds of ambivalence trying to find expression in either the novel or the philosophical profession), she discovers the field of politics, *before* Sartre, through and beyond the intimist adventure.[6] Her "engagement" is outlined in a letter to Sartre on October 8, 1939, in which she expresses "remorse" regarding Bost, her lover, and others from a generation about a decade younger than Sartre and herself: it is "satisfactory when one's thinking of oneself" to remain inactive out of disdain for politics, to accept war as a "cataclysm" without complaint, but this stoic indifference is irresponsible with regard to others, she says in sum. Well beyond "*individual* obligations," Beauvoir is thinking about the "general," the "social," the "political." Sartre replies: "And I suppose these ideas immediately come to the mind of a father, because the paternal function immediately introduces the social in the relationship with the child."[7] And now Beauvoir is . . . a father, the initiator of the very idea of engagement, which she will not hesitate to attribute to Sartre, later, since he will see to its elaboration and propagation after 1941.

This is not the place to untangle the share of the denial of erotic ties, culpability, and ethical superego choice or to point out their necessary coexistence. Such an operation would be hazardous, as it would be with subjects undergoing the psychoanalytic adventure, and it is uncertain—indeed, impossible—with those who have avoided it. If I am assembling these reminders of female suffering, male envy, and the denials that have marked Beauvoir's existentialist, fictional, and ethical choices, it is because I am aware that the situation of victimhood and its phallic counterweight have been and continue to be the daily lot of the feminine condition throughout history and even today. That those favored by birth, fortune, social class, or family can now denounce the so-called victimization of women by third-generation feminists, indeed, by Simone de Beauvoir herself, seems nothing but hypocrisy, at best, an optimistic fantasy of concern only to those expressing it. The denunciation of female misery in Beauvoir's writings before and after the Second World War had the ambition of a fateful political battle, in the sense of overturning the fate of humanity. Because her shocked outcries as well as her male desires, including the sadomasochistic cruelties endured by the imaginary family that gravitated around Sartre and Beauvoir, accompanied the struggles of modernity, effectively crowned by contraception, the right to an abortion, and the right to equal employment for women, still in progress. Without false modesty or hypocritical angelicness, it is worth remembering that the progressive advances of our century, perhaps more than others, were paid for in excesses, extravagances, and incommensurable burnings.

Of course, in the words that deplore a young girl's menstruating body, I can read an identification with the aggressor: as if the author had internalized the gaze and the experience imposed by technological and productivist society on and against this female body, her own. I can also read this Beauvoirian *lament* against motherhood, for example, as a desire to acquire a competitive agility, the incisive, penetrating force of a brother, a man. When, in an interview with Alice Schwarzer, Beauvoir says she loves women's breasts but is never attracted "until the waist," I could, if I chose to, recall Marcel Proust's assertion, through Doctor Cottard, that "women derive most excitement from their breasts."[8] Or, if the author of *The Second Sex* inspired less sympathy in me, I might evoke the denial, comparable to Beauvoir's, formulated by President Clinton himself, when he claimed not to see anything sexual in the pleasures of a pipe or cigar.

Phobia, then, of the female and notably maternal body, denial of female homosexuality—to protect herself from conventional confinement, legal proceedings? Because of the impossibility of integrating them into her Hegelian-Marxist, engaged, existentialist system? Or, more cynically, because of a taste for power, social conventions, and, ultimately, social calculation? Reading her, following her struggle, accompanying her in her defenses and sorrows, I remain convinced that Beauvoir never stops getting burned by what she says and what she cannot say, that she makes it possible to convey if not the truth of desire than certainly its trembling. With her we are far from the flood of pornography in which we are currently awash, but just as far from the rationalist repression with which certain universalists today defend their virile ambitions, mocking the varieties of maternal experience, for example, as if childbirth spelled the decline of the feminine condition. To listen to these self-proclaimed Beauvoirians, we might assume their credo to be "Every real woman is a man," a variant of "Behind every successful man is a woman." Nothing of the sort with Beauvoir. Her universalism, the libidinal foundation of which I have pointed out, is constantly being reconstructed.

Especially since the ambiguity of Beauvoir's denials cannot be entirely justified by the social and political breakthrough they were able to achieve. Her meanness toward women, objects of her desire and jealousy, her melancholy, revealed in *La Femme rompue* (*A Woman Destroyed*), and the cruel tenderness applied to the dying Sartre's diminished body in *La Cérémonie des adieux* (*Adieux: A Farewell to Sartre*) reveal the regrets of a missed motherhood and the missteps of the militant. The admission, almost, of difference. The kind that scares universalists: difference, for better or worse. The sexual difference that Beauvoir does not posit as a political or philosophical claim but that emerges in her existential experience of *a relationship falling apart*.

The Male-Female Relationship, Revised and Corrected

Beyond its Greek, Jewish, and Christian antecedents, the modern relationship was founded by bourgeois ideology, called "enlightened" insofar as it was as forged by the philosophers of the Enlightenment. It is to Rousseau (1712–1778) that we owe its contours and values. *The New Héloïse* (1761) describes a society and mores in a state of decomposition, to which Roxane and Saint-Preux fall victim. In response to this debacle, *Émile* (1762) invents a new reality: a relationship in which the sexual relationship, because it is founded on nature, is declared possible.

To measure the sexual meaning and social impact of this invention, we should look at it through the reflections on mores of previous centuries and their link to despotic power. Rousseau has to be read in light of La Boétie (1530–1563) and his *Discours de la servitude volontaire* (*Discourse of Voluntary Servitude*) as well as Montesquieu's *Lettres persanes* (*Persian Letters*) and *L'Esprit des lois* (*On the Spirit of the Laws*). In this perspective the Rousseauist relationship seems to propose an alternative to sensual jouissance in which the polygamous oriental sovereign is abolished as well as its counterpart, prefigured in the decline of monarchic power.

Starting in the sixteenth century, and particularly in the seventeenth and eighteenth centuries, interest in seraglios on the part of authors and the French public was quite lively.[9] The harem master seems less a man than a householder, indeed, "a dead man" caught between tyrannical mothers and obsequious eunuchs, a flabby man whose supposed phallic power is only power by default among his multitudes of women as in politics.[10] Travelers and philosophers refer complacently to this foreign setup because they see in it the archeology—if not the essence—of what is displayed before their eyes in French society: the collapse of political power, the lack of sexual relations. Geographical distinctions, historical facts, structural impasses? To observations of the fantastic impossibility of the sexual relationship and the crisis of despotic power, *the new relationship* would be the miraculous formula meant to establish a two-sided subject, a guarantee of the parent-child bond and the state-citizen bond. We already know—and Rousseau's texts show—that this formula is not tenable; it is contested in terms of debauchery, perversion, and crime. The "new harmony" the relationship represents will soon appear to be a façade, "a surface mechanism, hiding a hell of debauchery and perversion."[11] It is Sade, especially, who will herald the flip side of the Rousseauist model, and Diderot, in a more enlightened way, more sensual than scandalous, but no less unsettling.

The feminine novel, from Madame de Staël to Colette to the *Story of O*, has not ceased to investigate the difficulty of the bourgeois relationship. As for Beauvoir, she did not unveil its impasses, melancholies, and erotic fires any more audaciously or more originally than her female colleagues. Starting with *She Came to Stay*, it was *jealousy* that seemed to be her main target: a major unconscious admission of her fascination with the male phallus, which women have trouble eliminating without the experience of psychoanalysis, as well as female homosexuality envious of the jouissance of the other woman, the indestructible rival. And the exclusion of women from the political struggle, which, according to *The Blood of Others,* only has room for dead women.

Yet from *She Came to Stay* (1941) to *The Blood of Others* (1945) with its epigraph by Dostoyevsky—"Each of us is responsible for everything and to every human being"—a new hand is dealt: as Danièle Fleury shows, the theme of intimacy seeps into that of solidarity, which will now dominate, while being infiltrated in turn by the narrator's admission of her failures and weaknesses. But the genre is found: at the intersection of the intimate and the political. The damp folds of psychology, enhanced by the dialectics of the struggle to the death between consciousnesses, are dried in the winds of History: the Popular Front, pacifism, the Occupation, Resistance, collaboration, the deportation of the Jews, communism, syndicalism, etc., penetrate the imaginary with *The Blood of Others*. A witness to her time and the philosophy of engagement, the philosopher continues to deconstruct the relationship—here, Blomart and Hélène, the latter mortally wounded in an act of resistance determined by Blomart. The blood of others or the blood of a woman? The freedom of desire in *She Came to Stay*, the freedom of political engagement now, are paid for by the death of the other, always a woman, and consequently the death of the relationship.

But there is more. This surpassing of intimism—which might have calcified into a call for militant, even universalist, repression, as in Sartre's doctrine, which ultimately declared literature was a neurosis one had to renounce—was itself surpassed. The tireless walker Beauvoir was kept starting down new paths and creating new ties. Was the absolute tie, as in the Song of Songs or Rousseau, defeated? Whatever the case, it would yield to a plurality of ties. Sartre would remain a tutelary pole; Algren would be enlisted, from a distance, to unlock the jouissance of the body, as would a few other men. And jouissance would keep being written—or not being written, as her detractors would say. In any case, it would keep being said so as to be conveyed: parental responsibility required it, as suggested by the letter (mentioning Bost) that was a call "to politics."

This eloquent, adaptable, shifting vitality—what is it exactly? Infidelity? Vice? Manipulation? Abuse of others? Hysterical cruelty and lies used as antidepressants? Perhaps. No doubt. Beauvoir nevertheless keeps herself at the heart of her investigation as both experimenter and guinea pig, distant observer and dissected prey. She spares herself as little as she spares others. She does not stop searching in thought that situates her, or displaces her, in the world rather than language. "I am not of your opinion"—these words spoken by a Colette heroine, Renée Néré, guide her in her relationship with the male partner, with the exception of Sartre, perhaps, with whom she contests not openly but rather by remaining tenderly at odds until his dying day. Without making claims, but recognizing her debt to the superiority of her "dear little one," the *vous* she knows how to use with him, while also protecting him, and following her own path with disarming restraint.

The most remarkable thing in this experiment is that the couple thus deconstructed is not erected as a model (though there are—and will always be—militants to follow what they believe to be their example). But what have Sartre and Beauvoir shown if not the impossibility of the male-female union, with and beyond a concern for maintaining the bond of gratitude and respect between autonomous individuals? And this final politeness that is concern for another's physical integrity and work, which may include a caustic look and a spot-on word. A bond of thought, an exchange of ideas beyond erotic harmony and disharmony: a relationship, in their fashion, was a debate.

The mad love, the passionate exaltation celebrated by the surrealists and in a different way by mystics like Georges Bataille, are relegated after Sartre and Beauvoir to the archives of history, to childishness and the mirages of narcissistic regression. These two put a fissure in Religion, because they put a fissure in the idyll of the relationship, which still sustains the society of the spectacle, as image requires. The couple fissured in the light of day? Perhaps, not really, with all that was left unsaid, the censoring, the victims. But do you know of others that hold up in the light of day? In hardcore sex, or crime, perhaps.

In this display of the relationship, possible in the impossible, I see not heroism but generosity. This is the most suitable word for an art of living that maintains the possibility of a dialogue between two autonomous individuals, with and beyond sex, in the eyes of the world and as a resistance against totalitarianism or terrorism, the deflagration of bonds. Not the Rousseauist couple as a pedestal of state power and procreation, but the couple as a nuclear dialogue, as a space of thought. It's uncertain, it's risky, and it requires a good deal of intelligence so that freedom does not irremediably become a vehicle to murder. The couple as a space of thought, or thought as a dialogue between the two sexes: isn't this utopia itself? The universal, fraternity, all the myths of national, native, and group cohesion split in two. How many of us are capable today of this esteem, this discord, this generosity that endures in time in thinking?

What Good Is the Novel?

Whereas in *The Words* Sartre ends up making "words" his central target, before relegating belles lettres to neurosis, Simone de Beauvoir does not seem to notice that thought, engagement, life itself, and writing, after all, are the work of language. The volubility of her letters, the interminable accumulation of details in which she seems to savor interest that today escapes us, and with which she brusquely saturates her correspondents (Nelson Algren or Olga Kosakiewicz, for example, did not necessarily ask to hear so much about her private life with Sartre)—are they really made of words? Or of an incomprehensible verbal drive that nothing can stop, just as nothing could slow the frenetic pace of the walker reveling in open spaces? The insatiable curiosity of the top student, the eternal girl who conquers her freedom by comparing writing and philosophy to perfection. Who uses them as if they were automatic reflexes, while also managing to push the investigation of the self and the quest for liberty ever further. Beauvoir's rare remarks on the art of speech and literature reveal her fine intelligence, but never an essential preoccupation for what is commonly called "form." If her interest is retained by a virtuoso of the French language like Colette, for example, we seek in vain, in the philosopher's admiration, her recognition of Colette as the creator of some of the most beautiful, poetic French prose. If "Colette is above all a great writer," Beauvoir is quick to get rid of her by saluting her as a warrior who was able to make "her pen her livelihood." And by noting the liberties taken with young girls and young people by Colette's narrator or characters, "her spontaneity"—her "balanced and generous mother"—without suspecting the writer's projection into her model: before becoming an anthropologist and regretting that, although she brings an "attentive love" to nature, Colette, like Katherine Mansfield and women in general, seem to be incapable of grasping nature in its "inhuman freedom" because of an inability to contest the "human condition," something never taken on by a woman, or rarely! Exit the monstrous Colette along with her art, her complexities, and her abysses!

Before critics take on the scholarly style of the *Sartreuse* (as Beauvoir was known), Sartre encounters this in the remarks of Brice Parain, the "reader" at Gallimard of *She Came to Stay*: it is "their" common style that will be targeted, misunderstood, accused of being "lax," with dialogue that is "philosophical, slangy," that "jumps to conclusions," "that's basically ours."[12]

Woven together this way, Beauvoir's novel, if it is writing, seems to be its author's reconstruction of the self, a self-analysis and a social message more than a "work of art." The modesty of someone, unable to rival a Virginia Woolf or a Colette, who knows it and does not wish to? Certainly. But Beauvoir's novels are also the opinions of a philosopher, of a woman of her century: opinions about *existence* versus *Being*. Like walking along a railing separating and protecting you from the abyss. In the context of French literature, which for centuries has excelled at the sophistication of forms themselves transmuted into content, and even more in the formalist context of the New Novel and structuralism, Simone de Beauvoir's hefty tomes had very little chance of appealing to a "hip" crowd. The pantheon of belles lettres was not opened to her, in spite of the Goncourt for *The Mandarins*; her novels were "part of" the work of a "great intellectual." They impose themselves at present, however, in order to justify her thought, from which they are inseparable.

With Beauvoir, the novel is an act of existential affirmation by which the unbearableness of the intimate is transmuted into political stakes. In our troubled times, I for one am persuaded that this hybrid genre in which Beauvoir risked her private life not only reconnects with the origins of the novel as a dialogic and polyphonic text, but that its risks and infelicities are salutary in the face of the French novel's confinement in autofiction and the complacent narcissism that would be its substance. Because it is by the footpath of fiction, its things half-said, its displacements, that Beauvoir manifested another facet of her generous vitality: her capacity to embody a political philosophy of freedom in the microcosm of the intimate.

I began by speaking of Beauvoir's universalism and I return to it now. Didn't the final ruse of political fiction thwart the philosopher's universalism by exploring incommensurable singularities—her own, ours—beyond sexual difference and an ethics of ambiguity? And what if it were this weakness of the theoretician, her adventure as a novelist, that preserved her from the ridicule others later felt compelled to assume, becoming a leader of a group, movement, or feminist sect? The woman destroyed can be seen in the women conveyed to us in her novels. They destroy her feminist status, but sustain *The Second Sex* in what is irreducible in every woman, and every man, making it, more than a myth, an invitation to singularize the political and politicize the singular. And in this, an experiment we lack and urgently need, Beauvoir remains unique, exceptional, and unequaled.

9

FATIGUE IN THE FEMININE

Fatigue in the feminine reminds me of Colette's words in *The Vagabond* (1910):

"... That woman about whom we cry:

—She's made of steel!

is simply made 'of woman'"[1]

In other words: there is a feminine endurance that is not a phallic, metallic hardness but a suppleness and plasticity; it may result in fatiguebut also temporarily in the amorous exaltation of the hysteric or the unshakeable abnegation of the mother; it is appeased indefinitely in the serenity of the female mystic, the female writer, and sometimes the (male or female) analyst.

A Fatigue of Sexuation

To present these figures of feminine fatigue, I will say that psychosomatic fatigue in women—when not the tip of the iceberg of depression, and even if easily confused with it—is a fatigue of sexuation. The tired woman is exhausted by sexual difference; her complaint is rooted in *her inability to choose the sex of her object of desire, because she has failed to work through her bisexuality.* This would be a specific variant of feminine fatigue as I understand it in my clinical experience, but I would say that, ultimately, this fatigue of sexuation underlies all fatigue in women.

Indeed, the tired woman is not the eternally frustrated conversion hysteric who "makes us" her somatic symptom in order to assert her womanly body, even at the price of physical suffering, an irrefutable reproach: to avenge herself for an unsatisfied desire, to make up for an amorous separation, or to manifest a narcissistic humiliation. No, the chronically tired woman is not sure of her sexual identity, because she does not know whom she loves: "A man or a woman, papa or mama, I don't know," she says, in short; and this uncertainty of the sexual choice of her object of desire or love object leads to constant indecision in her existential and professional choices. This conscious or unconscious uncertainty as to the choice of the partner's sex seems to be more tiring for women than for men due to *psychical bisexuality*, which Freud already noted came to the fore "much more clearly" in women.[2] Indeed, the chronically tired woman I listen to on the couch complains constantly about the people around her who are "pains in the neck," as if by chance, tedious people who "sap her energy": her mother, her sister, her boss, not to mention her partners, men or women she "tries out" tirelessly but who never fail to "get on her nerves," she says (for lack of satisfying her undecided sexual desire?). All the impossible objects that cause her to experience as fatigue what I understand to be her lack of passion for a defined object, cut and uncoupled from the parental duo, combined father-mothers whose conflicting sexuality is at once overinvested by the patient and unacceptable to her.

Yet we should not confuse her with the homosexual woman who has opted for phallic identification and summons all the force of her libido to face her partner or repair the inconveniences of existence, of which there are no lack; dynamic, if not jovial, at least militant, this androgyne has tireless resistance and gives herself no respite, except in severe depression.

The woman with fatigue I am talking about is a homosexual woman who is unaware of it or is at least hesitating: her unconscious takes pleasure in the arcane realms of psychical bisexuality, but she feels such fascination and repulsion toward the united parents that she is exhausted pursuing this mirage of a *total object* whose *toxic hold* is supposed to spare her from choosing an object of desire of one sex and therefore from choosing one sex for herself. Everything that is not part of this toxicity of the fusion with what is revealed to be a mirage of combined parents is perceived by my exhausted woman as boring—it annoys her, gets on her nerves, is a pain in the neck, saps her energy, is tedious; she doesn't like anything, she's tired.

I believe there is a complaint of fatigue in the feminine that is a complaint of sexuation and should not be confused with the depressive complaint. I will try to clarify this based on my conception of the female oedipal phase, which I consider to be a two-sided oedipal, first devoted to the mother, then to the father.

If it is true that this two-sided oedipal gives the feminine subject an exceptional plasticity (which Colette diagnosed in her own way as endurance not made of steel but "of woman"), it is no less true that many women do not manage to accomplish the multiple subjective positions required by this polyphonic structure. As a consequence of these failures, whose specific causes I cannot analyze today (trauma inflicted by disagreement or parental separation, a depressive mother, the mother's operational functioning, the father's hysterical seducer behavior, etc.), the female subject is fixed defensively at one or several possible postures of this oedipal trajectory, which I will retrace here. And this veritable psychosomatic mutilation is perceived as a lack of being and as lassitude—indeed, as an inability to survive.

The Two-Sided Oedipal

I situate this complaint therefore in the context of female psychosexuality, which goes through two versions of the *oedipal*.

I call the most archaic period *oedipal prime*, which goes from birth to the so-called phallic stage (between the ages of three and six). I should remind you that while emphasizing what is commonly called "phallic monism" (namely, the idea that "a single genital organ, the male organ, plays a role" in the infantile genital organization of both sexes), Freud notes, in his later writings, a particular relationship between a little girl and her mother: adhesive and intense, almost inaccessible to analysis, because embedded in preverbal sensorial experience, which the founder of psychoanalysis compares to "the Minoan-Mycenaean civilization behind the civilization of the Greeks."[3] This foundation of a more marked psychic bisexuality in women is nevertheless far from the idyll of "being" before the drive-related "doing," as Winnicott would have it. Immediately eroticized, oral-anal-and-genital, the primal *mother-baby girl* coexcitation points to what I call *the woman's endog-*

enous homosexuality, which I consider to underlie Melanie Klein's "projective identification" and remains the repressed center of feminine psychosexuality throughout the life of the subject, just as inaccessible to analysis as the "rock of castration," if not more so. It is marked by this intrusion of the adult, and more particularly of the mother, in the life of the neotenous *infans*, which many analysts have found to be at the origins of infantile sexuality. The infant is seduced and seduces through the skin and five senses, offering himself or herself through the orifices: the mouth, anus, and vagina for the girl. Seduced, orificial, broken into: Minoan-Mycenaean sexuality— or *oedipal prime*, as I call it—is that of a sexual being, the "polymorphous pervert," anticipating . . . the woman's penetrated being. Yet, in spite of this break-in, *oedipal prime* is no less active and reactive: the emission of excrement, vocalizations, and gestures punctuate it aggressively. But while penile excitation in the boy (later reinforced by the phallic phase) is superimposed on the break-in specific to this "feminine position" (which continues in the male subject with the desire to possess the father's penis orally and anally), *oedipal prime* in the girl involves a more complex ambiguity.

On the one hand, the little girl's "ego-skin" (D. Anzieu) and the "orificial ego" (J. André) are offered to the seduction-passivation that engages the narcissism of the two women (mother and daughter), united in reciprocal projective identifications (more or less unconscious for the mother), as well as masochism and its sadistic abreactions: on the part of the girl, devouring the breast along with the penis, an outpouring of excrement, and so on; on the part of the mother, taking pleasure in the powerlessness of the newborn baby girl, in her orificial offering, when not ignoring them to defend herself, or, indeed, violating them to avenge herself.

On the other hand, this orificial break-in, this breaking and entering in the little girl's *oedipal prime*, is compensated not only by clitoral excitation but also by the precocious elaboration of a link of *introjection-and-identification* with the seductive and intrusive *object* that is the mother. I believe Melanie Klein was the first to suggest that under optimal circumstances the libidinal investment of the mother's hollow body as well as her own body is metabolized in the child into "depth."[4] As for me, I would note that, through introjection, the girl installs the seductress mother within: the excited cavity of the interior body is transformed into an internal *representation*. This starts the slow and long-lasting work of psychization that will be accentuated by *oedipal two*, in which we recognize the female tendency to favor psychic [stet] or amorous representation-idealization in counterpoint to drive-related erotic excitation. This precocious psychization also seems to be an early mechanism of the absorption of somatic fatigue: we find it again in the experience of the female mystic, the female writer, and the female psychoanalyst (and, of course, in the male psychoanalyst, insofar as his unconscious remains open to the "Minoan-Mycenaean" *oedipal prime*).

This feminine psychization, favored by a mother/daughter resemblance and the projection of maternal narcissism and depressiveness onto the daughter . . . is frequently complicated by the mother's serious depressive symptomatology: then the mother-daughter coexcitation is neutralized, when it does not disappear behind perfunctory care or harden in abandoning indifference.

To sum up, *oedipal prime*, on the one hand, leaves the girl with a precocious psychization of the object that the young ego introjects while at the same time identifying with it; on the other hand, because of this identification with a closed-off or evasive mother, there is a request for a *real link*, in the Lacanian sense of *impossible link*, for possession and dependence regarding this same object.

This *real need for a link* is like the recto of the cloacal verso, the daughter claiming an insatiable, imaginary premium for oral, anal, and vaginal pleasures submitted to (rather than acted upon). It is doubled by the attachment of the mother to her infant daughter: not a phallic prosthesis, as the boy is, but a chasm of masochistic or depressive latencies. The implacable need for a real presence, a protective link, is manifested in the tireless, necessarily extenuating request the woman addresses to her male erotic partner: the one who will rarely be a "partner" but more exclusively a "lover," whom the woman asks to understand her and to always be there, as if he were . . . a real/impossible mother.

Following neurobiological maturation and satisfying experiences of separation with the object, the phallic stage becomes the central organizer of the thought-sexuality copresence in both sexes: the subject may move on to *oedipal two*. The child who has already developed language and thought is no longer content to invest his organs and their excitability but associates the cognitive operations he applies to the external world with the internal movements of his drive-related excitability. From now on, he sees that papa is not only the one he wants to kill in order to appropriate the mother, but the one who possesses what must be called a separability: he is a third figure regulating the mother-child sensorial dyad, a *symbolic father*, authority of *law* and the *forbidden*. The bearer of a penis, the little boy invests this organ of pleasure all the more since it is first and foremost that of the father, whose organizing role in the familial and psychical world the child is now in a position to recognize.

This decisive encounter between the mastery of signs and sexual excitation is also produced in the little girl to weld her being as speaking-and-desiring subject. It is no longer oral or anal excitation but clitoral excitation, above all, with or without the perception of the vagina, that dominates this period that I call *oedipal two*, where, unlike the boy, the little girl *changes objects*: the father replaces the mother as the target of desire. Let us examine in detail the ambiguity of this change.

On the one hand, like the boy, and every subject of speech and law, the girl identifies with the phallus and the father who is its representative. But at the heart of this phallic assumption, she is nevertheless at a disadvantage. Deprived of a penis and depreciated by this fact in all known cultures, she adheres to the phallic order by bearing the unconscious trace of *oedipal prime*, of her polymorphous sensoriality, devoted to the desire of the mother and for the mother. Thus the little girl gains access to the phallic order—which is erected on the foundation of the "dark continent" or the "Minoan-Mycenaean" continent—according to the "as if" modality, the "illusory," the "I'm playing the game, but I know I'm *not in it*, because I *don't have it*." Consequently, if she is not stuck in the pose of the virago, the necessary phallic position of the woman constitutes the female subject in the register of *radical extraneousness*, constitutive exclusion, and irreparable solitude.

Moreover, while being a phallic subject of speech, thought, and law, the girl retreats not to the passive position, as is commonly said, but to the receptive position, in order to become *the object of the father*. A phallic subject of the symbolic order as a speaking being, as a woman she nevertheless wants to receive the penis and have the father's child, taking the place of the mother whom she wishes to evict, now a genital rival with whom the daughter never stops settling scores that go back to the original coexcitation in *oedipal prime*.

Following the twists that access to *oedipal two* imprints in the female subject, we understand the irreducible extraneousness a woman feels in the phallic-symbolic order. At best, that foreignness takes on the aspect of an enigma: "What does a woman want?" Freud is not the only one to ask. It may be refined in revolt and insubordination: Hegel salutes woman as the "eternal irony of the community." The constitutive exile of a woman in the phallic-symbolic order may prove unsuitable and then be deflected into chronic depressiveness and intractable melancholy. Or run aground in the suicidal aftermath of the "refusal of the feminine" that anorexia and buli-mia are: morbid symptoms in which the gaping excitability of the hollow body persists, unable to defend itself against the intrusion of the maternal-paternal seduction except by stuffing up or blocking the erogenous zones.

Because it is two-sided, ambivalent, and tortuous, the oedipal phase of the woman might be thought of as *incomplete* or *interminable*: Freud says it clearly (through his phallic optic) by noting that, unlike the oedipal of the boy who "sinks" under the effect of the castration complex, the oedipal of the girl is only "introduced" with the castration complex (in what I call *oedi-pal two*) and only endures with the feminine demand for a penis or a child.[5] In my interpretation the *feminine oedipal* does not "undergo catastrophe," but completes eternal returns due to the pregnancy of oedipal prime under and in oedipal two and leads the female subject to an eternal psychosexual incompletion: tiring, exhausting hesitation between unstable, undecidable objects of desire (as "marked" psychic bisexuality requires).

On the other hand, when a woman manages to complete the complex tourniquet that oedipal prime and oedipal two impose, she may have a chance to acquire the solid maturity a man so often lacks, buffeted as he is between the phallic pose of the "macho" man and the infantile regression of the impossible Mr. Baby. For, having assumed and elucidated the multiple facets of her two-sided oedipal phase, the female subject, like a portrait by Picasso, obtains an astonishing psychosexual plasticity: I am tempted to see this as the key to the endurance that indeed has nothing to do with steel. Colette, again: "A woman can never die of grief. She is such a solid creature, so hard to kill!"[6]

Human history since the last glacial period[7] has found two "natural" solutions to allow this grueling path (oedipal prime + oedipal two)—which society requires the female subject to realize somehow—to end in plasticity rather than collapse: these are motherhood and hysteria.

The Mother

When the *mother* manages to go beyond her control over the child as a phal-lic prosthesis and to disimpassion the link to the genitor-father, beyond the time of desire which is that of death, a cyclical time opens for her, a time of new beginnings and rebirths and a certain serenity. In the *real presence of this other* that the child is for her, both *phallus* taken from the father and real *body* in a narcissistic doubling of her own infantile sensuality as constituted in *oedipal prime*, the woman finds the conjunction of her symbolic essence (phallic thinking subject) and her carnal essence (mother/daughter sensual duality, genetrix reduplication). Nothing is impossible for a mother who succeeds at her psychical bisexuality: a tireless "good fairy," she does not notice that she is depleted in the small cares lavished on her loved ones. Like the mother coming for consultation who was worried (but was she really?) because, after getting divorced, taking care of a mother afflicted with Alzheimer's and a son who was operated on for a brain tumor—no less!— she broke her ankle but felt no pain or fatigue: "My cousin told me that that wasn't normal, that I should be seen, what do you think?" she smiled, almost naively.

The Hysteric

As for the hysteric, her erotomania tries to resolve her interminable oedipal and the bisexuality it commands through amorous exaltation: the infinite quest for an object whose absence is filled by the God of monotheists. Isn't the "successful hysteric" the one who does not succumb to conversion or depression, an indefatigable Diana, huntress of ideal objects, who narrowly misses paranoia by tirelessly persecuting more or less androgynous idols, whether men or women? The genius of Freud could not have been more inspired than when he tried to put an end to his patients' ill-being by transforming their loves into transference love. "It's useless to try to look for a two-sided Object that can't be found," he is basically saying, laying his patients down on the couch. "Let's maintain this transferential link, which you can't do without, but let's deconstruct it constantly, in the hopes of arranging more tolerable familial, professional, and social connections for you." Relying on this new found/created object, which is the object of transference, it is then, as we know, a matter of working through the time and space of the oedipal: reconstructing the psychical complexity, if need be, causing it to come about. In the best of cases there is a true modification of the psychical structure, so that its survival depends as much, if not more, on the capacity of psychical construction/deconstruction than on the quest for an improbable object of satisfaction. The psychization induced by the analytic process balances the race to the object, the inside defatigues the outside, the "interior castle" relieves exterior conflicts. Proust knew this already: the important thing is not the value of the beloved woman but the depth of the lover: not the object but the psychical working through. The writer compared himself to those strollers or readers who live "surrounded by our own soul."[8] We could say: their psychical space protects them from ills as well as from fatigue.

The tired woman, on the contrary, is a failed hysteric or a mother without conviction: she has such a hard time choosing between *letting herself go,* as the object of a sadomasochistic break-in in *oedipal prime,* or *wearing herself out, trying to seduce* in the solitude of the stranger proper to *oedipal two,* that she risks seeking refuge in the analytical cure. A last resort if there ever was one, where psychoanalytical speech causes to resonate, pell-mell, the echoes of the unspeakable intimacy with mama and those of elective symbolization through a father who understands her and makes her understood. While continuing to complain *to* the analyst about the analyst himself (or herself), who is tiring in turn: now a mother, now a father, never the two together, never the total object that the tired woman would so like to meet in someone—an absolute object that would fulfill her, without any loss, a nonobject, actually, nothing but a toxic exaltation to ward off the fatigue of sexuation; and refusing, with this very complaint, to choose the sex of her object—or to choose herself as a subject of a single sex. In regard to current social values, she is too modern to be content being "your basic" mother or hysteric and not modern enough to be content with perverse acting out.

Fatigue in the feminine has led us to the frontiers of psychoanalysis and history. Can a woman live through her psychic bisexuality, constructed by oedipal prime and oedipal two, without getting mired in fatigue or stuck in the role of the victim magnified by her abnegation or in that of the fatal seductress who doubts nothing, to say nothing of the virago favored today by the deculpabilization of homosexual mores as well as the promotion of superwomen in politics and elsewhere?

Posed this way (and for lack of a response), this question leads me to mention a few profound reworkings of the amorous link by which men and especially women have found a way to appease the neotenous psychosexual vulnerability and a way to appease fatigue. I will mention three that seem to me to be remedies for psychosomatic fatigue: reworkings of the amorous link through *mysticism, writing,* and analytical *countertransference.*

Mysticism

Saint Teresa of Avila (1515–1582) succeeds where Schreber fails: she manages to fortify her body, subject to frequent epileptic fits and grueling

headaches, through faith in a God who is not a persecuting God but a loving spouse who stands by her—like a permanent mother doubled by paternal wisdom that does nothing less than speak through the mouth of Teresa
herself. Teresa ends up sheltering this perfect object of her bisexuality, this
loving Lord, in her own center, since what she calls the "interior castle" in
her heart is inhabited by the Lord himself, whom the Carmelite admits to
us she has managed to . . . "checkmate."⁹ Might this mystic who is "checkmating God" be an atheist? The only possible atheist: not ignoring that
God is love, because the human subject is constructed in his connections to
the love object, without which he founders; but constructing oneself *through*
and *beyond* the object of love: taking it into oneself through the intervention
of "humility," as she specifies; identifying oneself in him by absorbing Him
in herself? If Teresa succeeds where Schreber fails, it is not only because the
mother superior very lucidly asks her Carmelite daughters to be women as
well as men, but because she avoids fatigue by loving herself in the object
of love, which amounts to saying that she loves herself *without* an object of
love: she loves nothing other than everything, the Everything that she is
herself, through an incessant inspection, first, vocal (prayer), then essentially silent (meditation), and finally, above all, written, so as to be clarified
and shared, an exercise in which one can easily see the ancestor of analysis.
Starting here, Teresa is no longer sick or, at any rate, her maladies no longer
matter. Between the ages of forty-seven and sixty-six, in fewer than twenty
years, she managed to found sixteen convents: is this being tired? No, this
is ecstasy. Or else a castle streaming with water, the exquisite fluidity of
the soul, whose suppleness she compares to "liquid stone," when not to the
metamorphosis of a silkworm. The castle—a chrysalis becoming a butter-
fly: What better image of feminine psychical plasticity in the meanders of
the two-sided oedipal, endlessly revisited!

Writing

We do not have to be mystics to arrive at this absorption of the object that
is perhaps the only possible freedom vis-à-vis the object of desire, without
succumbing to its control or resigning oneself to its melancholic loss: a joy-
ful freedom. If freedom is the modern version of happiness, as Simone de
Beauvoir says in *The Second Sex*, Colette—closer to us than Teresa of Avila
and in a different way—conquered it by melding all possible loves into the
"mental hermaphrodite" she claimed to be, so as to rid herself of it: "The
open sea, but not the wilderness. The discovery that there is no wilderness!

That in itself is enough to sustain me in triumphing over my afflictions."[10] Or again: "Love, one of the great commonplaces of existence, is slowly leaving mine. . . . Once we've left these behind, we find that all the rest is gay and varied, and that there is plenty of it."[11]

There is no fatigue in this writing, through which a gigantic feminine Self loves itself in the French language (for the first and last time?), Sido's mother tongue, consuming flora and fauna, cacti and cats, filling the dimensions of the universe.[12] Flowering (hatching?), constant rebirth: "Turning over a new leaf, rebuilding, being reborn, has never been beyond my strength."

Analysis

The Freudian path is entirely different. By implicitly inviting his disciples to participate in constant, endless transference-countertransference, oedipal prime and oedipal two, inside and outside, men and women, and several patients a day, an indefatigable psychical plasticity is demanded of us by the psychoanalytical experience. This amorous suppleness, this infidelity that we reenact from one analysand to another, is only tiring if we get caught in the trap of countertransferential identification, and if we allow the fluidity of the analytical process, required for a "good analysis," to become petrified. On the contrary, if we manage to keep our attention "floating" and our unconscious always ready to travel through the meanders of the various oedipal stages, prime or two, feminine or masculine, drives and meanings, and vice versa, and in different ways with each analysand, I do not think it is a matter of an aptitude for regression, or the efficacy of a lightened (protective rather than tyrannical) superego, or even a mania to switch objects perversely, specific to psychoanalysts; but a back and forth between agencies of the *psychical apparatus*, so many stations in the *history* of the speaking subject, which, by virtue of being revisited in this paradoxical amorous link that we call transference-countertransference, is relieved of the passionate hold (or its lack) that is grueling for its protagonists. Continually at play in the plurality of the links with our patients, transferential-countertransferential love, accompanied by its elucidation, mobilizes and favors our psychosexual plasticity. Can we imagine a better antidote to our fatigues? Neither "checkmating" the object of love, as the mystic would have it, nor love as "one of the great commonplaces of existence," as the writer given over to her sublimation would say; but a plurality of real-imaginary-symbolic transferential links, attentive to the two-sided oedipal phase of the woman, that accompany the feminine in man as well and give the most subtle among us this gracious maturity and fresh vitality we see radiate from certain women, at ease in their psychical bisexuality. Analysts of both sexes deal with it tirelessly in their listening and their interpretation: tireless guardians, because tireless builders of psychical space as open, incomplete, interminable structures. How? By not being made "of steel" but simply "of woman."

PART 3

PSYCHOANALYZING

10

THE SOBBING GIRL; OR, ON HYSTERICAL TIME

Father times, mother spacies.
—James Joyce

While the clinic of hysteria seemed to be getting banal, I thought, on the contrary, I detected a true possession there. I shared this feeling with André Green, who said, "Read my article 'Destin des passions.'" In it he wrote, "Madness is our hysteria today."[1] The reflections that follow were inspired by this reading.

Beyond the various definitions and categories of hysteria, Freud already leaves us with a certain coherence of the *psychoanalytical conception* of this ailment: crossed identifications and the prevalence of repression, at play in the oedipal conflict and the oral and phallic registers. We know, moreover, that, starting mainly with "conversion hysteria" and "defense hysteria," Freud not only works out his central conception of *an unconscious*, which he situates as an "other scene" at the heart of psychical life, but also notions such as "phantasm," "symptom," and "word-presentation/thing-presentation." Following the work on hypnosis, the analyses of hysterics attest to another relationship of the subject to *reality*, thanks to the new Freudian conceptualization. And although the link between *hysteria and memory* had long been observed (I will return to some of Freud's famous definitions regarding this), analytical thought today has still not sufficiently centered its exploration of hysteria on the fact that, if "reality" is modified in the hysteric, this modification goes hand in hand with a *modified time*.

Now, it has recently been noted that memory disorders are designated as the major manifestation of this affliction in psychopathological works on hysteria. I will not discuss the distinction between "hysterical personality" and "hysterical symptom" here, but I will mention two nosographic features, to start with, highlighted by the *DSM-III-R*: somatization and dissociative states.[2]

Although we are currently witnessing a veritable explosion of hysterical nosography (certain researchers distinguish no fewer than ten groups of symptoms, relying on at least twenty-five distinctive traits, and the *DSM-III-R*, mentions more than twelve complaints under the heading "somatization"), the *temporal criterion* seems to stand out for a number of observers as essential in characterizing hysteria.

Thus dissociative states are related to psychogenic amnesias,[3] and I agree with the authors who do not establish a structural difference between these dissociative states and somatizations.

As for me, I would like to interpret these assertions in light of Freudian theory and my clinical experience. I will base my remarks on three studies I have devoted to the problems related to today's subject: "Countertransference: A Revived Hysteria," "The Scandal of the Timeless," and "On the Extraneousness of the Phallus; or, the Feminine Between Illusion and Disillusion."[4]

It would seem hysterical amnesia translates an intense drive-related conflict that affects the *functioning of thought* but is rooted in the mother-child *primary coexcitation*, which in the hysterical subject does not require an elaborative value of seduction but a *traumatic value*.

I would emphasize the fact that this traumatism of the "primary maternal" cannot be approached directly, but only through an analytical consideration of hysterical thought in its "dissociative," "extraneous," indeed, "hypnotic" aspects.

These reflections will lead me to four scenarios (among others) in which hysterical time is manifested—the amnesiac dissociative state, somatization, the "scene," and passivation. I will conclude with a few questions about the notions of the *unconscious* and *time*.

A Double Personality

Oriane came to see me one year after her brother died in a car accident. She seemed serene but phobic and planned to leave her job as a special education teacher in Belgium to start a bachelor's degree in philosophy and start psychoanalysis in Paris. The analysis broached her difficult relationship with her father, as well as her mother, not to mention her grandparents, who sent her money to support her in Paris; we also dealt with the vagaries of academic competition and, above all, tensions in the relationship Oriane had formed with José, her former supervisor in Belgium. Oriane's controlled narrative, which seemed to expect nothing from me, filled each session unfailingly and contrasted with *the stifled tone of her voice*, breathless and marked by silent gasping, which I perceived as a *sob*.

It took a long time to formulate the strange dichotomy that Oriane's speech offered me: a sort of "dissociative disorder" and the copresence of two personalities. "I lack a single personality," she would tell me later. One of them launched into a quest for knowledge in full rational control, the other wept for the brother who was killed. No allusion to this brother, or death, ever entered the discourse explicitly. When certain complaints due to José's painful "absences" or "disappearances" seemed to reactivate the latent depressive state, I mentioned the loss of her brother in my interpretation; I went so far as to associate Oriane's almost constant gasping for breath with "what happens when one grieves for a dead person." Oriane reluctantly agreed but never spoke of the accident again, or the memories of twenty years spent with her brother, except to evoke scenes where she found herself *alone*, in conflict with both her parents: as if her brother had always been gone.

Today we have a tendency to describe hysteria as a state of psychical dissociation ("dissociative disorder") distinct from psychotic *Spaltung* (or, splitting) and different from confused states. Some authors report cases of hysterical patients with a "double personality"—the rigorous student of the morning and the prostrate depressive of the afternoon, for example, struggling against deep sexual and narcissistic traumatism.[5] Oriane presented this sort of dissociation, but synchronically, so to speak: on the couch she was two people at the same time—a highly capable intellectual *and* a depressed sister. This simultaneous dissociation, manifested by both registers of her speech (on the one hand, the meaning of the narrative, on the other, intonation, breath), was based on a selective memory disorder ("memory gap," "lost memory").[6] Not that Oriane forgot about the death of her brother; she simply couldn't remember it—but what did this simplicity consist of? The impossibility of *remembering* rather than *recognition*: apparently it was not a disorder in the encoding of information—though some of Oriane's very emotional states might have suggested that. Nevertheless, the otherwise intact mental functioning suggested that Oriane was not suffering from a foreclosure of the reality of her brother's death, but from a memory gap due to the "negative attention" focused on the brother's accident. I could only speculate on the passionate causes for this psychogenic amnesia, because nothing would prompt Oriane to reveal the time of this death or, beyond that, the dead time that twenty years of her life with her brother had become since.

Digression on the Timeless

"The hysteric suffers from reminiscences,"[7] Freud said, but we often forget to add a corollary regarding the temporality of the unconscious also left to us by Freud: "The unconscious ignores time."[8]

The value of this Freudian assertion on the timelessness of the unconscious, which continues to raise questions, is multiple, and I have tried to tackle this in a more theoretical way elsewhere. Here I would like to underscore that "the unconscious ignores time" is also an observation Freud owes to hysterics' paradoxical relationship with time—hysterics being the favored objects of his observations at the beginning of the analytic discovery—as well as to the dissociative state covering a psychogenic amnesia (the case of Oriane) and the somatization (to which I will return) that still characterizes hysterical nosography.

I propose the hypothesis that *hysterical amnesia* is a major figure of the *Zeit-los* (the timeless), probably the first Freud discovered in hypnosis. Hysterical amnesia breaks through the linearity of conscious time (the linear time of thought), through the afflux of contrary drives and their presymbolic offshoots: the semiotic (infralanguage: rhythms, alliteration, breath, vocal gestures, cries, digestive and respiratory spasms, and so on) and sensations, thus tying the unconscious to the biological.[9]

When Charcot describes hysterical paralysis as an "ideal" paralysis, because, he says, the "*idea* of movement is already the movement," the "*idea* of the absence of movement, if it is strong, is already motor paralysis realized";[10] when Janet explains morbid thought as a "narrowing of the field of consciousness," we are dealing with the *how* of the symptom. By digging under the phenomenon *before* and *elsewhere*—in infantile memory and drive-related experience—Freud unveils the *why*: it is traumatic memory that generates the hysterical symptom; "the hysteric suffers from reminiscences."

Perhaps it is now possible to associate these two currents of interpretation—the "why" of Freud and the "how" of Charcot/Janet—to account
for this paradoxical temporality that characterizes hysterical states (beginning with "dissociative states," "conversion," and I would add the "scene"
and "passivization"). To simplify, let's say that, as a result of the drive-
related conflict that traumatizes the psychical apparatus, the hysterical ego
opts for one "idea" instead of another: the ego forgets one of the agents of
the conflict, and so with the agent goes the act; the hysteric forgets their
time. This *defensive amnesia* adheres to a fragment of the field of consciousness and the preconscious (Charcot's "ideas"), considered inoffensive; but
it leaves intact the drive-related motions mobilized in the traumatic conflict
that take the regressive path of the primary process (in Oriane the *infralinguistic* expressions of mourning and suffering through sobbing). The time
of the subject is thus found selectively amputated from the intense time of
the trauma and therefore the analogous passionate states, more or less dis-
tanced from the major traumatism. The subject is literally in a passionate
timelessness while still proving capable of conscious, social activities, intact
and thus temporal, but that, deprived of this drive-related substratum, take
on a somnolent or histrionic appearance.

I would add that this temporal dissociation is accentuated *in the woman*
because of the specificity of her phallic phase and her oedipal phase, which
I have written about elsewhere.[11] Though the female subject, like every
subject, in order to be a subject, measures herself by phallic desire, the trial
of castration, and the murder of the father, the little girl experiences this
access to the phallic and/or the symbolic in a strange, foreign, illusory way.
Due to her privileged link (negative or positive, but privileged nonetheless)
with the "primary maternal" and the "mother-baby coexcitation" prior to
the pleasure principle,[12] the phallic, oedipal, and symbolic parameters of
subjectivity are connoted in her from a coefficient of "illusion" and "extraneousness." From then on, the little girl and the woman will "play the
game," often better than men, but not without a disenchanted distance
that can result in the women who fascinated Hegel (women as the "eternal
irony of the community") as well as cold technocrats, machinelike "manag-
ers" obsessed with power and devoid of reverie.

When the hysteric invests *thought* (access to which is ultimately consoli-
dated by the phallic and the oedipal), this thought does not necessarily take
on the split aspect of the "false self" or even the "as if" personality. However,
due to lost passionate time, *hysterical thought presents itself as a defense*, whereas

more exactly it is *dissociation that is the very structure of hysteria*. Suddenly, terms like *inauthentic, false time,* and *ignored time* come to the analyst when hearing this thought produced by the dissociative state, which Oriane exhibited in a paroxysmal way. Yet a certain analytical listening that would too quickly describe this hysterical (amnesiac) thought as a "defense" or "false self," to immediately target the forgotten/dissociated drive-related conflict, risks a countertransference that is itself defensive and that underestimates the *libidinal value* of this amnesiac dissociation, which, understood this way, can reveal itself to be a fertile seam in the unfolding of analysis.

It is this amnesiac thought and its false time oblivious to lost passionate time that the analyst should, in my opinion, start from—and not from the trauma itself, which remains dissociated and unapproachable—to have a chance at accessing the personal drama, and, only later in the cure, move toward its working out. The hysteric who suffers from reminiscences and ignores time confronts us with thought that has lost the time of passion. And we should take this amnesiac thought, if not as true than at least as likely, *pretending* in order to mask the real, because it carries with it the offshoots of the passionate unconscious, still entrenched in the timelessness of passion itself. Dissociated offshoots, certainly, but it is up to us to hear them in their double adherence: to the apparent defensive ego and to the hidden forgotten ego. In other words, analytical listening (transference and countertransference) should be able to revive this mad forgotten/dissociated passion by respecting the protective speech of the trauma, which is very different from a hystericization-dramatization of the cure. The difference consists in the fact that listening and interpretation closely follow *hysterical thought* as it presents itself in its specificity—by which I mean its "falseness," its "hallucinated truth"—and, by taking this dissociation seriously, threading through its labyrinths, will in the long run bring about the forgotten time of the traumatic passion. If the analyst does not play the game of dissociated/amnesiac thought, if he does not take it seriously, without holding to it exclusively but also without underestimating it, if he doesn't start down its meanders patiently, neither true nor false but likely—it is to be feared that the hysteric, through an intellectual and/or cognitive tendency toward histrionics, will seduce the master/analyst over whom she aspires to reign, and analysis will become interminable and therefore unsuccessful.

Psychoanalysis is a clinic-and-theory of the sexuality/thought copresence. This does not only mean that we analyze the unconscious drive-related conditions of the advent of thought and its accidents; it means that we constantly work out the models for a *stratified* (heterogeneous) psychical apparatus whose thought is subtended, set in motion, or checked by plural logics, to the point of a "remainder" of an unrepresentable excitability, a "biological rock."

Let's not forget that Freud invented the specific temporality of the unconscious and that of the cure in *counterpoint* to the dissociated temporality of the hysteric. I encourage you to consider this proximity—analytical time/hysterical time—for a moment in light of Bergson.[13] He defined *abstract time*, in which the consciousness of the speaking being lives as "a succession of immobile sections," opposing it to *duration*. Now, this "abstract time" cut up into immobile sections, which seems to be the ordinary time of everyone, finds its fixed and grimacing expression in hysterical temporality. In fact, it is in the *amnesiac* thought of hysteria and in its hypnotic temporality that time presents itself in immobile sections (think of our analysands' various "scenes," "conversions," or "selective memories"), immobilized as they are by the passionate suffering whose sadomasochism goes back to the crazy link to the crazy mother,[14] which maintains itself outside time.

The analytic interpretation, on the contrary, is placed on a "vector" (Bion) by its listening, so that it continues to hear the *open totality* of the various times the hysteric dissociates and immobilizes. From then on, analytic interpretation does not oppose abstract and/or hypnotic time but rather affixes to it a new temporality it introduced into modern culture: analytic time. Always open to the timeless, the time of analytic listening, in Bergsonian terms, would be the time of "movement as mobile sections." But how do we go from a "succession of immobile sections" to "movement as mobile sections"? The analyst has no other means to open the "immobile sections" of dissociative states than to mobilize the series of unconscious or unrepresentable dissociated passions in transference as well as countertransference. This mobility, tuned in to a well-tempered countertransference, constitutes the "qualitative change" of the analytical process, which sometimes—rarely, but it shouldn't be excluded!—allows the hysteric to emerge from dissociation/somatization and restores to him/her the *mobility of duration*. Do we need to emphasize the fact that this passage from the immobile to the mobile, from abstract time to duration, is to be handled with caution? If not, the hysteric quickly takes herself for the analyst, indeed, for analysis itself. And there she is, an established member of some society, continuing to control the hypnosis, and, above all, not allowing herself to be threatened by duration!

Hypnotic Thought: Anality

Oriane's dead brother was named Christian, and though she only uttered his name once, at our first meeting, I for one did not forget that it was on my couch, Kristeva's couch, that Oriane allowed her sobs to pour forth from a time other than the time of her speech—sobs accompanied by tears that literally flooded the pillow at each session, though the content of the patient's speech was perfectly controlled and in no way dramatic. Moreover, during the rare exchanges we had standing up, to schedule changes or vacation time at the end of the session, Oriane abruptly effaced the mourner to become suddenly and perfectly serene, showing me her other, controlled, superegolike ego, free of sobs.

This young girl's *amnesiac thought*, which unfolded in her narrative (again, dissociated from the *sob*), was not necessarily intellectualizing or flatly operational. Oriane rarely spoke of her studies, while suggesting the importance she accorded them; she did not speak of her accomplishments or competition with women, as I have heard from other female patients. With the mental and emotional control of a very mature little girl, she conducted the anamnesis of the oedipal triangle: a "drab, insignificant but authoritarian" mother, a father who was "a good guy, clearly a skirt chaser, but no one talked about it, those things aren't discussed in Belgium," her maternal grandparents, especially the grandmother who "spent her time reading" and whose distant tenderness and bourgeois distinction became a model for the little girl early on. Very quickly in analysis, the attention I call amnesiac in Oriane (because it was accompanied by the tearful nonattention brought to bear on her brother) became fixed on *the anality of the father and the daughter*.

The family's last name lent itself to scatological connotations, and with repugnance Oriane mentioned her father's anus, the "dirtiness" of a Don Juan doubled by the impression of "uncleanness" and "bad odors" that had "always disgusted" her. We might think of Melanie Klein's thesis, according to which the girl's superego is more forceful than the boy's due to her greater tendencies to introject and keep the father's penis within, even if it is bad, and this starting with the oral period, but more certainly still in the anal period, by confusing the vagina and the anus.[15]

A dream from this period: Oriane is in her bathtub, she is very small, perhaps even a baby, her mother is giving her a bath. It was "a state of grace," but suddenly the dreamer notices that her father is sitting on the toilet and defecating; horrified, Oriane wakes up. After my interpretation, "a dirty guy," she went on to her relationship with José, her ex-supervisor. I understood at the end of many sessions saturated with obsessional details concerning their meetings—the male and female friends they had in common, professional and affective complicities—that José was a married man, that he was black, and that he treated Oriane with brutality, but that she found him "less banal" (*sic*) than other men she had known, especially since José was very impressed by Oriane's study of philosophy.

The sadomasochistic link of inferiority-superiority with the father/man was displaced onto me during this phase of analysis. Another dream of Oriane's: walking in an unidentified city, which may have been Brussels, or a foreign, unfamiliar city that looked German, or perhaps even Eastern European. An old lady slips into a puddle of mud, which Oriane sees from behind, and she rushes to help her get up and wipe off "the filth she is completely covered in." Then she sees the face of the old woman: "It was you," she told me; "Pretty ragged-looking, I must say," she added unkindly, an exceptional respite between two sobs. I said: "A dirty woman the way there are dirty men? Or else a tender grandmother?" She went on to discuss the fear she had of seeing her grandmother die soon, because for the past few months the old booklover had been afflicted with a serious illness, which was catastrophic, because, as I learned then, it was the grandmother who paid for Oriane's analysis (Oriane had depleted all her funds and no longer gave lessons). Manipulated manipulator, the dissociated personality Oriane delegated to me on the couch included transference in the same logic of the anal manipulation that underlay the elegant presentation of her thought and allowed her to assert a certain control over . . . me, her mother, her grandmother, and a large part of her history. This, while nevertheless allowing herself access to certain aspects of her unconscious. Though dominated by the superego, this dissociated and amnesiac part of the hysterical personality is not reduced to it and acts as a complex entity with its own ego and its own id. I will come back to the superegolike dominant assuring her solidity.

We were completing the third year of analysis, when Oriane announced that she had received her master's degree with honors and that her adviser had suggested she be published. "You will be an author, a name," was my interpretation, which could be understood in transference-countertransference as well as in her phallic aspirations of symbolic control. Oriane went on: "My father was afraid that our name would die out with the death of Christian; that was more painful to him than the death itself. Now, thanks to me, the name will live on." I heard her brother's first name for the second time, a name so close to my own last name, followed—finally—by the account of the accident Oriane had repressed, or rather *dissociated*, all these years.

I will never forget this session: the change in tone, the gradual disappearance of the sob that would never return, and the detailed, though confused, account of events. I learned that Christian went to Spain with family friends in a car and was seated next to the driver. The exact circumstances of the collision with a truck would never be clarified; the driver was slightly injured, and Christian was the only fatality. Breathing normally, Oriane declared it "a suicide." Since the description she had just given me did not seem to justify this conclusion, I repeated: "A suicide." Then came the story, jumbled, angry, agitated—which took up several sessions—of the relations between the brother and sister.

At the time of the accident, Christian was twenty, and Oriane twenty-two. They were a twosome, like "twins," she said. "People confused us, especially since I looked like a boy and he sort of looked like a girl, but not the way you think, just very delicate, very sensitive." The idyll ended one year before the accident: Christian began to go out with a friend of Oriane's. "I realized that I found my brother's penis disgusting, his face had become obscene, something salacious." I thought of the anal father, the "dirty guy." She said: "I told him he disgusted me. I was disgusted with myself for not seeing what he really was until then. I was afraid of being like him, afraid that people would see me the way I saw him. I told him that, in his place, I would commit suicide." I said: "He didn't commit suicide, but, in his place, you would have committed suicide." Oriane told me she didn't know why she had spoken to me about Christian's suicide. Logically, it was impossible, of course, and to be honest she had never thought of it, but she felt very bad after the accident and had "a sort of fugue," fleeing to her grandmother's house and not speaking to anyone for three months. A psychiatrist placed her on sick leave for six months. Oriane had not mentioned any of this to me until now, because she had emerged from it, *id* had erased itself, she never spoke of it to anyone, not to her mother, obviously, who was beside herself with grief, "and there was no way we could utter the name Christian

in front of her; as for speaking about it to you, that did not present itself."
I thought perhaps "that did not present itself," because Oriane was afraid
and ashamed of her passionate ego, identified with the brother, at once beloved and disgusting, a desiring phallic ego, both desirable and menacing;
because another part of her ego was still in "fugue" on the couch itself, by
"forgetting" Christian; because she wanted to protect me—the way they
protected mama at home—from the drama and the risk the girl who so
identified with her brother ran in turn of being carried away by death, this
time no longer accidental but suicidal.

Starting with this session, Oriane gave me the impression of emerging from hypnosis. For almost four years after her brother's accident, she
had subjected herself—as the hypnotized woman submits to the will of the
hypnotizer—to an "ideal" or at least "second" image that was not suggested
to her from the outside (as in a session of hypnosis) but from a dissociated
part of her personality, which had taken the upper hand, attracting all the
attention to a certain reality and ejecting the fraternal passion in the amnesia of the sob. Oriane was emerging from a self-hypnosis.

The Oriane of the first part of analysis, dominating the sob through
her hypnotic thought based on anality, made me think of the patient under
hypnosis discussed by Charcot: "The ideas imposed under these conditions
(those of hypnosis), deprived of control over this aggregate of ideas that
we call the ego, can, thanks to the one who has brought them into being,
acquire an extreme intensity, an almost limitless power, as often takes place
in our dreams."[16]

Translation: The ideas imposed on Oriane by her dissociative state
(equivalent to hypnosis) can, thanks not to the hypnotizer but to the anal
personality of Oriane herself (controlled, realistic, following the introjection of the paternal penis), acquire an extreme intensity, an almost limitless power, as often takes place in our dreams.

Yet we emerged from the "power" of the first Oriane, amnesiac regarding Christian, evolving in a refashioned memory, like a dream or hypnosis, but assuming the appearance of normative and realistic behavior and
thought; and we entered another "dream"—in the time of twin *passion*, evac-
uated until then. It was not long after crossing this passionate lost time
that we could rejoin the archaic antecedents that predisposed Oriane to
becoming a hysterical personality with "dissociative states."

Thus I would say hypnosis is the hysteric's natural state—though it
might seem paradoxical, because we all know that late-nineteenth-century

psychiatry induced hypnotic states in hysterical subjects with the goal of getting them to emerge from amnesia and access forgotten memory. I suppose even Freud was no stranger to this way of seeing things, when he renounced hypnosis as a means of therapy: indeed, he wrote that his patients were in "self-hypnosis"[17]—implying that it was not necessary to add "suggestion" through the intermediary of a hypnotizer. Psychoanalysis would be born precisely from this move away from hypnosis and self-hypnosis. By relying on hysterical self-hypnosis, from *Studies on Hysteria* to Dora's homosexuality and the maternal link hidden there,[18] and "analysis terminable and interminable,"[19] Freud traces a path that traverses hypnosis and ends up in properly analyticalduration: that of the *verbal act of free association* caught in transference/countertransference, which, though insufficiently theorized and not without evoking the skepticism of Freud himself, ends up seeming to be the only thing likely to extract the hysterical subject from his/her dissociative states.

The Minoan-Mycenaen Dream

The "umbilical" aspect of Oriane's second dream regarding the "dirty old woman"—which marked the third phase of analysis—was, as you might imagine, the symbiotic state of the baby Oriane with her mother, before the birth of Christian. This archaic temporality that Freud suggests through the metaphor of the "Minoan-Mycenaen" civilization—and that, while common to both sexes, is more intense in the girl—is not necessarily the peace of "being" Winnicott speaks of: the supposed serenity of the "is" of the breast/ego prior to the tension of all drives that "do" (i.e., the opposition between "being"/"doing").[20] The biexcitation of Oriane and her mother, as the baby bit the breast of the woman who took refuge in her daughter to flee an unfaithful husband, made me think more of the "ruthless love" (Winnicott) that somehow, for the daughter and for the mother, is as absolute as it is merciless. This possession—source of an endogenous[21] madness in every nonpsychotic person—is worked out during the phallic phase, through the oedipal, and. thanks to the superego, in sadomasochism, the desire of knowing and the development of thought that construct conscious time. I support that, in the hysteric, the merciless passion of the Minoan-Mycenaen maternal link threatens conscious and/or temporal reality in the form of these dissociative states in which traumatic psychosexual conflicts are fated to amnesia, inasmuch as they are tributaries of their prototype, the crazy link to the crazy mother.

Oriane's mother had to have surgery, because her breast had gotten infected (that, at least, was the story), and Oriane had become a real "vomiter": anything, certain foods, being jolted in the car, could prompt her to empty the contents of her stomach, preferably on her father's jacket; he got in the habit of carrying another, a "spare," just in case . . . This continued with the birth of the little brother, and it was only when Oriane was assured that she was the true leader of the pair, the "boy manqué" of the family who clearly dominated the truth, that the vomiting was absorbed in the rivalry with "dirty men."

The mother, crazy about her daughter (or son—I will return to this with Charles, another analysand), is neither psychotic nor phallic, nor even seriously depressed. Certainly frustrated or somewhat depressive, she invests her child-penis with a possessive passion that makes up for her own castration, which the little girl (or boy) keeps engraved in an unconscious that is outside representation, outside time: the notion of the unconscious itself becomes problematic, though it is worked out in listening to hysteria, inciting thoughts of an *extrapsychical somatic excitation that cannot be represented*.

The superego and thought, as J.-L. Donnet recently described, are defenses against depression, issued from identifications as much as from the id.[22] The superego punishes a fault to spare itself the distress of loss and, by "delimiting the site of self-destruction," also allows the virtuality of an appeal to the object whose correlate, I would add, is the functioning of thought: culpability saves thought, though not without endangering it, sooner or later. The thought and superego of the hysteric are particular in that they must *also* "delimit the site of self-destruction" vis-à-vis mad love, the ruthless love of the crazy mother. Hysterical thought is constituted precisely by utilizing the play of primary processes (displacement, condensation) as well as secondary processes, provided they are based on dissociation: by rejecting ruthless love outside representation and outside time. In short, the hysteric's superego delimits the site of self-destruction by means of self-hypnosis and/or amnesia.

The hysterical fixation on the penis and the paternal anal penis, source of disgust, fear, and fascination, is parallel to *the investment of thought*. This hysterical thought with strong superegolike connotations is then experienced as an *internal extraneousness*, because incorporated and indispensable to the subject so as to delimit the site of self-destruction carved out by the archaic link to the mother. One could argue that the paternal penis, like thought, is always already there and that, by biting the maternal breast and vomiting, it is already the paternal penis that Oriane desires and attacks to take its place with the mother. Though I accept this "always already there" of triangulation, I think that the (male or female) hysteric confronts us with a particular version of it. The hysterical subject conserves sensorial prelinguistic traces (thus, anterior to the "idea," as Charcot would say, but also anterior to the representation of things or words), intense sensorial traces of the link with the mother. In relation to these traces, the *penis*, as the representative of the desirable object as well as *thought*, takes on the value of precocious counterinvestments, but counterinvestments just the same. A *dissociation* occurs, early on, between this aspect of desire, on the one hand, and sensoriality, on the other, with its substratum of drive-related representatives. The hysterical subject desires the penis and/or thought, and acquires them, but is swallowed up by the maternal receptacle that this penis gratifies or attacks. The phantasm of a phallic mother or a sadistic mother who "beats a child" is born of the subsequent guilt of having left behind this body-receptacle in order to desire the father. In other words, the *phantasm of the phallic mother* or sadistic mother is a montage of the superego that establishes a *logical order* (active/passive, master/slave, etc.), which is fanciful and imaginary but satisfies fear and desire. This phantasmatic order replaces the *initial coexcitation* of mother and baby, without representation of objects, even partial, and the wild disorder of which depended on the incompleteness of the baby (biological destiny) and love deprived of a third party, the ruthless love borne by this mother who is crazy about her offspring ("Minoan-Mycenaen" violence).

In adolescence Oriane replayed the Minoan-Mycenaen devouring in a bisexual rivalry with her brother; with the help of adolescent drives she also elaborated the breaking and entering undergone/inflicted with the primary *maternal object* that found itself transposed by the adolescent phantasm into this well-known dramatic scene where we find the *phallic mother* and *androgynous identity*. Alas, the death of her phallic double had brutally shattered the narcissistic and phallic totality in which Oriane had managed to translate— without sticking to it too closely—the primary coexcitation. *Thought* had survived this accident, but the *primary passion* reexperienced in the identification with Christian had imploded and ejected itself from the conscious realm. The hysteric forgets the real passions that nevertheless continue to consume her, and she is not only pretending to be somewhere else: she *really is* somewhere else—*verisimilarly* somewhere else. "Being somewhere else" is indispensable to her precisely in order to safeguard this psychical apparatus constituted as a result of phallicism, the oedipal, and superegolike investments, which certainly do not measure up to the Minoan-Mycenaen attraction, but that endure, because, regardless of Freud, who suspected women of an inaptitude to the superego; the more the superego is false the more perched it is on coexcitation and . . . sure!

The Conversion-Event

Conversion is an *event* that divides time: by dividing the story of the hysteric, conversion cuts itself off and rejoins the timelessness of dissociative states by somatic means. I consider conversion *amnesia incarnate*, and so I will not adhere to the distinction the *DSM-III* makes between the "hysteria of somatization" and "hysteria of dissociative states." For me, both obey the same "negative attention" that aims to push away a drive-related conflict linked to psychical bisexuality that is rooted in a traumatic relationship with the primary maternal.

Albertine complained of a complete lack of memory—she claimed to forget everything, which, she said, was problematic at work and, she added provocatively, risked making analysis impossible. Selective memory trouble, if there ever was, which I noticed after five years of analysis, when I took a trip to Israel that forced me to rearrange our schedule temporarily. Albertine's mother lived in Israel, and my patient told me she was a survivor of Auschwitz—a little girl who had escaped a raid and been sent abroad by cousins—while Albertine's grandparents must have died in Auschwitz. Albertine did not like stories: she had chosen images, because "it's immediate, you either get it or you don't, right away, there's no padding," and she hated psychoanalysts' explanations, which she was familiar with because her sister was a "shrink": "These people give you all the causes, but tell you nothing about the event: why does a teenager suddenly start shooting into a crowd or run away; that's what counts—not the before or the after."

Albertine's "event" wavered for a long time between headaches, sore throats, and stomachaches but finally settled on abdominal pains, apparently uterine. Tensions, anxiety, a sense of abandonment, then of revenge, of anger turned inward: "A force goes through me, I'm on the verge of coming, but I never really come, either with a woman or a man"—Albertine said she was bisexual—"only with my vibrator; but when it comes over me, the pain, I mean, there's no way I can think about the vibrator, I feel nauseous, then pain transfixes me like a knife pushing into my stomach." This sort of painful erection sometimes lasted hours: Albertine's time was literally punctuated by this anal phallic thrust that resisted the unconscious phantasm of being the boy of the family, the mother's little page/lover; just as Albertine resisted envy over her pregnant sister's stomach; phantasm and jealousy that analysis made conscious without however lifting the somatization. "Stomachaches like a pregnant woman" (Me). "You're the one who says so; I don't care about that" (Albertine, indifferent). "A tension in my entrails" (Albertine); I repeat her words: "A woman with a hard-on." "I wouldn't say no, but I prefer breasts to the penis, I've already told you a thousand times" (Albertine, annoyed).

Along with others,[23] I believe there is a not only masochistic impulse but a sadomasochistic one in the girl when she leaves the primary homosexual relationship in order to invest the father in the progression toward the oedipal. In fact, in the course of her passage from the mother to the father, the girl is at the apex of her sadistic-anal drives and sets up sadomasochistic scenarios with the mother: the aggressive desire to leave the mother, to disengage from the hold of the anal mother, generates guilt and sadistically mobilizes the anal penis of the girl as well as her phantasmatic phallus, which then becomes a uterus. The tension of the uterus, on lease from the colon (the "vagina on lease from the anus"),[24] participates in this drive-related montage that remains timeless (Zeitlos)—preceding the phallic/symbolic identification and the benefit of temporal thought that results from it. So much so that, as we have noted, the girl who becomes a boy phantasmatically protects the father from his own anxieties of castration (Albertine's father lived in the family home with a childhood friend, "just a friend, a very timid man"), while avoiding the culpability of incest with the father and posing as the idealized homosexual object of this same father—and not only as the homosexual and heterosexual object of the mother.

The conversion-event must have lasted until the conflict with the little sister analyst was actualized in transference (in a dream Albertine planted a knife in this unfortunate girl's throat), and Albertine mentalized her ambivalence toward me under the aspect of a threat of suicide: since I could do nothing for her (I didn't love her), there was nothing left for Albertine to do but commit suicide. "You're hesitating between penetrating me with your knife or punishing me by destroying yourself." Albertine did not let me go so easily. Missed sessions, threats of suicide, confused e-mails: but the somatic symptom was on the way to disappearing.

A dream she related at the end of this depressive phase shows the psychical working out that introduces psychical time instead and in place of conversion. Shortly before her appointment, Albertine suddenly felt weak and had to lie down for a nap. While I was waiting for her, she had this dream: "There was a child, I don't know what sex it was, it might've been a girl, but she was wearing the pants of an Italian page, it looked like from the Renaissance (*sic*). The child wanted to pee standing up, but the mother said such things weren't done and prevented it. So the little boy/girl rushed forward, head first, and, like a bomb, blew up the woman's stomach." Albertine told me this dream when she came back to see me, after the session she "missed," during which she had it. I told her that she fell asleep because she needed to know that I was waiting for her; that I was all alone with no baby in my stomach and no one on the couch, and that she could come at her convenience, capricious as a young page, to ram into me and finally let all her anger against her pregnant mother explode. This anger, which until then she only allowed herself to manifest by making her own stomach explode. She laughed, defending herself: "I didn't tell you the end of the dream. The woman was transformed; instead of exploding, she calmly came back to life. I saw that it was the cousin who had gotten my mother out of Germany, and she was carrying the child I didn't recognize in the beginning of the dream in her arms, the one I thought was me but that was my mother, a little girl being saved."

One cannot resent a mother who is an escapee. One cannot even make love to her. One suspends the contrary drives and knots them in one's own stomach—a love-hate with no object except for the inside. A psychical and prepsychical inside, a pain outside consciousness and outside time. The hysteric decidedly suffers from a dissociation between excitability and its cognitive congruence: to the by-products of this dissociation, Freud gave the name the unconscious.

"Scenes"

It seems we no longer see the hysterical arc, either in hospitals or on the couch, yet the so-called hysterical scene has not disappeared. By that I mean what sessions only show us in the calmer retelling afterward, fortunately: the analyst is never present for it, except perhaps in certain paroxysmal dramatizations of transference.

Odette remembered being a baby who could not hold her head up—she was told this, but thought she remembered it as well, so that at the age of two or three she recalled being "wilted, like a piece of fabric, spineless," sitting next to her big sister on a train, during one of the family's "many moves." I would attribute certain motor difficulties, and notably *axial dystonia* as well as the backache the hysteric suffers from, to an archaic perception of maternal *hypotonia,* a corollary to her depressiveness: if the *skin* marks the borders of the ego, *muscle tone* and the *verticality* of the spinal column immediately precondition the autonomy of the subject vis-à-vis the other, and record the failures. "With my mother, it was always like we were communicating vessels: I feel exactly what she feels, though I'm not sure of the opposite. Communicating vessels that only go one way must not exist." Of her military father, who was blown up in his tank in Indochina when Odette was sixteen, she reports a scene; she held out her hand to make a promise: "I promise to do my homework after our walk." The military man twisted her fingers as well as her ankle, a gesture that forced the young girl to fall to her knees, and the paternal voice ordered: "You will do what you must!"

Her first analysis ended with a paranoid outburst—Odette described it as "very emphatic, with a silent analyst," where she interpreted things on her own, "perhaps too much, I understood everything." "Mr. X (the analyst) had taken my husband's side, they both treated me like I was crazy, the neighbors whispered behind my back that I was incapable of taking care of my husband, my children; the housekeeper had taken control at home; I was relegated to a corner; I'd been rejected everywhere. X ended up telling me, if that's the way it was, I could leave his couch as well and stop analysis." Odette came to see me a few years later, and we began our sessions face to face over the course of two years. The persecutions returned, less frequent than before, as well as scenes like this one, which she told me "afterward": "I arrived at the country house by car, harried, tired. My husband, who had been there for two weeks, was not waiting for me, had not prepared anything, and had left to visit his sister in a neighboring village. The walls seemed transparent to me, I had no bones, I saw myself sink, I became a puddle of water. That's when Jean arrived. 'Still tired, poor dear,' he said in his condescending way. To him I'm worthless, a nobody. Then I felt the puddle rise up, a hurricane, a tornado, and a voice that tore through my throat; I don't know what I said to him. I must've slammed the door and went to bed. In the morning he said, 'You're as crazy as ever.' That may be so, but now I understood: my scenes are my health, without them I would just be a puddle."

The overinterpretation favored by the silent cure had demolished the defenses of an ego, its "skin" (Anzieu) uncertain and even its skeleton unable to stand erect. The absence of "transitionality" in transference/countertransference exposed the patient to her original phantasmatic scenarios, notably the most archaic, persecution. In the aggravating circumstances of such an "emphatic" analysis, hysteria, confronted with uncontained excitation, had yielded to its paranoid foundation: the patient saw herself persecuted by all and sundry and had no other shield against excitation except for the *scenes* acted and undergone in pairs: with the husband, the analyst, the mother—who ended up merging into the same persecuting paranoid object. Archaic scenes experienced but not made secondary through the copresence of verbal transitionality.

The *scene* is not an *action*: whereas an action unfolds in time, the scene involves a sensoriality outside time that is pathos filled—semiotic, in my terminology[25]—and that mobilizes motility, the voice, gestures, and "thoughts" in quotation marks, *extracted* from their status as thoughts. Then these "thoughts" are organized by the primary processes and thrown out like *bad objects* to the persecutors thus persecuted in turn, the patient having the impression of finding security through the elimination of the bad inside *as well as* outside.

Not without empathy, but through it, we went on to *reconstruct a transitionality*—explication, mentalization, indeed, theorization—to reconstruct the contours of the ego, beyond the crumbling of the original repression in empathy. The perverse innocence of the destructive empathy the patient experienced in her earlier analysis ("I was precipitated from empathy into an innocent destruction where I talked about everything all by myself") gradually began to yield to what cannot be called innocence but the pernicious harm of a conflicting formulation.

The *transitionality* of language in psychoanalysis is different from that of the baby and mother in that, in addition to playing and innocence, there is the added struggle to the death (*the work of the negative*) between two cognitive strategies that are revealed to be two contradictory desires: that of the analyst and that of the analysand. There is a chance not of avoiding but of voiding the struggle, this drive-related death that is the product of the hallucination that destroys thought. The *verbalized interpretation* implies a choice between the various meta-psychologies at the analyst's disposal, a choice that severs and thereby liberates unconscious thought from the traumatic scene where it was stuck.

Passivation

I could have spoken of male patients instead of female ones to describe my listening to the hysteric: notably regarding "scenes" tinged with paranoia, at which the male subjects I know excel. I have saved, not without a certain taste for paradox and desire for concision, the case of a male patient—Charles—to discuss a last variant of hysterical temporality: passivation.

Charles presented a "photo-obsessional" symptomatology without a characterized obsession. Doubt and inhibition, rather than compulsive rituals, hindered his personal and professional life. He stayed in his relationship for the sake of his child. Charles made a few attempts, without conviction, at relationships with young female colleagues; dabbled in politics; took a writing workshop. Repressed homosexuality and an identification with his mother—"like a deer in the headlights, unprotected," he said, at the first session—supported this well-defended structure, using analysis "not to touch it." What? The phallic identification with the father seemed a prosthesis, a "false self" that Charles maintained to keep up appearances, while admitting to me—via his dreams or sometimes by telling me in our sessions about the short stories he was writing in his workshop—his disgust regarding his own castration, which had come to be identified with the disgust once inspired in him by the cloth sanitary napkins spotted with blood that his mother let soak in a basin. A drastic image of his castration, this Charles-as-Bloody-Rag confided a much more profound traumatism than one we might imagine for a little boy abandoned by the mother-deer. "A bloody rag for others to see," I suggested. Charles continued with a memory: "I'm sick in bed, maybe three or four years old, my mother takes my temperature, I have my legs raised and a thermometer in my butt, she has a neighbor come in and leaves me in this horrible position. I die of shame under this man's gaze, I don't dare say a thing."

Memory-screen or phantasm, the desire and/or horror of being sod-
omized by this man was attributed to the mother—not so doelike after all,
not so castrated as all that, a mother with a phallic thermometer inflicting
"bloody" anal castration on a son who suffered doubly: of being identified
with feminine castration (the weakness of the doe, the dirtiness of the napkins) and being tormented by the phallic fantasized feminine excitation—
both insufferable.

Charles missed several sessions after this memory. When he came back,
he spoke to me of "a passive, I would say morbid, state," during the two
weeks he missed his appointments, punctuated by his fear of being attacked
by . . . homosexuals on the train. "The first homosexual who attacked you
was your mother," I said to him. "And you are afraid I will expose you the
way she did." This sentence of the analysis led to important modifications
in Charles's relationships with women. His heterosexuality seemed to become less of a cross to bear.

Both the anal retention and inhibition of the obsessional straddle hysteria. The passion of being the mother's passive object may be the aberrant
madness the obsessional's inhibition and ritualistic doubt are trying to contain. The subject suffers from the castration of the mother, with whom he
confuses himself, but, even more, he suffers from maintaining the belief in
the omnipotence of the sadistic phallic mother: a sadomasochistic suffering
that is his secret jouissance and that he hopes to preserve against analysis, if need be, by serving as his own analyst (I was fantasized as a phallic
woman who could torment him, expose him—especially in my publications). Charles had been through five years of analysis before consulting
me, and the dream of the mother with the thermometer only appeared in
the fourth year of analysis with me. He needed all that time to be less afraid
of telling me that I could be a mother "like that": he could then include that
mother—his own or myself—in the transference narrative, instead of keeping the trauma enclosed in the passivity of his circumspect person, doomed,
he believed, to failure. I agree, therefore, with H. Troisier who believes that
in the phantasm of "a child is being beaten" the beater is female, and the
fear/desire of being penetrated by the mother goes back to the primary coexcitation, later attributed to the anal penis or the penis, quite simply, so to
speak, of the mother.

I am less certain that this phantasm in women marks an *evolution* toward
the oedipal, an obligatory passage toward oedipal maturation: many girls,

including Albertine, remain fixed in the position of the female homosexual "punished, loved, penetrated by the mother."[26] On the other hand, this fixation on the masochistic position of being beaten/penetrated by the anal penis of the mother commands the failure of the castration complex and induces a hysterical position of passivation of the *male* subject toward men as well as women: we find it underlying many male obsessional neuroses, and I have tried, in my reading of *The Rat Man*, to point out the hysterical oral link to the mother, the violence of which is suggested only in Freud's *Journal*—but not in the text of the case histories.[27]

I have tried to present four modalities of hysterical time:

- self-hypnosis, source of amnesia
- conversion
- "scenes"
- passivation

These lead me to a few general remarks, the boldness of which I know I am not the first to express, as many researchers of the SPP (Société psychanalytique de Paris) have already started down this path:

1. The unconscious was invented to relieve the hysteric of the noncongruence between excitability and cognition. By way of this "other scene," the nontime of the drive is metabolized into representations and primary processes, still outside time but able to be formulated in temporal conscious representations. This always incomplete translatability invites us to understand Freud's sentence, "Hysteria is linked to the place,"[28] not only as a dependence on home, landscape, and setting, but on the maternal place, which is a place of passion. Now consider how Freud's sentence resonates with this one by Joyce: "Father times, mother spacies." Here, the *space* of passion (of the primary maternal) turns into the memory of the *species*, ontogenesis into phylogenesis. In short, hysteric temporality encourages us to reformulate the unconscious—beyond the timeless drive and its semiotic and sensorial offshoots—by including the prepsychical.

In other words, by listening to hysterical time and other contemporary clinics, a *contemporary version of the unconscious* appears to be emerging that includes the prepsychical and even Being.[29] Far from being the hysteric's trick of recovery in transference with the master-analyst, this unconscious *aug-*

ments the hysteric, just as the monster characters at the end of Proust's *Time Regained* are augmented: the outsize temporalities that are in play create monstrous intimacies. Moreover, and symmetrically, if the analyst's listening were to be placed in the vortex of this hysterical temporality, the analyst would run the risk of dissociative states. And access to this mad passion that is absorbed, with the serenity due to philosophy, by calling it Being.

2. I have naturally wondered if my personal interest in the crazy link to the crazy mother did not come from the fact that I was spared this configuration, "in favor," dare I say, of another, destabilizing in other ways: a mother neutralized by her latent phobia and, in addition, split in two, indeed, three, by a lineage of matrons (grandmothers, great-aunts, and so on) in the image of Santa Maria Metterza in the painting by Leonardo analyzed by Freud. To have been satisfied and frustrated by not *one*, but *two or three* possible mothers, I am probably impressed by the frightening impact of *unique* "ruthless love." As a result, I am among those who consider the emphasis on "the primary maternal" an excessive return of the deus ex machina—when not the goddess-mother—in psychoanalysis. If I have resorted to it, however, it has been to point out that this archaic maternity is not the absolute cause in the ultimate anthropomorphic representability adjoining the other side: the prepsychical/biological. By coming up against the real mother and the phantasm of the phallic or anal mother, hysterical time leads us to the coexcitation of the two primary protagonists. Moreover, beyond their *passion*, hysterical time leads us to the strictly *inhuman* components of this excitation. I understand this "passionate primary maternal" in the pure sense Freud attributed to the concept of "metapsychology": it is the ultimate irrepresentability. Didn't Freud write to Fliess that he was looking for "a *biological*—or rather *metapsychological*—" solution (emphasis mine), the synonyms biological and metapsychological contrasting with the "psychological" solution brought about by "the theory of wish fulfillment"?[30]

Though forged in transference by the speech of free association, a temporal action, hysteria defies it and checkmates the end of analysis, perhaps even "analyzability," in a different way than psychosis. Knowing this, the analyst does not disavow metapsychology or the clinic for all that. To those who worry about the end of History, we can say that, since his pact with hysteria, Freud opened another temporality: that of the spacing of Being in the *event*, which, for the analyst, is nothing other than *passionate madness*.

"Dissociative states" like conversion, scenes, passivations, and other components of the hysteric syndrome testify to the fact that, while threatening desire, thought, and time, it is indeed this madness, not to be confused with psychosis, that constitutes the secret motor of the human condition. Having led Freud to invent the unconscious, hysteria reminds us that the madness of this unconscious can never be explored enough.

11

HEALING, A PSYCHICAL REBIRTH

Illness—notably cancer, which is our topic of discussion today—is being increasingly "contextualized": we consider it not only as the deterioration of an organ but also as the *symptom of the organism* as a whole and, beyond that, a *symptom of the subject*. An organic ill-being, indeed, a subjective ill-being, is being expressed—finding its sign, its language, in illness.

First Therapies

From then on, healing consists in refining the specific treatment of the tumor, mobilizing all potential medical research and hospital care as well as dealing with the illness in its entirety. Going back to etiology and struggling against the illness in the present, to slow it and, if possible, stop it. More and more, slowing the progression of cancer—which has been achieved over the past few years—and stopping it have led medical professionals to become involved in the *psychical context* of illness: to assist the patient in overcoming the depression that has either preceded the appearance of the cancer or developed after its appearance.

Many studies show *connections between cancer and the depressive state* (whereas we do not find any, or very few, between cancer and stress or anxiety). There is often psychotherapy for the patient's depression as well as for the family's: outside the team treating the cancer or sometimes with a psychotherapist included on the team. Similarly, cognitive or group therapies are proposed, as well as therapy for children or adolescents whose narcissistic image and even the investment of thought are often damaged by the trial of illness and treatment. We wonder about using a particular *antidepressant* likely to inhibit the development of cancerous cells in the course of treatment. Finally, a sensitivity to *pain*—during and after anticancer treatment—has also been linked with endemic depressive states due to illness.

Depression, which is manifested by a psychomotor slowing, expresses a psychical disinvestment of the vital processes: ties are cut (ties of speech, erotic ties, and, ultimately, in suicidal tendencies, the tie to life). Treating it is therefore very difficult and fully mobilizes the analyst or therapist's countertransference, well beyond the empathy required in treating neuroses. Because treatment of depression consists of reestablishing ties—reestablishing the narcissistic image, the erotic tie, restoring language, so many necessities that call upon the *maternal* function of the therapist. But also, and very quickly, the subject must be allowed to revitalize *all of his/her own resources*: of binding and *unbinding*, of love and *hate*, of trust and *aggressiveness*. Analysis becomes a *space of revolt*, and, if it does not become that, psychical life cannot be reborn. The therapist is then the Father, Law, and Savior—so many frontiers, limits, and taboos to transgress and appropriate, which the child encounters on the path to the constitution of his psychical apparatus, that depression has compromised and must be refashioned.

I am focusing on depression because this symptomatology is observable at various stages of anticancer treatment. But, insofar as it is long-term work, listening to depression also allows us to refine our conception of recovery: the length of the analytical cure provides an example of this complex concept of healing, not as a circumscribed act that results in a *definitive state* (health) but as *a process with twists and turns in time*. To the definitive idea of "healing" resulting in a "state of health," it would perhaps be truer to appose, if not oppose, the durative idea of "care." A variant of the myth of creation—a Latin variant—tells how the first man was modeled from a small bit of clay by the god Care. When the fundamental work of Care was terminated, Jupiter—father and god of Light—approached and claimed paternity for creation himself. After a long quarrel between Care and Jupiter, the obscure work of Care would be recognized provided Jupiter could give his name to the result obtained by the cares of Care: so he called the work of Care "a man." And so, in the light of Jupiter, there is a body called "man," whose essence and intimate being results from Care, confused with the darkness of time.

More concretely, the *duration of treatment* (which should not be neglected when aspiring to a *state of recovery*) created the pair of cared for/caregiver. A complex pair involving tranference-countertransference. A couple in the inevitable amorous and dramatic sense of the term. Medical professionals encroaching on the field of psychoanalysis—within certain limits. The limits of transference are often crossed, and it is impossible to fix them in an absolute way; they vary according to patients and caregivers. But one rule remains: without denying transference, it should be contained and oriented toward a specific psychotherapy. But how do we prepare medical personnel for this goal? We are confronted with the need to train health professionals in psychology and, more generally, in the human sciences. This might make us miss the era when doctors could write, like Chekhov or Céline. After a long eclipse, a certain opening to the logics of the mind seems to have returned over the past few years in students of medicine. I have even met psychiatrists—on the couch—who are not content to prescribe Urbanil or an MRI but who want to take the risk of reading *In Search of Lost Time*. But when will we see the "sciences of the mind" in the medical curriculum? When will we see the rudiments in the curriculum of caregiving professionals? We can always dream.

The trial of caring for the terminally ill meets and aggravates the difficulties of the personalized approach internal to the cure. In particular, the attending physician is invested with the supreme power of the *subject supposed to know*: though phantasmatic for many patients, this power is no less real. The amorous transference then passes to a new power: the doctor is the possessor of life and, therefore, of the mystery of death. Needless to say, respecting the patient's beliefs in this extreme situation, more than in others, is only proper, especially if *the doctor's endurance regarding his own death* is put to the test because of the rather intense transferential pair he has formed with his (male or female) patient. It is not a question of becoming a priest or a spiritual adviser, or explaining the latest scientific developments regarding dying or euthanasia. Benevolent listening appears to be the most appropriate treatment for these final states: the dying person expects *not so much a response as to be heard.* This seems simple, but in fact involves a psychical availability that few of us possess. Because it depends on the complexity, richness, and stability of the psychical space of the doctor himself. To find the words and signs of this "listening" or "hearing" is not that easy: we touch on our own ease or lack of ease with death and our capacity to find the right words. You understand that I am not necessarily encouraging doctors to practice analysis but, at the very least, to read novels.

Medicine or Philosophy

Depression underlies many somatic illnesses, including cancer, and it is not only—as the general practitioner and psychiatrist observe—a motor slowing or psychosensory anesthesia. This tableau, which gathers specific symptoms but remains reductive, and which has prevailed for about ten years, actually corresponds to the social demands and models the patient assumes of his general practitioner or psychiatrist: "one" is really "sick" when one is unable to act or work. The patient will only confide these aspects, rather than others, to his doctor, as if it were understood that the psychical state is of no interest to this model, this opinion, at the source of the diagnosis. Indeed, the psychical state is often relegated to an intimacy considered old-fashioned, only appropriate to religion, sects, literature, and the arts. We should not be surprised to note that the *sadness* of the depressed person only appears starting with a certain journey . . . on the analyst's couch, the analyst being one of the rare people, if not the only person, who is prepared to listen to psychical suffering. We understand that healing, seen as a process of twists and turns in time, demands that the caregiver, whoever he is, not misunderstand the need to gain access to what some consider a chimera, but is revealed to be one of the centers, if not the main center, of the process: the soul, which sometimes must be restored, if not restructured, so that the patient can once again have a psychical life.

Do you have a soul? Whether philosophical, theological, or simply incongruous, the question takes on new value. In the face of neuroleptics, aerobics, and the remote control, does the soul still exist?

As you can imagine, as a psychoanalyst, I cannot *not* stress the importance of this "organ" that is not like the others. Whether you call it *psyché,* as the Greeks did, or anima, as the Latin Stoics did, doesn't matter; the essential thing is to take into account this irreducible enigma that is impossible to localize. I spoke of this in *New Maladies of the Soul*,[1] but I would like to revisit this subject with you, because our meeting encourages it.

In Freud, the "psychical apparatus" is a theoretical construction irreducible to the body, subject to biological influences but essentially observable in the structures of language.[2] Anchored in biology through the drive, but dependent on autonomous logics, the *soul*, now the psychical apparatus, produces (psychical or somatic) symptoms and is modified in transference. Yet it would be a mistake to think that psychoanalysis plays on the mode of a hypertrophy of the psychical: no primary dualism here, on the contrary. The energetic substratum of the drives, the determination of meaning by sexual desire, and even the inscription of the cure in transference, understood as a reactualization of earlier psychosensory traumas, are the many components of psychoanalysis that cross the frontiers of body/soul and work on objects that traverse this dichotomy.

Basically, there is no life without psychical life. Whether it is intolerable, painful, deadly, or jubilatory, psychical life—which combines systems of representations that traverse language—provides access to the body and to other people. Through the soul, you are capable of action. Your psychical life is nothing other than discourse in action, harmful or salutary, of which you are the subject.

Now, a current crisis is situated precisely at this point: look around and you will see, psychical life is atrophying, the soul is dying. Modern man is in the process of losing it, and suffering is taking over his body: he is somatizing. But, you might object, modern society does offer recourse—neurochemistry, for example. And so it is the body that must conquer the invisible territory of the soul. A bitter observation if there ever was one: modern man's psychical life seems to have been taken hostage between somatic symptoms (illness and the hospital) and the placing into images of his desires (reverie in front of the TV). No more psychical life then. Does this prefigure a new humanity that has gone beyond metaphysical inquietude and concern for the meaning of being, with psychological complacency? Isn't it wonderful that a person can be satisfied with a pill and a screen?

Yet the path of this superman is not self-evident: relational and sexual difficulties, somatic symptoms, the impossibility of expressing oneself, and the malaise engendered by the use of language that ends up feeling "artificial," "empty," or "robotic" lead *new patients* characterized by difficulty representing to the analyst's couch. Whether it takes the form of psychical silence or various signals experienced as empty or artificial, this deficiency of psychical representation in sensory, sexual, and intellectual life may have a negative effect on *biological* functioning itself. The call is then made to the psychoanalyst, in various forms of disguise, to restore *psychical life* and allow the *speaking body* optimal life.

Healing? Yes, provided we do not forget that healing involves psychical rebirth.

12

FROM OBJECT LOVE TO OBJECTLESS LOVE

After a variety of philosophical and methodological developments on the *object*, allow me to offer a few reflections inspired by the microcosm of the psychoanalytical clinic and to offer a few concrete examples borrowed from religious and literary experience. The following will deal with the object as seen through a reading of Freud and Freudians and its place in the writing of two women—St. Teresa and Colette—with resonance for the present.

Object relations are at the heart of the psychoanalytical theory and clinic. The subject of the drive (whether the life drive or death drive), the subject of desire, the subject of love are constituted, suffer, or experience pleasure because of the object or through it. Whatever the variants of the psychoanalytical approach to the subject (the ego, the self), objects vary but inevitably constitute their indispensable correlates.

Freud supposes, it is true, an autoeroticism and narcissism that make the neotene a monad incapable of this link to the object, which is only worked out later. As for Melanie Klein, she conceives of a self immediately linked to the "part object" (breast-and-penis) in the violence of the projective identification that characterizes the "schizoid-paranoid position," then a "total object" that only comes about with the depressive position, the mourning and separation from the real mother through psychical representation, which the child becomes capable of toward the end of the first year and supports language.

In the wake of Klein the approach to psychosis familiarized us with "fragmented" and "split" objects, and the term *object* itself was replaced by *alpha and beta elements* (Bion), *pictograms* (P. Aulagnier), my own semiotic and symbolic *signifying process,* and, in a more playful or maternal way, the *transitional object* (Winnicott) and the never satisfying, always elusive *objet petit a* (Lacan) in the metonymy of desire.

With these variants the configuration of the object changes, and it is this change that specifies the economy of the subject himself: the specific structure of the subject depends on the specific link to an object, which is itself specific. I will briefly mention five possible cases in point: the *abject,* the anorexic object, the object of mourning, the object of fatigue, and the amorous object.

The Abject

The lasting dependence of the neotene vis-à-vis the maternal container provides the conditions for this fascinating and unbearable relationship between the child and his mother that I have called the *abject,* with a privative "a."[1] Neither object nor subject, the *infans* and its genetrix, who is not an "object" either, much less an "Other," for the newborn, attract and reject each other: a devouring and a vomiting, a swallowing and an excretion, the pure and the impure. The "feminine position" of both sexes is dependent on this abjection, which is not only a passiveness or a victim state of seduction-invasion but a reciprocal situation of attraction-and-repulsion. The "rock of castration" and "femininity," which Freud tells us are the "most difficult to analyze" in subjects of both sexes, seem to me to be more accessible to analysis than this *abjection of the self and the other* on which femininity and castration rely in the sense that they are their mask. Art and literature know something about this, since catharsis, which Aristotle tells us aims for Beauty, is nothing other than a purification: similar to the purification of the abject, also known as "taint," in which all religions specialize. L.-F. Céline became its explorer: *Journey to the End of the Night* is teeming with idiotic men and abject women, while *London Bridge,* as you may recall, drowns the mother and son in the seasickness provoked by a raging sea. This does not prevent the author from succumbing to the process in question, when he abandons the fictional working out of the abject in order to replace it with the ideology of a scapegoat borrowed from the unhealthiest of French ideologies and fixes in the character of the Jew his limitless panic before the impossible object of desire of the neotene that persists under the mask of the writer.

The Anorexic

Less ideologically than organically, the anorexic is an idealist who sacrifices her body to an ideal phantasmatic object (papa-mama merged under the severe gaze of the superego); here, she withdraws, to judge herself: a piece of trash, a cesspit with orifices, soiled as much by what penetrates as by what comes out. Disappointed with all objects, incapable of supporting the object within, because no object can live up to the object, which she wants to want her entirely.

The Bereaved

On the contrary, the bereaved subject, though connected to the anorexic, as a double, a sibling, cannot leave the object behind: "the shadow of the object fell on the Ego," Freud writes in "Mourning and Melancholia." And this metaphor is not just an image evoked by Nerval's "black sun of melancholia." It suggests that the real object does not have much to do with mourning, anymore than it has to do with depression. But that its shadow—a murky mixture (a shadowy confusion, precisely) of love and hate—places me alongside the dearly departed and plunges me into an ineffable jouissance of tears. Which condemns the analysis of depression to an analysis of the unconscious hate that the depressed/bereaved subject sustains in place of the lost object.

The Fatigued

More modestly, so-called psychosomatic fatigue—about which contemporaries complain frequently, when not an acknowledged depression—is sustained by an uncertainty of the object of desire. "I don't know who I love: a man or a woman, papa or mama," the chronically exhausted man or woman says, and this uncertainty of sexual choice leads to indecision in existential and professional choices, which are "a pain in the neck." Chronically tired people complain endlessly of the "pains-in-the-neck" who surround them, as if by chance, or the annoying people who "drain their energy," as they may say: impossible objects that cause them to experience as fatigue, quite simply, a lack of passion for a definite object, cut off and uncoupled from the overinvested and unacceptable parental duo. An apparent lack of passion that hides a suppressed, frozen passion for the united parents.

These accidents of object relations lead us *a contrario* to the miracle of the love relationship.

The Lovers

A miracle, indeed. As I wrote in *Tales of Love*,[2] the love object absorbs my narcissistic needs, erotic desires, and most phantasmatic ideals, like the ideal of eternity. The resulting amorous object is thus a phantasmatic construction, which becomes the subject's absolute pole of stabilization, magnificence, or exaltation: the cornerstone of enthusiasm. But it is also the place where stability carries within it the risk of dissolving, either through an excess of manic excitation facing the constraints of limits and reality or through the risks of abandonment, separation, or rupture.

That the amorous relationship is madness all of world literature is there to remind us. I will only mention the wisdom of the rabbis who, having glimpsed love's promises and abysses, hesitated including the Song of Songs in the Bible, a text supposedly written by Solomon around the seventh or ninth centuries B.C. It was included around the first century, under the pressure of what was to be Christianity, which did not take long to establish the subject dependent on the object of love. Freud is the consequence and elucidation of this. A new knowledge of the imaginary and its objects began, for better or worse.

Object or deobjectification (*désobjectalisation*)? If you have followed me, you know that this is the problem raised in the economy of the subject/object confrontation, if one chooses not to veil one's face before its fragility, notably under the veil of repression. Object or deobjectification? This is the problem explored by mystics as well as by adventurers in aesthetic sublimation, as illustrated by two great female figures: St. Teresa of Avila (1515–1582) and Colette (1873–1953).

St. Teresa of Avila: "Checkmating" God

In her *Life* the young Teresa—an excellent writer—describes herself as torn between her erotic desires and her cultural, worldly, and monastic resistance. Intensely spiritual and violently political, she describes herself in the same breath as unhappy and epileptic (of course, the term *epileptic* only appears in the writings of modern neurologists who have examined the description of her states): Teresa trembles, loses consciousness, bites her tongue, spends days in a coma; she is taken for dead; she is almost buried. Until an illuminated mystical current, the *alumbrados* movement, allows her to discover the state of prayer. And she convinces herself not only that Jesus loves her but that this extraordinary "love object," as we would say, never leaves her, that He (Jesus) is always with her, that she is His wife, no less, and that her words are nothing but the words of her love object, Jesus, or God himself, words she is content in her humility to repeat.

You may recall that President Schreber, who so intrigued Freud, suffered because he loved a persecuting God. I think Teresa succeeds where Schreber fails: she loves an object that loves her. This is precisely what her exorbitant faith consists of: and this confidence, given to the object and received in it, reunites her with herself. No more contradictory passions, no more crises, no more comas. Teresa is beside herself; but by loving herself in the Ideal Object, she is beside herself in ecstasy: without a position, infinite, floating in an incommensurable Other who has lost all contours that might delimit an object, and that, as a result, is hardly an Other and, instead, an infinite *alter ego* that sends back infinite self-love.

Love as therapy: there is nothing better. However, we cannot grasp the complexity of this mystical ecstasy if we do not follow Teresa to the extremes, where this self-love abolishes the love object itself. In all consciousness Teresa relies on her humility, using it to get rid of the love object in person and consume it in her exaltation, which, once started, has no cure. In her *Way of Perfection* the mother superior calls this "checkmating God."

Comparing prayer to a chess game, she explains (I am quoting from the Valladolid manuscript): "The Queen is His strongest opponent in the game, and all the other pieces help her. No queen can defeat Him so soon as can humility. It drew Him from heaven into the Virgin's womb, and with it we can draw Him by a single hair into our souls."[3] And: "any one who does not understand how to set the pieces in the game of chess will never be able to play well, nor, if he does not know how to give check, will he ever succeed in effecting checkmate. You may blame me for speaking of a game, for such things are neither played nor permitted in our convent. . . . Still, they say that sometimes the game is lawful, and how well it would be for us to play it, and if we practiced it often, how quickly we should checkmate this divine King so that He neither could, nor would, move out of our check!"

Is this mystic who is checkmating God an atheist? The only possible kind? Not ignoring that God is love—because the human subject is made up of connections to the love object, a process Freud clarified—not feeling below God, but beyond Him? By checkmating Him, taking Him in through humility, identifying with Him to the point absorbing him? "And doubtless, the greater our humility, the more entirely shall we possess Him, and the weaker it is, the more reluctantly will He dwell within us."[4]

As I said, Teresa succeeds where Schreber fails: loving oneself in the love object, by confusing subject and object, which amounts to loving without a love object, just loving, loving nothing other than everything, the Everything that she is.

There is no need to be a mystic to get to this point. In a different way, but not that much different, Colette completes the journey from object love to objectless love, in writing, not faith, through the process of sublimation. How?

Colette; or, How to Succeed Where the Pervert Fails

1. Self-love

The subject of sublimation (artist, painter, musician, writer, etc.) overinvests his own means of expression (language, music, painting, dance, etc.), which is confused with a real object, when it does not replace it and become a veritable object of self-love. The self loves itself in its outsize creations that annex external objects, and this neoreality absorbs but also limits the drive-related satisfactions of the ego. It is in this way that the child loves himself by loving—and/or by learning his mother tongue. But the same logic of sublimation, joined to working through, sets up the chimera of the analytic session, for example, and also constitutes the *hyperworld* of aesthetic creation.

This hyperworld, this chimera, while essential to aesthetic creation and the analytic cure, are no less a part of the possibility of the "self-love" that unites us today, however modest or unconscious it may be for some under the effect of repression and the banalization of existence. But my focus here will be the specific variant of self-love in aesthetic sublimation based on my reading of the work of Colette (1873–1954).

As you may recall, in these pages, an enormous self loves itself, which extends to plants, animals, and all folds of Being. It is ultimately confused with a maternal figure, also enormous, "Sido, or the cardinal points," made mythic, and just as idealized after the author's fiftieth birthday as fascinating, contested, forgotten, or neglected before.

The *medium* of this neoreality that is Colette's imaginary universe is not even perceived by the writer as a literature or a language—those are overly formal, partial, inept terms for referring to the experience at hand: "The greatest living French prose writer , me? Even if it were true, I don't feel it inside, do you understand?" This *medium*, the literary text, is combined with Colette's enormous ego so as to order the world as she sees fit: literature is then the "alphabet," the "monogram," the "arabesque" of the world.

The alchemy that presides over this amorous recreation of the world and/or the self is complex; I tried to decipher it in the third volume of my *Female Genius* series, *Colette.*[5] Today I will focus on the element of *perversion* in the subject's recreation of self-love.

The erotic and thanatic drives are disentangled in the process of sublimation, as Freud already noted. Freed from the taboos set up by the parents, braving the frontiers of genders and generations, desires target *all* objects. It is in *homosexuality* and the *incestuous liaison* that Colette would find the laboratory of a limitless self, to which the savory language of her first texts, the *Claudine* books (from 1900 to 1903), had already given her access, and whose definitive style—crystallized with this transgressive erotic experience and its aftermath—would be the innocent and sovereign consecration.

Apparently, the writer was trying to avenge herself for the abandonment she had been subject to: the infidelities of her two husbands, Willy and Jouvenel. Against Willy's betrayals, Colette discovers her lesbian inclinations for one of her husband's mistresses, before being encouraged by the unfaithful philanderer to console herself with the Marquise de Morny, known as Missy. Rather quickly, however, the student proves a virtuoso in the matter and a lucid observer as well, capable of keeping her distance: a few decades later, *The Pure and the Impure* (1932–1941) would show this. If it is true that aggressiveness freed this way targets the Law of the Father, that it is a "père-version," as Lacan wrote, it was her reconciliation with her mother that would conclude the experiment of this transgressive pleasure for Colette. The incestuous relationship with Bertrand de Jouvenel, thirty years her junior and the son of her second husband, Henry de Jouvenel, would be the second and last instance of acting out by the writer, who would consolidate her narcissistic reassurance as an author in her sublimatory adventure.

In fact, the incestuous phantasm precedes the reality of the relationship between Colette and the son her husband had with Claire Boas. The character of Léa is not duped by the nature of the relationship she has with Chéri, the "naughty little boy" she "adopted."[6] *Chéri* was published in 1920, the relationship with Bertrand, to whom Colette dedicated the book ("To my beloved son"), begins later, starting in 1921.

However, while *realizing* the fantasy, it is now above all a matter of *rewriting* the infantile. Rewriting it in a completely different way than she did with the *Claudine* books, since the mischief of the first writings is now followed by the gravitas of a celebration.

2. Perversion or Sublimation?

A calmer self emerges, after *La Maison de Claudine* (*My Mother's House*, 1922), which will culminate in the writing of *Break of Day* (1928) and *Sido* (1929). Incest is revisited, contemplated, illuminated by the work of writing; culpability is expressed and traversed.

Colette's unconscious knows that the phantasmatic source of her osmotic style, the coalescence of sense and sensibility, language and pleasure, words and things, and what she calls a "monogram of the inexorable," is now unveiled: this source is nothing other than control over the object (the mother, every partner) and the outside (the world), beyond prohibitions, without limits, borders, or taboos.

Apollinaire thought it apt to describe Colette as "perverse," then retracted the adjective and replaced it with "mischievous" ("a soul more mischievous than perverse"); he did not hesitate to compare the writer's provocative audacity to the tragic immodesty of the first Christians: "It was thus that Roman martyrs entered the arena, freed from a sense of propriety."

You might expect a psychoanalyst to answer the question: "Colette, perverse?" My answer: "Certainly, a little, not at all." Colette writes, where the pervert seeks to climax: this is her success, beyond the pain she complains about, which exhausts the pervert. From Willy by way of Missy to Bertrand de Jouvenel, perverse acting out punctuates Colette's life. But she transforms it: first by using acting out as a self-analysis, by living-and-meditating on it in her writing, where it takes on a definitive reality, a fictive neoreality, at a distance from the real, untrue, and sublime. Writing then seems to be a substitution for erotic desire, a transference of pleasure from sexuality into all sensations and, simultaneously, all words.

3. The Metamorphic Body: A New Mysticism?

Indeed, *another* jouissance comes about as soon as Colette begins to write her *Claudine* books, prompted by Willy, but proving sovereign with the publication of *Sido* (Colette was fifty-five when the book of the same name was published): it suggests this *reversal of perversion in sublimation*, so that the perversion itself is absorbed, without disappearing, and gathers there, but as purity. In certain circumstances, men as well as women are capable of this other, transsexual jouissance, and we know writers who excel at it: Proust, Joyce, Nabokov, each in his own way, to only cite a few moderns. Or it may be that this femininity, if it is specific to this other jouissance, is also the secret of *all writing*: its "purloined letter," so to speak. Cutting across genders and language—inhuman, cosmic.

Today psychoanalysis—at least in its developments most concerned with truth—has abandoned the normative thinking that marred its fundamental notions (notably, that of perversion) and considers a number of "perverse" behaviors obligatory passages marking the complex construction of the personality. The bisexuality claimed by Colette is part of that. Several psychoanalytical treatments show that homosexual relations occurring in the life of a person who does not necessarily consider himself homosexual, either in the course of analysis in transference with his analyst, or independently of her, indicate a dissociation between the masculine and feminine identity of the subject, which is a common but repressed feature in most of us. In this amorous trust with a homosexual or incestuous partner, a paradoxical relationship may be produced that Winnicott calls an "ego orgasm," similar to ecstasy, that establishes "the capacity to be alone."

Some relationships, apparently perverse because they mobilize bisexuality or incestuous drives, comprise this sort of ego ecstasy. Sexual excitation is often present but remains subjacent, unless it is denied; it can also be effaced completely and yield to a primary affective abandon to the other (initially the mother).

If the body thus described is endowed with an exuberant sexuality, it is because it is disseminated through an extravagant sensoriality, eager to absorb and be absorbed.

Indeed, Colette's writing does not focus on the organs, much less the sexual organs: in Colette all senses are sexual organs. Except, unlike our ordinary perception, the moment she feels the elements, the elements feel her: loving/loved, subject/object, Colette describes a gigantic orgasm of the feeler *and* the felt. The barriers between the five senses, like the threshold between intimate perception and the external reality motivating it, are only pointed out to be overcome: footbridges, yes; barriers, never: "whatever I pass through—new countries, skies pure or cloudy, seas under rain the colour of a grey pearl—something of myself catches on it and clings so passionately that I feel as though I were leaving behind me a thousand little phantoms in my image, rocked on the waves, cradled in the leaves, scattered among the clouds . . . But does not a last little phantom, more like me than any of the others, remain sitting in my chimney corner, lost in a dream and good as gold as it bends over a book which it forgets to open?"[7]

4. *Passing Through Love*

Of the excitability of the feminine body, Colette brings a knowledge that, while singular and inimitable, is nevertheless a fact of society: the emancipation of women and the feminist struggles of the twentieth century. Colette did not see herself in that—which in no way devalues the fact that feminists see her life and work as an encouragement to their boldness—but her writing is part of a mutation of civilization more than social and political struggle.

Since the Song of Songs, women have invented the speech of love. Without mentioning them all, we must underscore that their works, known or marginal, constitute the circumference of this garden of feminine loves, at the center of which Colette holds court. Not that she went to the limits of burning desire: other women certainly exceeded her in terms of erotic temerity. She did not necessarily assemble experiences of untold richness or universality. But Sido's daughter managed to display the varied and painful spectrum of her loves in an Eden, a speech of *well-being*. Approached eagerly, monstrosity itself is tamed by Colette then restored to us, bearable and bracing.

The writer brings her vision to the insoluble question of the male/female relationship: no solution, nothing but a new experience to decode, to question, to tame.

Neither metaphysical nor sociopolitical, Colette's way of *being in the world*, which culminates in writing *of* and *in* the flesh of the world, implies an observation of the impasses and fertility of the amorous link, with its homo- and heterosexual valences. It attests to *a profound modification of the concept of the couple*, and feminists have not been wrong to see this upheaval as a courageous beginning to feminine freedom. But the essential part of Colette's message—resistant to all sociology—has to do with a transformation of *subjectivity* itself, of the risky equilibrium that places it between sense and sensation, law and passion, purity and impurity. Neither the imperative of the reproduction of the species nor that of social stability—both guaranteed by the couple—guide Colette's thought. Nothing but a constant concern for the emancipation of the subject, with priority given to the female subject, who wishes to attain her sensual freedom so as to maintain her curiosity and creativity in a plurality of connections.

Isn't Colette's passing through love also and above all a passing through religion? Her fury against religion is manifested in the texts of her youth, but her revolt calms down in time. And in observing the infinite but always passionate detachment from the amorous link that she proposes, replacing it with an amiable, floral, animal passion for Being in language, we follow the profound sense of her atheist convictions. Neither illusions nor fantasies are abolished in this proximity—unprecedented in French—between the imaginary effervescence and the stylistic labor that relates it. But in writing experienced this way, there is no enduring absolute object, no salutary center, no marker extraneous to passion. There is still passion, but it adheres to the adjustment between the felt and the said, the lived and the represented, the loved and the expressed. The sublimity and monstrosity of Colette reside in this total absorption of any transcendence through the arabesque, the alphabet, embroidery, the monogram, in this permeation between the flesh of the world and the French language that is her style.

If the object is the thing posited/exposed and accepted by me, then the absolute Thing, or *Res*, is certainly God. Would objectless love then be an exquisite atheism? The only possible kind, with full knowledge of the facts?

What is left of the subject, in this case? An interminable passing through as well, writing, ceaselessly written, always "to be continued," as Colette notes, a luminous trace. To be contemplated in the face of fundamentalisms and other veils clouding the present, which politics does not dare consider in its subjective and objective abysses.

DESIRE FOR LAW

The talk we've just heard suggests that law is a consecration of the desire of certain individuals or groups (the desire of gay people to marry, for example). This is no doubt an important function of the law. A psychoanalytical approach, however, illuminates another of its functions: one that favors the individual's creativity. In our civilization, freedom is the culmination of the individual with respect to human rights, and the law guarantees human freedom in relation to collective freedom. It might surprise you to hear that this problematic is not foreign to psychoanalysis: in fact, I would say, far from being a vision of man and a therapeutic experience that "liberates desire," as a certain anarchic vulgate of our practice would have it, psychoanalysis, since Freud, demonstrates the copresence of desire and Law in the psyche.

Prohibition and Rebirth

This copresence of desire-and-Law is produced according to different figures to which I will return. However, I should point out the specific meaning psychoanalysis gives the notion of Law. It is not a matter of judgment or a moral code: The unconscious, Freud writes in *The Interpretation of Dreams*, "does not think, calculate, or judge at all, but limits itself to the work of transformation."[1] Similarly, listening to unconscious desire, the psychoanalyst does not judge or calculate; and, if he/she thinks, it is in a very specific sense, the fundamental sense of what "thinking" means: transforming, creating, modulating, and revitalizing the "psychic map" of the person who is giving us his trust, the speaking subject. In this process of transformation (of inhibitions, symptoms, and anxieties), we understand the Law as a Prohibition, Limit, or Frontier, if, and only if, this Prohibition, Limit, or Frontier *gives an accurate sense* to the life drive or death drive, here and now. To separate a mother from her child, to say "no" to the repetition compulsion of desire, to unveil the meaning of an unsettling dream: these are some instances of the Law in the psychoanalytical sense of the word. It is a matter of channeling desire without repressing it or denying it or destroying it, to frame it in such a way that it can find new ways of being optimally realized, so that the baby, child, adolescent, adult acquire more varied, more complex capacities for expression and life. You see, then, that the Law we are talking about is a symbolic act that prohibits, slows, and limits while at the same time inaugurating a new psychical action. On what condition? On the condition that this symbolic act, this Law, tell the truth of desire: in other words, that it be accurate, that is to say, formulated in such a way that the subject is capable of appropriating it so as to be reborn at a given moment, in a given context.

You may appreciate the difficulty of the task of the person exerting the law: he needs empathy with the subject he is speaking to, but also a distance that implicitly takes into consideration the "common good"] into which the subject is preparing to incorporate himself, as well as the singular freedom of this subject. In our civilization it is the Father who is presumed to have this proximity and distance vis-à-vis the primary emotions, which produce the Law in this mother/child dyad. Experience shows that the mother is also called upon to assume this difficult role, increasingly so in the context of modern families, with specific modulations, stinging failures, or dazzling innovations, now inscribed in our changing civilization, for better or worse. Obviously, any analytical interpretation, whether proffered by a man or woman, has this symbolic value of Law and is consequently related to the "paternal function."

I cannot comment today on every variant of the *relationship to the Law* that characterizes various psychical structures. The hysteric is pleased to seduce the Law; she is even prepared to revolt against paternal prohibitions to be more accepted by authority. The obsessional neurotic will strive to conform meticulously to the Law, exhausting himself in rituals of fidelity to the point of inhibition, to the point of immobilizing his own desires, indeed, his thought. The pervert enjoys provoking the Law, not really to abolish it but to put himself in the place of the power he supposes it has and to exert it arbitrarily, violently, to the death. The psychotic is assuredly the most tragic figure: he lives without Law, psychosis "forecloses" the Law—the structuring prohibition is inaudible to him, either because the Father was not able to formulate and transmit it or because psychosomatic difficulties have caused reception of this speech to be deficient.

From this vast field represented by the desire/Law copresence in psychoanalysis, I will present two examples of two major problems in the relationship of desire and Law, as I understand them in psychoanalysis as well as in current politics.

1. On what condition is the Law received as just and therefore acceptable? In other words, on what condition does Law become authority?
2. How does the subject who is supposed to exert the Law become involved in abject transgressions? In other words, under what conditions does the Law induce its own transgression?

The Authority of Just Speech

A patient came to consult me, after a few years of psychoanalysis with a colleague, which she considered unsatisfactory, if not failed. Anne had undertaken this treatment following a slight depression that, in the course of analysis, had turned into a serious depression, so that the treatment was conducted with tranquilizers prescribed by a psychiatrist and sessions of analysis with my colleague simultaneously. The psychoanalyst in question, faithful to a rigid interpretation of the analytical rule, did not agree to the patient's request to speak with her face to face: did he understand it as a desire to seduce, to regress? He had the patient recline and thought it would be a good idea to subject her to frustration, separation, analytical silence—variants of frustration or prohibition. The rare interpretations he offered were received as accusations, reproving judgment: they aggravated the remorse and culpability, and when they addressed the patient's unsatisfied desire, desire for her brother, desire betrayed by her unfaithful lover, Anne received them as "dull" and "mistaken": "When I got up from the couch, I saw a little man with empty eyes, a thin body, exactly like his words, so empty and thin that they stopped my tears," she told me at the first meeting. In short, Anne confided that she could transfer neither her desires nor her aggressiveness onto her therapist, that she wanted to protect him from what she felt was a weakness—just as she protected her mother whom she considered to be mistreated by her father. Consoling or accusatory, but a "poor man" she could not even cry in front of, like the "poor woman" her mother was: "I don't cry in front of my mother; she's the one who cries." Wanting to console her, the therapist had responded to her apparent request, but this did not reveal Anne's unconscious desire—far from it. The young woman wanted to liberate herself from the image of her mother as a victim, from the weight of the misunderstood, mistreated woman. Neither consolation nor accusation, Anne looked in vain for speech that would express the truth about this sacrificial family circle, to allow her to detach from it. It was this speech she wanted unconsciously: accurate speech, to the point of causing pain so as to liberate her from the pain she could not express. Speech, finally, capable of making Anne cry from the truth, before she became "another woman," as she said. This was speech that could have been received as a regenerative symbolic Law. Lacking this, Anne experienced her attempt at analysis as a regression to her infantile dependence vis-à-vis her mother. Without this Law, which the interpretation of her analyst should have offered, Anne's desire wilted. Not only did she lack the desire to continue analysis, she also lacked the desire to go on living: which promptly sent her into melancholia.

This episode allows us to see that the meaning we give the Desire-Law copresence requires psychoanalysts' complete availability to their patients and great psychical suppleness, so that the analytical work is done by two. Anne also invites us to consider that authority (indissociable from the Law, in psychoanalysis as elsewhere) results from a subtle adjustment between the *request* of those who need the Law, on the one hand, and, on the other, the capacity to name the ill-being being treated, beyond the request, to the point of the *unknown desire* that makes the requester cry. It is not a matter of simply avoiding the request, of forbidding or frustrating it, to allow the patient to think and live in an autonomous and free way; nor is it a matter of indulging in these sufferings; it is a matter of naming the familial and personal ill-being with a justness that we consider here and now to be bearable for the analysand, despite its harshness: so that the analysand can recognize herself in it and free herself from it through new desires. The interpretation then serves as symbolic Law in the sense that it reorganizes the drive-related chaos that generates anxiety, confers meaning on desire, and allows it to be renewed in connections to come.

I imagine the value of this Law in psychoanalysis leaves jurists perplexed. Yet, it seems to me, beyond the microcosm of psychoanalysis, that it is not without interest for the social field. Because if we do not want the Law to "go unheeded" but to root itself in the life of the City, Anne's experience, in search of a speech of "just authority," merits our attention.

I thought about this recently in the context of the National Council on Disability, which we created to deinsulate disability in France,[2] to change the outlook of the French and to try to catch up in terms of personal assistance to the disabled. A law in this sense is currently being prepared, shuttling between the Senate and the Assembly. Whatever the amendments expected by the interested parties, it is obvious that the fate of the disabled in France cannot be improved if we do not accompany this law with speech that has authority because it is just, as my patient legitimately wanted. Speech that is addressed to everyone, to the disabled and, above all, to those who are not, and that speaks to them *in truth*. Not in order to say, "We are all disabled," which would be an absurd claim that would deny the suffering and the irremediable. Nor to say, "This could happen to anyone," as if we could only feel solidarity if there were a threat to us. But by trying to share the vulnerability, inseparable from fraternity, that we too quickly forget in the modern world besotted with pleasure-performance-excellence. By accompanying the legislative debate with a media campaign, a national debate that would show how the fear of psychical and physical death inhabits us all and makes us react with indifference, indeed, arrogance, to this discrimination unlike others that is disability. It has been difficult, to say the least, getting this debate started, which is nevertheless an indispensable corollary to the establishment of the law. Hopefully, these reflections will allow us to make clear that no law can be effective if it is not accompanied by speech capable of touching on the unconscious fears and desires this law encounters on its path.

Torture and the Image

International news offers a dramatic example with which to touch on, if only briefly, the second problem: indeed, there is no better illustration of the perverse exercise of the law than the tortures at Abu Ghraib Prison, involving a few "lost sheep" of the American contingent in Iraq. Specialists in international law, political scientists, and sociologists have already said everything about this abjection. As for me, I will say that the conscious application of legal procedure, through its laxity and negligence, allowed the transgressions, when they did not demand them: the military police of this prison never acquainted themselves with the Geneva Conventions; moreover, the brutalities against the prisoners were part of a sophisticated system taught to British and American intelligence specialists, meant to break down "resistance to interrogations," notably by including humiliations of a sexual nature. Question: what individual, "instructed" this way, can refuse to take part in these perverse practices? However brutal, my question is meant to show a psychoanalyst's vigilance, because I am convinced that certain deviations of modern society, known as the "society of the spectacle," and the "deculpabilization of transgression," risk increasing the number of "lost sheep". I do not know what the results of the psychological examinations of the guilty parties at Abu Ghraib were, but, to hear their reproaches, these young people from Maryland or Pennsylvania, Lyndie England— from whom feminist parity did not request so much zeal—and her friend Charles Graner, do not seem so distinct from the average American, or even the average inhabitant of the global planet, the humanoid "instructed" by television reality shows worldwide, and various sites on the Internet.

The young people of Fort Ashby are banal subjects of the planetary village I refer to generally as "Santa Varvara": subjected, on the one hand, to rational and even puritan technical training that allows them to rise through the ranks of their profession with rigor, they receive, on the other hand, through the images and permissiveness of the modern City, the message of a total disinhibition of their drives. Thus they find themselves split between two regimes of Law: ferocious professional constraint, on the one hand; no integration of the prohibition in emotional life, on the other. Beneath a failure in the functioning of the army or a particular administration, it is the (paradoxical, to say the least) integration of symbolic Law in the entire psychical apparatus that has failed: a matter of a failure of the integration of *Law into desire*, which is supposed to be completed in the context of family, school, and religious or moral constructions.

The drama of Abu Ghraib tragically reveals that our civilization not only fails to produce this integration of symbolic Law in the deep layers of the psyche governing sexual pleasure, but that, perhaps, it has aggravated this disintegration of the Law and desire more than previous civilizations. Of course, we know that torture does not date from the Iraq war: the Shoah, the wars of Algeria and Vietnam in the very recent past are there to remind us of this. Of course, the work of the Marquis de Sade already reacted in the face of the revolutionary Terror, through a refinement of tortures culminating in irony. Of course, thanks to the Milgram report, we know that, when asked to take part in the torture of their fellow human beings, only 10 percent of people tested refused.[3] But today we are experiencing a new version of the malaise of civilization, a version without precedent. Never before has the high level of technical perfectionism required from such a large number of people such an effort of coded apprenticeship, of conformity with the law, but a law reduced to *regulations* organizing the efficiency of a system and its underlings, a law calling for surveillance, concentration, and self-control: in short, ferocious repression turning the functionaries of the "new world order" that we are into robots. The desire for Law has become a desire subjected to a supposedly winning set of regulations. In counterpoint to this coded Puritanism and these regulations, the rush toward uninhibited satisfaction explodes. Never before has the influence of the image over the body laid our sadomasochistic drives bare so lightly: the rule is for robots to have a blast, film themselves, and communicate through discharge in all innocence! The desire for the other is deviated into a manic jouissance that is sustained by the sexual victimization of others.

Faced with this aggravated schizophrenia, it is not a matter of asking for a "return to values": conservatives of all stripes have tried this to no avail, and fundamentalists (notably Islamic) are already preparing future kamikazes to purify the miasmas of Abu Ghraib.

On the other hand, we lack the words, instruction, and discussion that would allow us to reflect on the urgent measures that should be taken to try to remedy this psychosis, this split, this abyss that today separates *desire for Law* from *desire for the other*. Unless it is too late.

14

LANGUAGE, SUBLIMATION, WOMEN

In response to this invitation to discuss some of the aspects of André Green's work that have marked me, I will begin with an admission of personal debt: my personal history has not ceased to cross your path, dear André Green, through the clinical and theoretical problems I will try to articulate here before you. Through your amiable listening and your generosity as a thinker, and without being my analyst (but who can be sure?), you have already supported me for thirty years: supervisions, seminars, not to mention those sessions without a label in your various domiciles, late into the evening. First, I must thank you: briefly, to avoid the emotion that comes over me at moments like these, but without falling into ingratitude out of a sense of modesty.

The three problems I will formulate here will examine the resonance of your research as an analyst with the significant advances of contemporary thought, as I see them, in three areas to which my own work is attached:

- theories of meaning: linguistics, semiology
- logics of sublimation
- female sexuality from the perspective of what Freud called the "sex/language asymptote."

These are not "questions," strictly speaking, but rather "free associations," reflections inspired by your works, and perhaps hypotheses that I would like to present to you today for your commentaries: your echoes, agreements, and reservations have always helped me and, I am sure, will help me again today to move forward and, to say it with pathos, to live.

Language and Affect

In your first book on affect, when you developed the idea of a "primary symbolization of affect,"[1] I understood that you saw affect as a *primary sublimation*, as analytical experience revealed it to you. The regressive path of affect, you say, is not only a discharge oriented toward the interior of the body, but also a "capacity to retain," an "inhibition of the drive with an internal goal." Affect participates in the dynamics of *drive-related introjection* (which is experienced as shame, fear, joy, etc.), an already symbolic process (which I call semiotic), the degree zero of symbolism, similar to motivity and perception. This investment of the drive is *objectalized*, and, as a result, it is the primary form of *sublimatory creativity* that characterizes the speaking being. In other words, the investment called *affect* creates a transnarcissistic object: that is why we feel alive provided we feel affects.

If I am breaking down your concept of the "double reversal of the drive— toward the object and toward itself" this way, it is because it seems to share a kinship with various kinds of modern research beyond the psychoanalytical clinic—post-Saussurean, inspired by psychoanalysis, with an emphasis on the "heterogeneity of the signifier" (for example, my proposals of a "double register of meaning": *semiotic* (drive related) and *symbolic* (language); Culioli's linguistics, which works with the presupposition of a semiotic meaning subjacent to the signification of a given national language; indeed, Derrida's notion of the *architrace,* which he suggested in response to the Freudian *psychical apparatus* (neither pure discharge, nor simple memory trace).

In this context, your sense of affect as "primary sublimation" shows that the latter is at once the *condition* for later modalities of the signifying process (gradually elaborated in the child and stratified in successive and interactive layers in the adult subject) and the *double inseparable from language* (in the sense of *tongue,* an object of linguistics that—obsessively?—isolates the signifier/signified pair of affect).

Understood this way, your conception of the heterogeneity of the signifier seems to me to have two consequences, which I will ask you to comment on, if you would:

1. While for Lacan the unconscious is "structured like a language" (linguistic imperialism over the unconscious), and, inversely, for Freudians loyal to the *doxa* of the first Freud, the unconscious is pure drive (censor of the initial linguistic environment that immediately modulates the infantile unconscious in the familial and transgenerational framework), you place affect at the interface of the artificial dichotomy of drive *versus* language. This theorization comes from analytical experience and allows it to flourish. Your listening to narcissism and early ties to the object, in sum, led you to decompartmentalize psychoanalysis and linguistics. We know the benefits that psychoanalytic listening would draw from this: following the patient's discourse "as closely as possible" but without being limited to the formality of the signifier, *interpreting* desires *and* affects, object (*objectal*) links *and* pre-object (*preobjectal*) states, in transference as well as in countertransference. I won't belabor the point; all those who have taken your seminars or had you as a supervisor know what it means to be "close to the discourse" to interpret affect, revealer of narcissism, and the desire trapping Eros in Thanatos.

2. Outside of psychoanalysis your conception of language, based on the theory of affect and culminating in the notion of a heterogeneity of the signifier, seems to me to lead to a revolutionary consequence in the language sciences. Can we still speak of two separate agencies: psychic apparatus/language apparatus? If the signifier is heterogeneous (architrace *and* language, affect *and* linguistic sign), then it provides the link between these two artificially separated apparatuses. That is what we hear in psychoanalysis: a living discourse. But if that is true, it is no longer legitimate to separate linguistics from psychoanalysis. And this reworking, outlined in work like Culioli's in linguistics or mine in semiology, is of interest to the fate of language sciences. In psychoanalysis it is perhaps the best response we can give to Lacan's *problematic* gesture, which was an opening (opening the unconscious to language) and a trap (enclosing the unconscious in a particular state of linguistic science).

Sublimation and Perversion

As an innovative reader of Freud, you propose a theory of sublimation that is striking in its originality, both in terms of your interpretation of works (Shakespeare, Proust, Nerval) and your strictly theoretical elaborations. I will examine the latter, supported by your interpretation of Freud's text, *The Ego and the Id.*

Since sublimation is a narcissistic retention of the life drive over the productions of the ego, it is an *investment of the investment* and therefore liberates the death drive toward itself and toward others (a few examples of this are Nerval's suicide and Proust's asthma, sadomasochisms that culminate in modern art). Starting from there, you observe:

—on the one hand, the "drive quality [*pulsionnalisation*] of Ego defenses," the psychological effect of which is to freeze time, to obliterate the other and the connection to the other;

—on the other hand, a parceling of the other: the one who is reduced to a part object of satisfaction (example: Proust, homosexuality, and fetishism).

In sum, you highlight a sublimation with two sides: the death drive is activated by sublimation, and the paradigm of perversion assuming ego defenses favors sublimatory processes.

My research (on Proust, Colette, Céline, and others) has led me to believe that this paradigm of perversion might be the foundation for the subject constructed on the mode of sublimation. There would be no sublimatory creativity without a certain perversity of the mother/child link. Isn't the dead mother the mother of an artist?

An example borrowed from Proust, once again, supports this hypothesis, which I draw from your work: the character of Odette and her relationship to time. While all the male characters at the *bal de têtes* grow older and melt like wax dolls, Odette is the only one who does not age. Several passages before the end of *Time Regained* show us Odette de Crécy, the cocotte who became Odette Swann and ends up ennobled as Odette de Forcheville, as a possible phantasmatic double of the narrator's mother, inaccessible and seductive, cold-hearted, complicit with the Jewish community, whose body is forbidden but intrusive through grooming, perfume, and trinkets. If Odette—the attractive and seductive version of mama—eludes time, is it because she is the first object of affect, the pretext of the first assimilation in the productions of the ego? Not the object created/found by the phantasm of the neurotic, but "my object" absorbed—swallowed orally— and refashioned anally in the "investment of the investment," captive of my language, my creation? A narcissistic-and-erotic double of the ego subject of sublimation, of the ego outside time, capable of being timeless and therefore likely to leave in search of time?

Figure 5.1. Giovanni Bellini, *Virgin and Child* (1470).
Pinacoteca dell'Accademia, Bergamo. *Bridgeman Art Library*

Figure 5.2. Giovanni Bellini, *Madonna with Two Trees* (1487).
Galleria dell'Accademia, Venice. *Bridgeman-Giraudon*

Figure 5.3. Giovanni Bellini, *Virgin with Standing Child* (1487). São Paulo Museum of Art. *Bridgeman Art Library*

Figure 5.4. Giovanni Bellini, *Young Woman Holding a Mirror* (1515). Kunsthistorisches Museum, Vienna. *Eric Lessing/Magnum*

Figure 5.5. Giorgione, *Venus Sleeping* (1508–1510). Gemäldegalerie Alte Meister, Dresden. *Bridgeman Art Library*

Figure 5.6. Fragonard, *The Useless Resistance.* National Museum, Stockholm. *National Museum of Fine Arts*

Figure 5.7. Courbet, *Sleep* (1866). Musée d'Orsay, Paris. *Photo RMN/copyright © Hervé Lewandowski*

Figure 5.8. Rodin, *Iris, Messenger of the Gods*, bronze. Musée Rodin, Paris. Copyright © *Musée Rodin (S. 1068);* *Ph. Christian Baraja*

Figure 5.9. Picasso, *Woman with Pillow* (1969). Musée Picasso, Paris. *Photo RMN/copyright* © *J.-G. Berizzi, 2005 the Picasso estate*

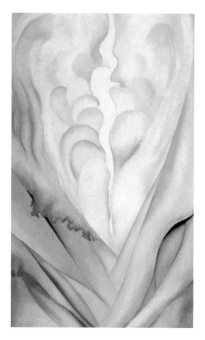

Figure 20.1. Georgia O'Keeffe, *Flower Abstraction* (1924). Copyright © *Georgia O'Keeffe Museum*

Figure 20.2. Georgia O'Keeffe, *Black Iris III* (1926). Copyright © *Georgia O'Keeffe Museum*

Figure 20.3. Georgia O'Keeffe, *White Sweet Peas* (1926). Copyright © *Georgia O'Keeffe Museum*

Figure 20.4. Georgia O'Keeffe, *Pink Sweet Peas* (1927). Copyright © *Georgia O'Keeffe Museum*

A Few Consequences of This Comprehension of Language and Sublimation for the Woman-Mother

Your conception of "thirdness" makes the Father not a ferocious father of the primitive horde, a hardening of the oedipal father; not a Name-of-the-Father; but a third object, a "reunion of the analysand and the analyst." Perhaps closer to the Father of primary identification (which Freud mentions briefly—too briefly—in *The Ego and the Id*); a third party between the child and the mother, with whom the future subject will identify in a "direct and immediate" way—*direkte und unmittelbare*; a loving and nonaggressive father; a father of the "yes" beyond the "no."[2]

The oedipal triangle understood this way allows us to approach the construction of the maternal imago in a particularly original way, through the "negative hallucination of the mother." That is, the child internalizes the *absence of the mother* and not the object: "the maternal object that nothing can represent."

This orchestration of the problem is laden with consequences. I will pass over the connotations this "negative hallucination of the mother" may induce in Mallarmé scholars (the object of poetry being the "flower absent from all bouquets") and in Catholics (more than a woman who is forbidden sexuality, isn't the Virgin an absence in the configuration of the trinity of Father/Son/Holy Spirit? The "hole" around which the filial/paternal symbolic revolves?). And I emphasize this: the "internalization of the absence of the mother" depends on the proper integration of the oedipal. Mama belongs to papa; I am left to console myself with her absence by withdrawing into "her" *représentance*, which is "my" *représentance*: affect + language + idea. That is what you call the integration of the "oedipal couple," which opens the way to the *représentance*/representation of the dramas of the oedipal. We are still within the consequences of the "double reversal": the ego invests the oedipal couple in the optimal manner, which allows it to invest the investment, that is, its own psychic functioning, and to become a speaking being.

Question: what are the optimal conditions for this to come about? Isn't it a certain eroticization of the link to the mother *and* the link to the father, in other words, a *mère*-version and a *père*-version? Which Freud suggests when he distinguishes the (loving) Father of primary identification from the (forbidding) oedipal Father? On the other hand, the founder of psychoanalysis is more discreet in terms of the mother. Now what about the mother in this dynamic who allows the "investment of the investment"?

While the oedipal forbids this for the *infans*, it is "eroticizing and eroti-cized enough" to allow it to invest the investment by making it narcissistic. There would then be a split of the maternal function, between eroticiza-tion and prohibition, in the link to the child. Source of maternal madness, inevitable psychic reserve of maternal hysteria?

Religious myths weave their fabric around this split: in Christianity, the splitting of Mary between the "hole" of the Trinity *and* Queen of the Church, between absence *and* immortality, between "Woman, what have I to do with thee?"[3] and the Nativity-*Pietà*.

Because it assures the support of primary sublimation, the mother/woman is destined to the hystericization of her desire (in the interval of excitation-frustration): she is torn between the Irrepresentable (a role the "Dead mother" aggravates, according to your terminology)[4] and the part object that allows itself to be used as "perverse object."

The sexual and professional liberation of women today makes the working through of the maternal split I have just discussed, based on your writings on maternal madness, difficult and perhaps impossible: a work-ing through that made the existence of a humanity endowed with a com-plex psychical apparatus, with an "interior life" capable of sublimation and working through, possible. To turn the spotlight on the modern deficien-cies of the paternal function, doesn't modern psychoanalysis lack an audible discourse to draw attention to the difficulty of the maternal vocation in this modern civilization with its discontents? I would stress that this difficulty goes beyond an appeal to Winnicott's "good-enough mother," the unbear-able dynamic of which your work allows us to understand anew.

15

HATRED AND FORGIVENESS;
OR, FROM ABJECTION TO PARANOIA

In distinguishing hatred from aggressiveness, keeping in mind that hatred is older than the love erected on top of it and that the object of hatred (unlike the object of love) never disappoints, Freudian psychoanalysis introduces two fundamental mutations in the exploration of the speaking being, the measure of which we have perhaps not yet taken. On the one hand, in contrast to religious or humanist moralism, the psychoanalytical experience reveals that hatred—in its multiple variants—is coextensive to human destiny. On the other hand, simultaneously, psychoanalysis assigns itself the redoubtable privilege of accompanying and untangling this destiny.

These two mutations continue to provoke misunderstanding and resistance.

At the Foundations of Original Repression

By saying the exciting word, *hatred,* we are still confining the incontrovertible psychical event to symptom or pathology. I will take a different path, which, however provocative it may appear, is no less intrinsically faithful to the negativity Freud considers the motor of psychical life; its complex genealogy remains our only recourse in the face of the many (destructive and constructive) destinies of hatred. I would submit that multifaceted hatred is inseparable from human destiny, and from the speaking being, in other words, the human drive as energy and sense. To support this, I will take you from the original repression, where the first indications of neotenous demarcation are manifested with desire for the other and desire of the other (through the other and the other's meaning), which I call *abjection*, to the most intolerable symptoms of psychical negativity that explode in paranoid hatred. What I would like to suggest is that there is no other way to approach an outburst of hate except to conduct an anamnesis of it, to the point of the abjection it is repressing. But, if this is the analytical attitude in the face of hatred, what about the fate of hatred in interpretation? Does hatred disappear in interpretation or does it operate there as well?

In my earlier clinical work, attributing to neoteny the co-presence of hatred and desire indissociable from speaking humanity, I called abjection the initial and foundational experience of the newborn confronted with separation from the uterine container, and then from the maternal body, making every object of speech and thought a prototypical object.[1] As an intertwining of affect and meaning, abjection has no definable object, strictly speaking. Between an object not yet separated as such and the subject I have yet to become, abjection is one of those violent and obscure revolts of the being against what is menacing it and what appears to come from an outside as well as an exorbitant inside, an "abject" cast beside the tolerable and the thinkable: close, but inassimilable. The abject that I experience in abjection is not an ob-ject in front of me, which I might name or imagine much later. Nor is the abject an *ob-jeu* (the term is Francis Ponge's) or a *transitional object* (could Winnicott's term be a synonym for the poet's playful *objeu*?). The abject is not a correlate of the ego (as the *ob-jeu* or transitional object is), which, by offering me support concerning someone or something, would allow me to be fairly detached and autonomous in the long run. The abject has only one quality of the object—that of opposing the I. But while the *ob-jeu* or the transitional object, by opposing me, gives me equilibrium in the fragile web of desire for meaning, the abject excludes me and pulls me to where meaning collapses. "Something" I do not recognize as a thing. A weight of nonsense that has nothing significant about it and yet crushes me.

Fascinating and unsettling, it solicits desire, but desire is not seduced: frightened, it turns away; disgusted, it rejects. Not that!

Aversion to food is the most basic, most archaic form of abjection: it sends us back to the expelling body of the expelled baby. Spasms and vomiting protect me. I use them throughout my life, in my repugnance—the intermittent retching that will distance me from, and allow me to avoid, objects and extreme situations that I experience as menacing and dangerous: defilement, sewage, sordidness, the ignominy of compromise, in-between states, betrayal. Fascination and rejection at the same time, abjection is the jolt that leads me into the abject but also separates me from it.

When the skin on the surface of milk—inoffensive, as thin as a sheet of cigarette paper, as inconsequential as a nail trimming—is presented to my sight or touches my lips, a gagging and a spasm lower still, in the stomach, in the belly, in all my viscera, makes my body tense up, bringing tears and bile, making my heart beat and causing beads of sweat to form on my forehead and palms. Vertigo blurs my vision, and nausea rises up against this creamy film, separating me from the mother and/or father who present it to me. This perhaps insignificant detail, which they appreciate and impose on me, this trifle turns me inside out, eviscerates me: they see I am in the midst of becoming another at the price of my own death. In the path of abjection I give birth to myself through the violence of sobbing and vomiting. The silent protest of the symptom, the noisy violence of a convulsion, immediately inscribed in the symbolic system of the family triangle, but in which, not wanting or being able to be integrated and respond, it reacts, abreacts: it abjects.

If I am offering this very unliterary phenomenology of abjection, it is to persuade you that abjection is the "degree zero" of hatred, present well before the so-called paranoid-schizoid position described by Melanie Klein. By soliciting both the subject and object, not yet separated from each other, and revealing that external objects disgust the subject on the path toward constitution to the point of a loss of self, abjection is a recognition of loss, the basic lack of all being, sense, language, and desire. Therefore I prefer not to use the term *paranoid-schizophrenia* to refer to these outposts of the infantile psyche, but to describe the psychical dynamic that may subsequently end in a "paranoid-schizoid" structure by the more connotative term of *abjection.* It has the advantage of linking the intertwining of love and hate to the trauma of separation as well as to original repression and of suggesting its structuring role in the course of psychic autonomy, before the subject has the means to deal with the subsequent pathological realizations of love/hate fusion/defusion.

We have gotten used to slipping too quickly over a concept in psycho-analysis that is now a fetish: the object is an "object of lack." Yet if we imag-ine (and I'm using the word *imagine* on purpose, because it is the work of the imagination that establishes the interpretation of transference and coun-tertransference), if we imagine, then, that the experience of lack, which follows separation, is logically and chronologically prior to the being of the object and correlatively to the being of the subject, then we understand that the only psychosexual significance of *lack* (a noble, ascetic term) is ab-jection. That is, abjection is the only possible narrative of the experience of lack. Isn't this precisely what literature, religion, and mysticism tell us?

By situating abjection this way, as logically and chronologically anterior to the paranoid-schizoid position, I am not forgetting the mother or the father. On the contrary, I imagine the *infans* of human beings as having swallowed its parents too early, before being crystallized into a subject in the face of objects: it scares itself "all by itself" in this ultraprecocious oe-dipal stage and, in order to find a way out, it rejects and vomits all gifts, all objects. Essentially different from "unsettling strangeness," and also more violent, abjection is constructed on the impulse of revolting against one's family in order to posit them as such: it is the psychosomatic avant-garde of the future oedipal revolt. I am driven to expel my progenitors and in this way I begin to create my own territory, bordered by the abject.

It could be that, in place of maternal love, I swallow a void or rather a wordless maternal hatred for the words of the father: then I will try end-lessly to purge myself of both of them in anorexia—an extreme figure of abjection that will be fatal to me. Or it could be that the inaugural abjec-tion of the neotenous is fixed in phobia. Fear then cements its enclosure around the phobic ego; a prison is built, dividing the world of others, which in reality will never come about except as a fleeting, hallucinatory, ghostly world in my foggy, fugitive, shadowed speech. Or, finally, it could be that the inaugural abjection of the subject ends in paranoid hatred: the most redoubtable, most deadly of all.

For now let's turn our attention to these borders of one's own that are the abject and abjection. If we agree that the abject and abjection manifest the "degree zero" of what will be perceived later as variants of hatred, and that they continue to underlie these variants, we may be better able to un-derstand why it is difficult to find an antidote to the symptoms of hatred themselves.

The logic of abjection places us at the border of the nonexistence of the subject and the hallucination of an inassimilable object: apprehension of a reality that would annihilate me if I recognized it, the abject can appear as the most fragile sublimation (from a synchronic point of view) or the most archaic sublimation (from a diachronic point of view) of an object still inseparable from drives. A pseudo-object, the abject would be the object of original repression. What is original repression? I will simplify: it is the capacity of the speaking being to divide, reject, repeat, without a division, separation, the constitution of subject/object (this will occur with secondary repression). In other words, starting with neoteny, a psychosomatic negativity fashions the human being, where mimesis (which makes me homologous to another so that I can become myself) occurs secondarily. Before being *like*, I am not, but I am content to separate, reject, abject. A precondition of narcissism, abjection nevertheless accompanies psychic diachrony and its evolutions throughout psychic life, to which it is coextensive and that it constantly renders fragile. The rather beautiful image in which I am mired or recognize myself, for example, is based on an abjection that cracks when the permanent watchman repression eases up.

To go a step further: the abject, in which subsequent manifestations of hatred lie dormant, and which constitutes original repression, confronts me with my earliest attempts to demarcate myself from the maternal entity, even before existing outside of her, thanks to the autonomy of language. Why this hiatus between primary and secondary repressions, why this time, this slowness that fixes the drive in abjection, latching it to the body, to the unnameable, making it resistant to analysis? Neuronal maturation requires it, biology has often said. Let's add maternal anxiety ("maternal madness"), which cannot be appeased in the triangle of the oedipal symbolic and overexcites and maintains my abjection. I come about as a subject through a violent and awkward demarcation, always threatened by a relapse into dependency on a mother struggling to recognize the paternal symbolic agency and to be recognized by it. In this hand-to-hand combat the symbolic light of a third party helps the future subject continue the war, reluctantly, with what, from the mother, will become an abject. I become this subject by pushing away, by rejecting: by pushing myself away, by rejecting myself, by ab-jecting. The abject and abjection are my guardrails, the beginnings of my culture, my beginning of culture.

Here we are at the borders of the human universe in formation. At this threshold there is no unconscious; it will be constructed when representations and the affects linked to them (or not) form a logic. Consciousness has not yet transformed the fluid demarcations of still unstable territories into signifiers, where an I in formation is constantly losing its way. If the abject is already the beginning of a sign for a nonobject at the borders of original repression, we understand that it exists alongside the somatic symptom, on the one hand, and sublimation, on the other. The symptom: language that forfeits, structures an inassimilable foreigner in the body—a monster, a tumor, a cancer. Sublimation, on the contrary, is nothing other than the ability to name the prenominal, the preobjectal, which, in fact, are only the transnominal and the transobjectal. In the symptom the abject invades me; I become it. In sublimation I hold it: the abject is bordered by the sublime.

Paranoid Hatred Has No Subject: It Erects Two Objects Face to Face and Protects Them from Abjection

Having touched on this fate of negativity in analysis, I thought I would be able to understand the paranoid hatred that brought a man into my office. Before telling you a few details of his treatment, I will sum up the conclusions to which I came.

Pierre was a difficult patient I hesitated taking on. His raging hatred, which would one day necessarily be turned against me, scared me less than his narcissistic closed-mindedness: it made his "insights" (which at first seemed quite intelligent) superficial, bookish, and insignificant in fact— clever defenses that prevented any questioning of the self. At times he hated himself as much as he hated others, but he never questioned himself. He had been "at war," "since birth," with "people," he said—a category he grimly detested because he found it stifling. Besides, "people" were constantly plotting—against him, no doubt—at the office but also in newspaper articles and on television shows, where he recognized himself without being named, and, needless to say, at home with the "manipulative complicity" of his wife, he was sure. The passionate description of various strategies constructed by "people" against him occupied every session, and Pierre took lively pleasure in denouncing the hatred of which he was the object, by pouring out torrents of *pure hatred*—by which I mean hatred without a trace of ambivalence—against these haters. His wife could no longer stand this "permanent state of war"—she, too, quite naturally, was assimilated to these hateful, hate-filled "people"—and, tired of being accused of conspiring against him, started analysis and ultimately divorced him. She told him that he "needed his enemies," that his "hatred of others allowed him to live," and that he "sought out this hatred and would invent it if it didn't exist."

The systematic determination of Pierre's stories, which detailed the real or imaginary "people" fueling his hatred, may have confirmed Freud's diagnosis on the subject of President Schreber ("what lies at the core of the conflict in cases of paranoia among males is a homosexual wishful phantasy of *loving a man*."[2] Pierre's history and discourse led me to think that this obvious "center" concealed a genealogy and destiny of the "love-hatred" that transference with a female analyst would uncover. More than an erotic appeal to a dangerous man thought to be compensating for the weakness of his own father, this passionate hatred, to which my patient seemed to be attached like a drug, revealed a much more inaccessible dependence.

I felt persecuted in turn: not only did Pierre end up convincing me of the ugliness of "people" and of the world in which we lived, but his wife had already made the interpretations that were on the tip of my tongue! Did he come to consult me in order to prevent me from speaking, out of hatred of analysis? Or else was he revealing the unbearable truth of the speaking being whose hatred uncovers what was concealed? Having made a few fruitless attempts to publish his work, "Reflections on World Politics," Pierre nevertheless began to shield his transference with me in a temporary idealization of my status as an "envied intellectual," which allowed us a certain degree of working through.

The persecuting hatred that inhabited him then revealed its alchemy: faced with a father who "went from failure to failure," Pierre had never had the chance to confront an identifiable adversary. He was convinced that his father was part of the mass of ugly and uninteresting "people" and that his mother, who was entirely focused on her only son, reserved her concern and anger only to castrate him. The affect was then displaced, for many years, from men ("people") to the mother, an "abject character," Pierre asserted; Pierre's assertions, however, did not convince me; the more he condemned his mother, the more his erotic desires became focused on a cousin his mother's age who became his mistress. This incestuous relationship was revealed to be a partial narcissistic reparation that allowed him to express his hatred toward the analytic cadre, against my colleagues and against me, though he did not appear to be conscious of it. After particularly violent sessions, Pierre would calm down, become quiet, and, before leaving, confide: "Analysis is one of the rare places I feel I become peaceful, like a newborn." Was analysis becoming less stifling to him?

Eventually, the failed political scientist took up painting. Pierre expressed himself outside the sessions, then, by means of a different language, with "unclean" (improper), "dirty" materials that finally allowed him to appropriate what was "proper" to him: his "dirty nature," he said. He spoke to me of his paintings, describing them as "sort of portraits" of "people" whose hatred he hated, "horrible characters," who would finally lead him to paint himself, he said, laughing, "as a horror," "a tender horror, after Francis Bacon." Aspiration to greatness had taken another form, apparently less hateful but no less megalomaniacal. Pierre could now begin another phase of his analysis; he could begin to speak of his disgust for women, his homosexual fantasies, his rivalry with me, his digestive and intestinal symptoms, and even his memories as a vomiting baby and as a little boy who was made fun of because he was still not potty trained, which made his mother laugh, while his father called him "disgusting." He could begin to speak of the shame he felt about his body and the shame he felt due to his liaison, though restorative, with his older cousin. His paranoia was infiltrated by a perverse pleasure, showing itself in the way he actively experienced his abjection and that of others: naming it, sharing it with me, attacking me with it, and perhaps contaminating me.

In transference I was alternately solicited, in place of the abject mother, to become an object from which Pierre would finally be able to separate, and in the role of the oedipal father, from whom he sought the symbolic support his own father had not given him. When we terminated analysis, the "hatred of people" had not ceased to persecute him; he did not deprive himself of "waging war on the human race," as was now said complacently by his . . . mistress! The state of hatred nevertheless seemed less invasive, an epiphenomenon among others on the waves of a psychic life that was now vaster and therefore more painful, closer to personal secrets, old wars, rejections, jouissance, and archaic defenses. Thinking of him, I was able to write *Powers of Horror: An Essay on Abjection*. A few years later, having come across and read this book, which made no explicit reference to him, Pierre sent it to me for a dedication.

The paranoid hatred seemed to be a defense against maternal control, making the subject regress to the point of abjection, where the borders between the ego and the other are erased. Against this abjection in which the "I" tries desperately to merge with the maternal feminine, hatred—in the guise of defense—crystallizes two objects (not two subjects) that are dangerous for each other. "'I' am, only if I am dangerous for a dangerous other—a fellow creature," says the paranoiac. "I am dangerous," the apotheosis of negative narcissism, makes narcissism safe. But it does not guarantee "my" autonomy (the other before me is just as dangerous as I am; attacking and attackable, we are inconsistent, men reduced to "people," like Pierre's devalued father). Paranoid hatred has transformed the uncertainty of abjection into a reversible dyad, sadomasochistic communicating vessels, but it does not assure any lasting independence in terms of identity. The armor of the hateful warrior is the temporary hiding place for a nonsubject who—if he finds the path of analysis—asks only to be born.

This patient awoke many negative affects in me, even the "theme" of abjection itself; I borrowed the term from his vocabulary. And yet, beyond the trap of the "crazy truth" into which he led me, I had the feeling I had given him something, too, through interpretation and the transferential link. And this gift, which was neither love nor hate but simply a patient interpretation of the psychical movements subjacent to his "state of war," broke the chain of persecutions in which his psychical negativity had been stuck and inserted it into the openness of psychical time—the gift of a new way of being.

That is what led to my conception of psychoanalytical interpretation as a postmodern version of forgiveness.

On Interpretation as *Pardon*

When Freud claims that he "succeeds where the paranoiac fails,"[3] he surely means that psychoanalysis dismantles the persecuting hatred the paranoiac devotes to the other and that comes back to him like a boomerang. But the founder of psychoanalysis does not ignore the privileged link a psychoanalyst has to the other, in transference and countertransference. I succeed there: I'm there, too, but I succeed. In addition to this triumphant claim, the entire Freudian oeuvre allows us to understand that, if there is success, it is rooted not in the evacuation of the hatred inherent in the link to the object, but in the patient dismantling of various cogs of drive-related, imaginary, and symbolic negativity that sweep away the subject's links to the other: from sadomasochism built on repressed homosexuality, by way of the horror of the maternal feminine, to the borders of the "proper" and the "improper" where the self, fascinated and repellent, is confused with the parental container.

Religions were constituted precisely as "catharses" or "purifications" of variants of "evil," which were nothing other than various destinies of hatred. In fact, if we consider the religious experience over the course of history, we see that, when religious man is not strangled by fundamentalism (and even when he is), he is invited to purify himself of his defilements. These involve various "substances" at the limits of the "proper" (clean) and the "foreign" (strange)—ultimately referring to the maternal body and blood of primitive religions; purification may be sought through food taboos (in Buddhism as well as Judaism and Islam); one may be purified of murderous hatreds, whether sacrificial or fratricidal ("Thou shalt not kill"). A veritable archaeology of the negativity that constitutes psychical life comes into view through religious history, which can offer the gift of pacifying meaning, but, under an ideological superego, generate hateful conflicts.

If we think of the destiny of hatred this way, from the emergence of the human to the original repression complicit with abjection and the various symptoms that constitute hatred of the self and our ties to others, we see that it cannot be altered by love, for hate and love are bundled in coexistence. Love cannot be the antidote to this fascicle where love and hate coexist. Once again, old religions already found another solution: forgiveness. Not "an eye for an eye, a tooth for a tooth," or judgment, or even love, but forgiveness. Through forgiveness, time for vengeance is suspended, allowing a rebirth for men, always already petrified by hate, before the metamorphoses of abjection begin again.

Contrary to what the uninitiated might imagine, the forgiveness of theologians does not erase the horror of hatred, much less the horror of the ultimate variant of hatred, which is murder, anymore than it judges them. As St. Thomas Aquinas said, forgiveness is neither sorrow (meaning: it does not imply a complacency with abjection and horror) nor loving tribunal, but the act of "bestowing a gift" that "prevails over judgment."[4] It is about temporarily suspending the time of the ego, which is the time of hatred, by applying a sinful meaning to hateful acts, referring to the mercy of the Absolute Being: God. Pascal says the same thing in his own way: "The self is hateful. . . . Only God should be loved."[5] To pardon the self that remains in destructive negativity consists not of allowing it to "work through" this negativity indefinitely but giving it sense and nonsense, provided it is in the Name of God Almighty.

If psychoanalysis succeeds where the paranoiac fails, it is not because it teaches us to "love the Self," or even to "love others" (as we say so lightly) under a godless sky—which is already not that easy. The Freudian revolution consists of replacing this forgiveness, through *the interpretation of variants of hatred* that feed a symptom, invented to stop the time of judging in the

name of the dogma of love (of God or our fellow man). Indeed, Freudian vigilance in the face of the multiple destinies of hatred has revealed
that the imperative of the Supreme Being, like the moral imperative, is
maintained by the dogma of absolute Love as a defense against its double,
Hate. It also discovered, as a result, that forgiveness—which forgives in the
name of a Supreme Being free of hate—inevitably and inexorably catches
the forgiven subject in the nets of the defusion of drives, sadomasochism
and abjection, by which fundamentalisms and their inevitable clashes are
sustained. It is only through the endless analysis of the lack of being, of
the asymptote between sexuality and language, and the defenses mobilized
against them, that analytical interpretation, including transference and
countertransference, can give sense to the successive and stratified stages of
negativity, from abjection to hysterical "love-hatred," or paranoid "pure hatred," and vice versa, endlessly: that is the message of "analysis terminable
and interminable."

If we try to situate this Freudian legacy in a broader cultural context,
we see that the analytical ambition of succeeding where the paranoiac fails
(untangling the "crazy truth" of hatred) is inseparable from another ambition: succeeding where *theological forgiveness* promises the rebirth of the subject in a new temporality. Religion "fulfills" this promise only by subordinating the faithful to its dogmas and/or referring them to the beyond. Yet
this promise of forgiveness gives faith that forgives its greatest appeal.

I do not think religion fascinates only because it maintains illusions.
More than that, religion that forgives, that claims to guarantee the psychical rebirth of forgiven believers, corresponds to a vital need in the speaking
being: that of opening up psychical time. Religion that forgives is greeted
as a promise that assures psychical life. In the modern age, this is what af-
flicts individuals whose psychical space is threatened with destruction by
the rise of technology and sexual liberation (to which the "new maladies of
the soul" attest).[6]

And so I say that Freud succeeded where the paranoiac fails, because he
set in motion the modern, endless, postmoral variant of forgiveness, which
is nothing other than interpretation. Let's call it *pardon* to (*par*, through,
don, a gift) highlight the giving of sense to the senselessness of unconscious
hate. Interpretation is a pardon: a rebirth of the psychical apparatus, with
and beyond the hatred that bears desire, which religion is and is not aware
of and from which it defends itself. Interpretation is a pardon whose ambition, through the refinement of its models and formulations, is to make

psychical rebirth possible. The gravity of this pardon is perceptible in analytical listening that neither judges nor calculates, but is content to untangle and reconstruct. Its spiraled temporality is realized in the intersecting times of transference and countertransference. This pardon *renews the unconscious*, because its temporality inscribes the right to narcissistic regression in History and in the Word; thus, only this pardon confronts the other side of desire—hate. It does so without fighting it or submitting to it but also without ceasing the deconstructive elucidation of "love-hatred." There is no transcendental authority, just the interminable variants of transference-countertransference and, ultimately, the immanence of transcendence here on earth.

In these postmodern times of religious clashes, which are times of endless war, it might be useful to remember that psychoanalytical interpretation, by revealing multifaceted hatreds, offers itself as the ultimate lucidity of pardon, which psychical life needs in order to continue living, quite simply, without necessarily absolutely ceasing to hate.

16

THREE ESSAYS; OR, THE VICTORY OF
POLYMORPHOUS PERVERSION

To read the three prefaces to successive editions of *Three Essays on the The-ory of Sexuality* (1905), a modern reader notices that Freud is increasingly aware of the scandal he introduced by "enlarging the concept of sexuality," so much so that he is careful not to mention the key concept that is the book's strength—the "polymorphously perverse predisposition"—and in-stead "cloaks" himself in . . . Schopenhauer and Plato. Along the way, Freud takes a cultural historical perspective, inviting us to read the text in all its scope, as both immediately therapeutic and inextricably historico-political. He notes that not "every point" of his psychoanalytical theory has known the same fate and that, while on the horizon of the First World War, which disquieted people and his own thought, one accepted the unconscious, re-pression, psychical conflicts, etc., "one" continued to resist "that part of the theory which lies on the frontiers of biology," i.e., the *sexual instinct*: the au-thor does not mention the term *drive* in the prefaces any more than the concept of the "polymorphously perverse."[1] From these silences, and my rereading of the Freudian text, I am allowing myself the following short-cut: the sexual drive is polymorphously perverse; there is no drive except the polymorphously perverse. That is the essence of *Three Essays*, which was disturbing then and continues to be disturbing. This seems to be Freud's conviction in 1920, and it is also mine today. I will explain, keeping in mind recent developments in (French) psychoanalysis.

1. Topical Questions

If recent developments in psychoanalysis have favored the study of border-line states, depressive states, and disobjectifying regressions, and despite various remarkable approaches to perversion,[2] I would say we have a tendency to make perversion banal, when not obscuring the word itself under the pretext of avoiding both normative thinking and blame. Thus, rereading *Three Essays* leads me to these questions:

• Hasn't psychoanalysis, like a society in fear (the fear of war, Freud implies in the fourth preface, but also fear in the face of blended families, sexual liberation, new forms of media-friendly and fundamentalist terrorism, etc.), followed a tendency toward the repression of *sexuation* (which Freud already suggested)? Are we ignoring sexuation in its inevitable polymorphous perversity, which nevertheless remains the basis of analytical listening, theoretically? Doesn't rejection of the notion of the "drive," which mobilizes a number of colleagues, or the emphasis placed on *being* to the detriment of *doing*, betray if not rejection than at least discontent in the face of the polymorphously perverse drive? That would take the cake!

• If this is the case, haven't we confused the loss of symbolic authority, which characterizes advanced democracies, and the sexo-narcissistic exhibition of the polymorphously perverse, in which the society of the spectacle revels, with the support of a psychoanalytic "benevolence" that ends up making us lose the sexual edge in countertransferential listening to which *Three Essays* testifies, precisely? *Three Essays*, in any case, does not yield on the libido, this *Lust* that is at once *tension* and *relief, desire* and *pleasure*, "internal foreign body," psychosomatic urgency. Haven't we yielded on the libido because repression is fractured—as families fall apart, there is a lack of paternal-symbolic-political authority, and TV shows like *Star Academy*[3] flatter the narcissistic omnipotence of neotenes—and ancestral barriers of modesty, disgust, and morality, thought to metabolize infantile perversity, are receding to give way to "the idealization of the instinct"?[4]

• For millennia the history of civilizations has shown us that human beings are not content with repression but take the path of *idealization* and *sublimation* to socialize the "polymorphous perversity" that inhabits them: aestheticizing metamorphoses, religious patchworks, support of the polymorphously perverse by the market, patronage, marketing, sects, community, etc. Today, however, for the historical, technical, and cultural reasons I mentioned, *repression* is being modified under the effect of *idealization* and *sublimation*. A modification never before recorded (though Freud was careful to point out historic eras favorable to perversion: the religions of Moloch or Astarte in the Semitic East, in particular). The result of this is the specific feature of the inhabitant of the third millennium, less the "classic neurotic" than the "polymorphous pervert," precisely, skilled at surfing from channel to channel. "Channels" or "networks" that are less and less "significant" and more and more complacent in terms of the drive and its idealizing negotiation: whether embellished seduction (celebrity magazines) or the exploitation of hardcore sex (à la Catherine Millet) or, conversely, seedy despair (à la Michel Houellbecq), where the polymorphous pervert becomes a pervert, quite simply—the ultimate mirage, the secret fascination of the consumers of fantasy we have become.[5] The shadow of the pervert has been cast on the polymorphous pervert. More than ever, the conditions seem ripe for a new mysticism where we might place the new polymorphous pervert who, compared to Freud's, has this new feature—he does not want to know: he has traded in his role as a "seeker" of "sexual theories" for that of a consumer of images, beginning with his own.[6] Thus he exhibits his polymorphous perversity in all innocence and insolence, the only consequence being the listless ennui of the impotent libido now complacently attributed to the Western individual or its opposite, namely, the manic excitation of the criminal or drug addict. All this against a background of generalized indifference on the part of all parties concerned and their audience, which has seen it all.

• In this context it is not easy to interpret the polymorphous perversity expressed on the couch without seeming to be a backward-looking person who "discriminates" against the right to difference. However, in *Three Essays* we find neither complacency nor normative judgment: Freud simply *names* the polymorphous sexual drive (bisexuality, cannibalism, voyeurism, exhibitionism, sadomasochistic anality, etc.) and makes it *desirable* precisely when the subject in prey to the drive appears *vulnerable* and, for that very reason, not omnipotent, but having a drive quality that can be shared . . . with the analyst, to begin with. As if, underneath the obsessional neurotic he made us believe he was, Freud was hiding a polymorphous pervert—but was he really hiding it? A man of the Enlightenment, profoundly attached to the *link* that creates *meaning* through the *libido*, which psychoanalysis still hopes to safeguard and renew, Freud diagnoses an accident of the libido and meaning in psychosis, but psychosis does not really interest him. *Three Essays* nevertheless announces that the social link is not simply a pact of neurotics but that "aberrations" are hidden in the guise of psychoneurotics: in other words, in the beginning there was "abnormal sexuality."[7] And thus symptoms do not arise solely at the expense of the so-called normal sexual drive, but "are formed at the cost of *abnormal* sexuality; *neuroses are, so to say, the negative of perversions.* The sexual instinct of psychoneurotics exhibits all the aberrations which we have studied as variations of normal, and as manifestations of abnormal, sexual life."[8] To say it another way, *Three Essays* proclaims that the main problem of connection—symbolic, social—is perversion.

• A hundred years later, the observation made by *Three Essays* remains: the social link is polymorphously perverse and often criminally perverse, but we cannot ignore that modern history itself continuously makes this Freudian "theory of sexuality" patently clear. So what does this change? The challenge, for psychoanalysts, is all the more serious and perhaps insurmountable: is our listening, our interpretation, in tune with this Freudian truth, according to which the speaking being is intrinsically a polymorphous pervert? How, as analysts, can we "be" (of this theory, of this polymorphism) without succumbing to the agonies and delights of the libido, while sharing them through the drive of countertransference and the words of countertransference? Isn't this the only way to one day complete an optimal cure, a path Freud sums up by quoting Goethe: "From Heaven, across the world, to Hell"?[9]

• And so *Three Essays* sends us back to the polymorphous perversity of the analytical position itself and of analytical interpretation above all. Before addressing this last point, I would like to present a reading of the Freudian vision of perversion as revealed in *Three Essays* and as intrinsically linked to idealization and sublimation.

2. Perversion, Sublimation

If the drive is polymorphous-perverse, it is not only because it begins, in the child, with partial satisfactions of the erogenous zones (oral, anal, genital, bisexual, sadomasochistic, etc.). It is because, at the origins, there exists a *copresence between soma and psyche*, drive and meaning, drive and language. This position is not a modernist artifact of structuralism, though it is thanks to structuralism that I am speaking of it. This polymorphism-sublimation copresence can be found in Freud himself, as I have shown elsewhere.[10]

Freud removes the culpability from perversion: we are all perverted through our infantile past and we remain so unconsciously in adulthood. But he by no means avoids the question of the transformation the *polymorphously perverse child* must undergo or the conditions that lead to this transformation. The inscription of polymorphism at the foundation of the sexual drive nevertheless results in paradoxes that have rightly been formulated; the best known is this: psychoanalysis not only considers that perversion does not exist, but that we are all perverts! One of the contemporary indicators of this situation is the debate currently stirring in psychoanalytical societies throughout the world: can one be homosexual and an analyst? The most difficult part of this dilemma is assuring oneself one is an analyst. The second, less known, is the polymorphism-sublimation copresence. Due to the "mental factor" always already internal to perversion and polymorphism, satisfaction with the object, albeit partial, is always unsatisfying and returns to an investment of the "mental factor," thus, my own capacity to see-know-say-think. Object dissatisfaction is intrinsically relayed by investment of the investment: the ultimate, and inevitable, autoeroticism.

Starting with *Three Essays on the Theory of Sexuality* (1905), Freud defines perversion as an *extension* or a *lingering*: "Perversions are sexual activities which either (a) extend, in an anatomical sense, beyond the regions of the body that are designed for sexual union, or (b) linger over the intermediate relations to the sexual object which should normally be traversed rapidly on the path towards the final sexual goal."[11] There is a sort of "sexual overvaluation" that elevates activities involving parts of the body other than the genitals to the level of sexual goals. This behavior is specific to the child and has to do with the strong narcissistic investment of his own body, taken as an object of satisfaction in all the erotogenic zones (the mouth and anus, but also the skin and the five senses, which place the baby in contact with the first object, the mother). If, for this very reason, the child is a "polymorphous pervert," the mother is one, too: "A mother's love for the infant she suckles . . . is in the nature of a . . . love-relation offering possible satisfaction of wishful impulses . . . which must be called perverse. . . . [And] the father is aware that the baby, especially if he is a baby boy, has become his rival."[12] Disciples of Freud point out after him that, because of neoteny, the baby is inhabited by an "early anxiety" or "primal phobia," paving the way for the "appetite for excitation" (*Reizhunger*) and its always uncertain, always sub-stitutive satisfactions. This "appetite for excitation" in search of an object of satisfaction—itself always unsatisfying—is thus the inevitable destiny of the drive in human beings, the true economy of what Freud saw as a primal perversion. And what if the notion of perversion itself was not a "counter-phobic" concept and perversion instead concealed . . . *mère*-version!

All this is very familiar to the Psychoanalytical Society of Paris. What is less discussed is the perversion-sublimation link. Yet the complicity be-tween perversion and sublimation does not constitute the slightest com-plexity or mystery of this psychoanalytical vision of our psychosexual-ity. Freud introduces the term *sublimation* in *Three Essays* precisely when he evokes the gradual dissimulation of the body that goes hand in hand with civilization and art, which detaches interest in the genitals so as to direct it toward the body as a whole culminating in the desire to know.[13] Later I will discuss the development of psychoanalysis after Freud and how it deep-ens this polymorphous-sublimation entanglement, thereby elaborating the heterogeneous character of the drive, always already biology *and* sense, as far back as we go in the development of the *infans*. And it is this copresence of pleasure and sense that makes all satisfaction necessarily partial, incom-plete, repetitive, before a traumatism fixes it in perversion pure and simple. Freud's texts reveal this drive-sublimation copresence that is the essence of human polymorphism.

But let's return to the book that unites us today.

According to *Three Essays*, far from being due solely to the force of drives or external agents (seduction, abuse), perversion in its own logic *idealizes* the drive from the start; which amounts to saying that perversion is, at its very source, a mental construction that mobilizes a "mental factor": "It is perhaps in connection precisely with the most repulsive perversions that the mental factor must be regarded as playing its largest part in the trans-formation of the sexual instinct. It is impossible to deny that . . . mental work has been performed which is the equivalent of an idealization of the drive."[14] Are perversions creations, works of art *avant la lettre*? Freud offers two hypotheses to explain this early entanglement of the drive and ideal-ization in perversion—two hypotheses that concern the role of the *latency* period and the *superego*.

Our capacities for sublimation are particularly developed during the latency period that extends from the age of five to preadolescence, after the apex of the oedipal. The acquirements of infantile sexuality are then repressed, and genital sexuality is not yet prepared, so that one can envision latency as a period of "preparatory pleasures." These imply erotogenic zones and partial drives that do not end in genital realization, and therefore provoke states of displeasure and anxiety, but also, and at the same time, opposing mental forces that transform drives into daydreams, hallucination, idealization, sublimation. "It is possible further to form some idea of the mechanism of this sublimation. On the one hand, it would seem, the sexual impulses cannot be utilized during these childhood years, since the reproductive functions have been deferred . . . On the other hand, these impulses would seem in themselves to be perverse—that is, to arise from erotogenic zones and to derive their activity from instincts which . . . can only arouse unpleasurable feelings. They consequently evoke opposing mental forces (reacting impulses)."[15]

This remark of Freud's, which links the fate of sublimation to that of latency and thus to the partial satisfaction characteristic of perversions, implies that, while the adult tries to avoid genital sexuality, he inevitably reencounters the time of latency with its partial pleasures, their tensions, and their compensation through sublimation. Nevertheless, before latency, sublimation-idealization takes root in the origin of psychical development itself. There is a "primal creativity," a "primal sublimation" in relation to the ideal Ego in every small child, who is already constructing a sort of "fetish" based on his osmotic desire for the mother and on the desire of the mother herself: this is Winnicott's "transitional object." A blanket or a toy that already represents an area of illusion between the child and his desires, the "transitional object" protects the subject from the anxiety of separation. Have we sufficiently emphasized the polymorphous character of the transitional object? I try to, by reading Winnicott alongside the *Three Essays*. I believe the acquisition of the symbolic function itself—the passage from equations to symbols-equivalences—presupposes a sublimatory activity that invests vocalizations as objects of secondary pleasure, without which there is no development of language and thought as autonomous areas.

After this aurora of sublimation, the latency period constructs a complementary process, that of a "supersublimation" leading to the ego ideal (and no longer to the ideal Ego), opening the way to true cultural activity. These different degrees of sublimation are so many "stations" that require artists' attention in their search for lost time, the ideal time of heavenly satisfaction: we find this theme in Colette and Proust, to give only two examples.

A complex and always enigmatic process, sublimation sets in motion a desexualization and defusion of drives. *We should emphasize desexualization.* In the course of sublimation the drive changes aims and objects: instead of aiming for the satisfaction of erotogenic zones, the subject's activity affords ideal pleasures, satisfactions attached to the ideal beauty of people, things, and the subject's own productions, composed of words, colors, or sounds, which become representatives of narcissism and the ideal Ego. Is this deviation of the genital and even sexual aim of the drive toward a desexualized idealization a sort of reconstruction of polymorphism or a fixation of polymorphism in perversion? We can suppose that, in the sublimatory dynamic, what is established in place of sexualization is not its repression, but a displaced eroticization: that is to say, there is no sexual release even if the excitation is maintained, notably, by means of the ideal beauty of people, objects, and productions. An experience of omnipotence often accompanies such an experience: an omnipotent, manic ego constructs a universe that must indeed be called *imaginary*, made of pleasures that are only *representations*, though experienced libidinally. What's more, these are the ego's own representations, which do not depend on any "object" or "other" external to it; for that very reason, the imaginary creator experiences them as more powerful than any other pleasure, unlikely to be lacking, indeed, imperishable. This imaginary omnipotence lacks nothing: this sort of sublimation is a fixation of the subject within his infantile omnipotence, where, if there is a subject, he lacks nothing, if not precisely lack itself.

As for the superego and its role in the search for pleasure and beyond that in perversion, a change occurs in Freud's thinking. Where initially Freud conceived of the pleasure principle in the negative, as an avoidance of displeasure, with *The Ego and the Id* he posits pleasure as a positive principle obtained through the superego's injunction. The ego represents the external world and the reality principle and is opposed to the pleasure that reigns without restriction in the id, while "the super-ego stands in contrast to it as a representative of the internal world, of the id."[16] Here we are confronted with a new function of the superego: far from being an inhibitor of pleasure, as it was according to Freud's initial observations, the superego, which is intimately related to the id, is not only a defensive agency but encourages jouissance—Lacan would call it a *pousse-à-jouir*. In the same perspective, we understand that if the superego is represented by the father, perversion as a transgression of prohibitions is not only a challenge directed at the father but also a completion of the injunction: "the Superego says:

'*Jouis!*'" and perversion is a . . . *père*-version. Lacan invites us to consider divine authority (in monotheism, at least) and Christian "redemption" itself as a sadomasochistic submission to the father, a *père*-version, while at the same time suggesting that the very charged term *perversion* be abandoned by psychoanalysis. *Père*-version? Or *mère*-version? Both, based on the difficult, indeed, impossible, independence that we as "neotenes" assert vis-à-vis our genitors and our problematic freedom in place of the indispensable symbolic Law that makes us speaking beings.

Another experience of pleasure emerges in the wake of these deeper investigations of psychoanalysis by Freud and his disciples, defined as a jouissance (Freud uses the term *Genuss* rather than the *Lust* of *Three Essays*). It refers to the state of sexual satisfaction analogous to death, because the expulsion of sexual substances corresponds to the separation of the soma from the germ-plasm: after satisfaction, "Eros has been eliminated" and the "death instinct has a free hand for accomplishing its purposes."[17]

Jouissance appears to be an experience of objectless satisfaction, similar to primary narcissism, according to Freud. Traces of it can be found in the artistic experience, as well as in mystics, drug addicts, and . . . women. "In women too we must postulate a somatic sexual excitation and a state in which this excitation becomes psychical stimulus—libido—and provokes the urge to the specific action to which voluptuous feeling is attached. Where women are concerned, however, we are not in a position to say what the process analogous to the relaxation of tension of the seminal vesicles may be."[18] Lacan amplifies and diversifies this Freudian advance—not only does he emphasize the difference between pleasure and jouissance, but he distinguishes in the latter the phallic jouissance of the man (and the woman, since women identify with men, in fantasy and clitorally) from another jouissance.

If our pleasures are fundamentally perverse, if our jouissance depends on it, and if pleasure and jouissance are closely linked to our capacities for representation, then the perversion that attracts us in works of art is that which is addressed to the universal logics inhabiting us all as "polymorphously perverse." A separation anxiety presides over our development as supposedly free and autonomous individuals: the anxiety of a "primary disidentification" with the maternal container, inherent in the sexual drive, itself specific to all beings who speak/sublimate/work through. The pervert has the particularity of being *stuck* in this separation anxiety as signified by the father: the latter does not necessarily threaten to deprive the son of his organ, but represents to the male or female child his/her incapacity to fulfill the mother genitally. To battle against this unbearable aspect of "dis-identification," the pervert is mobilized in a frantic, often exhausting, quest for paroxysmal satisfactions. In this context oral satisfaction—at the foundation of so many addictions—may be experienced as the equivalent of an original intrauterine alimentary satisfaction: orality is already developed *in utero*, before any other activity (at fifteen weeks, the fetus sucks his thumb; at sixteen weeks he clasps his hands and explores the uterus).

Every perverse act, then, is not merely an attack against the procreative couple and a desire to retrieve the original mother/child coupling, but an effort to dominate the genital universe through the creation of another world. To the "impure" chaos (as Colette would say) of genital sexuality and all sexuality that includes it, a neoreality would be opposed: "my" secret universe, "my" hidden intimacy, "my" necessarily dissident work, violating the order of the world and what I perceive to be its unbearable excesses, so as to replace it with a heavenly serenity. As vengeance against both the mother and father, such creativity, in its megalomaniacal and narcissistic thrust, contains a more or less unconscious hatred of reality, and, if it is linked to evil, it is because it involves the hubris of the destruction of the parents' world. Infantile creativity versus parental creativity is a matter of investing the child's orality and anality more than genitality: anality "idealized" and "sublimated" into "perfumed paradises" and exquisite smells occupies a central place in the reconstruction of Colette's new "house of Claudine," as it does in so many sublimatory works; it proves essential in all "productions" of the aesthetic "objects" that embellish the first productions of our bodies—excrement.

We can now understand the perverse reaction as a manic reaction to a denied depression: rather than accepting the loss of the object and engaging in the work of mourning, the subject appropriates—in perverse fantasies and acting out—substitutes for satisfaction, ersatz replacements, which he hypercathects. Many depressions, like certain cases of mourning, are accompanied by orgiastic abreactions of a perverse nature, while the analysis of perversions reveals a painful melancholia in the background that is often impossible to work out. Joyce McDougall has analyzed the alternation between mania and depression in the theater of the perverse.[19]

By immobilizing the perverse subject in a fixed organization (a particular incestuous or fetishistic representation), the stable perversion assumes the role of a protection against the subjacent destructiveness and possible

acting out: destruction is tied to a certain sexuality that serves as a bar-
ricade and prevents the infinite unfolding of hatred. In a similar way, the
creation of aesthetic objects preserves the one devoted to it from the drive
defusion proper to sublimation. The creation of aesthetic objects, especially
when they are appreciated and enjoy public approval, link destructiveness
to creative work that can be transformed into a true vocation. The effort of
creating, the *oof!* of effort, as Colette says, the "rule that cures all," while imposing ferocious discipline on daily life, is laden with supplementary pleasures, because it becomes a barrier against the destructiveness of the death
drive, depleted like a wave against a jetty.

3. Interpretation and Perversion

If I have lingered over this polymorphous perversion-sublimation copresence, it is to let it resonate with the share of polymorphous perversion in
analytical listening and interpretation.[20]

The act of interpretation consists, first, of abandoning oneself to the
pleasure and pain of libidinal identification with the analysand; then,
quasi simultaneously, of dissociating thing-presentations from word-
presentations. First, oral-anal-genital osmosis: cannibalism, control, voyeurism, exhibitionism. Then, and/or simultaneously, I interpret. Is it by
interpreting that I truly dissociate from my polymorphism? My distance is
certainly not a repression, but rather a sublimation. Because, by naming, I
establish word-presentations in their arbitrary autonomy as signs, distinct
from the perceptions-sensations I nevertheless continue to share with the
analysand in my libidinal identification-disidentification. The interpretation sets up my words as fetishes and leads the patient to play with his own
words-signs-fetishes; these are given back to him, as play objects to begin
with, as from a mother to her child. That way, starting with sensory fixa-
tions, the analyst works first with sensorial games, then words, but certainly
not word-concepts; rather, in the moments of grace of the analytical process, word-pleasures, word-things, word-fetishes.

Therapists of autistic patients have noticed the aesthetic pleasure patients take in using their first words, more charged with sensations than
ideas.[21] Beauty is necessary to psychical growth and the blossoming of
thought, provided the analyst can create it as well. As for me, I tend to
reflect on the sadomasochistic share of the patient's aesthetic performance,
who receives or refuses, destroys, cannibalizes, or defecates on his analyst's

interpretation. It is so important to reflect on the polymorphous sadomasochism hidden within the analytical interpretation itself, rather than simply being content to diagnose "the violence of interpretation"!

I observe a blocked psyche through a hole in my consciousness, temporarily opened in soma-psyche, drive-meaning flesh. My fusion sows the seed, and I know it needs my distance. This way, this other flesh can perhaps become someone else, a subject, from my named pleasure. The violence of libidinal, sensorial naming is obligatory, and it is beneficial within the cure. How can we create out of discontinuous fragments—dissect a *sign* to reveal an *object* of desire—without imposing on the polymorphously perverse continuity our own desire for names and therefore objects? The desire of the other that I am for the analysand proceeds in the manner of a sculptor: he "takes away" and trims in the continuous and analogous libido of the polymorphous pervert; he can only do harm, cause injury. More benevolence and tact are necessary, notably in cures that mobilize the splitting of the analyst and that rely on his own sadomasochistic latencies. It is in the precincts of the rhetorical art and latent perversion of the analyst himself that we find this optimal interpretation that may lead the analysand not only "from heaven to hell," as Goethe said, but vice versa, endlessly. Without ignoring the polymorphous pervert, or fastening him to an idealization of his drives, but leading him toward what Freud seemed to consider the optimal destiny of our polymorphism (which the postmodern era is placing in check): that is, the *desire to know* that keeps the psychical apparatus open. Part of the originality of Freud's discovery was to recognize polymorphous perversion, to recognize himself in it, and to play on it until teasing it out. So that the *polymorphously perverse children* that we all are will be accompanied by the fewest possible *perverse crimes*.

Lacan said that the "true" religion (Catholicism) had triumphed and *had* to triumph because it was built on sexual polymorphism, indeed on perversion itself, inseparable from sublimation.[22] Along with *Three Essays*, I would like to think psychoanalysis could, if not triumph then at least endure, provided that it recognize "the fundamental perversion of human desire" on which it is founded, thus leading perverts of the third millennium, who do not want to know, to this optimal destiny of polymorphism that is the *desire to know* without ceasing to *imagine*.

The desire to know without ceasing to imagine: A hundred years after *Three Essays*, I would call the real triumph of polymorphous perversion the psychoanalyst.

PART 4

RELIGION

17

ATHEISM

I grew up in the shadow of icons and for a long time observed the faith of my father, an Orthodox Christian and seminarian; he cultivated this faith, it seemed to me, as an intimate revolt against Communist atheism and as an aesthetic religion. Two months before the fall of the Berlin wall, he died at seventy-seven, killed by "socialist" medicine, which would not administer costly medications to aged persons but transformed them into guinea pigs for their surgical experiments. The horror of this atheism requires no commentary. The debates with my father, necessarily oedipal, left me with an interest at once passionate and critical in an experience of faith that continues to be informed, and tends to be refined, by contact with scientific, philosophical, and, above all, psychoanalytic thought.

Since Freud, and even more after him, the speaking being appears irreducible to his biology, but capable, starting from it and with it, of representing and symbolizing his functioning and activities with others, sexuality being the hinge of this metaphysical dualism, its unimagined artifice and necessary refashioning. Human beings' apperception of their complex aptitude for representation and symbolization is at the basis of what has been imagined, since the dawn of the hominid, as a "beyond," "spirituality," or a "divinity." Generally, we call atheism the fact of denying this meta-phor of the "divine," which was hypostatized as a "supreme cause" or "su-preme good," or simply the fact of attacking the institutions that celebrate it, whether flexible or dogmatic. Such an attitude often hides an even more brutal denial, that of the capacity of representation-symbolization that Christianity celebrates in its own way by proclaiming, "In the beginning was the Word." In addition, supposedly militant atheists often proceed by the same causalist and creativist religious logic, erecting a biological or po-litical ideal in place of the "divine."

On the contrary, true atheist thought would suppose, as Sartre sug-gested,[1] a depletion of transcendence from and in transcendence. In other words, it would be a meticulous and painstaking analysis of the aptitude itself to represent, symbolize, and think. The psychoanalytical experience, on the one hand, the construction/deconstruction of meaning by arts and letters, particularly in their modern incarnation, on the other, can trace the royal road of this particular atheism. How does *id* think? What are the variants and modalities of our capacity for representation? What damages them? These are the questions that mark the thought of an atheism with-out nihilism.

Religions have explored this heterogeneous continent in their own ways. They have accumulated vast stores of knowledge on the human soul and its relationship to the world and to others, notably and especially in the form of fables, illusions, or imaginary constructions. This pantheon can only be interpreted by considering the internal logic of the facts, commentaries, and logical consolidations and then addressing them in light of the modern knowledge of the speaking being and his world—necessarily provisional and in progress.

And so I was interested in the various purification rituals of religions in societies without writing as well as in Hindu food taboos, Levitical food taboos and defilements ("Thou shalt not cook a kid in its mother's milk," Exodus 23:19), and finally in the Christian revolution that situates abjec-tion in the word, the symbolic, and the link to the other ("It is not what enters the mouth that defiles the man; but what comes out of the mouth, this defiles the man," Matthew 15:11).[2] What emerges is a veritable geneal-ogy of the psychical construction of men in their environment, the sacred appearing as a celebration of the passage, of the border between two struc-tures or two identities (inside/outside, woman/man, child/mother: the list of taxonomies is endless, but these practices and their evolution are always structured by a concern for coherence and identity).

Similarly, a deeper study of theology, notably Marian, allowed me to note how Christendom went on to truly construct the maternal experience—in the guise of what some consider a "goddess-mother" in Christianity and others deplore as a "victimization" of femininity—at the intersection of biology and meaning. Recognition of virginity as an unthinkable externality, a challenge to the logics of beginnings, causes and effects; valorization of maternal love with its ecstatic as well as painful latencies; recompense for feminine paranoia, avid for power and sovereignty; encouragement of the infra-verbal, "semiotic" link between mother and child, on which the incestuous experience of art is built, and whose patron is Mary, mother of Art: these are a few of the advances of Marian worship, on which the subjectivity of men and women in the West was built and without comprehension of which this subjectivity would remain inaccessible.[3]

Finally, and to conclude for now, certain fundaments essential to modern humanism, such as notions of "freedom" or "personal dignity," go back to theology. We have to rethink freedom as self-initiation (self-beginning), as rooted ontologically in the *initium* of birth according to St. Augustine and haloed with the superiority of contingency in Duns Scotus's *haecceitas*, to meditate on the risks that freedom is running in a modern world of robotization, programmed births, and mass production.

Religions, in short, seem to be a recognition of what Freud calls *das höhere Wesen in Menschen*, "the higher side of man" in which the subject's freedom is inscribed.[4] This recognition guarantees religions a function of truth beyond the consoling fascination they provide, at first, in any case. Religions recognize human beings' capacity to create meaning while at the same time denying this intra- and extraphysical dynamic its value as open and renewable knowledge, so as to erect it in a hierarchical system of values. As protective and consoling value systems, religions assure certain human freedoms, but this conquest comes not only at the price of a persecuting exclusion of others (other religions and dissidents) who do not share the same system of values. Graver still, it comes at the price of sexual repression reinforced by the divine threat, and that leads in the end to the inhibition of critical thought, i.e., thought plain and simple. Generating neurosis on the personal level, religion also reclaims it, by way of belief itself: *credo*, to give one's heart in exchange for a reward, the supreme version of which is Eternal Life granted by the heavenly Father.[5] Especially since the neurosis favored by religious prohibition is accompanied by authorized transgressions, in which the perversion (*père*-version?) of the believer is satisfied. Christianity excels at swinging between inhibition-repression and freedom-perversion.

In the favorable economic context of Western democracies, and especially with current evolutions of Protestantism and Catholicism, it makes its way toward a moralism that tolerates difference and is concerned about exclusion. On the social level it is not radically distinguishable from humanist moralism,but in addition has the advantage of benefiting from tradition, from its security and comfort. Which is to say that atheism, if not confined to the unrest of elites, has a long road ahead of it to rise to the challenge.

THE TRIPLE UPROOTING OF ISRAEL

EXODUS, EXILE, RETURN

According to the biblical account, the foundation of Israel is nothing but a constant uprooting: exodus, exile, return. This instability, suggested at the origins from the start, this *founding voyage* that from the start disseminates the essence of the chosen people, brings lamentation and consolation, and, for the first time in human history, uproots human beings from their soil to reunite their nomadic community in the only possible covenant, which in the end is only symbolic. Because it is the Word of God alone, and fidelity to His commandments or sins against them, that now trace the fate of those engaging in this pact instead and in place of earlier ritual sacrifices. A universalist messianism is already sketched out: the "deported," those absent "from home," are assembled only in the Word of God and in the Book that is a witness to it, and if Yahweh is the shepherd of Israel, going to find exiles like a shepherd and bringing them back home (Ezekiel 34), it is to give them a "new heart" (Ezekiel 36:24–28) by leading them to their fold (Isaiah 40:11; 52:12)—a place of scripture, a spiritual place more than a geographical and political one, where ultimately the infinite covenant of *all* can occur. This theological version of the resurrection of the nomadic people (Ezekiel 37:1–14) will be made explicit by the Christian message when it displaces the "Holy Land" itself and even the blood ties among communicants in a gathering for later or never, a community beyond, a theophany in the heavenly homeland (Hebrews 11:16), a world detached from the world: "in spirit and in truth" (John 4:24), through Christ when "lifted up" (John 12:32), whose Kingdom, while in this world, is not "of this world" (John 17:16).

The history of the world understood as the history of technology would enclose those who shared this constitutive exile in a painful fate: depriving them of a habitat; excluding them from sedentary, agrarian, and industrial communities; suspecting and persecuting the foreignness of this people of God, withdrawn into its Law and nomadism; projecting into its flaws, admitted in the face of the world, and into its symbolic endurance, also on display, the terrors and deep hatreds secreted by the paranoia of men and women in every society. More specifically, and with an unprecedented brutality, European history ended up crystallizing this fascination-repulsion elicited by the people of the Bible in the horror of the Shoah, the consequences of which we continue to live out today. And yet these days it is still the history of technology that makes the biblical logic of exile not a suspect adversary of nations supposedly sure of their identities but a source of reflection for foreigners of no return who are becoming the inhabitants of our globalized planet. The third millennium is detaching from its roots and, without eradicating them, invites us, or forces us, to make and remake our lives continually, elsewhere, beyond the frontiers of familial-national-ethnic-religious identity. Then we can recognize ourselves as strangers to ourselves and perhaps find a way to move beyond the belligerent and suicidal fury that characterizes our era, constituting new pacts, new ways of sharing.

In this context the "exilic" message of the Bible and the New Testament naturally lends itself to multiple readings. Some see it as an invitation to heal the wounds of the uprooting, exclusion, and persecution by building and fortifying solid and inviolable enclosures: to constitute, in the face of the enemy and insecurity, these protective "holy lands" that nation-states with exceptional circumstances are, religions sure of themselves and dominant in their fundamentalist essence as well as indigenous havens of all sorts: linguistic, racial, ideological, aesthetic, sexual (gender, sexual preference), preferably isolationist and discriminatory.

Others, on the contrary, read it as an invitation to include in identity itself the foundational wandering constituted by the triple uprooting of exodus, exile, and return. To deepen it, to construct it in absence, through separation and loss, by traveling through their own memory as well as through a multiplicity of cultures and beings. The new political ethics, trying to find itself today in disasters threatening the survival of the planet, tallies with this *second possible reading of the biblical message*. The microcosm of psychoanalytic investigation uses the same logic: from Freud to his modern disciples, the analytic experience discovers that the child becomes a subject of speech, thought, and meaning when he is able, under certain biological and familial conditions, to lose his mother as well as her narcissistic and phallic omnipotence, and from this foundational "exile"—"separation," according to Freud, "depressive position," according to Melanie Klein, "lack," according to Lacan—to find the object and the other again in psychic representation and language, by means of the imaginary and the symbolic, in what might—under these conditions alone—become the precarious freedom of the human condition. Moreover, our acts of creativity, which are the rebirths of our subjectivity throughout life, demand the capacity not to renounce the self but to stay away from the old Self or "object," so as to give it a different meaning in new ties, new transferences, a continuous "transitional space" (D. Winnicott), which is the private side of civilization, and culture.

Listening to my analysands—who transfer themselves from the place of their birth to the new and provisional tie of the psychoanalytical process, who lose themselves in their symptoms and stay away from themselves but also lose me and stay away from me in order to open new passages, passageways, transitions, rebounding from what they think of as their "own" being toward "other" people, objects, projects, words, thoughts (endlessly, indefinitely, in an uncertain and open community to come)—prompts me to pick up the Bible. Exodus, exile, return: they "speak to me" in our common (yet different) concerns to live a life of possibility, not secularized but on display, sustainable, and therefore creative, in a world where exodus has become generalized and where hostilities between natives and exiles have never been so brutal or unbearable.

Exodus

To read the biblical account, a story of immigration is at the origin of Israel: whether Abraham's (Genesis 12:1, "Now the Lord said to Abram, Get out of your country, from your family and from your father's house, to a land that I will show you") or Joseph's (Genesis 37, 39–40, 50), "it begins" with a voyage, with the entrance and exit of certain groups of the future Israel, lasting several centuries, from the Hyksos period to the thirteenth century B.C. Joseph's "short story" or novella offers the theological version: Joseph ("the one who succeeds at everything"), son of Jacob and Rachel, sold by his brothers and brought to Egypt as a slave, becomes a grand vizier whose agrarian policy is so astute it saves the country from famine: which encourages his brothers to settle on Egyptian soil. It is Israel as a whole, and its twelve tribes symbolized by this account, that Joseph brings into Egypt and that Yahweh will liberate.

As one trip leads to another, in the logic of wandering that replaces that of the origin, this entrance will be followed by an exit: Joseph gives a foreshadowing of the exodus. Yahweh calls Moses and sends him to Pharaoh to obtain . . . the departure of the Hebrews. The mission is a failure and leads to a new intervention by Yahweh, which is decisive this time: on the night of Passover, he smites all the first-born of Egypt, which provokes . . . the immediate expulsion of the Hebrews; who end up . . . crossing the Sea of Reeds thanks to a miraculous intervention by Yahweh, again! This account very probably transposes the oppression and exodus under the reign of Ramses II, as well as various earlier expulsions and flights, blended into one single Mosaic exodus, from which the people of God are born. Whether by a single act of God or through Moses working in His name, the epic account celebrates an act of salvation: leaving Egypt and the covenant of Sinai (Exodus 1–15, 19–40). The rupture, the persecution, and the departure are followed by the feats of crossing the sea and the desert, so that finally, in Sinai, Yahweh makes the descendents of Jacob who escaped Egypt "His people" (Exodus 19–24). The pact intensifies and supports the wandering, and it is in the balance and tension between the two that the identity of Israel is constituted: God proclaims His will through the Decalogue (Exodus 20, 1–17) and the code of the covenant (Exodus 20, 22–23, 19), while the people respond by engagement (Exodus 24, 1–11): "And [Moses] took the Book of the Covenant, and read in the audience of the people: and they said, All that the LORD hath said will we do, and be obedient."

And as though to accentuate the infinite meaning of the voyage, to make clear that the wandering is structural, the biblical text tirelessly repeats the image. "They" do not hesitate to fall short of their promises, and their disloyalty provokes the wrath of God: "The LORD said to Moses, 'I have seen this people, and behold, they are an obstinate people. Now then leave me alone, that My anger may burn against them and that I may destroy them;

and I will make of you a great nation'" (Exodus 32:9–10). Then there is the renewal of the covenant, a second proclamation of the Ten Command-ments, and finally the institution of a sanctuary and vocation that will make the people a true religious community inhabited by Yahweh: "Then a cloud covered the tent of the congregation, and the glory of the LORD filled the tabernacle. . . . For the cloud of the LORD was on the tabernacle by day, and fire was on it by night, in the sight of all the house of Israel, throughout all their journeys" (Exodus 40:34–38).

It couldn't be clearer: the original displacement will endure, and is even the sine qua non for the covenant to endure, or recur: the covenant that alone constitutes the clashing identity of the weakening and wandering community. A covenant in law, a symbolic pact, an ethical requirement im-possible to sustain, whose transgressions prepare for new ruptures, new de-partures, new exiles. The *traveling being* is established structurally right away: whatever the injustices of the persecution inflicted by external oppressors and enemies, it is through *the biblical pact, itself contingent on wandering* that the subject is constituted as essentially uprooted *and* infinitely symbolic. Entrance-exit *and* covenant: this logic imprints both the instability and es-sential flaw in each of the faithful who subscribe to it and a promise of solidity and protection that is only obtained in the expectation, accepted by each, to contemplate one's indefiniteness, infiniteness, and the problematic of moral perfection in times to come.

Exile

Restored by prophetic discourse, exile is inseparable from its rhetoric, full of threats and promises. Isaiah, Jeremiah, and Ezekiel speak of a distress that seems to be punishment for sins denounced countless times, a nega-tive theophany as well as a promise of renewal and a divine presence whose glory is not enclosed within the Temple but mobile, accompanying the faithful like an invisible sanctuary. In 734 several cities of the kingdom of Israel undergo persecution and deportation (2 Kings 15:29) and in 721 the entire kingdom is deported to Assyria (2 Kings 17:6). But it is the depor-tations to Babylonia ordered by Nebuchadnezza, following his campaigns against Judah and Jerusalem in 597, 587, 582, for which the term *exile* is re-served (2 Kings 24:14; 25:11; Jeremiah 52:28).

Prophetic speech is not taken in by promises and divine miracles, and if it continues to wait for a certain completion of God's designs, in which it still believes by definition, it also continues to denounce illusions, to threaten those who persist in sinning, and to repeat that exile will last. Why? For Isaiah, Jeremiah, and Ezekiel, exile is coextensive to the very condition of the people of the covenant, because the requirement of divine election is grandiose and the sinning in which the great compromise themselves measures up to this requirement. Exile and prophetic speech seem to be two sides of a structural necessity: we must be conscious of the incurable perversion of human beings and use the reality of deportation to transform it into an incitement to psychical evolution, to make it the image of a wresting away of oneself, of a never-ending journey toward the difficult principles of the covenant.

"And you have done worse than your fathers, for behold, each one follows the dictates of his own evil heart, so that no one listens to Me. Therefore I will cast you out of this land into a land that you do not know, neither you nor your fathers; and there you shall serve other gods day and night, where I will not show you favor" (Jeremiah 16:12–13). What sins is the prophet condemning? The sins of leaders mired in base political calculation instead of serving the divine covenant (Isaiah 8, 6; 30, 1); the sins of the rich who betray the common fraternity through violence or fraud (Isaiah 1:23); the sins of the people as whole, idolatrous worshippers of "foreign gods" (Jeremiah 5:19), immoral beings "from the least even to the greatest given to covetousness" (Jeremiah 8:10) who have made Jerusalem a bad place: "The word of the LORD came to me: 'Son of man, will you judge her? Will you judge this city of bloodshed? Then confront her with all her detestable practices'" (Ezekiel 22:1–3). Isaiah's incantation on his "friend and the vineyard" is one of the most florid metaphors of this prophetic desolation, free of illusion before facility and complacency, convinced that shadows and anxieties inhabit the heart of ignorant men: "My Well-beloved has a vineyard / On a very fruitful hill. . . . He expected it to bring forth good grapes / But it brought forth wild grapes" (Isaiah 5:1–2). This faithless people will be chased from its land and scattered among all peoples (Deuteronomy 28:63–68): but the diaspora itself will be the sign of failings *and* the precondition for improvement, simultaneously. And Jeremiah, prophet of doom, one of the most intransigent, will stigmatize the idolatrous and the swindlers as well as the credulous souls who coddle themselves with illusions of peace: "They dress the wound of my people as though it were not serious. 'Peace, peace,' they say, when there is no peace" (Jeremiah 8:11).

Never peace and always exile: these remarks, rarely heard in Palestine, had to be understood as an inexpugnable truth by the exiles of Babylon.

Because the prophetic discourse fighting against "sin" is certainly a call to moral elevation and fidelity to the covenant. But, to the ears of men chased from their home, deprived of social complicities and familiar gratifications, relegated to solitude and the need to work on themselves constantly to be able to survive with dignity in the midst of a hostile environment, this discourse sounds like a revelation of the essential flaw in the human condition: it is received as a questioning, a breach in plenitude, a path to forge, a voyage into the dissatisfaction of desire and the vigilance of thought. The exiles in Babylon were the first to understand that the psychical working out of exile—of separation, loss, incompleteness—was the path required to reconstruct their living, demanding, and creative psychical space and that this constant psychical reconstruction would allow them to confront existence without lapsing into "sin," remaining vigilant and attentive beyond moral prescriptions. Isn't the foreigner, the exile who is not under his family's gaze, also someone who may succumb to moral compromise, violence, delinquency? Just as he may become—if he continues to listen to his incompleteness, as the prophets suggest—this acute consciousness, this opportunity, this night watchman whose melancholy is lessened in a gamble on the constantly reconstructed meaning of a possible life.

Dolorous Christianity had to exalt the culpability echoed in the exile/ sin duo of the prophetic threat, and we are not counting the faithful consumed by sin in this sacred fire. We would have to wait for another kind of listening, intransigent yet benevolent, in the breaches of agnosticism—that of Freudian psychoanalysis—for exile, as the prophets reconstruct it, to reveal the constitutive uprooting of the human condition.

Return

Far from being limited to threats, the prophetic incantation itself was coupled with a salutary comfort: the promise of renewal, the tenderness of a God who castigates and scatters but also consoles: "How can I give you up, Ephraim? How can I hand you over, Israel? . . . My heart churns within Me; My sympathy is stirred" (Hosea 11:8).

Hope is the other side of exile, and its only reality that of *listening*: without soil or political or economic power, the deportee who has renounced sacrificial worship gives himself over to the reading and commentary of sacred texts and, in the liturgy of the synagogue, finds communal comfort in prayer. The return can only be a return to the meaning of the divine word:

the exile then foreshadows an Israel whose ambition is to be the "light of nations" (Isaiah 42:6) and announces the universal eschatological reign of Yahweh: ". . . Egypt . . . Cush . . . the Sabeans, men of stature, shall come over to you, and they shall be yours" (Isaiah 45:14).

But this barely sketched out universalism requires a *second exodus*, above all and absolutely. The exile is encouraged by the prophet and his God to return home: he is assured that his exile will end and that, with a new heart and a new spirit, he will inhabit the land of his fathers: "For I will take you from among the nations, gather you out of all countries, and bring you into your own land. Then I will sprinkle clean water on you, and you shall be clean; . . . I will take the heart of stone out of your flesh and give you a heart of flesh" (Ezekiel 36: 24–26). In fact, the edict of Cyrus promulgated in 538 allows Jews to return to Jerusalem: and these survivors of captivity (Ezra 1:4) give the Jewish community a new spiritual élan, the second exodus in this sense being the motor of a veritable resurrection of the people of Yahweh: "Thus says the Lord GOD: 'Behold, O My people, I will open your graves and cause you to come up from your graves, and bring you into the land of Israel. . . . I will put My Spirit in you, and you shall live, and I will place you in your own land. Then you shall know that I, the LORD, have spoken it and performed it,' says the LORD" (Ezekiel 31:12–14).

With the resurrection continually to come, the voyage is endlessly written. Prophetic speech suggests it: sorrow to he who settles on dead soil, ignoring the infinite effort, the voyage restarted over and over that God asks of those who listen to him, so that their bones can live again! The return is a promise, provided we read it as part of a triptych of the voyager's path: exodus, exile, return—never an end in itself. Echoes of the prophetic threat invite us to include it in an endless uprooting that is the condition for the resurrection, itself endless: the return is an image of uprooting, a second exodus, a prelude to another exile, another return . . .

"'Peace, peace!' when there is no peace"—Jeremiah's cry is the most illuminating desperate speech any exile has ever given. Because it opens up time (our time, biblical time, and that of the *global era* after *modern times*), a time when necessary uprooting can make its way toward the appeasement of men in the extreme rigor of thought, imagination, and culture: always beyond separation and loss, in the voyage outside oneself toward others. To think that at the heart of the crisis, which transcendence and humanism are now undergoing, we might have regretted the "loss of habitat"! To think that we wanted "to save ourselves," wanting nostalgically to conquer a *habitat* that would finally be familiar, stable, reassuring! On the contrary, the strangers that we are in the globalized era of wandering can do no better than continue to listen to Jeremiah: do not succumb to the illusion of a soothing haven; the biblical prophecy was only a beginning; keep moving!

19

WHAT IS LEFT OF OUR LOVES?

After "God is dead," which at first sounded like liberation, after its martyrdom in Auschwitz and the gulag and in the planes that crashed into the Twin Towers in New York, we know that a single religion remains: that of Love. It is enough to turn on any screen on our globalized planet to see it: reality shows probe the secrets of love, soap operas fan the flames, quarrels, and tears of love, actresses and actors become bodies that sell love, when actors do not kill their actresses (the reverse has yet to be added to the repertory), always out of love, and for real—in any case, that is what is happening. That is life.

More than two thousand years ago, rabbis hesitated including the Song of Songs in the Bible, the amorous song attributed to King Solomon, uttered through the mouth of a woman, which would become the model of the romantic discourse of modernity. I tended to disapprove when I was younger and not yet psychoanalytical enough. Rereading these sage ancient debates today, it would be pretentious to say I understand them, but I'm getting there. I thank all those who have made this translation of my writings into Hebrew possible for the first time, and I will try to explain myself briefly.[1]

It is true that as an adolescent I already wondered what the glamorous word *Love* might actually mean, since it seemed everyone who used it, around me or in books, gave it a different meaning—an obscure meaning that could only be shared in its dazzle. I succumbed to love, naturally, and my sixties and seventies were as romantic and erotic as yours. However, I dare say it is not age that is making me more "rabbinical" today, but listening to history and the new maladies of the soul.

We attribute the subjective exaltation of the Western subject to romantic sentiment and to the focus of metaphysics on romantic sentiment, which ends up enclosed within its own psychical space and cultivates narcissism and egotism, the modern nihilistic ravages of which we are all too familiar with: destruction of values and other dismissals of the Concern for Being. I would say, on the contrary, that humanity has been made more lucid by the fact of finding Eros and its twin, Thanatos, at the source of the mental activity specific to the human race, the Western philosophical and aesthetic experience, from Plato by way of Judeo-Christian-Muslim monotheism, the troubadours, humanism, romanticism, not to mention Sade and Proust, a long trajectory to which I devoted *Tales of Love* (1985). More lucid, not better, certainly, but often more ambitious, active, cynical, and cruel, as well as more caring, compassionate, perverse, and complex. Human, too human, surely—the reason Nietzsche revolted—but "human" in the sense that, beyond any personalist complacency, the love of God inspired the inhuman ecstasies of St. Teresa as well as the laughter of Mozart and the extrahuman polyphony of Bach.

When Love gives itself an absolute object—after creating psychical space, as the carrier wave of language and the vector of inquiry that constitutes thought—and is strangled in the celebration of the Identical and the Absolute, in the veneration of dogma or the possession of Truth and the Other, thus signing the death sentence of thought and life, this Love becomes the troubled water that (I imagine) made the rabbis hesitate around the first millennium. I agree with them. Or, to be more precise, I agree with the most concerned, modern, cosmopolitan, i.e., paradoxical, among them—none other than Sigmund Freud, when, at the dawn of the twentieth century this time, he laid Love down on the couch.

It is not enough to say romantic passion is a neurosis, indeed, a psychosis, to denounce the sentimental impasses in which the speculative bubble has submerged human beings in the globalized world, or to lance the abscess of fundamentalism in which religious fanatics pour the coffers of various mafias who rejoice. Despite its patient listening, despite its detailed interpretations that engage countertransference (we might as well say the analyst's love), psychoanalysis itself is not protected from the loss of control that the narcissistic psychosis of fundamentalists generate. Any more than it is protected, in a more ordinary way, from mental laziness. But it keeps watch over itself, too, and that is already a lot. Beside it, against it, or in complicity with it, could art and literature, philosophy and science, each in its own way, help x-ray, help weave and unweave this amorous tie without which human beings make no sense, but in which the sense of the human condition is also enchained, blinded, wasted?

Let's consider three female geniuses: Hannah Arendt (1906–1975), Melanie Klein (1882–1960), and Colette (1873–1954).

Arendt, while eager to defend the singularity of the "who" threatened by totalitarianisms, did not take refuge in solipsistic incantation. Against the isolation of philosophers, whose "melancholic tribe" she mocks, and against the anonymity of crowds, in which "one" is dissolved, this theoretician of imperialism and anti-Semitism, the persecutions of which she underwent, this woman "faithful and unfaithful" to Heidegger, this student of Jaspers, whose first work was a thesis on "The Concept of Love in St. Augustine," calls for a political life capable of assuring the originality of every person in the bonds of memory and the narrative destined to others.

Klein, meanwhile, radically transforms the Freudian hypothesis of an original narcissism and posits an "ego" from the beginning of the baby's psychical life capable of "object relations" (with part objects) before the object relationship to the "total object" following the "depressive position." "Repairing," i.e., loving, speaking, and thinking then become possible.

Finally, the amorous Colette, endlessly betrayed and endlessly betraying, declared herself beyond romantic passion, "one of the great banalities of existence" from which one had to escape, provided one was capable of participating in the plurality of the world—in a fulfillment of the ego through a multitude of "gay, varied, and plentiful" connections.

These philosophical, psychoanalytical, and literary female adventures— as experiences of the collapse of political, psychical, and aesthetic connections, and unconsciously of amorous ties—have surveyed the destruction of states, thoughts, and lives. With the conviction, however, that, in spite of everything, *ties can be reconstructed.* In politics: through pardon, promise, and discernment. In psychoanalysis: through the working out of the death drive that ruins the possibility of thought. In literature: through finding the *mot juste* that savors and shares the flesh of the world. So many variations on love. Differently and conjointly, Arendt, Klein, and Colette relieve it of its fanatic core and, by defusing it, transform it into availability, proximity, psychical, political, and aesthetic creativity.

Can this love attained by the genius of Arendt, Klein, and Colette—a gay, varied, and plentiful love—still be labeled *love?*

A report on television told the story of a song in six countries in the Balkans, my place of origin. The single melody everyone in this region knows had become the basis of six different texts celebrating six meanings of love, a spectrum that went from eroticism between a man and a woman to a prayer addressed to Allah to a warlike exhortation to conquer a threatened territory and uncertain national identity. Each of the nations surprisingly enamored of this song, each of the singers transfixed by the words of his/her desire, thought he or she was the origin, source, and truth of this melody, at times languishing and tender, at times quick and saucy, at times vengeful or flirtatious. Each was persuaded that the neighboring and opposing version was a usurping of this national purity that each was alone in possessing, as a result of which the singers (sometimes female, more often male) in love with their song, itself in love with the beloved and/or God, said that they were ready to go to war with their neighbor so as to allow their own voice, history, and . . . love to triumph. "Make love, not war," we chanted, not so long ago. Is anyone still unaware that this antinomy is not one?

I am persuaded, and I think I have demonstrated with Colette, that the path of romantic connection realized by this writer is the private face of her atheism: vindictive and showy in her youth, serene and firm in her maturity.[2] Colette's deconstruction of the amorous link, which is the basis of faith, probably constitutes the most precious, most unexpected gift she bequeathed not only to feminists but to our civilization as a whole, which clings to passionate neurosis as if it could rise up as a substitute for the loss of transcendence and values.

Similarly, I would like to think that when Sartre conducts his philosophical inquiry to the ends of atheism—which he calls "a cruel and long-range affair"—he suspects that the double of this ambition is situated in the experience of the relationship he forms, already with his mother, no doubt, but above all and scandalously with Simone de Beauvoir. Far from the romantic idyll devoured by amateur existentialists, it was also a deconstruction of the amorous link, bound by cruelty and melancholic tenderness.

Eroticism—the religion of eighteenth-century France, more so than other eras and other cultures, whose modernity knew a limitless explosion— is not this maniac incapable of love who ruins families (moralists have stigmatized it as much as churches have, if not more so). However varied the figures of Love throughout history and civilizations, and despite the Platonic and religious tendencies that try to encapsulate it within a single idealization, Eros and Love cross paths, cross swords, ignore each other, and reconnect: mystics know this; Freud came to explain it.

From then on, the risky path of love—which is neither an inability to love nor the intellectual denial of affect, any more than its brutal exaltation in "hard sex"—is a working out of eroticism in search of its sense and nonsense. A search, a working out, a passingthrough: they sketch the profile of a humanity to come, fragile and lucid. A nonidealized humanism, yet available to others. Utopia? Certainly. What else remains, if God is love and He fuels desire to the death?

Art and literature and, more specifically, the novel, have assumed the role of alchemical crucible in this civilization dominated by the romantic imaginary: they compose and decompose the laws and figures of the amorous adventure. What is a novel? The unbearable elevated to the savors of language. Novelists revel in it, distilling it in the labyrinth of romantic intrigue. But what is left of "love's unbearableness" after a century of psychoanalysis (however few those with access to this experience are, and however debatable certain practices may be)? Everything, transcended in a state of weightlessness. As well as certain mysteries: the impasses of politics, the enigmas of sublimation, the virtuosity of great crimes. In all these knotty issues, love conceals its failures, which are nevertheless the companions inherent in its fate.

Because the insolence of the Freudian discovery was to show this: there is no love but failed love. Nevertheless, far from despairing, the disenchanted and still resistant atheism that results creates new ties, modulations of this indispensable *pleasure to the death* that the speaking being feels in otherness and sharing. Pleasure to the death that the moderns, when they manage to analyze its logic, temper and defuse. If we dare hope to one day be done with the fundamentalist terror the amorous knot contains, we will have to tirelessly analyze this bond that allows speaking beings to be: the bond of maternal, paternal, adolescent, conjugal, professional, political, religious, familial, group, national, endless love! The way out of religions is not the Jacobin or Stalinist materialism imposed by the massacre of believers. If it were possible, it would require patient knowledge and a meticulous dismantling of the amorous ties: mama-ego, papa-ego, sister-brother-ego, God-ideal-future-singing-tomorrows-or-not-paradise-success-relationship-glory-posterity-bank-account-ego . . . In short, a surpassing of my relation-ship to the Object and to the Other that only exist if (and only if) this Ob-ject and this Other are an Object and an Other *in* Love—sensorial, sensual, intellectual, religious, aesthetic, living Love.

The dispassionate humanity reborn from this experience would not necessarily be boring or robotic. Perhaps it would simply have a gay, varied, and plentiful lucidity. And it would preserve the laughter of Love: to the point of making light of Love itself. Apparently, the Jewish God is a laugh-ing God.

Freud (a much more scientific mind than his ancestors, the rabbis, sus-picious of love) wanted to believe in a humanity rid of its illusions: without really believing in it. As for me, I would like to preserve one illusion: that of a humanity capable of laughing, out of love, and making light of love.

PART 5

PORTRAITS

20

THE INEVITABLE FORM

She was twenty-nine in 1916: a beautiful young painter who had studied at the Art Institute of Chicago and the Art Students League in New York, visited great exhibitions by French artists and Alfred Stieglitz's art gallery in New York, and traveled across the country teaching painting at various art schools.

His name was Alfred Stieglitz: a famous avant-garde photographer who established a highly regarded art gallery at 291 Fifth Avenue, a fervent supporter of European modern art who aspired to elevating American art to the same heights, or higher.

Stieglitz-O'Keeffe: A Couple with Four Hands

Stieglitz sees Georgia O'Keeffe's work in January, exhibits it at 291 Gallery in May, and never leaves her again. In 1917 he begins to take photos of her. Georgia will be the most photographed woman in the world: in twenty years (1917–1937) Stieglitz made more than three hundred photographs of her. Georgia's face, Georgia's body, Georgia's hands: the photos tremble with eroticism, delicacy, pride—is O'Keeffe a "vamp"? The style of the photography changes, the model is serene, serious, grave—is O'Keeffe the enigmatic muse of modern art?

But that is not all. The model is an artist. She has one exhibition after another, her talent is asserted, she has her own glory.

The couple marries in 1924, after Stieglitz's divorce, and, remarkably, neither of the two stars goes crazy. Romantic sorrow or some turmoil was expected—Georgia's suffering or Stieglitz's jealousy, for example. No. After a bad patch in the early 1930s, she makes a Virginia Woolf–like decision, but one that is triumphant: more than a "room of one's own," O'Keeffe builds a world of her own, in New Mexico, where she will have her house, her friends, her universe, and where she will often spend half the year.

The intensity of their life together—in any case, before the 1930s, marked by travel, then by Georgia's attachment to New Mexico—allows parallels to be drawn between the conceptions and aesthetic practices of both artists.

More theoretical, more prolix (Stieglitz is reputed to have been an excellent storyteller, capable of subjecting a listener for hours to tales woven from parables, fables, and speculation), a prolific letter writer (we note that he neglects punctuation, as does Georgia, replacing periods with dashes), Stieglitz seems to find just the right word to apply not only to his own photographs but to O'Keeffe's paintings as well; she works alongside him, autonomous and close at hand. Then, after his initial style influenced by symbolism, Stieglitz distances himself from that current. Advocating the right to individualism in photography, he decides that the camera's necessary and inevitable objectivity can and must be submitted to the expression of the photographer's character and ideas. He asserts the autonomy of photography as a medium "distinct" from painting, and his photographs become assemblages of form, a search for "pure form," "objective truth" detached from the recognizable environment, increasingly abstract and sober.

Yet the gaze that chooses and delimits conveys the artist's presence: this is Stieglitz's quasi-mystical preoccupation. Inspired by Bergson and Kandinsky, he aims for nothing less than the fragmentation of time into dividable units. The artist brings the camera closer to his objects/targets, cropped and enlarged as if under a microscope, and aims to express not the state of the world but that of the photographer. The cloud series, entitled quite simply "Music: A Sequence of Ten Cloud Photographs," followed by "Prints" and "Equivalents," are called on to express emotion like music, to make "the objectivity of subjectivity" visible, because that is the goal of the "photography of ideas" Stieglitz is in the midst of promoting. Along the way, modern American photography finds its founding father in Stieglitz, while Georgia O'Keeffe's art resonates with Stieglitz's passion for the object explored in detail, spotlights and sequences that can be organized in a harmony of forms and that through an arrangement reveals the artist's passion. Objective or subjective? The form of a world captured by an irreducible, ineluctable, individual passion—form according to Stieglitz and O'Keeffe—emerges as "subjectively objective." Inside and out, this form signals the presence of subjective experience in the world and restores the world's singular intimacy.

Consider Stieglitz's photos of Georgia's hands (1921). Delicate fingers lightly graze a bunch of grapes: it's Cézanne, female desire through hands, this body part that combines the greatest industrious innocence with the slyest erotic suggestion.[1] O'Keeffe's two hands climb an invisible stem; and there are so many other hands—from above, from below, suspended, raised, floating. A veritable poem, objective and intimate at once, on the erotic ties that attach both artists to each other and on this mysterious formation that is the art proper to each, obviously manual. Formation—in other words, the creation of forms—is revealed as autoeroticism for both, the artist's control over the body, work, and Eros, indivisible. Stieglitz affirms that his photographic constructions are "something that already take shape in me," and Georgia points out that he "always photographed himself." A hypnotist of his models? Perhaps. But he is not alone: Georgia O'Keeffe also "hypnotizes" her flowers and shells, transposing into known forms the unknown lines of force of her own world.

Of all the images Stieglitz and other photographers have left us of this strange woman, who lived her life like a work of art and experienced her work as life, the one I like best is from 1929 by Stieglitz himself, "Georgia O'Keeffe—After Return from New Mexico."[2] Leaning against a big car or a small truck (we see its back window and the spare tire beneath it), Georgia stands erect, looking proud, detached, somewhat provocative. Her face has an austere tenderness, which seems to contemplate an inviolable and inevitable interior world. Her hair is pulled back; her long, bare neck gives her the air of a dancer. The eroticism comes from her hands, which introduce the nervous grace of a suspended motion.

Woman, lover, model, artist, Georgia O'Keeffe combines all the roles women have had in the history of art and modern art, and that have often relegated them to a painful marginality. While she excels at each of these roles separately, she combines them with an elegant intensity, perhaps un-precedented and unmatched. Her unique vital and aesthetic complexity has a simplicity that defies the interpretations she has always provoked.

Perhaps this instant melding of lived experience and perfect form in the work of a woman explains why she is so little known to the French public. As if the analytical and suspicious genius of the Hexagon were stupefied before this energetic demand for sensation, breath, solitude, and the un-speakable unknown. Her disdain for words, her declarations, positioning her as impenetrable to language and resistant to the critical speculations incited by her work, no doubt contributed to creating a distance from the more measured currents of modern art. Like a wild force surging up from the nature of the new continent, in communion with colors, wind, sound, flowers, flesh, bones, mountains, canyons, and plains, Georgia O'Keeffe seems to brush up against the adventure of modern art and, in a flash, with-out an intermediary, attain a sort of sublimated holiness, a clear and un-avoidable perfection. Like a new Emily Dickinson, without words: floral, astral, vivid.

A Naive Artist?

More appropriate than the word *art*, the word *experience*—dreamlike, unset-tling, disarmingly naked—would be more suited to her rigor and the poly-valence of her aesthetic adventure. Because it allows us to go beyond the apparent lightness conveyed by the canvases that would reduce Georgia O'Keeffe to a *naïve* artist. Indeed, the question raised by the great parsi-mony of representations signed O'Keeffe is complex: is the whole artist, particularly the whole female artist, *in* the painting—its colors, its contours, its composition? Or, to see the whole artist, or at least "most" of the artist, or the "best" of the artist (male or female), is it essential to *read her life*, know her sensations, her breathing, her battles with words, to reread her letters and retrace her history?

With the insolence of great artists who rarely feign modesty, this woman seemed to consider painting to be the visible, almost indifferent face of a complex experience of an overall organization of forms, over which she was sure to have control, most of the time.

"I feel that a real living form is the natural result of the individuals ef-fort to create the living thing out of the adventure of his spirit into the unknown—where it has experienced something—felt something—it has not understood—and from that experience comes the desire to make the unknown—known—By unknown, I mean . . . The artists form must be inevitable—You mustn't even think you wont succeed"[3]

And:

"I must say to you again that I am very pleased and flattered that you wish to do the show for me. . . . I do not know why I am so indifferent."[4]

This creation of forms based on an experience at the limits of the self is no doubt common to every aesthetic adventure. Far from erasing it, modern art brought it to the frontiers of mental identity and to a new incandescence in the violence of pleasure or pain (Picasso, Matisse, and, in a different way, Pollock, De Kooning, and Artaud testify to this). But the formalism that modern criticism is consumed with scrutinizing only examines the tip of the iceberg: concentrating on the technique of the works alone, it ends up forgetting the phenomenal expenditures that make them come about. The challenge that the aesthetic experience levels at formalist reason, but also at psychological shutting down, is even more intolerable when the work confronts the viewer with the appearance of an almost oriental serenity, impenetrable, uninterpretable. No malaise? No sexuality proclaimed or displayed? Is the artist puritanical, too covert? Or does she have a certain "unconscious stinginess," as someone accuses her of having,[5] leading to a new series of hypotheses: excessive restraint of her "rich inner supply," "defensive egotism."

O'Keeffe was familiar with the great European artists. In 1908 she visits the Rodin and Matisse exhibitions. In 1941 she shows with Picasso at Steiglitz's gallery, An American Place. Picasso is sound, music—in 1916 she writes: "That Picasso Drawing is wonderful music isn't it—Anita—I like it so much that I am almost jealous of other people even looking at it—and I love the Gertrude Stein portrait—the stuff simply fascinates me—I like it all."[6] Marcel Duchamp is a close friend of Stieglitz and O'Keeffe's, whom they admire deeply.

What is the common denominator of these sacred monsters who usher in and dominate the twentieth century? Their challenge to sexual and moral conventions is equaled only by an unflinching self-discipline that, with every new work, molds the person into a new form, a new visual felicity.

And so, once upon a time, there was a couple, Stieglitz and O'Keeffe. I assume the symbolic and professional harmony, and the mutual respect for one another's art, would be accompanied by a deep erotic complicity. The archives of the couple and Stieglitz's unpublished photos may hold some surprises for us—or not. But we can read Georgia's delicate attention, her acknowledgment of a debt toward the person who revealed her talent, and at the same time this formidable, tender, but absolute independence of mind that she demands from the start: "Stieglitz is in great form—working like a beaver. . . . His work is always a surprise to me—one feels there can be nothing more for him to do—and then he away he goes" (GOKAL letter 29, 1923, p. 173).

Does she love him because he gives her the sense of being, and the chance to be, the best, the first? Georgia has no qualms asserting this ambition . . . with the precious ability also to know how to be self-effacing:

"I like being first—if I'm noticed at all—thats why I get on so well with Stieglitz—with him I feel first—and when he is around—and there are others—he is the center and I dont count at all" (GOKAL letter 27, 1923, p. 171).

Or this: "[M]y funny little Stieglitz—He is grand—so grand that I dont seem to see family about or anything else—I just seem to think—to know—that he is the grandest thing in the world—and wonder how I ever was able to stay away from him for so long" (GOKAL letter 50, 1929, p.196). Similarly, regarding the sense he has of her work: "It is almost as tho Stieglitz makes me a present of myself in the way he feels about it" (GOKAL letter 53, 1930, p. 200). And later: "I see Alfred as an old man that I am very fond of—growing older . . . —Aside from my fondness for him personally I feel that he has been very important to something that has made my world for me—I like it that I can make him feel that I have hold of his hand to steady him as he goes on" (GOKAL letter 94, 1940, p. 244).

It is Georgia's uncompromising sensuality that is asserted in this polyvalent complicity between the two artists. Georgia likes to paint, take walks, drive her car, breathe the icy mountain air, rave about a pattern in a carpet, praise the qualities of Native Americans or Mexicans, listen to the sound of colors. Strange, this frequent translation of the visible into the audible, at the expense of words, judged inadequate—to breathe, constantly breathe, the force of life. Did a mural commissioned by Radio City make her anxious? Was she depressed? The "blues" don't last long: Georgia finds the fault lies with the wild, strange buildings of New York, "and my kind of work is maybe a bit tender for what it has to stand in this sort of world" (GOKAL letter 62, 1932, p. 207). And then she throws herself into an exploration of the world, which is to say, herself, on a trip that seems like a prayer, toward the southwest of the United States and toward regions unknown to her: she wants to crawl "far far into a dark—dark hole" (*GOKAL* letter 59, 1932, p. 205), to venture faraway and find "some thing of the outdoors" (*GOKAL* letter 61, 1932, p. 207).

A Kind of Triumphant Feeling

From now on, Georgia O'Keeffe will lead a divided existence: one part of the year in New York with Stieglitz, the other in New Mexico where she will set up house at Alcade, then Ghost Ranch, and finally at Abiquiu with Maria Chabot. "I am divided between my man and a life with him—and some thing out of doors—of your world—that is in my blood—and that I know I will never get rid of—I have to get along with my divided self the best way I can" (*GOKAL* letter 61, 1932, p. 207) There is no doubt this adventure is a wild joy she consumes with relish, like Mexican chili or raw steak: "Maybe you think me a lunatic—maybe I am one—the sort of state I find myself in is so pleasant it doesnt seem quite normally human" (*GOKAL* letter 51, 1929, p. 198). She admits having a "kind of triumphant feeling" about life, which does not preclude dark times, but that, beyond an animal-like quality the artist may have—she calls herself a "petted baby" and a "well fed cow"—still harbors some wisdom: "The vision ahead may seem a bit bleak but my feeling about life is a curious kind of triumphant feeling about—seeing it black—knowing it is so but walking into it fearlessly because one has no choice—enjoying ones consciousness—I may seem very free—a cross between a petted baby and a well fed cow—but I know a few things" (*GOKAL* letter 54, 1930, p. 201).

And this sentence, finally, against the critics who judge her as ethereal, "like some strange unearthly sort of a creature floating in the air—breathing in clouds for nourishment— . . . when the truth is that I like beef steak—and like it raw at that" (*GOKAL* letter 26, 1922, p. 171).

Georgia likes to laugh: she says words don't get through to her unless she finds them funny (*GOKAL* letter 78, 1939, p. 228), she tells several of her correspondents that they make her laugh, earnestly or ironically (*GOKAL* letters 112, 116, p. 263, 267), and sums up: "And of course I like my life" (*GOKAL* letter 117, 1961, p. 268).

How does one show proof of this limited and limitless happiness, centered on the self and shared with another, plunged in one's own feelings and diluted in the great outdoors, an increasingly strange, savage, faraway, outside world that she will try to discover, while also knowing that what is at stake is a dreamlike and sensual inner world?

The "Hand-Sewn" Word

She judges words harshly, preferring life. "Words and I are not good friends at all except with some people—when Im close to them and can feel as well as hear their response—I have to say it someway— . . . Ive been slaving on the violin—trying to make that talk—I wish I could tell you some of the things Ive wanted to say as I felt them. . . . The drawings dont count—its the life—that really counts" (*GOKAL* letter 8, 1916, p. 150).

What's worse, after six weeks of illness, confined to her bed: "It is as if I have a strange oily skin of some sort that words dont get through at the time they might disturb me—they don't seem to get through until I think them funny" (*GOKAL* letter 78, 1939, p. 228).

Yet she writes often, and her strange correspondence reveals a language manipulated like a plastic material. In place of periods, the manuscripts contain squiggles, which are reproduced as dashes in print. As if harnessing the breath of a body carving or sculpting the raw material of sentences. The syntax emerges more or less transformed: sometimes intact (in "professional" or "business" letters), sometimes broken into isolated words or fragments of clauses. Like salvos faithful to an emotion that refuses to be enchained: avoiding paragraph breaks, they remain upright, immediate, massive. The eye focuses on the emotion; the emotion is the focal point of this invisible camera organizing the experience. From now on, perspective in painting and syntax in language are useless, because they imply distance. Georgia O'Keeffe does not put herself at a distance; she is presence itself, arranged, stylized; with her, distance is internalized and seeps into the delicacy of lines or the clarity of colors when she paints. But when she uses words, the artist is almost obligated to resort to a pointillist, irregular sentence, at times blunt, at times ambiguous, to remain faithful to her immersion in the lived material.

Take, for example, this description of her carpet. She looks for her metaphors in the sonic universe, in what is felt, animal-like, and links them together in rhythmic, staccato syntagmas:

"The sound of the wind is great—but the pink roses on my rugs! And the little squares with three pink roses in each one—dark lined squares—I have half a notion to count them so you will know how many are hitting me—give me flies and mosquitoes and ticks—even fleas—every time in preference to three pink roses in a square with another rose on top of it" (GOKAL letter 13, 1916, p. 156).

She writes the way you would arrange colors on a surface or in three-dimensional space. But the seeming carelessness has nothing lax about it: as in her painting, the spontaneity is polished, carefully groomed, "hand-sewn."

"If it wasn't something that is very much in the world . . ."

Let's return to the paintings that began my acquaintance with Georgia O'Keeffe and that you see in this catalog.[7] If I have taken a detour into the context (her life, her letters), it is because the immediate simplicity of the work may leave one with the impression of decorative art or, at best, a kind of Asian spareness. Indeed, *Abstraction IX* (plate 8), *Blue Lines X* (plate 9), a fleshier variant of which is found in *Drawing V* (plate 113) and *Blue, Black and Grey* (plate 117), *Blue No. III* (plate 12), and *Blue No. IV* (plate 13), and the opulent and simultaneously ascetic curve of *Winter Road I* (plate 115) all suggest the influence of Chinese and Japanese art. Parallel to this asceticism, *Starlight Night* (plate 18), *Red Cannas* (plate 22), and *Red Canna* (plate 23) are scarcely or naively stylized watercolors, while *Grapes on White Dish—Dark Rim* (plate 36), *Plums* (plate 37), *Apple Family III* (plate 38), and *Pattern of Leaves* (plate 39) seem to go from Cézanne toward a more photographic realism. However, starting with this period, Georgia O'Keeffe begins the surprising series of *Specials* (plates 10, 11, and 46) and *Series I* (plates 29, 30, and 31) that reveal an oneiric world. Dream landscapes? Volcanic craters? The earth's rugged crust, a canyon? Or, more prosaically and intimately, the radiant membrane of the female sex, up close, enlarged, fold over fold, foliate and sensitive?

I choose this last vision—the one I prefer, the one that touches me, so to speak. And I can defend it "objectively," by referring to the watercolors of the same period entitled *Nude Series* (plates 24, 25, and 27). Here, the female torso is presented in a classical manner, externally this time, explicitly attracting the artist's gaze. Of course, we can respect the play of abstraction and admire the curves as such—pink, green, or blue funnels converging exquisitely; cream-colored semicircles floating on pink waves, split by a dark blue slit; or a melody of pink, blue, and green glistening in yellow and orange: *Pink Moon and Blue Lines* (plate 34); *Music—Pink and Blue, II* (plate 35). Contemplating the work without seeking "what it evokes": a turbulent and delicious dream of colors with no adequate translation in any language besides that of color and form, because its unique and absolute code is nothing other than this color and this form. O'Keeffe is a priestess of color.

"Color is one of the great things in this world that makes life worth living to me and as I have come to think of painting it is my effort to create an equivalent with paint color for the world—life as I see it" (GOKAL letter 55, 1950, p. 202). She rejects interpretation, by the way, and the undoubtedly excessive decodings of critics; she claims to be shocked by the sexual symbolism people think they see in her paintings and calls for simple objectivity regarding her art. It's not even abstract, she says at times; it exists "objectively" in the world. The proof? If people like her art, it's because they find elements of it in reality. As for "writings," "books," etc., on painting, they are inadequate; but one is obliged to use them to get "people" to come and see the exhibition itself.

"My work this year is very much on the ground—There will be only two abstract things—or three at the most—all the rest is objective—as objective as I can make it—He [Stieglitz] has done with the sky something similar to what I had done with color before—as he says—proving my case—He has done consciously something that I did mostly unconsciously—and it is amazing to see how he has done it out of the sky with the camera—.

I suppose the reason I got down to an effort to be objective, is that I didn't like the interpretation of my other things— . . . —I only want you to write anything you want about anything that is—You see—you are read— this part of the world is conscious of you—a book has a much better chance than a picture because of its wide circulation—so the picture has to send out the printed word to get people to come to look at it—" (GOKAL letter 30, 1924, p. 176).

"What you say about what other people will paint because of what I paint doesn't bother me at all—If it wasn't something that is very much in the world—nobody would be trying to put it down" (GOKAL letter 32, 1924, p. 179).

Yes, of course, O'Keeffe is right, and a plural reading of her visions is called for: fantasies, abstract dreams, lunar landscapes, lakes, mountains; they are all there, seen from a distance or under a magnifying glass. With a single constant: the unwavering and proud assurance of the curved, vague, and serpentine line. And the frankness of color that is displayed in and of itself, whether vivid or pastel halftone, running the gamut in the space allotted, harmonizing strangely with the layer of color alongside it. The greatest chromatic violence ends in the greatest harmony.

And yet I come back to my preferred vision, which does not seem to betray the emphasis O'Keeffe placed on the force of her sensations or her vital appetite for "rare steak." With time, the *Specials* and *Series* flourish: membranes expand into sumptuous flowers that barely hide or, if you prefer, provocatively invite examination of the slits and lips. Go back to *Flower Abstraction* (plate 44, fig. 20.1), *White Sweet Peas* (plate 50, fig. 20.3), or *Pink Sweet Peas* (plate 51, fig. 20.4). Do you see anything "special"? Is it all natural, pure, and floral? Look at *Black Iris III* (plate 49, fig. 20.2): do you see "the moist entrance to the dark valley," as a Chinese poet might say?

The Moment of Flowering

Georgia O'Keeffe is a painter of female eroticism; it is present, conspicuous, and invisible at once, in its natural and proffered appearance; no transgression, no perversion; the jouissance is permanent, a constant blossoming diluted in appeasement, neutrality, quietude. It has nothing to do with cold detachment, but simply with a neutral and internalized distance, able to wait for its moment to bloom. Passion filtered through repression. It knows how to hide and sometimes fade away. The hiding place? Shells, mussels, closed or subtly cloven, or wide open, exposing gelatinous flesh against a background of tendrils of seaweed: *Closed Clam Shell* (plate 52), *Open Clam Shell* (plate 53), *From a Shell* (plate 62), *Seaweed* (plate 63), *Tan Clam with Seaweed* (plate 64), *Clam and Mussel* (plate 65), *Slightly Open Shell* (plate 66), *The Broken Shell—Pink* (plate 91).

We could look at these closed, opaque "objects" the way we might read The Oyster or *Soap* by Francis Ponge. O'Keeffe would then appear to be a "thing-centered" visionary of still-lifes enlivened by nuance and chromatic intensity, which Ponge did through wordplay. Or perhaps the more explicitly ecstatic, implicitly erotic context of the American woman/artist invites us to rediscover the discreet passion concealed in the polished pebbles of the very pagan Ponge.

After a descent into feminine viscosity, let's return to the surface of flowers, to look at the milky white lilies of *Lily—White with Black* (plate 68), *Two Calla Lillies on Pink* (plate 70)—the scarlet corollas of *Red Poppy* (plate 69)—the satiny petals against the blood-red background of *Red Hills and*

White Flower (plate 96)—or the yellow green fringes, in creamy gray—*An Orchid* (plate 97).

You see flowers, simply flowers, but after our undersea voyage they may seem less external, less decorative. Do you see the white turn iridescent, sensual, nuanced, the red burst forth from orange into garnet; the loud, exciting shades of an intimate jouissance—visual, certainly, but also sonic and tactile?

Imagine these flowers as internal bodies, the sensitive, inward blossoming of the ecstatic young woman Alfred Stieglitz photographed: "Georgia O'Keeffe—After Return from New Mexico" (1929).

Yet a paradise like this has its purgatory, and naturally it must remain sublime. First there is blackness: the membranes and holes darken in *Jack-in-the-Pulpit No. IV* (plate 80), red folds become wine dark in *Jack-in-the-Pulpit No. V* (plate 81). Finally, a brush with death, real or imagined, leaves Georgia O'Keeffe with a smooth mark. The dry whiteness of bones, especially when embellished with grayish pink, turns death into eternity and avoids decomposition, just as the flowers, offered and opulent, avoid pornography in full sensual light.

The voluptuous membranes, the abundance of petals, the slightly open shells of the beginning yield to the cracked skulls of cows or horses and other bovine bones: *Cow's Skull with Calico Roses* (plate 75), *Horse's Skull with White Rose* (plate 82), and so on. Adorned with artificial flowers, these surrealist visions are nothing more or less than a mockery of death wedded to celebration: they neutralize the horror of the former and the splendor of the latter and imply the (serene or sinister?) permanence of artifice. And art.

When they take the form of jawbones with massive teeth topped by a luminous egg (or gland)—*Red and Pink Rocks and Teeth* (plate 95)—we remember the artist's appetite for life: an oral Eros dominates the still-life. Likewise, the series of red or gray Hills (plates 86 and 100) assume the aspect of a living fabric, a mons veneris filled with blood and fluids rather than a mineral conglomerate.

A Sculptural Quietism

Antonin Artaud went to Mexico to find new horizons, through peyote, for his Theater of Cruelty. Georgia O'Keeffe seems to find a sculptural and quietist taming of death: without the tragic element, ordinary and inevitable, but also irradiated with a wild jouissance. As proof, the face of this strange old woman, weathered by the sun and wind, sculpted, looking at us with distant irony in her later photographs from the 1980s.

Skulls and bones are Georgia O'Keeffe's sculpture. They show death as anatomical as well as embellished, present, implacable, and . . . nonexistent. The bones emerge under her brush as an ethnological exploration among Native Americans, "remarkable people," and as a challenge to the extenuation of modern art. Not morbid reflection, but the assurance of venturing into the unknown and into a time that unfolds against the grain, incommensurable: "I brought home a lot of bones—cows head—a horses head—and what not—and painted them with artificial flowers—a new way of trying to define my feeling about that country—and they seem to think that painting bones is news—News quite apart from Art News—It makes me feel like crawling far far into a dark—dark hole and staying there a long time" (*GOKAL* letter 59, 1932, p. 205).

The skulls and bones do in fact transform time into a monument: nothing slips away, everything endures, life and death are calcified in the artifice of a calm, unusual vision. Georgia O'Keeffe thought that time and painting were incompatible, that painting was timeless (see *GOKAL* letter 64, 1932, p. 212).

Only Hans Holbein the Younger, in the pictorial tradition, was able to keep his distance from death, and even to make light of it in solitude, without compassion. We remember his *Dead Christ*, with no access to the Resurrection, his *Danses macabres* that made all of Europe laugh as it reemerged from the specter of Thanatos.

But you probably had to be a modern woman to decide that the sparest and most final image of death was the pelvic bone: this basin at the bottom of the spine that houses the lower abdomen and the sexual organs, and that, deprived of flesh, is nothing but a coarse ring—the void itself. No more flowers in place of the genitals, but a simple, bony hole that lets in the blue of the sky and a dazzling sun. The Pelvis series (plates 99, 102, 103, and 106), and the "horns" that accompany it, recall the Taoist representation of the sky, the Pi, a circle of jade with a hole, symbol of male emptiness.

Stieglitz dies of a heart attack in 1946. That year Georgia O'Keeffe paints *A Black Bird with Snow-Covered Red Hills*: there is no red, obviously, just a frozen white hollow, an icy basin flown over by a serpentine blackness. Georgia is fifty-nine.

The term *death* is too dramatic in our culture to refer to the luminous serenity that emanates from a dead pelvic region painted by Georgia

O'Keeffe. For a woman who had no children and from whom we get the sense all her creative passion went directly into giving birth to colorful forms, this celebration of a pelvic ossuary is a new triumph over the anxiety of death, the ultimate affirmation of a happiness entirely absorbed in aesthetic accomplishment. "And of course I like my life," she writes. Read: to the point of death, which I transform into aesthetic eternity.

Later works depicting *Sky Above Clouds* (plates 118, 119, and 120)—more metaphors of the beyond—are quite simply accumulations of pelvic bones over the azure (plates 102 and 103), with an inversion of the blue and white. From now on, play has subsided, abstraction dominates, the geometry is perfect. Georgia O'Keeffe visits the beautiful sites of the world, goes to France. Naturally, logically, she marvels at the stained-glass windows of Chartres, is astonished by Sainte-Chapelle—"I never imagined anything like it"—and admires the Chinese bronzes at Musée Guimet, a Fra Angelico at the Louvre, and "an astonishing portrait of some French king [this is the native of Wisconsin speaking]—I will look for him again too" (GOKAL letter 112, 1953, p. 264).

O'Keeffe attained absolute form: intense but spare, convincing, ineluctable. Lucid and still eager to see, she continued to stylize, master, and be present before retiring in serenity and passing away in 1986 at ninety-nine. Decorative? She presents us with the decor of her tamed passion. Aren't the paths of internal experience unforeseeable? We can only try to gain access to them through contemplation.

21

A STRANGER

Can we really love—what we call love—Duras? I am intoxicated by her, but as I prefer the pain of clarity to the malady of alcohol, I frequent her novels with the symbiotic and cautious ambivalence induced in me by the most catastrophic patients. I have known more than one patient (both male and female) who let themselves become enchanted by their love of death, to the point of suicide. She did not mind when I used the word *sorcery* to refer to her complicity with the ravages of maternal hatred, with the ennui that takes the place of desire in the depressive, with this "nothing" that shimmers between two women, that ties them to each other in an umbilical way and floods the basement of endogenous female homosexuality. While Duras's groupies have reproached me for not recognizing her virtuosity as an artist, she saw my diagnosis as an homage.[1] Of course, she couldn't care less if her art was capable of catharsis or not, since what she wanted was precisely to contaminate the reader with her passion to the death, her passion for death. What did it matter if she was taken for a nihilist, a collaborator, a communist, if we let ourselves be carried away on the floodtide of her sadness, fomented in the remote precincts of a mythic Indochina, when not in the French countryside with a crazy mother, necessarily infanticidal and necessarily sublime? "Collaborators, the Fernandezes were. And I, two years after the war, I was a member of the French Communist party. The parallel is complete and absolute. The two things are the same, the same pity, the same call for help, the same lack of judgment, the same superstition if you like, that consists in believing in a political solution to the personal problem."[2] The history of our century passed through her pages, leaving only a ravaged intimacy. Is the source of suffering familial or historical? It doesn't matter, my general, both if you like, provided one can write and make it universal, better, contagious. It's a way of living, surviving, perhaps even washing away a political culpability. But is it literature? And what is literature? No one asks that anymore.

Deep down, we did not have the same sadness or the same history or the same loves—on the contrary. But we had a savage complicity, because we were both consumed by pain that did not fit with French rhetoric. Hervé Sinteuil, Duras's companion during the war, told me one day on the beach at Conch-en-Ré: "There is some of Duras in your writing." I'm not sure it was a compliment. Melancholia is not French, I know, but I learned that at my expense when I wrote *The Old Man and the Wolves*, a novel about mourning a father and various other extravagant injuries.[3] Duras was the only one to read me with the vague but inevitable friendship that unites translators: because within the same language they speak another language. To transplant the sensible time of a foreign country—childhood, passion, other people, other expressions—into the host language amounts to a transubstantiation of the suffering that connects exile, translation, and writing in a single fate.

If this is where you find yourself, the only thing that will give you a sense of a psychic life—which, true to its name, is what keeps you alive—is your own perception of the loss of self. Nothing but a language that can be translated/destroyed endlessly, drunk and spit out in the sincerity of dispossession—of uprooting.

Freud thought that mourning and melancholia bore the shadow of the "lost object"—whether it was a lover, a job, your dignity, this loss was fundamentally that of the mother. Duras's translucent heroines bear the shadow of passion. This is her discovery, this is her contribution to be added to the handbooks of the new maladies of the soul. The Durasians mourn passion. The "object" is not yet constituted or else it disintegrates; the two protagonists are drawn to each other and reject one another with merciless force, as implacable and absolute as the plenitude of Being. What if the wise men of Antiquity, who trained their inner eye on a wordless enigma, scrutinized this unnamable passion—rather than the calm dissipation of serenity? The survivors of Nevers, Hiroshima, Calcutta, or a dance hall on the edges of a desiccated sea testify only to this: well before *desire* and its sadomasochistic accidents, in a different way, *passion* is an alchemy of binding and unbinding that preserves nothing of our hypothetical identities. *Passion is our madness.* We are not all psychotic, but we can all be crazy. Crazy for one another (men and women, women and women, men and men), because we are crazy for our crazy mothers. The psychical pain of depressives is the impossibility of communicating this passion, this madness: one can neither express it nor insert it into social ties. This passion casts the rays of a black sun over our appearance as speaking (and supposedly erotic) beings—the fleeting reflection of a love involving no one on the borders of biological excitability. You can't do anything about it. Or . . . perhaps you can . . . after all in the best of cases . . . at your own risk and peril: you can try to write. This attempt, a matter of courage as much as vanity, manages to turn depression into exaltation—another more pleasant, more indulgent reflection of passion. A little more courage and writing becomes your new passion: in a different way, no less destructive than the first, but the only bearable one—you live to make it contagious.

Some use this transubstantiation as a Band-Aid: their secret is walled up, no horror, "the writer must not create sorrow in her books," suffering is refined into nothingness, erudition, beauty. Psychoanalysts believe denial leads to this one perversion: denial of ill-being sustains beautiful style. And publishing houses.

Others, on the contrary, surgeons of abjection or psychiatrists of borderline states, cultivate a loyalty to malaise. They enjoy holding their crisis close while upsetting the harmony of belles lettres and revealing their proximity to pathology. Duras is one of those traitors. Psychoanalysts are not the only ones to think the truth cannot be *entirely* said. It can be said by destroying—destroying itself, destroying literature. Out of a thirst for truth: "Destroy, she said."

The autochthon will always find this foreignness of questionable taste, as long as he indulges in a complicity with his own (usually hidden) madness.

Let's suppose the issue today were human madness. Duras thought so. She also thought there was nothing beautiful about it, but that it was communicable. And profitable. She invented an aesthetics of awkwardness: an elongated sentence, without sonic grace, whose verb seemed to forget the subject; last-minute additions tacked on to a rhythm that was not expect-

ing them; scholarly terms or superlatives bordering on platitudes; grandilo-
quence as first aid. Our so-called speaker does not write spoken discourse
but rather speech that is overdone as a result of being undone: the way one
might be undressed, or unmadeup, not out of negligence but as the result of
an insurmountable yet pleasure-filled ailment. What is she suffering from?

The sorcerer is a fearsome clinician. Let's take a look at her discoveries.

To start with, the Durasian woman is woman-as-sadness.

"How does a woman go about things?" asks the Vice-Consul.

The Secretary guffaws.

. . .

"I should play on her sadness," says the Vice-Consul, "if I got the chance."[4]

Tears are her eroticism, a faded, frigid secretion. "I cry for no reason
that I can explain. It's as though I were shot through with grief. Someone
has to weep, and I seem to be the one."[5] The ecstatic or morbid passion is
outside time and outside the self, impersonal: "Is it because of her tears that
she is lost to him?"[6]

The domain of this absolute lover is ennui, which cannot be shared.
Ennui, a desert without question, a ravishing without pleasure. "The only
times she did speak was to say how impossible it was for her to express how
boring and long it was, how interminable it was, to be Lol Stein. . . . Was she
thinking of something, of herself? they asked her. She didn't understand
the question . . . the infinite weariness of being unable to escape from the
state she was in was not something that had to be thought about."[7]

The astonishing precision of these "vignettes" nestled within Duras's
novels, in the hollow of melancholia, reveal the enigmatic presence of a
mother *without an image*. Barrage or torrent, this genetrix does not reflect
but is content to shatter the mirror, along with her daughter's reflection.
"There, suddenly, close to me, was someone sitting in my mother's place
who wasn't my mother . . . that identity irreplaceable by any other had disappeared and I was powerless to make it come back, make it start to come
back. *There was no longer anything there to inhabit her image.* I went mad in full possession of my senses."[8]

We cannot measure the cruelty of this absence in full presence, this
orphan in the glare of passion. The only thing left for a girl to do whose
mother has deprived her of an image is to try to inhabit this uninhabited
image, this mirage of original rootlessness, through a new, intensified cru-

elty: through vengeance. Hatred is the salvation of the melancholic, which leads to . . . writing. Hatred, the source of a silence that marks speech and transforms it into style, but also the source of the impossibility of writing. "She ought to be locked up, beaten, killed."[9] And: "I think I wrote about our love for our mother . . . the area on whose brink silence begins. What happens there is silence, the slow travail of my whole life."[10] Love and hate, hate and love: is hate the carrier wave of love? The writer imagines this and is perhaps the only one able to say so. "You think you weep because you can't love. You weep because you can't impose death."[11]

Here the opacity of Being is revealed not in the stillness of philosophers but in the omnipotence of an original unbinding: the attraction and rejection that bind mother and daughter, of which Duras made herself the somnambulistic explorer. More enigmatic, however, than the pleasure of destruction, Durasian suffering resides in the inability to write. "How strongly sometimes one feels one mustn't write," Max Thor says in *Destroy, She Said*, Max Thor and Stein being the two Jews eternally on the verge of writing.[12] Phallic impotence, if there ever was, which the woman-as-sadness deplores. However, unlike so many graphomaniacs who erect writing-as-a-prosthesis against the hatred and emptiness not recognized within but whose plot is repeated externally, Duras's texts do not wrest themselves from suffering but distill it into destruction, into a rage that is able "to fell trees, knock down walls," before fading into "sublime gentleness" and "pure laughter."[13]

The men in this adventure are foreigners: the Chinese man in *The Lover*, the Japanese man in *Hiroshima Mon Amour*, and the whole series of wandering Jews or diplomats. Foreigners, like the foreigner she is, closest to the unsettling strangeness at the depths of things. Desire, which is central, belongs to men, but it is always brimming with the strained, insidious passiveness of women. Sensual and abstract at once, the men are gnawed by a fear that their passion will never dominate. This panic is like an edge, axis, or reprise of the play of mirrors that allows women to display the flesh of suffering, for which their men are merely skeletons.

The end of the twentieth century—a lousy time for literature! Wars and crises, the "psychological" dissection of one's innermost depths, and philosophy's progress all revealed the subtle dramas of our adventures with meaning, and beautiful language returned to its role as amusing sketch or gratifying virtuosity. Caught between the drug of images and the demand for truth induced by psychoanalysis, when not corrupted by the reconstruction of defenses, literature becomes the rival—so often superior!—of the clinic. Before (even in *The Lover*'s erotic exoticism), Duras's novels were barely reconstructed self-analytical accounts in an uncertain, dreamlike narrative framework. Those who read them from the outside will see only the madness. Unless literature has another vocation: to expose madness in the light of reason. Neither understanding it nor concealing it, but simply denuding its "immense pain," without complaint, "as if singing."[14] "I went mad in full possession of my senses."[15]

The novel as madness in full possession of one's senses? This apocalypse, foreign to literature, is certainly not made to be loved. It is just there to keep us alert for the time that remains.

22

WRITING AS STRANGENESS AND JOUISSANCE

If it is true that only *great men* deserve to have exhibitions devoted to them by posterity, I can hear Roland Barthes laughing from here. Not a hearty laugh à la Rabelais or a sardonic laugh à la Foucault, but a smooth laugh that excuses itself for passing the throat, after having troubled the lungs, half-way between the compassion that believers in greatness deserve, according to him, and the regret of "not being among them." Because Roland was one of those rare cases, perhaps the only person I have known, who cultivated no faith, while also believing in the existence of what is at the basis of all cults, namely, love. That "the rose is without why" captivated him,[1] yet he still attempted to look objectively at its petals and delight in its fragrance without becoming intoxicated by it.

Of this human, too human, inversion of religion that is the romantic link between two people, he made an object of writing: not an altar of adoration to which literary ladies, whom he liked to make fun of, devoted their time, but a permanent inquiry into what, in love, had to do with discourse, and ended up being the higher side of dreaming. To take himself for one of "those men that other men call great" (a phrase of Colette's, from whom he practically borrowed the title of his last book) would have seemed ridiculous to him.[2] In the sense that it is ridiculous to posit oneself as the lover as well as the beloved in the lover's discourse: a ridiculousness that is lethal, but whose sentimental, erotic, and rhetorical components Roland Barthes enjoyed tracing, writing about, and analyzing. The inevitable pitfalls, inexorable vulgarities, and hyperboles that exalt and confound us—a lifetime or what we believe is essential about it. But what is essential? Here we are at the core of language and meaning once again, a semiological question if there ever was one. Let's go ahead and celebrate another great man with an exhibition—that goes without saying—but in a way that is closer to his ironic lover's discourse and his muted laugh.

He is what I remember most from what we called his "teaching": a sarcastic complicity that respected and defied his topics at once so as to deflect them more effectively and digress in some innocent detour—neither austere scholar nor venerated writer, neither authority nor innocent, just inquiry, always open, formulated as perfectly as possible, into the music of meaning and its impossibility. From "semiology," which he took out of the university, enraging the papers, to the Balzac of S/Z, from Sade to Loyola, from the reclusive French language of the provinces to the most aggressive utopian modernity, Roland Barthes sounded out everything he approached and made texts out of these things, restoring, then transforming their flavor—well before any "deconstruction" and in a completely different way—simply to approach them in his own modernity: in his modesty as a modern, making his way down paths leading nowhere, and in which we recognize our own, vaguely, inevitably, simply. Barthes, sophisticated, accessible.

That sort of teaching, if that's what it was, honored the student and elevated him to the dignity of a copresence in the thinking of the teacher, who, as a result, ceased to be a master thinker or, on the contrary, went far beyond one. As I have already had occasion to note, Roland Barthes was—and still is, as far as I know—the only professor and writer who *read* his students and readers. Read: not to see how he was admired as a professor or writer, but to discover the student or reader in his/her irreducible strangeness. This was the very thing Roland Barthes prided himself on—and praised in others—and that he greeted as another, indispensable, threshold on his own path.

That was how his text "L'étrangère" seemed to me when I read it, on a plane that was taking me far away from everything, submerged in one of those solitary states that will either make you sick or make you dispassionate.[3] Roland Barthes's writing opened the latter direction to me. No one has sketched a more accurate portrait of my work: Roland Barthes was able to point out my flaws and turn them into the promise of a merciless analysis of myself, language, and others (which he nicely termed "the French family"), fixed in an endogamous, irremediably closed passion. By detecting a fertile "strangeness" in my youthful alacrity, he gave me the gift of originality that I was not at all striving for. And, beyond that, he opened the jealously guarded Temple of French Letters and its signs to the sort of decompartmentalization that is only beginning, and whose good taste will always be disrupted by immigrants from Russia, India, or China, with the risk of conflict, but also with the chance of bringing the spirit of the Hexagon into the third millennium. I took this short text not as a love letter, as some have seen it, but as an encounter: in the sense of the impossibility that aureoles an idea when it inhabits you unconsciously and only reveals itself through the aptness of another word that recognizes you and then waits for you, ahead of you, at a distance from you. Ahead of me, ahead of Roland himself, and without him, to be constructed endlessly. My strangeness, in Roland Barthes's sense, was certainly in me, but it was his writing that crystallized the idea of my exclusion, as well as the contentment to be had in the detached, remote, testimonial thinking I tried to put together in my dorm room.

For him, it was perhaps the chance for a lexical find: the terms *stranger* or *strangeness*, which he had not used much before, became a favorite way of referring to himself, as he would do indirectly in *Roland Barthes by Roland Barthes* (1975) and just as indirectly in *The Pleasure of the Text* (1973).

I am lingering over these personal memories, because they seem open to a constant of Barthes's experience: his conviction that writing is strangeness, because it is jouissance, and jouissance insofar as it is strangeness.

Roland scandalized the guardians of Literature so much that they reproached him, as well as *Tel Quel*, for destroying literature when he defined *writing* not as *style* (Sacrilege! What would be left of Man without Style?) but as a *testament of exclusion*. It was not a matter of complaining that the person who writes is excluded from a milieu—the bitterness of this situation is always good for a laugh, at least since the Verdurin clan that so amused Marcel Proust, and today the Republic of Letters continues to cultivate that ancestral poison. Roland Barthes received attention, much more radically, for what he considered a "final alienation: that of his language. . . . He [R. B.] felt more than excluded: *detached*, forever assigned the place of the *witness*."[4]

Yet this later observation applies to his body of work from the start. *My-thologies* was nothing other than the fruit of this witnessing by a "detached" person, who sees France, for example, with its *steak-frites* and *abbé Pierre* from a "distance": observing it with tenderness and ultimately and very gently devaluing it, its national prejudices raised by analysis to the level of this ridiculous *noblesse*, which the author, in this case, calls an ideology, myths unbeknownst to themselves. The semiological adventure itself was just the invention of *another language* to create this distance from the jinx of the proper, beginning with the amorous fascination inflicted on us by the mother tongue, the national rhetoric learned at home and at school, and the official literature itself, once academic, today media friendly.

This Frenchman from the Southwest who practiced no other language—with the exception of the music he played on the piano and the painting he tried his hand at—asked himself, in his sedentary retirement, the question of Ulysses the navigator: how can one not be an autochton? Is it possible not to be one? Appropriating the code of semiology others practiced as established scholars, he used it to extract his own invention, his inimitable, semiological idiolect, which a few narrow-minded epigones tried unsuccessfully to reduce to dogma for several decades. As for Roland Barthes, he sought to "estrange himself," as Berthold Brecht said, something our impromptu semiologist was more than familiar with: to witness, with detachment, the adventures of meaning as they unfold, unbeknownst to us, in the French language and in everyday myths.

Was this witnessing a martyrdom? Not necessarily. A discipline, to be sure, with a good deal of inventiveness and detail, which is to say, finesse, and irony regarding the target (French, this text, this myth) as well as the tools (semiology itself, with its parataxis, intertext, and signifiers). Because he knew in the remotest depths of the French provinces from which he came, and which all of France now reluctantly understands, seized as it is by the challenge of the globalization underway, that *writing*—as he saw it, reading those who had risked everything (Sade, Fourier, Loyola)—was the only worthwhile upheaval, and he generously associated me with it. Because there is a *ménage*, which is the "stubborn refusal of another language," where the need to be native is rooted, and that some, he and I ("cavalier," "rickety," "offensive"), do not share. Because, unlike the natives, we had to invent writing as "another language": a "theory," in appearance; in truth a language, quite simply, "that speaks of a politically and ideologically inhabitable place."⁵ However unacceptable it might appear to some, for Roland Barthes, theoretical thought that changes the familiar point of view and the most audacious intimate writing are joined precisely in this place where he situated himself. Some, to this day, continue to disdain him as apolitical. Whereas, on the contrary, he suggests a radicality of the inhabitable that is demanding in other ways: is it ethical? Spiritual? Sexual? Nameless? Inhabitable.

This sort of witnessing, written in *an other language*, is not a martyrdom, because it is a jouissance. To write for one's own pleasure would just be masturbatory. On the other hand, an other language consists of creating a mobile space where the reader, the other, is not seduced in a trivial way (Roland Barthes writes: "cruised") but invited to take part in the possibility of improvisation: he enters the game, plays his own game, the game exists for several people.

"If I read this sentence, this story, or this word with pleasure, it is because they were written in pleasure (such pleasure does not contradict the writer's complaints). But the opposite? Does writing in pleasure guarantee—guaranteeme, the writer—my reader's pleasure? Not at all. I must seek out this reader (must 'cruise' him) *without knowing where he is*. A site of bliss is then created. It is not the reader's 'person' that is necessary to me, it is this site: the possibility of a dialectics of desire, of an unpredictability of bliss: the bets are not placed, there can still be a game."⁶

Roland Barthes was in some ways the Winnicott of French criticism: he invented critical discourse as a "transitional object," that is, as a space of indecision—a creation between author, critic, and reader. Who is the father, who is the mother, who is the child in this space of open possibilities? There is no answer, the lack of an answer is part of the game; check your identities (including your sexual identity) at the door and go see for yourself.

Have I been too quick to say that intellectual, theoretical work is a jouissance? You don't believe me, I can feel it. "Public opinion does not like the language of intellectuals. Hence he has often been dismissed by an accusation of intellectualist jargon. And hence he felt himself to be the object of a kind of racism: they excluded his language, i.e., his body. . . . A petit-bourgeois view which construes the intellectual, *on account of his language*, as a desexualized, i.e., devirilized, being: anti-intellectualism reveals itself as a protest of virility."⁷

Parenthetically: how is anti-intellectualism of this type revealed, when attacking the language of a female intellectual in this racial manner? As an

exhortation to pathetic confession? Romantic hysteria? Bovaryian senti-
mentality? Let's close this parenthesis.

Abstraction, when you are in the midst of it and have made another language of it, is "in no way contrary to sensuality." Barthes feels a "flush of
pleasure" in it; "he always associated intellectual activity with delight: the
panorama, for example—what one sees from the Eiffel Tower—is an object
at once intellective and rapturous: it liberates the body even as it gives the
illusion of 'comprehending' the field of vision."[8]

You are there: before a landscape that expands as far as the eye can
see—what one sees from the Eiffel Tower. You find the "concept," which is
a new idea conveyed by an unknown word. It's a *panorama,* you say. You are
seized by this foreign word, in the sign of another language. *Panorama* then
becomes "an object at once intellective and rapturous." Why? Because it
"liberates the body even as it gives the illusion of 'comprehending.'"

Comprehending is no doubt an illusion, like the lover's discourse itself.
Yet comprehending is formulating something in another language that detaches you from your sensible immersion, without separating you from it—
simply giving meaning to your pleasure or euphoria, a temporary, modest
meaning, but one that is more intense than the sensible vibrations to which
the other language still adheres and from which it is nevertheless detached.

The joy of Barthes is in the modesty of this temporariness that does not
leave the field of vision but, by protecting us from dazzle, gives us the gift of
seeing in total lucidity. Perhaps in these somber times of ours this apparent
minimalism of *the pleasure of thinking* is the only enlightened visibility (at the
antipodes of spectacular hallucinations) and the most serene jouissance (in
counterpoint to raucous transgressions) left for us to share.

PART 6

WRITING

23

THE "TRUE-LIE," OUR UNASSAILABLE CONTEMPORARY

When I learned French reading *Aurelien* and *Holy Week,* I never imagined I would speak to you one day about Aragon—about his gorgeousness and lies—in an era when Europe, freed of its iron curtain, would be integrating its former communist countries.

Needless to say, a figure as singular as Louis Aragon, the multifaceted writer, should not be confused with the exaltations or abjections of an ideology. As for psychoanalysis, as attentive as it might be to the alchemy of the imaginary, it alone cannot interpret a human adventure in which familial destiny, national memory, and global history cross paths. I thank Daniel Bougnoux for his affable confidence and his excellent works,[1] which have often guided me in my reflections, and I am pleased to accept his invitation to speak to you of the writer and the man, with an inquiry into the *origins.* It is to the impasses of *revolt,* however, that this inquiry will lead me. Because the essential themes of his engagement and work—while specific to Aragon the individual and his incommensurable singularity—may also illuminate the dramas of the twentieth century, caught between the most extravagant demand for freedom and the most massive oppression of this same freedom human beings have ever known. And beyond the communist adventure, the "true-lie"[2]—formulated and practiced by the man who was *fou d'Elsa* (crazy about Elsa)—assumes a new aspect today, made common by the media and exploited by religious fundamentalisms and their suicidal conflicts. Is the "true-lie" our unassailable contemporary?

I could have outlined the psychopathology of a born impostor, fatherless and motherless and destined from the cradle for masquerade and the "false self": a lover of women to the point of wanting to kill himself for one, who believed he survived because of another woman's beautiful eyes, who claimed to experience pleasure and to write the way he imagined women did, to the point of considering himself female before dying; a lover of men to the point of acclaiming the power of a dictator, serving him, using him; yet also capable of mocking these varieties of lust as well as their certainties, services, and roles—every role, every power.

The "case of Aragon" demands much more, however. Beyond the psychopathology he sets in motion, the writer calls on the brilliance of the French language, where he finds his true family, his *alter ego*. The mores of the Third Republic, which he detested, are his patent genitors. And in the political history of totalitarianism, the head of *Les Lettres françaises* would create his imaginary, untouchable traitor. Which is to say, to be Aragonian, the drama of the "true-lie" is the drama of the French imaginary as well as of communism. Fortuitous convergences? Or inevitable complicity? Let's go back to the "origins" and look at two books: *La Défense de l'infini* (1923–1927), part of which was set on fire in 1927, and *Blanche ou l'oubli* (1967).[3]

At the Familial Origins of the "True-Lie"

"I know of nothing more cruel in this lowly world than decisive optimists. They are obnoxiously spiteful people, and you'd swear they'd made it their mission to impose a blind reign of folly [Is he talking about himself?]. *I believe in the power of sorrow, injury, and despair. . . . I have wasted my life and that's all.*"[4]

In the man who treads the red carpets of Stalinist palaces, in the pen that signs the ukases of the PCF (the French Communist Party), in the compromises and flashes of brilliance of the poet, I see—I hear—the "sorrow, injury, and despair" of Louis the child. Who is he? How many are there?

Aragon was born on October 3, 1897, and died on December 24, 1982. We know about his mother, Marguerite Toucas, who was unmarried; her sisters, Marie and Madeleine; and their mother, née Massillon: the writer often refers to this maternal configuration formed by the grandmother and her three daughters in his (very gap-filled and guarded) autobiographical notes. A tribe of women of illustrious ancestry, an absent, globe-trotting grandfather, and a single concrete man, Uncle Edmond, the brother of the three sisters, scarcely present. Not only did Marguerite conceal the fact that she was expecting a child, she even pretended not to have conceived him. The newborn vanished for thirteen months, sent to a wet nurse in Brittany. He was not supposed to have been born in the Toucas-Massillon family, so when he meets his mother, he is passed off as her younger brother, and his grandmother is presented as the mother. Aragon's childhood, at once sheltered and dramatic, is subjected to the "true-lie" from the start. A poem entitled "Le Mot" (The Word) published during the Second World War after his mother's death, in a collection of texts on the Resistance (1942), evokes for the one and only time, as far as I know, a lyrical and shattering image of this mother, immediately associated with the uncertain birth of speech ("the word") on the verge of the "lie": "Le mot n'a pas franchi mes lèvres / Le mot n'a pas touché son coeur / Est-ce un lait dont la mort nous sèvre / Est-ce un drogue, une liqueur / Jamais je ne l'ai dit qu'en songe / Ce lourd secret pèse entre nous / Et tu me vouais au mensonge / À tes genoux / Nous le portions comme une honte / Quand mes yeux n'étaient pas ouverts / . . . / Te nommer ma soeur me désarme / Que si j'ai feint c'est pour toi seule / Jusqu'à la fin fait l'innocent / Pour toi seule jusqu'au linceul / Caché mon sang / J'irai jusqu'au bout de mes torts / J'avais naissant le tort de vivre . . ."[5]

> The word did not pass my lips
> The word did not touch her heart
> Is it a milk death weans us from
> Is it a drug, an alcohol
> I said it only in my dreams
> This heavy secret weighs between us
> You swore me to concealment
> At your knees
> We bore it as shame
> When my eyes were not open . . .
> To call you my sister disarms me
> If I feigned it was for you alone
> To the end played innocent
> For you alone until the shroud

Hid my blood
I will see my mistakes through to the end
Born, my mistake was living.

The mother of the poet was the great unspeakable that continued to haunt the virtuoso of French rhythm. But his nostalgic chateau hid another mystery: the invisible father (presented as a godfather or tutor) who, in the few memories of him, was brusque with Marguerite Toucas-Massillon and rarely crossed paths with the child. In *Souvenirs d'un préfet de police* (Memoirs of a Police Prefect), the memoirs of Louis Andrieux, he reveals himself.[6] Andrieux (1840–1931) became the chief of police of Paris after the fall of Napoléon III and conceived his biological son, also named Louis, at the age of fifty-seven. The whirlwinds of the Third Republic, known as "les Jules,"[7] come to life in the father's memoirs, and in his writings we savor the militant anticlericalism that characterized it, along with the administrative fragility and the omnipresent masonry that Andrieux takes part in and disdains. Grandiloquent, solemn, Aragon *père*, or rather, Louis Andrieux, represses the insurrection of communards from Lyons in 1871, aggressively pursues Bakunin himself, and infiltrates the anarchists around Louise Michel. Cynical? Certainly. Boring? Never. At eighty-seven, while his son is in the thick of surrealism (this is 1927), Mr. Andrieux continues to publish and learn, and even to defend theses on Alphonse Rabbe and Gassendi, resulting in a Ph.D.! And, two years before his death, he publishes an essay devoted to Madame du Châtelet, Voltaire's friend. We might ask which of them, father or son, was the surrealist!

This strange lineage—the musketeer dandy, author of *Paris Peasant* and *Treatise on Style*, traced back to a police prefect with "gusto" who embodied bourgeois France to perfection—has a certain beauty in the end. Beauty in the sense of Lautréamont, who was a precursor and constant source of inspiration for the surrealists and to whom we owe the famous phrase: "Beauty is the fortuitous encounter between a sewing machine and an umbrella upon a dissecting table." Indeed, there is a chasm between the two characters, Louis Andrieux and Louis Aragon, and yet an encounter, if we look at their respective styles as a place and its flipside, only accessible to a true spirit of dissection, after all, a suitable approach to both father and son. From the "Jules" of the Third Republic to the "little father of the people" that Stalin was; from libertine and puritan France to the dictatorship of the proletariat; from decadent rhetoric filled with Latin quotations to *La Défense*

de l'infini and back again—the road is not the shortest. But there is one, tor-
turous and brilliant, if you follow it in automatic writing, and if you break it
open in the end in an explosion, as Aragon did. A century is revealed there,
grandiose and comic, still concealing the complicity of adversaries and the
fascination exerted on us by fathers and sons, poets and cops.

It is the early1920s: "At every moment, I betray myself, I fail to keep my
own word, I contradict myself. I am not the person in whom I would place
my confidence." This is from Aragon's "Révélations sensationnelles" in the
review *Littérature*.[8] There was the First World War, mobilization, disaster.
Aragon, a medical auxiliary, meets Breton at Val-de-Grâce, becomes friends
with future members of the surrealist group, establishes the Dadaist group.
In March 1919 he signs a secret pact with Breton, filled with nihilist rage:
"The one who renounces, ruin him, discredit him, by any means necessary.
There is only one morality at this level of 'incapability': that of bandits. A
law that does not tolerate the slightest weakness, which is in the refusal of
the written law. . . . We will shatter the others. Until the day it is necessary
for us to go even further, one or the other will abandon one or the other in
turn. [Rupture is already on the agenda.] To know that the other will run
you down. To know. Therein lies the condition for action."[9]

It is in this context of the rejection of the "written law"—of social, familial, and national norms—that the first writings will appear: *Feu de joie* (1919),
an attempt to reconstruct the self through the imaginary character of Jean-
Baptiste A. (A. as in Andrieux, as in Aragon); *Anicet ou le Panorama* (1921),
an ironic chronicle of an apprenticeship of revolt in a group of conspirators
the artist opposes; *Les Aventures de Télémaque* (The Adventures of Telemachus,
1922), a dialogue between the Dadaist project and Fénélon's *Telemachus*, in
which paradoxical feelings emerge, not coded by classical psychology; *Le
Libertinage* (The Libertine, 1922), which presents itself as a debate with another text, a mask, a critical imitation with a strong mimetic element and
an effect of subtle detachment—Aragon makes his way through the dedi-
catees, mimicking them, and distancing himself from them; and *Le Paysan de
Paris* (Paris Peasant, 1924–26), which explores the city, the night, the feminine, and "the marvelous."

Aragon's writing in its nascent state is attuned to personal joys and anxieties, while also responding to the revolts of a generation shaken by the First
World War, the disaster of Verdun, and the economic and political crisis.
But instead of settling into social protest or naturalist narrative, Aragon
and his friends take the path of what I have called *a-thought*: with a privative

"a." Taking their cues from Rimbaud and Lautréamont, they reject "action [which] is not the sister of the dream" (Baudelaire), while freeing thought from the constraints of action and judgment. The rigid forms of bourgeois civilization are execrated, but, beyond the social order, a "metaphysical" revolt is being outlined: "My business is metaphysics"—this is *Paris Peasant's* profession of faith. By attacking not only *homo faber*, and the practical activity of workers always already on the path to robotization, but just as violently attacking conventional art itself: "These days there are several individuals prowling over the world for whom art, for example, has ceased to be an end in itself."[10] It is a matter of pursuing thought—unconscious desire and intransigent destructivity—that escapes toward the sensory, disavows the literary experience itself as amoral futility, and calls for a new way of thinking that only comes about in writing and touches on "the very essence of the Word" (Apollinaire): "I thus belonged from the earliest age to this zoological species of writers for whom thought is formed in writing."[11]

Ephemerality, humor, images, scandal, and a style composed of metaphors turned upside down by dreamlike free association will weave this rebellious *a-thought* together: "I call style the accent adopted by the flow of the symbolic ocean, reflected by a given man, that universally mines the earth with metaphors."[12] Consider this political credo: the speaker, "I," calls "style" the "flow" of the "symbolic ocean," a flow that is "reflected" by a "given man." Aragon writes "symbolic ocean" for the Christian "Word," for "God." The "given" man, an anonymous, indifferent man, like Louis A., Andrieux, Aragon, perhaps. And a universally mined earth. Mined by metaphor, displacement, transports-transferences-images. Writing of the whirlwind, the vortex an "I" calls forth and is temporarily appeased by, the testimony of a "given man," set adrift by the gods and the mined earth, impacted by earthquakes, tsunamis, the vertigo of our reference points, the instability of the ego, other people, words—metaphor is what is left to us.

This adventure—both the subjective revolt and the metaphysical project—will usher in three major themes: the *marvelous*, the *crisis of confidence in the imaginary*, and the unbridled *worship of female jouissance*.

La Défense de l'infini is inscribed in this context. Against the background of the author's stormy relationship with Nancy Cunard and the sexual and financial difficulties to which he was subject during this liaison, the risks of imaginary revolt and surrealist *a-thought* emerge brutally. While Breton continues to believe that the inner experience must be pursued and that it is possible to change the rights of man through art (as suggested in the first issue of *La Révolution surréaliste* [The Surrealist Revolution], December 1, 1924), Aragon stigmatizes literary activity as "vanity," and though he publishes Artaud's *The Nerve Meter* in 1927 with Doucet's funding, he seeks in politics a solution to the contradiction between social efficiency and irredeemable literary activity.

La Défense de l'infini

In short, this is truly a crisis of confidence in the imaginary: joining the Communist Party and writing *La Défense de l'infini* at the same time suggests that political choice might have acted as an unconscious counterweight to the risk of the imaginary. Indeed, in 1927, Aragon joins the Party and has a dramatic moment in his emotional life. It is as if political membership balanced out an unbearable affective and passionate disorder. This is the period of his tumultuous relationship with Nancy Cunard, which takes place in an elegant and cosmopolitan world in Paris, involving trips to various European countries (England, Holland, Germany, Spain, Italy). Then there is the breakup. The writer succumbs to a crisis of depression, destroys a large portion of his manuscript, "La Défense de l'infini," in Madrid, near the end of 1927, and attempts suicide in September 1928 in Venice.

Two motifs animate this text. The first is explicitly rhetorical and literary; it presents itself as a rejection of bourgeois ennui and the nausea provoked by the habit of telling "stories . . . for assholes," as the narrator bluntly puts it. Nevertheless, this anger is still expressed in a fictional style. If there is a *narrative*, it is subordinated to the *act of writing* at its most singular, solitary, and dreamlike and to a mastery of words that, like a substitute for automatic writing, generates characters and the fragmentary structure of a story made of "collages."

The second motif concerns the appropriation of the feminine as a revolt against the degeneration of Man (or, if you prefer, the father). The infinity in question is ultimately the account of an exorbitant jouissance transferred from the *woman* to the narrator's *writing*. The section entitled "Le Con d'Irène" testifies to this.

As I have said before, Aragon, Breton, and the surrealists all glorified the feminine as a new divinity, but Aragon gave this perspective a new slant. Irène is an ambiguous character, the narrator's double, a libertine, an idealized echo of the prostitute; however, above all, she exerts power over the others, including the narrator, thanks to words—an infinite power, power against the finiteness of love. This love, initially exalted, is devalorized in turn in favor of the only infinity that matters: the infinity of Irène's words. Does she create the words herself, or does she inspire them in the narrator? The ambiguity remains; the writer and the muse are almost assimilated; he is the woman and she is he; a splitting projects the libertine into the role of creator and assigns the writer the feminine role, suggesting the bisexual nature of the creator. Only Joyce in *Ulysses*, through a polyphony that rivals *Atheological Summa* attempted such an orphic appropriation of female jouissance. As for the disenchantment of eroticism, it is rare in French literature, which placed eighteenth-century libertinism at the zenith of the experience of freedom and generally prefers to glorify the sexual exploit. This Aragonian admission of weakness, impotence, and disgust is not in the style of the sexual liberation and exaltation of the erotic act practiced by other writers during the same period, which has permeated anarchist literature and art to this day (we have only recently started questioning the benefits of this "freedom": since media images have imposed *hardcore sex* as the "right-thinking" norm). Jouissance, in the narrator of *La Défense de l'infini*, is ultimately transposed to another plane; confronted with the sadness of eroticism, the narrator valorizes the magic of the word, "the prodigious metaphorical value that I attribute to words alone."[13]

And female jouissance can now be described in one of the most beautiful passages on this subject in French literature. Consider this description, full of physiological detail, sensation, emotion, and desire:

"So small and so large! It is here that you are at ease, man finally worthy of your name, it is here that you are back on the scale of your desires. Don't be afraid of moving your face closer to this place—and already your tongue, the chatterer, is restless—this place of delight and darkness, this patio of ardour, in its pearly limits, the fine image of pessimism. O cleft, moist and soft cleft, dear dizzying abyss. . . . Touch that voluptuous smile, trace the ravishing gap with your finger. . . . And now, all hail to thee, pink palace, pale casket, alcove a little disordered by the grave joy of love, vulva appearing for a moment in its fullness. Under the designer-label satin of the dawn, the colour of summer when one closes one's eyes. . . . Oof, oof. Irene is calling her lover. Her lover gets a hard-on at a distance. Oof, oof. Irene is about to die and contorts herself. He's stiff-pricked as a god above the abyss. She thrusts, he eludes her, she thrusts and strains. Oof. The oasis leans down with its tall palms. Travellers your burnouses rotate in the abrasive sand. Irene is panting fit to burst. He contemplates her. The cunt is steamed up awaiting the prick. On the illustory chott, the shadow of a gazelle. . . . Hell, let your damned toss off, Irene has come."[14]

Clearly, the imaginary is at a loss before the enormity of the project represented by translation—translation not of a "multiplicity of facts" but of female jouissance: admittedly phantasmatic but upheld as a variant of the divine incarnate.

Stalinism Versus Sensible Infinity

The senselessness of revolt consists of the ambition to translate into language this appropriation of original paradise, this loss of boundaries between the ego and the other, between man and woman, this effacing of limits and taboos beyond the speaking subject, the phantasmatic representation of which is female jouissance. In counterpoint, joining the French Communist Party in 1927 and meeting Elsa in the fall of 1928 are stabilizing and reassuring. Party membership will be effective in 1930 and consolidate the writer's identity. The impossible literary mission that involved competing with *phantasmatic female jouissance* will be replaced by a *cult of the people*: a sympathetic mission amongst the sovereign yet destitute people, the dark continent of oppressed sensibility and repressed organic power. While the popular miracle replaces the feminine marvelous, the police prefect is easily transformed into a dictator—the male cult of personality requires it!

Is this papering over of literary *a-thought*, of imaginary revolt, in party membership and belonging, a true-lie, a pretense, a mask, an artifact? Aragon's later years suggest it, as he gradually allowed his respectability to dissipate. Nevertheless, he maintained this role as member, militant, and dogmatic leader for a long time, drawing criticism from those who accused him of cynicism and conformism, whether dyed-in-the-wool bourgeois or liberal anarchists. Adherence to the Party, as well as conjugal "mad love," were no doubt his lifesavers after setting the manuscript on fire, the mirror necessary to assure his identity: "I" belong, because "I" do not know who "I" am; and because "I" do not want to be swallowed up by the jouissance of the other, "I" adhere, "I" stabilize myself, if only temporarily, "I" profit from it to continue living and writing. The alternation between revolt and adherence structures the surrealist period itself, the "group" assuming the role of identity support—before the Party takes its place and seals the strictures of *revolt* within *social demands*. With Stalinism, Aragon abandons *revolt* in the name of *engagement*, at times critical, at times servile, wanting it all, all the time ("toujours tout l'arc-en-ciel," Breton said of him), without belonging absolutely to any one identity, any one precise truth. This is what some of Aragon's commentators have called his successive and constant "betrayals." Betrayals that also allowed him to follow his path as a writer. After setting Infinity ablaze, writing could only be a constant betrayal/translation of styles, genres, postures, and tonalities.

At this point, in 1928, the impasses of Stalinism have just begun. There will be 1930, the congress of Kharkov, and the redoubtable adherence to social realism; then 1932 and the split with surrealism; *Le Monde réel* starts in 1933 until *Les Communistes* of 1949, and there is the conjugal and patriotic pathos of the poetic cycle of the Resistance—but should he not have done it? Who will cast the first stone at the alexandrines? In 1945 *Aurélien*; and finally—I say "finally" for myself, because it was a relief to see the writing catch its breath again—*Holy Week* in 1958. But *La Défense de l'infini* was no longer discussed and would not be republished until 1986 (in 1969 Aragon still does not mention Irene, but he describes the style of the novel he set alight in *Je n'ai jamais appris à écrire* [I Never Learned How to Write]).

The writer's virtuosity in the novel, characteristic of his later years, vaguely recalls the phantasmatic explosion that ignited *La Défense de l'infini*. *Blanche ou l'oubli* (1967) also confronts us in a new way with female desire and the incommunicability between the sexes. The fascination that Blanche (already present as a character in *La Défense de l'infini*) and Marie-Noire have over the linguist Geoffroy Gaiffier is accompanied by a new fusion between masculine and feminine, the narrator usurping the place of his heroines. The exception here is that Aragon, still wanting to grasp sensible infinity beyond language—"I would like to describe forgetting beyond language"[15]—nevertheless admits a sort of defeat. The sensible world resists the narrator, he will always miss the safety net of language, forgetting will prevail, the blank is inevitable, absolute: the feminine will be this elusive blank—this Blanche, unless it is black, this Marie-Noire. Writing is certainly a power, but it is above all the power to admit impotence, an admission of lack: "The novel begins where rules are dismissed . . ."[16]

"The novel is a science of anomaly."[17]

"This character of inexplicability, inexpiability, the absence itself of a serious attempt to justify the thing, all this contributes to giving the novel this light of anomaly that reigns at times over the television set . . ."[18]

The anomaly of the novel, the Party, and TV?

When "Joining" Replaces "Being"

To conclude, a few reflections to tie up the loose ends of this "true-lie," still being woven today, and from which we are not spared, as leaders of the liberal establishment would like to think.

First of all, Aragon's revolt against the familial unspeakable could not be an oedipal revolt: it is closer to the anti-Oedipus,[19] which opens to psychosis. Yet, far from the exclusion Artaud experienced in the insane asylum, the surrealist position seemed fairly integrated and seductive, with Breton in charge of esotericism and Aragon in charge of the Party apparatus. Nevertheless, we find the polymorphous instability of this modern Narcissus, this explorer of maternal language, in a nonoedipal tonality at the borders of suicidal depersonalization. Political engagement seems to be a replacement for tragic revolt, its papering over in the cult of the people—the mother of all suffering, under the iron rule of the "little father of the people" and/or the Party police. In contrast to the deconstruction of an uncertain identity, the unbearable "Being" of pleasure and anxiety that decided to join forces with automatic writing, there is "membership." This reversal of the quest for Being in Membership is supported by a will to atone for the father and the law, to struggle against the disappointment of depression, against the invasion by the feminine, against the capsizing into a-thought, of which *La Défense de l'infini* was such a perfect example and whose scars *Blanche ou l'oubli* still touches.

So, supporting Stalinism was revealed to be a passion with much more insidious roots. Take the invalid man in *La Défense de l'infini*. We can imagine a man like that restoring himself by supporting something strong: there is no longer a reason for being, but there is a group that embodies the reason of History. The reason of History is the counterweight to depression, and the Party of the popular masses becomes the manic version of melancholy. A "given man," reflected by the waves of the symbolic ocean, sees communism as "conscience incarnate," an absolute spirit "back on its feet."

In addition, a certain French materialism was not averse to the temptation of establishing a new cult, that of historical reason, which the Party indeed embodied. That a human group could materialize the Power which German idealism attributed to the idea did not fail to appeal to the descendents of those clamoring for sensuality and vilifying the obscurantism of cathedrals. The cult of the irrational marvelous, made substantive by woman, borders on the inconstancy and pluralism of the Baroque. But the cult of the rational marvelous that dialectical materialism represents, in counterpoint to the earlier marvelous, is reassuring, solidifying, and stimulating at once.

Here we are undoubtedly at the heart of what underlies all *belonging*: "I" do not know *who* "I" am, "I" do not know *if* "I" am (a man or a woman); but "I" am part of something, a member. Hannah Arendt, after Proust, writes that the French transformed Hamlet's motto "to be or not to be" into "to be part of or not to be part of" (*en être ou ne pas en être*). The French or the communists? Or perhaps: the more French you were, the more communist? Is this logic of conversion, which transforms "lack of being" into *membership*, so far removed from us (natives of globalization), as opponents of the true-lie would like to believe? Some support religious certainties, others ephemeral media-driven seductions—new versions of the true-lie.

Yet the thaw of the cold war, revisionism, the critique of totalitarianism, and the fall of the Berlin Wall did not simply "accelerate" History, as has often been said. They reactivated—and now allow us to reevaluate—the highlights of a much more personal and subjective revolt than that of militant engagement. Doesn't this revolt, confronting familial structure and sexual identity as well as the strictures of identity and language, constitute a true *mise en abîme* of the totalitarian temptation in which a number of "rebels" nevertheless compromised themselves? Alas, the horror of totalitarianism leads conservative minds to stigmatize libertarian revolt as an accomplice to the destruction of transcendental values that may have facilitated the advent of Stalinism and Nazism. On the contrary, the fate of Aragon proves that "membership" and "political engagement" are the consequence not of the "symbolic ocean" which *La Défense de l'infini* proposed exploring but of a shipwreck. His political investment appears to have been an attempt to mask the writer's powerlessness to pursue his "metaphysical business," which is nothing other than this "transmutation of values," the difficulty and urgency of which Nietzsche made clear.

Along with and beyond the true-lie, which was Aragon's (and many other people's) lot, this work of the negative also seemed to be a *profound questioning of the foundations of meaning and morality*. Various experiments in painting, music, and literature at the antipodes of "socialist realism" (Khlebnikov, Mayakovsky, Picasso, Malevitch, Tatlin, etc.) questioned the "already-there" of signification, images, and forms—to unveil their conflicting logics and unbearable identity. The Freudian revolution revealed the unconscious meaning of this trajectory by discovering the endemic madness of the human race in dreams. Taking these limits seriously, the ultimately psychotic limits of the speaking being who ventures—by accident (madness) or audacity (in art and thought)—to the frontiers of taboos and coded identities is what characterizes the culture of the twentieth century. Faced with new forms of conformism, we sense the gravity of this message.

The artist—to take only one example—may have difficulty handling all these risks alone. In the (indeed insane) ordeal of this experience, there is one security: blocking the work of the negative in turn, stiffening in the pose of the disciple, the faithful follower, the militant, and today the media-friendly artist or intellectual. This person opts for "another morality," arbitrary as well, even more so than the previously rejected one, because events are no longer questioned, doubts have been suspended, and doubt dissolves into forgetting to doubt. *La Défense de l'infini*, burnt; *Blanche ou l'oubli*, suppressed. Infinity then ventures into the oedipal-Oresteian revolt or else is forgotten in the whitewashing of red support. Often more lethal than the well-controlled morality of earlier societies, which equipped themselves with the filters of democracy and religion in order to channel the death drive, the new morality of political fundamentalism kills. In reality. And in culture, by denying the intrinsic negativity of meaning, its imaginary dynamic. The new believer, even if he is a writer, abandons his experience and submits it to the Cause. The cause of the people, the cause of Allah, when not the most infantile and therefore most protective cause: the cause of self-promotion in the society of the spectacle, with no guardrails.

To compare Aragon's drama to ours, we could ask the question another way: is Aragon's imaginary experience audible, readable, without the political support and "mediatization" *avant la lettre* that communist popularity procured for him and that gave him one of his reasons for being?

Or: is it really just a matter of amoral manipulation on the part of an imposter? A borderline state of unbearable identity: of the Self, of groups? A critical period in the Western conscience where the refusal of the pair formed by conscience and the norm stiffened into an institutionalized antinorm and anticonscience, even more restrictive and lethal than their traditional targets? Revolt running aground in radical oppression, unable to follow in thought alone, in lone thought, this archaeology of the sensed and the sensible, this debate in metaphysics and against it, that Aragon introduced in *Paris Peasant*?

One thing is certain: if we have surpassed this critical period and see its impasses today (which concern not only Aragon's compromises but all dogmatic engagement), it is not certain that we have not also lost the unsettling vitality of the revolts of the twentieth century. The opening to *a-thought* might be temporarily closed in media chitchat, the *soft-core* version of the true-lie.

24

MURDER IN BYZANTIUM, OR
WHY I "SHIP MYSELF ON A VOYAGE" IN A NOVEL

Don't look for it on the map, my Byzantium is a matter of time.
—Julia Kristeva, *Murder in Byzantium*

PIERRE-LOUIS FORT: One of my first impressions is that *Murder in Byzantium* is a cryptic novel, in both senses of the term: because there are elements to decode (a subtle intertextual game, discreet political and societal allusions) but also because, more profoundly, it seems to touch on something intensely personal, even more so than *The Samurai*, where the personal dimension was nevertheless quite significant.

JULIA KRISTEVA: It took me a while to find the character. It did start with *The Samurai*, actually, but I think in trying to appropriate the polyphony of "the novel" as a genre, I dealt with more secret territory in *Murder in Byzantium* than in my earlier books.

In this novel the reader finds themes that are immediately decipherable: the corrupt, criminal, and mafialike society of the globalized village referred to as "Santa Varvara"; the crusades of modern terrorists intersecting with the First Crusade that began in Vézelay and Puy-en-Velay, a political "historical" reflection (in the sense of the history of civilizations and the clash of religions) and, at the same time, a coded, as you say, descent into the folds not of the Ego but of the subject. What's the difference? The Ego reassures itself through display, the exhibition of its minidramas, while the subject's intimacy is diffracted into a mosaic of confessions, associations, and slips that destabilize the Ego's certainties as well as others'—the reader's. The subject's intimacy pierces through to that of others (characters are split, twinned, there are doubles, projections, there is a loss of self in crime but also in serenity—*Murder in Byzantium* is woven of all this). I'm not saying it results in any "transparency" or "glasnost"—it really is a a piercing through. Oblique, cubist, plural, an intermingled intimacy at the crossroads of my encounters, the languages I speak and write, the various times inhabiting them and inhabiting me, and my irreconcilable identities. If I feel more at ease in the novel of the subject than in the novel of the Ego, is it because of psychoanalysis? Or is it because of history, which made me an immigrant of Bulgarian origin, French nationality, European citizenship, and American adoption? The "ethical community" Kant envisioned as a new version of the *corpus mysticum* does not exist today and may never exist outside this intimacy of subjects in transverberation. At the very least, we can say that the globalized spectacle to which we devote our "disposable publishing" does not take this path.[1] Since the televised image amplifies what is already at work in the marketing of books, we can see that the market's rush toward the "transparency" of the blissful or suffering Ego-ego produces an effect of seduction and astonishment. The fascinated consumer hoping to bandage his wounds in fact paves them over; speech is no longer an enigma that might have meaning, but raw "data" used or manipulated in matters of power (whether the supposed "truth" of children at a trial or the mythomania of a so-called victim of the RER; even militants of sexual freedom end up militants of *starification* (instant celebrity) and horror—there is no return to a reflection on the self.[2] We are fabricating a terrorism of the ego, like a soft version of hard sex and technology that is also hard and necessarily militaristic. Is this inflation of the ego the revenge of our innermost depths against the black tide of fundamentalisms? The convulsions of the pleasure principle unleashed against the spasms of kamikazes enamored of the beyond? Is this a fleeting moment in banalized culture? Or a symmetrical pair that will prolong the end of history with the complacent participation of artists, writers, and intellectuals?

Now that *Murder in Byzantium* and its immediate reception are behind me, I feel as though I wrote this book in a dream: a fugue state against religious crusades and the crusades of the "Ego-ego."

PLF: A novel intended and thought of as *a novel of the subject*, then, as opposed to the *novel of the ego*?

JK: Writing is an unconscious necessity for me. I don't decide when to scrawl notes in my journal or cross out entire pages in bed at two o'clock in the morning. One of my patients admitted to me recently that he hesitated buying *Murder in Byzantium*, afraid that I would be like "one of those novelists who pose in their novels, as if in front of a mirror." This man, who was clearly in a phase of positive transference, said, "But you're nothing like that, you take the mirror down." Actually, *Murder in Byzantium* is at once a metaphysical detective novel, a historical novel, a lyrical narrative, and a social satire: the ego is broken down into multiple facets, and familial images are present but disseminated in a historic framework that includes ten centuries and a continent, from île de Ré to the Black Sea. . . . My press agent managed to "book" me on a television show whose theme was "Your childhood." Everyone was talking about their father, their mother, their noble descent, their French, English, Jewish, North African lineage. It was the sort of politically correct reflection we like after dinner, in the kitchen. I was trying to say that the truest image of "my story" was a photo taken with my father at a soccer match in Sofia. In this photo, which I found in the newspaper the following day, I was reduced to a little gray dot in the snapshot. But it was only with this cancellation of the *ego* that I was able to speak to the people in the TV studio of the intensity of what I had experienced: the love of my father, our disputes; the violent acts of communism that ravaged the school, the Church, the family; the revolt of the "democrats" against the "totalitarians," which was transposed to an athletic confrontation, the team of "Blues" versus the team of "Reds." . . . That was my story, the story of a *subject*, if you like, a subject that includes the ego, displaces it, traverses it, hollows it out, recomposes it, revives it. A story that can only be told if it passes to the other side of the mirror, if it follows the shifting of facets, roles. . . . Obviously, the moderator of the TV show "didn't like it" (which is what media heads say when they want to get rid of something: end of discussion!), so he edited me out. The day the prerecorded show was broadcast, I noticed with a certain sadness that nothing had been retained of my story of the "little gray dot." They preferred the other, juicier stories: an abused girl, academic failure, the drama of blended families, and so on. I told my editor I would no longer appear on television; now he has to think twice before taking the risk of publishing me.

P L F : Is this essential distinction between subject and ego linked to the fact that, as a novelist, you are also still a psychoanalyst?

J K : You ask me why I feel foreign to this indulgence many of my fellow writers feel for their old and current psychodramas? Why I enjoy dissolving, reconstructing, recreating not an entity (my "ego" and "my" loved ones) but a process of language, a processing of meaning and identities we call a "subject," precisely?

Whatever the problems and marginalization of psychoanalysis today, I am convinced that it has radically transformed human beings by changing our relationship to what we say. To what we hear . . . and we no longer write as we did before. Some people know this. Others act as if nothing happened. But the question is there: can one write a novel today "as if" psychoanalysis did not exist?

The free association of the analysand on the couch has spoiled an entire literature that was telling itself stories: stories of dreams, desire, ill-being. Because psychoanalysis begins precisely where the ego seeks itself, helping it come about, rehabilitating its conflicts, allowing familial dramas to emerge from oblivion; but also allowing the Ego to be reborn by releasing creativity, if and only if the ego has been able to question itself, as St. Augustine (precursor to Freud) already suggested. "Analysis" means "dissolution," the deconstruction of identity: a path, a break, alternating reconciliations and estrangements, and a "transubstantiation," as Proust wrote. By contrast, the narcissistic mirage, the specular worship of the ego favored by the culture of the media and the type of storytelling it fashions are very far away from this passing through of inner dwellings that Christianity initiated and that the novel brought to its apex.

P L F : There are echoes here of one of your first works of criticism, Le Texte du roman (The Text of the Novel),[3] which focuses on this genre.

J K : I was able to show, in this very technical and already old book, that novels—the genre of the "novel" generally, whether a novel of chivalry, a young adult novel, a psychological novel, etc.—are initiatory narratives that transpose here on earth, in a "horizontal" dimension, the "vertical" passion of Christ in search of the Father and Transcendence. The fabulous European novelistic adventure was made possible by the advent of biblical and evangelical subjectivity, Christian dissidence in the face of Judaism and with it, the focus on the passion of the man-God, the intersection of meaning and the sensory, and the incarnation of transcendence. Other civilizations have constructed narratives, myths, and fables; the novel is a post-Christian fact, the exquisite product of the inevitable and intrinsic decomposition of the biblical and evangelical continent in a humanist spirituality reminiscent of the Greeks: from Rabelais to Balzac, from Dostoyevsky to Proust and Joyce, at war against monotheism or in complicity with it. All of them are metaphysical novelists, dismantlers of metaphysics in the novel. Psychoanalysis itself is heir to this tradition: encouraged by the discovery of sexual pleasure, the illuminations and terrors of which were propagated by the eighteenth century, not to mention the romantic and naturalist forest of the nineteenth century.

So how is it that this novelistic speech—this fertile vein in which the European subject was constituted and through which he seduced the world—finds its source today in the literature of scandal, in the bandaging of sexual misery, or in the hero-worship of erotic exploits? Is this yet another apparently harmless yet profoundly symptomatic failure, the most spectacular yet, of the immanence of transcendence? Not that the latter is impossible. Listen, read: writings exist, labeled "literature" or "philosophy," in which incarnation is palpable, sense meets the senses, meditation is made flesh, and vice versa (French theory, Americans might say). Don't ask for a list of prizewinners or names: it has to do not with individual success but a certain position of the subject in the discourse of philosophy and literary criticism, semiology, psychoanalysis, etc., that mobilizes the imaginary and the body of the subject and is thereby radically distinct from the subjective cancellation by which scholarly discourse is characterized by definition. It has produced a curious phenomenon in France: reading Heidegger and Freud unlocks subjectivity in philosophy and the human sciences, and we receive this unlocking as an invasion of these disciplines by literature and style. "This is the modern novel," some have said, in the face of this dissemination of the imaginary in the discourse of the subject who is supposed to know. "Stop telling your little stories; this is the age of the deconstruction of genres by writing." We'll see.

Because the dissemination of the imaginary in scholarly discourse is not transubstantiation. The transubstantiation to which *In Search of Lost Time* aspired needed a narrative; narration was consubstantial to it. Why? The recounting of affects uttered by a subject who is necessarily in love, as every speaking being in search of a willing listener is, is an unbeatable antidepressant. The novel as an account of the subject uses the affects of the ego who is telling the story, telling its story—pleasure, anxiety, fear, violence, shame, seduction, etc., so as to activate them, to put them to the test of events. But it plays with them like cards in a game, as a body is used in choreography or the chords of a musical instrument in a concerto. Then affect, childhood memories, romantic trials, and personal history are sideswiped by the stakes and rules of the philosophical, ethical, and political game. The big story is transfigured by the little story. And it is indeed this crossing, this diagonal line, that makes up the real flesh of the novel of the subject, which is not an admission or a confession, but a questioning, a voyage, an invitation to distance oneself from original identities, insufflating an essential irony into the very heart of the tragic. But transubstantiation is inherent in the flesh of the novel; it extends to the music of words, the rhythm of the syntax, the tempo of telescoped narrative genres: with me, it's a lyrical-historical-political detective novel.

If we call the meaning that inhabits us divine, then the mutation of the place of the subject in speech conditions the mutation of the divine. The novel of the subject, seen this way, places us on the path of this mutation. St. Augustine was the first novelist of the subject, because he was the first to articulate the two fundamental principles of his transfiguration: *Quaestio mihi factus sum* ("I have been made a question to myself") and *In via, in patria* ("The homeland is the journey"). This seems to me to be the metaphysical agenda of a speaker in a novel: the deconstruction (of psychological themes, of characters themselves) and the displacement (of limits, of genres) flow from the Augustinian dynamic that transfigures the memory of word and flesh. And it is in the revolt against theology, but in its precincts, specifically, in the medieval carnival, that the first detachment of the subject of the enunciation vis-à-vis the certainties of the ego will be produced: through laughter, irony, the mask. The great novels of the subject mix Augustine and the carnival: Rabelais, Joyce, Dostoyevsky, and modern authors as different as Patricia Highsmith, Philip Roth, and Philippe Sollers with *Paradis* or *Women*...

PLF: I'd like to return to the idea of the "diagonal." At one point, you write in *Murder in Byzantium*: "No genre, only a diagonal passing through" (*MB* 67). Isn't this "diagonal passing through" the very essence of your book, a sort of total novel (if only by virtue of the multiplicity of points of view—I, he, the killer; the subjects addressed—political, societal, religious; the tonal variations—lyricism, humor, irony; aesthetic shifts as well as changes in tempo)? A novel with a "kaleidoscopic" aspect, as Bernard-Henri Levy put it in *Le Point*.[4] Is *Murder in Byzantium* playing *on* and *over* the diagonal line?

JK: Take the title of a famous work by Heidegger: *Paths That Lead Nowhere*.[5] The subject is this path that leads nowhere, if not to its constant surpassing. It is a diagonal line that cuts across the circle of the confinement of the self for itself. At the end of *Murder in Byzantium* Stephanie Delacour has a motto: "I'm shipping myself on a voyage" (MB 237). That is the meaning of the subject. But your reading, attentive to the various narrative points of view and the tonal variations in my novel, allows me to point out what strikes me as capital in the adventure of the novel. Unlike philosophical or intellectual discourse, the voyage of the novel, as I understand it, leads to a summit, that is, incarnation, which seems to me to be the essence of the Christian imaginary. Transposed to our field, incarnation supposes that every event of discourse (including, necessarily, an idea, a concept, that of the voyage) is inseparable from the passion of a living body: from its flesh, its perceptions, its familial, social, and historical bindings and unbindings. There is no event that is not somehow word and flesh, and the event itself is nothing other than the copresence of word and flesh. You know that the globalization of the virtual has abolished the event: via remote control, you can go from the collapse of the World Trade Center to the arrest of Saddam Hussein to gay marriage and so on, each sequence effacing the previous one in a vertigo of the nullification of memory and subjects along with it. The regime of the spectacle is a regime of the virtual, and the only event that seems to resist the remote control remains death: does the unfurling on the small screen of every crime and the trials that accompany it mean that humanity has become more homicidal than ever, that sophisticated technology allows one to be better informed about what has always existed, or that birth and death are the only values that retain the attention of our bodies made delirious by the acceleration of the spectacle?

The detective novel is the fruit of this explosion of the death drive in counterpoint to the virtual. Some cash in on it, others try to reroute it toward restlessness, revolt. I would say that, in this context, narration that condenses the accidents of passion with those of the battle of ideas, a novel that embodies ideas in the living flesh of mortals, produces events extraneous to the virtual sweep. This is a form of memory's resistance against forgetting: a possible resistance, because narrative speech confronts the major hallucinogenic life-death episodes that exacerbate the generalized spectacle and because elucidation itself is permeated by the substance of sensible bodies. Still, the disposable publishing world the book market has become allows potential readers to read and retrace the writer's path as each one sees fit. It is not impossible that a multiplicity of events might seep into our consumer slumber.

Murder in Byzantium begins with a murder that takes place in the Whale Lighthouse; then a woman is strangled by her lover before being drowned; then a mafioso is stabbed and an assistant professor is killed in an asbestos-filled tower; bullets fly in the cloister of the Puy-en-Velay Cathedral; and the Louvre itself is shattered in a terrorist attack. Lovers of detective novels write me to say that they find this imaginary Byzantium to have some of the breathless anxiety of a "hardboiled" detective novel or even a "completely twisted" detective novel. Some are sorry that the "detective" narrative thread is not only one; others are glad. Because another lyrical story line is mixed into the voyage, featuring the love affairs of Rilsky and Stephanie, of Stephanie and her son, and the relationship between Ebrard de Pagan and Anne Comnena. This story line intersects with the historical novel that evokes the extraordinary fate of the first female historian and first female intellectual, Anne Comnena, author of *The Alexiad*, and the fate of the spiritual guide of the First Crusade, Adhémar de Monteil, a story line that inserts a few unusual but necessary "characters," such as the cathedral of Puy and the entire court of Byzantium, into the modern "crusades." And since there is no subject without irony, irony is everywhere in this metaphysical detective novel: it inhabits Commissioner Rilsky as well as Foulques Weil, the French ambassador to Santa Varvara, and the narrator, Stephanie, when she sees herself as a double of the historian Sebastian Chrest-Jones. . . . So it is full of personal stories, "stories of the ego," if you like, but mixed together, played out or thwarted, put in perspective, disengaged, endlessly refracted. Ah, irony, a long history, with so many variants . . . the irony of Socrates, the carnival, the Romantics, Joyce . . . To play the ego card, yes, like a card in a game, on the path, the diagonal line that cuts across the circle of the confinement of identity, as well as the circle of oblivion . . .

PLF: I was under the impression that the "diagonal" might also be understood as a sort of "tangent." That is, one would touch on a multitude of things constantly without being inserted into or confined within a closed system. A diagonal line that would be an opening, both a passage

(Stephanie Delacour's "shipping herself on a voyage") and a tangent—touching on things without stopping there. The irony you just spoke of is part of this system. In the course of the novel, you establish an interesting distinction between irony that is revelatory ("elevation toward a truth"; *MB* 244) and ridicule that is destructive (suggesting "everything is imposture"; *MB* 244).

JK: The music of the novel keeps time with the rhythm of the novelist. I like a quick pace; speed is my element; I'm not fond of slowness. And I'm convinced that a quick pace—far from skimming the surface of the world, as we have a tendency to think—encourages flashes of brilliance, a cascade of epiphanies that illuminate one another, thus revealing the essential aspect of the speaking subject, that is to say, the subject's movement and basic singularity. This acceleration of the narrative, which is my approach, contradicts a certain use of the televisual image, which paradoxically slows the mind. I say paradoxically because we usually emphasize the "punch in the face" effect of the image, its lightning speed, its instantaneousness and immediacy compared to the linear unfolding of language, which requires duration. And yet, with the exception of a few instances of virtuoso montage, the images flooding TV viewers and moviegoers stop the flow of thought in a sort of hypnosis: whether these are "news stories" meant to seduce or horrify or an accumulation of commercials that cancel each other out for lack of being internalized. On the contrary, an accelerated narrative tempo that juxtaposes unusual themes necessarily brings new knowledge that some readers find compelling and others tedious, but, in any case, their reciprocal resonance prevents the reader from settling in, dispossessing the reader to the point of a dispossession of the self. The reader does not "recognize himself" as he might in, say, a sentimental or familial novel, but is initiated into the unknown of the time of others, the unknown of the time of the self. *Murder in Byzantium* is basically a novel about Time, about the diversity of the times we live in, perhaps more diverse now than ever before: the time of the first Crusades in the eleventh century and the modern crusades; the time of the cathedral in Le Puy and the Orthodox churches on the edges of the Black Sea; the time of Byzantium attacked by the Seldjukides in the east and the Latins in the west, and the time of the modern Byzantium that France is today, which is having a hard time having its difference recognized between the power of Santa Varvara and the terrorists of Bin Laden, the time outside time of the love affairs of Stephanie Delacour and the commissioner, or the time, also outside time, that makes Sebastian a killer of butterflies, a strangler, and Wuxian a bloodthirsty calligrapher, a serial killer purifier . . . This narrative acceleration, which proceeds by multiple disconnections, is calmed in a phrastic melody, similar to oral intonation, an interior monologue that slides on the surface of the French language to the emotive, sensitive, drive-related foundation of the syntax, words, and phonemes: in this infralinguistic hiding place that I believe to be the true habitat of foreigners like Stephanie, Sebastian, Wuxian, and Julia Kristeva. Irony profits from this lag between the meaning of language and the sense of the drive; it creates more distance. Starting there, the tonality of the book can oscillate between a sort of despair in the face of human history, which is indeed a criminal history, and the impassive detachment that is the affect of lucidity. The difference you point out between irony and ridicule is particularly evident in the central female character. Stephanie Delacour, the narrator, who makes ironic comments about Julia Kristeva, is not an adversary of Santa Varvara, since she goes back there after the attack on the Louvre, and she does not abandon her career as a journalist while making incendiary statements about the French media. Not rejection, but a distant participation: inside and outside, outside the inside. Her irony, in short, conveys a remote complicity.

PLF: This irony is used on many levels, first and foremost, regarding you (I'm thinking of the mises en abyme as well as the ferocious evocations of the two milieus in which you circulate, the academic world and the world of psychoanalysis). But it seems to me this is equally valid for all the milieus and all the characters.

JK: The carnival spares no one, not even close friends. Nothing escapes that ironic affection.

PLF: There is also a kind of dig at the media, which some thought was well observed, not only about the editing of TV programs, which you mentioned, but also more direct criticisms. Overall, what are your views of the reception of your work as a writer in the media?

JK: At this point, the media exploitation of a book (by television and newspapers) has nothing to do with literary criticism. "Communication" in the sense of "marketing" has killed literary criticism; the spectacle, which ignores the written word, is not interested in the writer. Even though I know that this is an implacable and inevitable phenomenon of society, I have a hard time getting used to it. With a few rare exceptions, which appear to exist more or less unconsciously in an ethics inspired by religion and seem old-fashioned, media reaction either takes the form of disparagement (a psychodrama is created around the writer as a person and, under the pretext of offering him the freedom to defend himself, pulls him down—naturally, without any intention to do him harm, just as a distraction) or, more banally—but this approach is less entertaining and therefore more grave—it takes the form of general peddling: you are warned at the start of the game that it will not be a question of your book, you understand, ratings *oblige*, everything is centered around a theme, preferably love and, if possible, family drama. Are you talking about an affective disaster (separation, betrayal, rape)? You have to have that in your arsenal, don't you? If not, why are you writing? You don't want to play the game? The moderator will turn to glare at someone, no doubt the person who had the bad idea of inviting you to this television studio. You are a dinosaur who showed up at the wrong place, at the wrong time . . .

PLF: Indeed, in a rather symmetrical way, during your interviews in the media there was a return to you as an academic and critic, a desire to restore you on your path, above all, in relation to Barthes, *Tel Quel*, psychoanalysis, your ethical and political engagements . . . broadly speaking, the novelist was just a pretext. One of the recurring questions had to do with the fact of having opted for this genre ("why a novel?").

JK: They try to reduce you to your sexual life, to extract confessions about people you frequent (if possible, famous people). What did you think of them? No sexual harassment? No quarrels with your spouse? But the essential thing is this: it is forbidden to mix territory; you are only allowed to "wear one hat." You are even more disturbing if you have the bad form to be a woman and to be labeled an "intellectual": the novel is not an intellectual pursuit, everyone knows that. One of the guardians of the literary temple had the straightforwardness to say that the doors to this temple would always be closed to me. So much the better: my religion is outside temples.

PLF: The doors to the literary temple nevertheless opened for *Murder in Byzantium* in *Le Monde*, *La Vie*, *La Croix*, *Le Point*, *Métropolis* . . .

JK: The "literary world" disgusts me, and I hear the bluntness of that remark, but why retract it? I will never be part of that world, and it doesn't want me either. There are necessary protective rituals, given the psychical risks inherent in writing, and that just as soon weave mafialike networks. The new Verdurins—editors, media, institutions, and academies of all sorts—are content to flatter neuroses during "the fall literary season" while scouring for the requisite familial dramas and scandals to lure the indefatigable "new bourgeoisie" who outlive every "new gadget"— the "new novel" or "new philosophy"—and to attract the necessarily depressed housewives, whom the "literary world" disdains but profits from, as the bottom line requires. This business would not work if it did not rely on a religion: the Verdurins officiate as priests of "beautiful language," which is their password, their code for initiates, their sign of recognition, to which they invite the buyer to succumb in turn. The pitiful cult of the splendid national language, which, as we all know, is threatened today. The one that was created in Europe in the late Middle Ages, that serves as our soul and our I.D. card in the current crisis of values, where nothing is left, *n'est-ce pas*, and in which the Verdurins recognize their education, their school, their family, their religion, their antifamily, their ersatz religion, and their "inrockuptible" deconstruction of "belles lettres." The one that does a poor job hiding the wars of taste, so many vital, existential, philosophical, political wars, wars of style, rhythm, incommensurable egos, of emerging subjects destroying the planet and all identity, and that does not count on any "milieu" to be recognized.

PLF: You spoke of time. Is Time the main character of *Murder in Byzantium?* Time in all its modalities, including the essential timelessness you highlighted in *Intimate Revolt?*

JK: Narration, unlike poetic enunciation, which captures an instant, situates me in a fleeting time, the time of passage and worry. The psychological novel and, more particularly, the self-centered minimalism being promoted at the moment by the book market, have cornered this complex novelistic time in narrow familial duration. But if we go back to the origins of the genre, from the novel of chivalry by way of novels of initiation and the great novels of the nineteenth and twentieth centuries (from Balzac and Dostoyevsky to Proust and Joyce), the time of the novel threads its way through familial destiny to accord with the time of nations. The novel recounts a national imaginary. We could even say that the national imaginary is constituted in the novel, where it goes beyond itself ironically or tragically to meet European and world history—with Kafka, Joyce, Philip Roth, Salman Rushdie, Sollers . . . Bizarrely, the minimalists of the ego have lost interest in this time; some even situate their psychological or pornographic exploits against the backdrop of

September 11, while carefully preserving themselves from the deluge of time. Time? No way! Time eats away at the spectacle; time may provoke thought. Time is too intellectual . . .

On the other hand, if Time is indeed the main character of *Murder in Byzantium*, as you suggest, it may be because I feel the third millennium is opening up a new temporality for us: both an unprecedented confrontation with the various national and religious times imposed on us by the clash of civilizations, and a suspension of time, an invitation to the "timeless." The main character, "Time," is coming along with me in my next novel. I discovered that Louis XV's watchmaker, a man called Passemant, built an astronomical clock set to 9999. This craftsman, who was also a meteorologist and a navigator, opened time to the darkness of time and placed it outside time, like a jewel on a chest of drawers at Versailles. This is the very emblem of the novel, as I understand it, and as I am trying to share with you . . .

The term *timeless,* which I analyzed in *Intimate Revolt*, is a Freudian notion that applies to the time of the unconscious: the unconscious is not aware of time; it is *zeitlos*, timeless, outside time. In *Murder in Byzantium*, the timeless is above all that of crime: the detective novel leads its readers precisely to this unbearable and fascinating place where the death drive interrupts duration. Crime fascinates us because it reveals a psychical functioning that allows itself to suspend time and that, in the instant of the criminal gesture, is itself excluded from human time. Sade's *120 Days of Sodom*, for example, builds to a paroxysm of violence the reader receives as a rejection of messianic hope: a breach in the time of faith that aims for human destiny's heavenly end, a breach in the revolutionary time of the supposedly enlightened classes. Is Sade the radical, unlikely precursor to the modern detective novel, which assumes the dark privilege of racking up murders (like Sade), but under cover of a judicial inquiry (a precaution Sade did not take)?

Our era is comparable in many ways to this eighteenth century, when violence, now called sadomasochistic, exploded in a society that didn't want to recognize it. But that, like ours, changed regimes: Christian morality, which came of age in a state of decomposition, recoiled before a rationalist but implicitly lethal and already terrorist bourgeoisie. The nineteenth century had to banalize this criminality, and English law, consolidating Protestant justice, had to allow women writers, notably, to focus their insatiable curiosity on the place of the crime. Female cruelty is nothing like men's aggressiveness or the male death drive: in women, destructivity is immediately eroticized, it is social, and, consequently, it is able to reveal the lethal other side of social connections . . . The Gothic novel, then the detective novel, were born this way without recognizing their debt to either Sade or the timeless unconscious. It doesn't matter if it's a "mystery novel" or a "detective story," if it is perfected in the psychology of psychopaths or specializes in the logical puzzle of the police procedural, alongside Thanatos or the superego, the detective novel is the only type of novel to deal with this radical evil that is murder and that abolishes human time, the time of life: radical evil is a catastrophe of time.

PLF: For you, is the detective novel composed of political philosophy or theology . . . ?

JK: The genre of the "detective novel" was imposed on me when I faced the violence of the political world personally, on the death of my father, killed in a Bulgarian hospital a few months before the fall of the Berlin Wall. A murder that did not involve the pathology of a serial killer, since an entire political system was invested with the same logic of contempt for human life, ordinary life, in a sly and much more insidious way than that manifested by wars, mass graves, gulags, the Shoah . . . Political life, life itself, beyond serial killers, seemed like a crime novel to me then. And then my novels—*The Old Man and the Wolves* (1991) and *Possessions* (1996)—necessarily became crime novels in which the pathological is mixed with the political. The timelessness of the killer instinct that ravages Sebastian Chrest-Jones and Wuxian damage both their own humanity and the history of humankind: killers, they are also political actors. Good? Evil? Undecidable, in the logic of purifiers who might have been Islamic fundamentalists . . . At this level of darkness, Commissioner Rilsky himself can't make heads or tails of it: will judgment itself be swallowed up by the timeless in our virtual world of judicial inflation and impotence?

The homicidal act revisited by the crime novel is obviously a projection of the now conscious violence of the narrator, and, when it gets through to the reader, the reader is in tune with his/her own sadomasochism. Reading meets the death drive, destroys the mask of surface identity, and confronts a menacing brutality, which the reader was not necessarily aware of before: that, for example, of a calligrapher drawing an ideogram (as Wuxian does on the back of a mafioso or on a small

poster sent to the police in Santa Varvara). This suspension of catastrophic time surprises Commissioner Rilsky when he identifies the target he is tracking: the upholder of the law and the criminal, the knife and
the wound are carried away in the same vortex.

In counterpoint, there is a splendid variant of the timeless: the unconscious spares us from these depersonalizations that damage our
capacity for control and cancel us out in the infiniteness of nature or
other people, in the infiniteness of the encounter. Thus, Chrest-Jones
is transfixed by the colorful flight of butterflies in a meadow, the scent
of roses in Plovdiv, and the ocher wind of Byzantium. But it is Jerry who
best embodies this sacrificial timelessness: the deaf boy on the margins
of society whose computer skills help Stephanie root out the serial killer
and who appeals to the adoptive mother/journalist with his extravagant
sensitivity, sparingly named, as in a haiku.

PLF: Darkness, ecstasy; the dark vortex and crime, sensitivity and justice;
sometimes both at the same time. At various points, in fact, the reader
starts to wonder whether Commissioner Rilsky himself is not the guilty
one. At that point we imagine you are playing with the traditional
mechanisms of the crime novel—split personalities, multiple facets of
identity.

JK: Of the many splits that make up *Murder in Byzantium*, Rilsky's is perhaps
the most fundamental and most contemporary. Is the commissioner the
serial killer's twin? Only in his fantasies? Or, like Mr. Hyde, very real as
the good Dr. Jekyll's villainous double? The reader is caught in a trap:
what if the commissioner is a nocturnal killer but unaware of this while
assuming his daytime function as a guardian of the peace? We cannot
escape contemporary history: at Abu Ghraib, and well before, upholders
of the law were torturers. Does the law protect us from murder, use murder, or, worse still, call on its own guardians to transgress it? This con-
tamination between law and perversion, which Lacan spells *père-version*, is
in the logic of the unconscious, but, at certain moments, is inserted into
political events themselves. Of course, some will try to convince us that
these deviations are the results of a few lost sheep, etc. Certainly. But the
question remains: Not only how the lost sheep thought they were authorized to run rampant and conduct sadomasochistic orgies, but what
unconscious shifts did this acting out obey? Rilsky, the commissioner of
Santa Varvara (in no way naive), is at the heart of this question. Or, we
could say, he's in the grip of this question.

PLF: Precisely—I felt this was highlighted in *Murder in Byzantium*: the fact that all the characters were in a sort of shaky psychological state, a state of contagion, of reversibility, and that, ultimately, the reader was led to wonder about the stability of his own identity and limits, to question his own certainties again, as if one of the great mysteries of this novel was also that of the psyche.

JK: Whether it's a "detective story" in the style of Patricia Highsmith or a "mystery novel" in the style of Patricia Cornwell, the detective novel shakes up our identity and makes us complicit in one human being's murder by another and the ultimate intolerability of this. As modern men and women master technology, the more this mastery liberates them from sexual and ethical taboos, and the less they master their identity. If the detective novel allows me to explore this shaky identity, as you say, "on the spot," I am prepared for it as much by my listening as a psychoanalyst as by the fluidity of the female psyche, not to mention the frontiers of living, with which I'm being familiarized because of my involvement in the vast domain of disability. I do not see the loss of identity—even the riskiest or most dramatic—as a threat, but as a current event that inhabits me and that I can therefore describe and confront. I know that it is unavoidable. You can't muzzle it; it's not enough to understand it; all that remains is to sublimate it . . . Indefinitely. The novel, as I understand it, is precisely the form most suited to this sublimation of our unbearable vulnerability.

In another era and in another way, a woman—St. Teresa of Avila—experienced and named this fluidity of human frontiers. All her metaphors are metaphors of water, cascades, and flow. Is she naming female jouissance (the loss of vaginal secretions, as her commentators have claimed) or is she letting her discourse be permeated with an oriental rhetoric, indeed, the rhetoric of the Spanish soil, battling desert heat by watering gardens and dreaming of trips to the antipodes? St. Teresa's speech is undoubtedly inhabited by the reality of the world. However, more profoundly, this woman was subject to intense psychical ailments that have since been diagnosed; she was ravaged by epilepsy; she was eager for pleasure yet faithful to familial prohibitions. But prayer recomposed her, and it was in the writing, itself fluid, of her conviction of being the Son of God's beloved lover that she found the suppleness necessary to have both a radical meditation practice and a radical body of work. Saint Teresa succeeded where President Screber failed: in her fluid writing her psychial uncertainty no longer seems threatening to her, no severe superego-God persecutes her, her inner dwelling place is not a fortified castle but an aquatic construction with fluid contours. So the shaky identity is no longer a handicap, Teresa can pose as *Madre*, reform the Carmelites; the amorous epileptic becomes a political woman and even escapes the Inquisition, which moderately appreciated this fluidity. It is true that it was the dawn of the Baroque, and the Jesuits followed this Teresian trembling very closely . . .

Our era of drones and fundamentalist decapitations is admittedly very far from this Salvation through the rustling of Love. And our survival is difficult in another way: if God is dead, can we still survive the loss of identity? *Murder in Byzantium* is a novel of the end of an era: we all know that a certain history is ending; the cathedral of Puy-en-Velay is now a museum, the Louvre itself is not protected from kamikazes, and the Chinese may be the next purifiers of our colonial miasmas . . . Still, *Murder in Byzantium* will not be subjugated by crime, Stephanie returns to Rilsky in Santa Varvara, terrorism does not immobilize her at all, she continues to search for fluidity in the detective-historical-ironic novel . . . And what if the sadomasochistic orgy was only one version of history, one face of monotheism, the one exaggerated and exhibited in the film by Mel Gibson? What if there were others? *Salve Regina*, for example? The Nativity as a symbol of eternal renewal, Sebastian taking refuge with Mary in Puy-en-Velay. Mary, a virgin and victim, compensated as sovereign queen of the Church but not exempt from a period of maternal melancholy. That is how artists, painters, and musicians have understood her, taking her away from looking inward, so as to undress her, give her a body, and start down the path to the female body and women's rights. As he travels backward through the Crusades, Professor Sebastian Chrest-Jones thinks of the right to the singularity of each man, since he is god, *Ecce homo*, man of passion and memory. A path of anamnesis, a return to the origins. But there is nothing sacred in either maternal origins or the regression to which it leads us; the historian will die the very moment he finds the origins; and a cathedral does not impress criminals. History, however, is reborn from its ashes, Stephanie will continue the novel, the novel is the only resurrection, the rebirth of those with no reference points, the promise of a flowering for those with no system, no home, for travelers . . .

PLF: A flowering . . . a Colette-like perspective, it seems to me, as you showed in *Colette*, the third volume of the *Female Genius* series, analyzing this phrase of the author's in which she emphasizes the importance of flowering: "It is in [flowerings] that, for me, the essential drama resides, better than in death, which is only a commonplace defeat."[6]

JK: In some ways. Flowering is sketched out from the start in the story-line that destabilizes the detective novel: the lyrical or ironic account of the love affair between Anne Comnena and Ebrard finds its way into the wild and no less amorous quest conducted by the historian Sebastian Chrest-Jones, in search of the same princess Anne (nine centuries his senior); he gets mixed up in the elliptical exchanges between Stephanie and her adoptive son Jerry, comes across Stephanie's letter, while she is overcome by the death of her mother . . . nevertheless, the true flowering for me was and remains this perpetual rebirth that is the appropriation of the French language, a language I learned in elementary school and that, all in all, remained foreign. To be reborn in it, to put the memory of my sensations filtered through other languages, other places, other times into French is like watering the soil, the flowers. This is what Stephanie means when she says: "always held back by the vowels, consonants, and syllables, I go to meet the ungraspable little flame underneath the outer covering of signs: humor and meaning, mean and naive goodness, fluid fleeting river forever changing" (MB 63–64).

PLF: This brings up the question of kinship, at play in *Murder in Byzantium* on several levels: on the fictional level—as in the relationship between Rilsky and Chrest-Jones, described as a "bastard," or Stephanie's relationship with Jerry or her own mother—and also on a personal level. If *The Old Man and the Wolves* was about mourning a father, as you have said, isn't *Murder in Byzantium* a book about mourning a mother (I am thinking in particular of the chapter, "Silence, My Mother Is Dead," which I know was added when your mother passed away), supported by an inquiry into kinship and origins?

JK: This novel was written over a period of eight years. It started with a daydream about my nomadic life: the strange pleasure I felt "feeling at home" in airplanes reminded me of my father's jokes, about how our family name, Kristev, which means Delacroix (of the cross),[7] meant that we were descended from the crusaders, bizarre people, holy but hardly commendable travelers . . . Byzantium emerged with the idea of weaving a detective novel into a historical novel. Inevitably, it implicated me personally—the transgenerational saga that traced my father's family back to our supposed ancestors, the crusaders, and consequently, to my native Bulgaria, by way of our powerful Byzantine neighbor, and Adhémar de Monteil's armies, which left from Auvergne and Toulouse . . . In the meantime, there was the tragic turning point of September 11. But it was my mother's death that made me reconstruct the entire novel. The various traumas that have punctuated my life, perhaps the caesura of exile, which is a sort of death and resurrection, and also the constant opening to the unconscious, which psychoanalytical listening is, make me live in the moment: a vertical time, suspended. I had the strange impression time had stopped for me. But the death of both my parents and the acceleration of recent history suddenly brought me back to passing time: from the current crusade to the ancient crusaders, as well as to my own lineage.

The initials of the last name Chrest-Jones echo my own, Kristeva-Joyaux, and Stephanie Delacour is her father's daughter, as am I. We are not the sort of women who strive to equal the power of males. Sure to have our place at the game, in the stands, thanks to daddy, beside him, with him, Stephanie and I could happily expatriate ourselves without risk in the invisibility of the image: which, these days, is worse than a tomb. I could write, like her, that "my father convinced me, even before I realized it for myself, that I was capable of being one of them, of fusing with his enthusiasm, all the while remaining definitely someone else and somewhere else" (*MB* 73). And, like my journalist, my mother helped me win a contest as a child in which we had to answer the question "What is the most rapid form of transportation in the world?" My mother's answer was, naturally, thought. Conflicts can always be resolved with a mother who thinks like that. Quarrels, disagreements? Of course. And yet, after my analysis, which continues on the other side of the couch, in the armchair of the analyst, through my patients' countertransference, I can leave in search of familial memory with the certainty of owing my parents more than just my birth but the extravagant ability to be reborn—an exorbitant claim, I grant you, which Colette already formulated: "To be reborn has never been too much for me."[8] If what results is a novel of origins, it is not really an inquiry into the source, to be glorified, but a composition-recomposition of the subject. Through Sebastian and Stephanie, who both resemble me, but are complete strangers to me (I have never killed anyone, except for a few butterflies, and I am not a journalist at *L'Événement de Paris*, for example), I am speaking of myself as if I were another: I have composed their genealogical adventures with certain elements of mine, but above all with features I have borrowed from others, from individuals more traumatized than me, or traumatized in different ways, in whose ill-being I project myself, since my unconscious takes me there, while remaining very close to the history of my people. "My people" meaning my family, to start with, but also the Bulgarian people, the Orthodox tradition, and Eastern Europe.

Yet the Europe that is mine today is above all France and the European Union, my adopted homeland having practically absorbed the former homeland: the main proof of this integration is that I rarely speak Bulgarian and no longer know how to write it. So *Murder in Byzantium* is a reconstruction of my individual landscape through the political landscape of Europe. Themes specific to the refashioning of the modern family have also been added. So Chrest-Jones, for example, is a "bastard." He is looking for his crusader ancestor beyond the uncertain genealogy he has been given, in a rather decomposed family in Santa Varvara, which makes this killer/historian the commissioner's nephew . . . You will also find a discussion of gay couples and their rights to adoption: Chrest-Jones is overwhelmed by the absurdity of all the positions at cross-purposes in this debate, leading us to wonder whether these sorts of confrontations are the sorts of things that lead to crime . . . But don't think Stephanie Delacour (the real narrator of this metaphysical detective novel, as you noted) is a conformist. Like Julia Kristeva, Stephanie is convinced that human kinship is moving farther and farther away from traditional norms and that this is inevitable. By adopting Jerry, the son of her friend, Gloria, Stephanie is continuing an investigation into motherhood as a vocation and gift beyond genetics, which began in my earlier novel *Possessions*. It's the symbolic function of the mother that preoccupies her, the imaginary and symbolic function, regardless of its transmission through ovaries and the uterus and even if there is none. Lineage, you say? We have to agree on what that means. It's not about celebrating one's origins or paying a debt to one's parents, much less denying it. The questions are raised, there is no response, and the reader is invited once again to "ship himself on a voyage," to submit to the pitching and tossing, the mutation not of history but of the human race.

PLF: Since we're talking about mutation and change, I will move on to immigration. In your novel, Sebastian Chrest-Jones, a historian, is a specialist in migration and, to use Stephanie Delacour's neologism, "ships himself on a voyage" as well. Isn't this one of your essential preoccupations? I am thinking, for example, of the questions raised in *Strangers to*

Ourselves. But the voyage proposed in *Murder in Byzantium* is much more than a geographical voyage: it is also a psychical voyage to the borders of identities, including crime. Reading you, the reader becomes a psychical immigrant; he invests this *sans-soi* (without-self) of the traveler in which C-J is immersed.

JK: While writing this novel, as well as after publishing it and listening to you now, I kept asking myself: "Who is ready to hear this?" Who will be interested in this immigrant humanity, which is mine and which I am trying to bring to life in this novel? In spite of recent upheavals that have induced various migratory fluxes, the history and culture of the Hexagon has protected the French from these nomadic beings, which I am and which my characters are. Should I write in English, in Hebrew? Indeed, my novels are more appreciated abroad, and yet French is the only language I write in now. Sometimes I share my fears with my editor: what's the use of trying to convey the nonbeing of a Chrest-Jones, a Wuxian, or a Stephanie Delacour to people who feel sure of themselves and rooted? But, since one does not write solely for others, and I have the exceptional luck to have an editor who understands that, I persevere. In reality, I can do nothing but devote myself to impossible causes. For example, foreigners, disability, Europe. Which all have this in common: these causes do not interest anyone. No, no, don't rile French people up with that; I've heard that. So why is it that I continue to *express* this immigrant experience, as you say, in French? Because that is the point of *Murder in Byzantium* too: to write in my immigrant French of the happiness and unhappiness of the uprooted. Oh, of course, I have good reasons: France adopted me more readily than other nomads; I'm even a "personality on the scene," as they say, though an "atypical" one; the Enlightenment of the eighteenth century and the fringes of recent avant-gardes have given me my moral framework, and I am fond of these people who are fairly simple, all in all, full of good sense and good taste, proud of their past, their social advantages and their houses in the country, who are trying to set the tone for this very problematic European continent, "inspired by fever and cancer," as Rimbaud said. But I do not have any illusions: the reality of immigrants is certainly not seen, and people do not see what I am talking about. I get the same impression when working on the impossible mission of changing the way disability is seen. If I dared to be direct, I would say: "You can run!" The media wants disabled people who are entertaining—fiery, compromising, if possible—for a party, a government, a good little scandal, why not? But sharing and acknowledging the everyday misery, the endemic vulnerability, the anxiety of psychical or physical death—no one's lining up for that, believe me. You might as well ask for a look at the wall of *mens sana in corpore sano* (a sound mind in a sound body), shaped by the preoccupation with pleasure/performance/excellence: the wall does not see the excluded, because the wall is what creates them! Did you say the disabled? Geographical nomads? Historical nomads? Psychical nomads? What next? All of that is very foreign to them—that's the word. Obviously, I'm exaggerating. There are still a few devoted believers, and a few people armed with a good superego that taught them the duty of solidarity with the marginal, just as we find partisans of Europe who appreciate this civilization and believe that their children's future is better assured by an imperfect Constitution than by petrodollars or fanatics of God. But this does not go very far. No. Even the most well-intentioned political men and women are caught in oblivion. Conclusion: I'm addressing a minority of people about things that are folkloric, I'm aware of that. And yet I threw myself into this saga of immigrants that *Murder in Byzantium* is with a sort of enthusiasm, the kind you have when, surrounded by walls, you knock, thinking in spite of everything, it might be heard one day, notably in French, from a book written in French . . . An illusion? Certainly, and I don't necessarily see it being fulfilled. But it doesn't matter: it had to be done, and I am happy to have done it in the French language. A message in a bottle, writing about time for time's sake.

PLF: Isn't Anne Comnena the heroine of the novel in a sense? Couldn't she be one of the illustrious ancestors of your three female geniuses (Arendt, Klein, and Colette)?

JK: I didn't think about it, but your idea is plausible. In fact, Stephanie Delacour shares Chrest-Jones's conviction that Anne Comnena was the first intellectual in the world, well before Simone de Beauvoir and even George Sand or Madame de Staël! It's true that I was dazzled when I discovered the work of this twelfth-century woman, but it does not seem to have made on impression on the media; the press barely noticed her existence in *Murder in Byzantium*. Instead they pointed out furious allusions to French society or Santa Varvara. Byzantium continues to be a blind spot, like the new Europe, by the way . . .

Anne Comnena was an extraordinary woman, who was born in 1083 and probably died in 1148—that, at least, is the year she finishes her monumental book, *The Alexiad*, a fifteen-volume history devoted to the reign of her father and thus the beginning of the Crusades. She was a completely exceptional woman for her times: raised on Zeus and Homer, Plato, Aristotle, as well as Jesus and the Virgin Mary—the Marian cult developed very early in the Orthodox Church. Like a military strategist, Anna describes the battles engaged in by her father's troops. But, like a psychologist and politician, she also mentions the court intrigue she took part in, in her eagerness for power, before distancing herself from it and devoting herself to writing. It's a unique testimony if we consider that there are no women in Western Europe capable of such performances and that at the time major historical chronicles of the Crusades were written in Latin by men who belonged to the Catholic clergy. Her later Greek overflows with filial piety; Anne is already a romantic who uses the melancholy of her Stoic ancestors to predict the collapse of her Byzantium, under assault by those uncultured barbarians, the Latins, and, above all, by the onslaught of the Muslims, even more ferocious and unbearable for her. Isn't it strange that no feminist has spoken of Anne Comnena until now? Why this lack of curiosity, at least in France? Foreign journalists, on the other hand, particularly Swedish and Norwegian ones, asked a lot of questions about her.

PLF: Your text is quite rich and erudite, notably in the historical sections and also as a result of the little intertextual winks (St. Augustine, Colette, Baudelaire, Joyce, Sollers, Quignard, Ricoeur, and even Saint-Exupéry). Is this the literate person's pleasure? An intimate and personal pleasure?

JK: I don't think erudition is foreign to the novel as a genre, in any case, not to the novel I lay claim to. It's true that the authors you cite and many others mentioned in *Murder in Byzantium* are part of the novel of my life; and I do not resign myself to the borders of genres that separate theology from poetry, for example. Ultimately, I recognize myself in this reflection of Hannah Arendt's, who was surprised that a woman's erudition could be considered the result of a constraint, because, for the author of *The Human Condition*, there was no greater happiness than that of thinking. What you call "winks"—Joyce's ironic passages on the Louvre, St. Augustine's reflections on the memory of the man of sorrow, or Pascal Quignard's amused look at our humanity of viviparous babies—are part of my joie de vivre.

PLF: You have your daytime activity as an analyst and academic and your nighttime activity as a novelist. Is plunging into that universe, that of the novel, a way of placing yourself outside time?

JK: "I know that in writing I have to blind myself artificially in order to focus all the light on one dark spot."[9] This was Freud's admission to Lou Andréas-Salomé, and it sums up the analytical experience for me. But it's also the way I write a novel. Night—this state of wakefulness between two dreams, not insomnia but a paradoxical lucidity, precisely—is necessary for me to "blind myself." Not understanding and not knowing, suspending the vigilance of the mind, letting oneself drift toward the "dark spot" of a sensation, perfume or brutality, expression, phrase, judgment, idea . . . perceived yesterday or engraved in one's memory and that take up all the space in the dark. To throw myself toward this dark spot the way I imagine a person leaping from the fifth floor would throw himself, looking for the last word to latch on to what is happening to him. A free fall and extreme shock, instantaneous and interminable. Capturing this *sans-soi* (without-self) in a phrase or rhythm is related to that moment of grace in analytic interpretation when, detached from my self and my reason, I am in osmosis with the patient's unconscious discourse, possessing it as much as it possesses me.

And yet, in retreat from this perilous empathy, there is an attempt to express this timelessness, a concern to convey it, convey myself, and share not a faith but a trust. This guarantees the link with the patient and the anonymous readers with whom *Murder in Byzantium* keeps company. "Devising it all for company . . . The fable of one with you in the dark. The fable of one fabling of one with you in the dark . . . Alone," Beckett writes in *Company*.[10] The time of loss, the time of restitution: analysis and writing alternate the two in an incessant pulsation. With this one enormous difference, that the novel—unlike analytic speech—is haunted by language and history. Expressing a fall, possession/dispossession in words, but always listening for this age-old music composed by a people with its taste and history. It is here that the *sans-soi* becomes social: the novelist is a *sans-soi* who infiltrates the social through the medium of language, inherited or chosen. Is this a contraction, a defense of *sans-soi*?

Durkheim already reminded us that today God is society. Fine. Then the novel as I understand it will be its mystic, God's as well as society's. I must admit to you the core of my inadmissible, nocturnal ambition. What other composition, if not the polyphony of the novel, could echo the psychosis that is the brute reality of globalized humans, as generalized criminality shows? In proximity and at a distance, in total lucidity? What other composition, if not the polyphony of the novel, could convey these psychical modulations that are different religions, in crisis today more than ever and consequently in fratricidal conflict? Without complacency and without the judgment of national identity, in total lucidity? For the analyst as for the novelist, religions are psychical modulations, don't you think? The Byzantine man is not the same as the Catholic man, he is not the same as the Protestant, he is not the same as the Chinese man, he is not the same as the fanatic of Allah. The characters in *Murder in Byzantium*—Anne Comnena, the Orthodox, Sebastian Chrest-Jones, who brings together Catholic Europe and Protestant Santa Varvara, while remaining in love with Byzantium, and, of course, Wuxian, the wayward Taoist turned purifier—are musical variations added to this religious orchestration, in counterpoint to actual wars, stirred up by the sophisticated weapons of the Pentagon as well as the mythomaniacal fabulations of riders on our trains. And what if the novel were this propitious place where what was at play was not the clash of religions and assassins, but their passing through, their recasting into a bouquet of psychical landscapes impossible to stabilize or abolish but explored in an attempt to sublimate them?

I said *the novel*, because if it's true that a reformulation of psychical diversity is needed (if we want to avoid not the end of History but a History heading implacably toward the destruction of the planet and human beings), this reformulation has to do with the imaginary—certainly not with the sciences, even the human sciences, and certainly not with religious discourse, today tense with worry about their identities, despite the wishes of the pope, who at present is perhaps the most advanced of religious men. If it is true, as I think it is, that globalization and its religious crises signal not the revival of what is religious, but its nervous breakdown, the inevitable moment of its decline, already announced by Nietzsche, it is the novel that will be—that is—the favored terrain where this interminable end may be put into words. I'm not thinking of best sellers that enjoy falsifying religious history and replacing it with the more digestible opium of esotericism, in the style of *The Da Vinci Code*, but the novel that is constructed as a novel of the subject. Obviously, those addicted to the ego will find the novel of the subject "too intellectual." Unless they get through their fear of travel and wrest themselves from the prison of the soul in which they have been taught to protect themselves, in which they become sedentary. And provided they agree to "focus all the light," including that of intelligence, on the multiplicity of dwellings that make up the "dark spot." Because it is here that jouissance and death are joined, from this that religious wars profit and this that the metaphysical detective novel reveals.

PLF: [On] Religion . . . I was thinking of that phrase attributed to Malraux that said: the twenty-first century will be religious or it will not be. *Murder in Byzantium* in fact leads the reader to reflect on this assertion.

JK: Ah, religion! The psychoanalyst will tell you that it replaces death, the fear of death, with an absolute master, the ideal Father who assures you of life in the hereafter. The man, Malraux, tormented by death, turned toward hope, toward the idealization of the Father, and could not help but feel a resonance with all forms of religion secreted by the twentieth century and foresee the hysterias of times to come . . . The mystic does not take exactly the same path. The male or female mystic (they often lay claim to a psychical bisexuality) is not content to deny death by means of hope or idealization. They identify with death, which is fundamentally the separation from the maternal container; they confuse themselves with lack. Paradoxically, to relive death itself allows the mystic to detach him- or herself from the lost mother without getting attached to the ideal Father who promises life beyond death. The mystics take pleasure in this inhuman autonomy, no mother, no father, which is also, consequently, areligious, indeed, asocial, and necessarily apophatic: that is, their thought is a negative thought, resistant to rational systems. This path is therefore a constant resurrection, while also being experienced as an acceptance of death: another mystical paradox formulated by Meister Eckhart as well as by Heidegger, when they identify God and nothingness or being and nothingness, and St. Teresa of Avila, when she affirms to her sisters that they can and must "checkmate God." For me, this imaginary experience, that of the novel of the subject, is obviously situated in the vicinity of these adventures. By creating a character, by transfusing myself in the flight of butterflies above the Rhodopes or singing *Salve Regina* in the cloister of Puy-en-Velay, I abolish the separation, and I construct ideal models against anxiety, against and with the death to come. Such mystical moments are found, as I have said, in the process of analytical transference/countertransference, but they are bordered and framed by the knowledge of the psychical apparatus that psychoanalytical knowledge elaborates at the crossroads of medicine, philosophy, and aesthetics. None of these safeguards exist in the novel-

istic writing of "the fable of one fabling of one with you in the dark." If
not the constraints of the musical craft, the exquisite infidelity faithful
to the chosen language. And thus this voyage through negative thought,
an apophatic voyage, through the thoughts accumulated in the history of
my life of travel, in the conflicts underway, from social life to the clashes
of religious configurations. You see then that the metaphysical detective
novel that crystallizes this way is not an "aesthetic religion," though it is
saturated with delicious sensations and cadavers, maternal caresses and
rotten mafia, vicious serial killers or purifiers. If it mobilizes hysteria, in
the sense that it fills my body with visions, and if it is projected into the
varieties of monumental history, through its open narrative structure,
the novel lends itself to questions, reversals, revolts, to suspense . . . In
the metaphysics of knowledge, religion, or mysticism, through the novel
I ship myself on a voyage

PLF: One may "ship oneself on a voyage" in music, too. It was not spoken
about much in the interviews that were done. Music accompanied you
as you wrote the novel; we also find it in the novel, brought to the fore
by Stephanie, who speaks of Scott Ross's "touch." There is also a music
one perceives in the lyricism: certain passages of your novel are in fact
extremely lyrical (and at the same time denounced as such in a mise en
abyme: "qu'il était lyrique le petit oncle . . ." for example). Is music at the
heart of *Murder in Byzantium*?

JK: Music has been part of my life for a long time. The songs of my father,
who was an excellent tenor, greeted me in the cradle, and I would listen
to him as a soloist or in the choir of his church (Orthodox, naturally)
or at concerts. My sister was a cellist; I heard her play from morning to
night in the next room, I admired her gifts no less than the draconian
discipline that is the carrier wave of musicians' jubilation and that led
her to the Moscow conservatory. Philippe Sollers is the most musical
person I know, and our son David has a perfect ear. I do not have these
talents, but I am a receptive and fascinated audience member. In *Murder
in Byzantium* music is present as a final transition of the sexual relationship: Stephanie Delacour finds a new lover and makes love with Scarlatti
played by Scott Ross, and *Salve Regina* by Vivaldi or Palestrina complete
Sebastian Chrest-Jones's reconciliation with himself and his history in
the Puy-en-Velay Cathedral.

Freud admitted in a letter to Romain Rolland that he was as closed
off to music as he was to mysticism: he thus admitted, along with his

personal limitations, a fear of drowning in an infralinguistic maternal regression, a fear of relinquishing nascent psychoanalysis to the "swamp of occultism," etc. We are no longer at this point. As for me, when I listen to music, or when I think I am integrating it into my thought, my writing, I see it as a perpetual framing of vital excitation: breathing, the beating of the heart, the pulse of sexual pleasure. But it is an atemporal framing, in contrast to the sexual organ, which is subjugated to the time of the release. Sound that is thought—i.e., composed by the human voice or an instrument—seems to me to be the ultimate sublimation of the sexual relationship, its absolute transposition into human history as well as into the inhuman flesh of the world. Hence this "oceanic feeling" that music provides, the intermingling of a restrictive technique and a sensitive experience, intimate and foreign at once. I see music as a sublimated vital sharing, in modesty and the greatest detachment. To try to transmit this by means of the language or plot of the novel is obviously utopian, but I need to let myself be carried away by music when I write. Jouissance is not incompatible with elucidation, and this crest that I cling to in writing a novel is supported by music.

PLF: And painting! Orthodox icons appear in reproduction in this novel, which is not like other novels in that it contains geographical maps, images of churches and frescoes. You did an exhibition at the Louvre in the graphic arts department, Visions capitales, around the theme of decapitation; your study on Giotto is still read in universities, and your reflection "From Madonnas to Nudes" [in this volume] captures the celebration of two thousand years of Christianity.

JK: Is it because the voyage includes its share of betrayal? In any case, there is very little left of my Orthodox origins. But the icons, yes! An Orthodox icon is not viewed, it is embraced. You plunge into it, and your eyes are flooded by touch, smell, taste, hearing. The believer hears the voice of God, immerses himself in the harmonics of choral groups, plunging beyond the visible into the invisible, but with the sensorial profusion of the carnal body. The flesh, which Merleau-Ponty would rehabilitate in phenomenology after Christian mystics, was perhaps never solicited in monotheisms as strongly as in the Orthodox mass. Catholicism does not ignore it, obviously, but refines it in music, precisely. And as for the visual arts, it transforms iconic contemplation into figuration: the icons are followed by the *figura*, then realism, then its deconstruction, the fabulous destiny of Western painting. While icons immobilize

Orthodox man in the communion, delights, and dependencies of a medieval, pre-Renaissance humanity, artistic freedom will be Catholic and post-Catholic, Baroque or Protestant, but certainly not Orthodox. And yet the stagnation of the Byzantine icon is compensated by its syncretic sensoriality, an intense appeal to the senses, which everyone who participates in an Orthodox liturgy experiences. I am convinced that people's interest in Christian Orthodoxy is rooted not only in the fact that it addresses borderline states—depression, melancholia, mourning, loss of self, which Orthodox theology exalts, more than others, with the term *kenosis* (that is, the annihilation of the divine realized by Christ's descent into hell) —but also in the fact that Orthodoxy saturates these states in caresses, sounds, scents. I am made of this Orthodox sensibility, and if I discipline it in the daytime, I am submerged in it at night: my unconscious is an Orthodox land enveloped by a French atmosphere.

The pages of *Murder in Byzantium* you allude to try to make these phenomena, this body, resonate in the French language. Obviously, my guides on this path are the two most "orthodox" writers among the French: Proust, a Jew inspired by Schopenhauer, and Colette, a pre-Socratic from Burgundy. With this I hope you are sensitive to the modesty of my claim: Stephanie Delacour, who is my alter ego, admits that she does not inhabit the phonemes and syntax of the French language— a kingdom in which she will always be surpassed by Proust or Colette, to cite only those two—but she writes the melody of the sensory that flows beneath her sentences. It is this double of language, the invisible foundation of icons, that I have tried to translate through the rapid *tempo*, pulsing, slipping from the narration, through the multiplicity of characters, who correspond to each other and are confused as "doubles," through the complexity of the detective story that insinuates itself into the story of the court, which is historical, and, of course, through the omnipresent irony. It seems possible to reach this infralinguistic experience through sounds, words, and syntax, but even more perhaps through the polyphonic narrative structure, embedded in philosophical and political insertions.

PLF: In *Murder in Byzantium* one senses something that is not Proust, not Colette, but really very "Kristevan." A way of writing that is also found in the essays with lyrical sections. The chapter "Time for a Long Time" in *Time and Sense: Proust and the Literary Experience*, for example, is a very lyrical piece.

JK: I resisted my father's efforts to bring me into the Orthodox faith: until the age of eight, he never failed to bring me to church. Afterward, there was a revolt, and, very quickly, rupture. It may be that this childhood permeation has endured, an Orthodox sedimentation that pierces through the Cartesian French. The Orthodox faith, if you adhere to it, lets you touch the mystery of the incarnation not with a finger but with your entire body: the Word is made Flesh in an Orthodox church, no doubt about it. Catholicism is, in spite of everything, necessarily, happily, much closer to the idea. The Catholic Trinity based on the *Filioque* (the Holy Spirit proceeding from the Father *and* the Son), and not on the Orthodox *Per Filium* (according to which the Holy Spirit proceeds from the Father *through* the Son, subordinating the latter to the former), guarantees the extraordinary independence of the Son and the believer. All of theology feels it; it will rehabilitate Greek thought and arrive at a "blank theology" with Descartes, then modern philosophy. Nothing of the sort in my Orthodoxy, with its brioche sensibility, as one of its exegetes put it, in which God is unrecognizable, subtracted from Logos, accessible only in prayer. The depression that is ravaging our societies, in the West as in the East, seems to find more consolation in Orthodox ritual than in Catholic exigency, which nevertheless very reasonably creates charitable organizations, like Secours catholique and Quart-monde. Orthodoxy seems more comfortable with Good Friday than the *Gloria*, though it ostensibly celebrates the myth of the resurrection: you are constantly called to the melancholic or ecstatic crossroads between the body and the word, sense and the sensory.

When I finished my book on Proust, the moment I finished "Time for a Long Time," it seemed clear that my path through *In Search* had mobilized my entire body, that I had "reembodied" myself in the text I was studying, and so I tried to take note of that state: which you noticed. Why is that striking? Perhaps because a philosopher or an essayist coming out of the Sorbonne, the rue d'Ulm or [rue] de Sèvres, does not feel obligated, much less authorized, to be embodied in an "interpretation." I do not ask permission. Was it given to me by my Orthodox father, or by this Byzantine tradition I am trying to rehabilitate just as Europe is opening to the East with such difficulty and reticence, even if it will happen sooner or later . . . ?

I emphasize this resurgence of childhood in me, because the "lyricism" that marks my essays and persists in *Murder in Byzantium* is not something I owe to a willful decision or a philosophical influence. Of course, a whole phenomenological current, with Merleau-Ponty or Deleuze, excels at bringing forth the sensorial fundaments of expression. Of course, this context consoles me in my writing, but it does not engender it. It's all of my experience, "my Byzantium," from Bulgaria to Paris, as a mother, a psychoanalyst, a woman, a citizen, a linguist, a semiologist, and a teacher that has led me to an effort of thought, and this effort confronts me with the fragility of the sensory body. The sensory not as flaw or lack, but as the actual purpose of this enigma that is meaning: the secret of saying, of writing? I don't know, but this is where the imaginary I would like to transmit is situated: breathing space in this world where the word, including the novelistic word, is reduced to a seductive manipulation, when not raw technical data, a pretext for cruelty, murder.

You will notice that murder, or murders, are neither judged nor condemned in my Byzantium. Well, that's not only because the capacity to judge is disappearing little by little in the modern world: look at the inundation of trials and the failure of the judicial spectacle. Above all, it's because the true antidote to crime and murder is not judgment, but the sensory body: on the condition that it be said, written, and shared. Crime sees this speech as "lyricism," negatively or positively. But there is no other safeguard, no other protection against acting out of all kinds, than id: that, at least, is what I learned in Byzantium.

PLF: There is lyricism in the text, but there are also provocations: regarding the novel itself ("the novel as the rhetoric of the perverse") or politics. These provocations are not without irony, however.

JK: Oh, yes, take the terrorist attack on the Louvre. French diplomacy took a position during the Iraqi crisis that elicited a lot of sympathy across the world, and Stephanie Delacour herself shares it. Like Commissioner Rilsky, she seems fascinated by Foulques Weil, the atypical French ambassador in Santa Varvara. And yet the narrator sets up the sort of failure of French policies, since, despite all this prudence and precaution, Paris remains a target for terrorists: the proof is that the Louvre is shattered . . . according to *Murder in Byzantium*. The novel allows one to show that every "position," however laudable it may seem, is untenable, because it involves its opposite. And that is so not only because of the complexity of the political chessboard, on which various national and international interests confront each other, but because, in this freedom that is the novel of the subject, question and answer neutralize each other; the answer loses its character as a question and simply becomes saying. The irony comes from this, and this is where I see the essence of the novel. Look at Proust: when he sees himself as a mistreated Jew in French society, when he writes of the subtle or brutal exclusions that affect Swann or Bloch, and at the same time makes fun of Jews as he does every other group identity, and all those who would like to "be of"—a religion, a race, a nation, a salon, a sex—"little Marcel" reaches the novelistic summit as well as the singularity of being.

Is this to say that "the novel is the rhetoric of the perverse"? Stephanie says it with irony, which has its share of truth: for example, in global marketing, particularly French, the reduction of certain novels to an indulgence in sexual or moral transgressions. But my heroine also makes a wager: can one still sell a novel that is not reduced to *père-verse* seduction? A novel that does not ignore it but integrates it into the kaleidoscope of the subject, the mosaic that "ships itself on a voyage"? That's not certain! And yet this is the choice.

PLF: We spoke of Proust and Colette. I think while reading you I noticed two other authors, Dostoyevsky and Thomas Mann, who seemed to accompany you in writing *Murder in Byzantium*.

JK: Writing of night, disconnection, and regression, there are no moorings, rough drafts, or notebooks—no references. Composition comes in a second phase, also without a safety net, but more consciously musical. It is only while rereading an almost acceptable version of my text that familiar echoes, complicities, unsuspected influences become apparent to me. Thomas Mann, notably, with *The Magic Mountain*: the emergence of European time under the rust of families, historical duration, the First World War, and the tubercular bodies of the sanitariums, which symbolized a Europe already ill, yet alive in its memory, through its memory. The time of Thomas Mann resonates with this other European time I evoke, going back to the Crusades, and with the ailing body of the third millennium, which is no longer the phthisic of the early twentieth century but the psychotic of modernity . . . And, of course, Dostoyevsky, because, if *Murder in Byzantium* is a detective novel, it is indeed in the sense that *The Possessed* is a detective novel, a historical detective novel. Upon publication of the French translation of *The Possessed*, Parisian critics decried that this Russian was decidedly too intellectual, that his book was not a novel, but rather heavy theory that was incomprehensible. Sounds familiar . . .

Stavrogin, Kirilov, and other Dostoyevskian characters are criminals, and deranged, the precursors to the Bolshevik revolution through which the novelist reveals the great mystery of politics—psychical life, madness.

PLF: Thomas Mann, Dostoyevsky: writers of malady, madness, crisis. All this is in *Murder in Byzantium,* and yet the reader is left with a feeling of joy that is not in *The Magic Mountain* or *The Possessed* . . .

JK: Is joy an encounter between unrest and serenity? The central theme, the voyage—the voyage to the time of the Crusades taken by Sebastian Chrest-Jones; the voyage between Santa Varvara and Byzantium, between police inquiry and romantic quest, which Stephanie is writing— keeps the question open, exposes the reader to the impossibility of an answer and so to anxiety. This seems to be the only optimism possible at the present time and explains the success of detective novels: the detective novel says, "You can know" without necessarily giving the answer, but placing us in the investigation. The question, because it is more stimulating and more open than the answer, is our only promise. But where does serenity come from? Psychoanalysis teaches me everyday that one can offer tranquillity without offering a positive answer. The interpretation I offer a patient is never directive: it never responds to his request; it is content to revive his free association, his search for lost time and desire, and in this way appease him. It may be that my novel is woven in unison with this music: all the themes, positions, and characters are as positive as they are negative and disconcerting, and the insolence of this openness is certainly not a consolation, but leads to fleeting serenities.

PLF: *Tranquil* . . . In *Murder in Byzantium* you use this word in a sentence that sends us back to the fundamental questions, which for you are the journey and timelessness: "Tranquil, perfectly Byzantine—Greek, even— Sebastian now stopped. Perhaps it was the end of his journey. A possible end in any case. Time regained outside of time" (*MB* 180). What would it mean to be Byzantine, today?

JK: To thwart identities and complicate certainties, including those of the novel; to be heretical; to "ship oneself on a voyage." What dies in *my* Byzantium—in Puy-en-Velay, at the Café du Louvre, or in the restless wanderings of Stephanie Delacour and Sebastian Chrest-Jones—are beliefs. I am trying to write in the open; uncertainty is my Byzantine memory, and the novel a flowering of questions.

NOTES

Foreword

1. Roland Barthes, "Kristeva's *Semeiotike*," in *The Rustle of Language*, trans. Richard How-ard (Berkeley: University of California Press, 1989), pp. 168–169. Originally pub-lished in French as "L'étrangère" in *La Quinzaine littéraire*, May 1, 1970.
2. Named after Danish-Norwegian philosopher and writer Ludvig Holberg (1684–1754). The Norwegian Parliament created this prize in 2004 to celebrate "a re-markable, erudite body of work" and to fill the void left by the Nobel Prize in "the domains of the arts and humanities, social sciences, law, and theology."
3. Julia Kristeva, *Thinking About Liberty in Dark Times/Penser la liberté en temps de détresse*, co-published by the Holberg Prize and Université Paris 7–Denis Diderot, 2005. See chapter 1, this volume.
4. References to first editions appear at the end of this work.
5. Blanchard, "Julia Kristeva."
6. A reference to the corrupt fictional world described in her novel *Murder in Byzantium*. Julia Kristeva points out: "The reader will find themes that are immediately decipher-able: the corrupt, criminal, and mafia-like society of the globalized village, referred to only as 'Santa-Varvara.'" See p. 00 of this volume, in the section entitled "Writing."
7. Julia Kristeva, "Unes femmes," *Les Cahiers du GRIF*, no. 7 (June 1975); "Le temps des femmes," in *34/44: Cahiers de recherche de sciences des textes et documents*, no. 5 (1979), Uni-versité Paris 7, published as "Women's Time" in *New Maladies of the Soul*.

8. *Female Genius* is composed of three volumes: the first examines Hannah Arendt (1906–1975), the second Melanie Klein (1882–1960), and the third Colette (1873–1954). All three were published by Fayard and Columbia University Press. As Julia Kristeva explains in the first volume of the trilogy: "*Life, madness,* and *words:* the three women relied on them to become lucid and passionate investigators while drawing on their existence as much as their thinking" (p. xix, introduction, *Hannah Arendt*). The three volumes retrace their trajectories.

9. See especially "Roland Barthes and Writing as Demystification," in *The Sense and Non-sense of Revolt,* vol. 1: *The Powers and Limits of Psychoanalysis,* trans. Jeanine Herman (New York: Columbia University Press, 2000).

10. Julia Kristeva, *Time and Sense: Proust and the Experience of Literature,* trans. Ross Guberman (New York: Columbia University Press, 1998), *The Sense and Non-sense of Revolt,* trans. Jeanine Herman (New York: Columbia University Press, 2000), and *Intimate Revolt,* trans. Jeanine Herman (New York: Columbia University Press, 2002).

11. See "What Is Left of Our Loves?" this volume.

12. "Je me voyage" is the motto of Kristeva's heroine in *Murder in Byzantium.*

2. Secularism

1. "Considérons aussi que rien, en dépit de l'insipide tendance, ne se montrera exclusivement laïque, parce que ce mot n'élit pas précisément de sens." Stéphane Mallarmé, *Divagations* (Paris: Bibliothèque-Charpentier; Fasquelle, 1897).—TRANS.

2. Hannah Arendt, "The Origins of Totalitarianism: A Reply to Eric Voegelin," in *The Portable Hannah Arendt,* ed. Peter Baehr (New York: Penguin, 2003).

3. Liberty, Equality, Fraternity and . . . Vulnerability

1. Did you know, for example, that in the country of the rights of man, thirteen thousand disabled children who could have gone to school in 2002 did not? "Rapport d'information sur la politique de compensation du handicap" by Senator Paul Blanc, appendix to the session of July 24, 2002. That twelve thousand people with multiple disabilities receive no care and that a court of honor, formed by the organization Droits aux soins et à une place adaptée (Right to treatment and a suitable place), condemned the French state for "mistreatment and deficiencies" so as to draw attention to this scandal, with no tangible result up to now?

2. Julia Kristeva is president.

3. Jacques Chirac set three goals in 2002 for his five-year term: the struggle against dangerous roads, the fight against cancer, and aid to the disabled.

4. Last line of Sartre's *Les Mots* (The Words): "Tout un homme, fait de tous les hommes, qui les vaut tous et que vaut n'importe qui."—TRANS.

5. Cf. Stiker, *A History of Disability.* Published in France as *Corps infirmes et sociétés.*

6. As outlined in Mahéas's excellent synthesis, "Le role du pauvre au coeur de l'Église. L'expérience de l'Arche et le Mystère pascal" (The role of the poor at the heart of the Church: The experience of L'Arche and the Paschal mystery).
7. Written in November of 2002, published in Paris by Fayard in 2003.
8. Cf. Ameisen, *La Sculpture du vivant*.

5. From Madonnas to Nudes

1. Lévinas, *Ethics and Infinity*, p. 85.
2. Philippe Sollers, "L'Assomption," in *Théorie des exceptions*. See also "Le trou de la Vierge," an interview with Jacques Henric filmed by Jean-Paul Fargier.
3. Arthur Rimbaud, "Cities" in *Illuminations* (1873), trans. Wallace Fowlie, *Complete Works* (Chicago: University of Chicago Press, 1966), p. 241.
4. *The Virgin and Child with St. Anne.*—TRANS.
5. See his *Sleeping Venus*, 1508–1510, Gemäldegalerie Alte Meister, Dresden.
6. Olivier Widmaier Picasso, *Picasso: The Real Family Story* (New York: Prestel, 2004).

6. The Passion According to Motherhood

1. Green, "Cognitivisme, neurosciences."
2. Vincent and Ferry, *Qu'est-ce que l'homme?*
3. On the two-sided oedipal phase, see "Fatigue in the Feminine," this volume.
4. Vincent and Ferry, *Qu'est-ce que l'homme?* pp. 193–194.
5. Cf. Julia Kristeva, "Klein on Negativity" in *Melanie Klein*, trans. Ross Guberman (New York: Columbia University Press, 2002), and "Des Controverses aux Indépendants" in *The Freud/Klein Controversies, 1941–1945* (London: Routledge, 1992).
6. Cf. Winnicott, "Birth Memories," pp. 182–183.
7. Colette, *La Naissance du jour* (1928)—she is fifty-five years old—in *Oeuvres complètes*, vol. 3 (1991), p. 285; Colette, *Break of Day*, trans. Enid McLeod (New York: Farrar, Straus and Giroux, 2002), p. 16.
8. Colette, *Break of Day*, p. 3.
9. Ibid., p. 4.

7. The War of the Sexes Since Antiquity

1. Charpin, *Le Féminin exclu*.

8. Beauvoir, Presently

1. Simone de Beauvoir, *La Deuxième Sexe*, 1:31; *The Second Sex*, trans. H. M. Parshley (New York: Vintage, 1989), p. xxxv.
   References to *The Second Sex* will be abbreviated SS.—TRANS.

2. Emphasis mine.

3. Sartre, *Being and Nothingness*, pp. 503 and 504.

4. Cf. Moi, *Simone de Beauvoir*, p. 169. Published in a French as *Simone de Beauvoir: conflits d'une intellectuelle*.

5. Joseph, *Une si douce Occupation*.

6. An excellent analysis of Beauvoir's first novels in light of her evolution toward political engagement can be read in Danièle Fleury's brilliant thesis, "Simone de Beauvoir: De *L'Invitée* au *Sang des autres*, l'éveil à la solidarité" (Awakening to Solidarity, from *She Came to Stay* to *The Blood of Others*).

7. Cf. Sartre, *Les Carnets de la drôle de guerre*, pp. 135–136, with notes by Arlette Elkaïm-Sartre.

   This quote is from notebook 1 of the war diaries. Notebook 1 (*Lettres au Castor*) was added to the French edition but is not included in the English edition; the English starts with notebook 3 (*Witness to My Life: The Letters of Jean-Paul Sartre to Simone de Beauvoir, 1926–1939*)—TRANS.

8. Marcel Proust, *Cities of the Plain II*, vol. 2, *Remembrance of Things Past*, trans. C. K. Scott-Moncrieff and Terence Kilmartin (New York: Vintage, 1982), p. 824.

9. Cf. Grosrichard, *Structure du sérail*, published in English as *The Sultan's Court*; cf. Julia Kristeva, *Colette* (New York: Columbia University Press, 2004).

10. *Hommeau* (possibly short for *homme au foyer*), an obsolete expression for a domesticated, castrated man.—TRANS.

11. Grosrichard, *The Sultan's Court*, p. 178.

12. Sartre, *Quiet Moments in a War*, p. 176.

9. Fatigue in the Feminine

1. Colette, *The Vagabond*, trans. Enid McLeod (New York: Farrar, Straus and Giroux, 2001), p. 32.

2. Cf. Sigmund Freud, "Female Sexuality" (1931): "Bisexuality . . . comes to the fore much more clearly in women than in men"; in *The Standard Edition of the Complete Psychological Works of Sigmund Freud* (London: Hogarth, 1923–1925), 21:227.

3. Ibid., p. 226.

4. See Julia Kristeva, *Melanie Klein*, vol. 2 of *Female Genius* (New York: Columbia University Press, 2001).

5. Cf. Sigmund Freud, "Some Psychical Consequences of the Anatomical Distinction between the Sexes," in *The Standard Edition of the Complete Psychological Works of Sigmund Freud* (London: Hogarth, 1923–1925), 19:241–258.

6. Colette, *The Vagabond*, pp. 31–32.

7. Here we might recall Freud's reverie in "An Overall View of Transference Neuroses" (1915).

8. Marcel Proust, *Remembrance of Things Past*, vol. 1, *Swann's Way*, trans. C. K. Scott Moncrieff and Terence Kilmartin (New York: Vintage, 1982), p. 93.

9. Cf. Teresa of Avila, *Oeuvres*, 1:754–55.

10. Colette, *The Blue Lantern*, trans. Roger Senhouse (New York: Farrar, Straus and Giroux, 1963), p. 6.

11. Colette, *Break of Day*, trans. Enid McLeod (New York: Farrar, Straus and Giroux, 2001), p. 16.

12. Colette's first book about her mother is called *Sido ou les points cardinaux* (Sido, or The Cardinal Points) (Paris: Krâ, 1929).

10. The Sobbing Girl; or, On Hysterical Time

1. André Green, "Passions and Their Vicissitudes: On the Relations Between Madness and Psychosis," in *On Private Madness* (London: Hogarth, 1986).

2. Widlöcher discusses this in detail in "Hystérie, maladie de la mémoire."

3. Perturbation is the sudden inability to recall important personal memories, too marked to be explained by "bad memory" alone. See *The Diagnostic and Statistical Manual of Mental Disorders*, 3d ed. (Arlington, VA: American Psychiatric Association, 1987).

4. "Countertransference: A Revived Hysteria" in Julia Kristeva, *New Maladies of the Soul*, trans. Ross Guberman (New York: Columbia University Press, 1997); "The Scandal of the Timeless," a paper given at the Société psychanalytique de Paris (SPP) in Deauville, November 1994, and published in *Intimate Revolt*, trans. Jeanine Herman (New York: Columbia University Press, 2002); and "On the Extraneousness of the Phallus; or, the Feminine Between Illusion and Disillusion," a lecture at a colloquium on psychic bisexuality at the Toulouse chapter of the SPP in March 1995, and published in *The Sense and Non-sense of Revolt*, trans. Jeanine Herman (New York: Columbia University Press, 2000).

5. Cf. Widlöcher, "Hystérie, maladie de la mémoire."

6. Putnam, "The Psychophysiologic Investigation."

7. Breuer and Freud, *Studies on Hysteria*.

8. The unconscious, from *The Interpretation of Dreams* (1900) to *Metapsychology* ("The Unconscious," 1915), as well as the id (*New Introductory Lectures on Psychoanalysis*, 1932) enjoy a *zeitlos* (timeless) temporality, "outside time": the time of the drive that is manifested first as the *pleasure principle* targeting the realization of desires (notably in dreams, cf. *Interpretation of Dreams*); then, more explicitly, the *zeitlos* persists in *repetition* (repetition compulsion); finally, the favored mode of the *archaic*, the indestructible and the immortal prove to be "the most drive-related of drives," the death drive.

9. Cf. Julia Kristeva, "The Semiotic and the Symbolic," in *Revolution in Poetic Language*, trans. Margaret Waller (New York: Columbia University Press, 1984).

10. Cf. Charcot, *L'Hystérie* (emphasis mine).

11. Cf. Julia Kristeva, "On the Extraneousness of the Phallus," in *The Sense and Non-sense of Revolt*.

12. Cf. Luquet-Parat, "L'Organisation oedipienne"; Barande, *Le Maternel singulier*; Florence Begoin-Guignard, "À l'aube du maternel et du féminin," *Revue française de psychanalyse* 51, no. 6 (1987), and "Pulsions sadiques et pulsions épistémologiques," in *La Curiosité en psychanalyse,* ed. H. Sztulman and J. Fénolon (Toulouse: Privat, 1981).

13. Cf. Henri Bergson, *Matter and Memory*, trans. N. M. Paul and W. S. Palmer (New York: Zone, 1998 [1896]); *Creative Evolution*, trans. Arthur Mitchell (New York: Henry Holt, 1911 [1907]).

14. Green, "Passions and their Vicissitudes."

15. Cf. Melanie Klein, "The Effects of Early Anxiety-Situations on the Sexual Development of the Girl," in *The Psychoanalysis of Children*.

16. Charcot, "Leçon du mardi 17 janvier 1888," in *L'Hystérie*.

17. Cf. Breuer and Freud, *Studies on Hysteria*.

18. Freud, *Cinq Psychoanalyses*.

19. Freud, "Analysis Terminable and Interminable."

20. Winnicott, *Playing and Reality*.

21. Cf. André Green, "Passions and their Vicissitudes."

22. Cf. Donnet, *Surmoi*, vol. 1: *Le Concept freudien*.

23. Cf. Parat, "A propos de la coexcitation libidinale"; Troisier, "La 'position féminine' chez la femme."

24. "The genital appartatus remains the neighbor of the cloaca, and actually to quote Lou Andreas-Salomé, 'in the case of women is only taken from it on lease.'" Freud, *Three Essays*, p. 53.

25. Cf. Julia Kristeva, "The Semiotic and the Symbolic," in *Revolution in Poetic Language*.

26. Cf. Troisier, "La 'position féminine,'" pp. 1581–1583.

27. Cf. Julia Kristeva, "The Obsessional Neurotic and His Mother," in *New Maladies of the Soul*. Cf. also Sigmund Freud, "Notes Upon a Case of Obsessional Neurosis" (1909), in the Standard Edition, 10:151–318.

28. Cf. Freud and Jung, *The Freud/Jung Letters: The Correspondence Between Sigmund Freud and C. G. Jung*, trans. Ralph Manheim and R. F. C. Hull (Princeton: Princeton University Press, 1974).

29. Brusset mentions, before hallucination and acting, a "brute reality, out of reach" or an "indeterminate determination" (A. Green) whose status would be "ontological, a legacy in Freud of Schopenhauer's conception of Nature as will," in "Métapsychologie."

30. Cf. Sigmund Freud, Letter of March 10, 1898, in J. M. Masson, ed., *The Complete Letters of Sigmund Freud to Wilhelm Fliess, 1887–1904* (Cambridge: Harvard University Press, 1985).

11. Healing, a Psychical Rebirth

1. Julia Kristeva, *New Maladies of the Soul*, trans. Ross Guberman (New York: Columbia University Press, 1997), pp. 9–20.
2. From *An Outline of a Scientific Psychology* (1895) to *The Interpretation of Dreams* (1900) and *Papers on Metapsychology* (1917), this "psychical apparatus" takes the form of two well-known topics (conscious, preconscious, unconscious; superego, ego, id) and continues to refine its structures in successors to the father of psychoanalysis.

12. From Object Love to Objectless Love

1. See Julia Kristeva, *Powers of Horror: An Essay on Abjection*, trans. Leon Roudiez (New York: Columbia University Press, 1982).
2. Julia Kristeva, *Tales of Love*, trans. Leon Roudiez (New York: Columbia University Press, 1987).
3. St. Teresa of Avila, *Oeuvres*, 1:754. St. Teresa of Avila, *The Way of Perfection*, trans. The Benedictines of Stanbrook (London: Thomas Baker, 1919), pp. 88–89.
4. Ibid., p. 89.
5. Julia Kristeva, *Colette,* trans. Jane Marie Todd (New York: Columbia University Press, 2004).
6. Bertrand de Jouvenel, "La vérité sur Chéri," in Colette, *Oeuvres* (1986), 2:lv.
7. Colette, *The Vagabond*, trans. Enid McLeod (New York: Farrar, Straus Giroux, 2001), p. 74.

13. Desire for Law

1. Freud, *The Interpretation of Dreams* (1900).
2. See chapter 3, "Liberty, Equality, Fraternity and . . . Vulnerability," this volume.
3. Milgram, *Obedience to Authority.*

14. Language, Sublimation, Women

1. Cf. Green, *Le Discours vivant,* translated as *The Fabric of Affect.*
2. Freud, "The Ego and the Id," p. 26; cf. Julia Kristeva, *Tales of Love,* trans. Leon S. Roudiez (New York: Columbia University Press, 1987), p. 45.
3. Jesus to Mary in John 2:4—Trans.
4. Cf. André Green, "The Dead Mother," in *Life Narcissism, Death Narcissism,* and "maternal madness" in *On Private Madness.*

15. Hatred and Forgiveness, or, From Abjection to Paranoia

1. Cf. Julia Kristeva, *Powers of Horror: An Essay on Abjection*, trans. Leon S. Roudiez (New York: Columbia University Press, 1982).
2. Sigmund Freud, *Psycho-analytic Notes on an Autobiographical Account of a Case of Paranoia (Dementia Paranoides)* (1911), part I: *Case History of Schreber. The Standard Edition of the Complete Psychological Works of Sigmund Freud.* Vol. 12. Trans. James Strachey and Anna Freud, with Alix Strachey and Alan Tyson. 24 vols. London: Hogarth, 1953–1974.
3. "Letter to Sandor Ferenczi, October 6, 1910" in Freud and Ferenczi, *Correspondance*, p. 231.
4. Cf. Saint Thomas Aquinas, Question 21, "The Justice and Mercy of God," in *Summa Theologica*, part I.
5. Pascal, *Pensées*, 509–524, in *Oeuvres completes*, 1:763.
6. Cf. Julia Kristeva, *New Maladies of the Soul*, trans. Ross Guberman (New York: Columbia University Press, 1995).

16. *Three Essays*

1. Preface to the fourth edition of 1920.
2. Janine Chasseguet-Smirgel, Joyce McDougall.
3. *Star Academy* is a kind of French *American Idol*—TRANS.
4. Freud, *Three Essays*, p. 27.
5. Catherine Millet is the author of *The Sexual Life of Catherine M.*, a frank account of her sex life that was scandalous to some because she is also the editor of a well-known art magazine; Michel Houellbecq (*The Elementary Particles*) is a writer of fairly grim novels with louche characters—TRANS.
6. Keep in mind that Freud's polymorphous pervert was a seeker endowed with *Wiss oder Forschertrieb* ("the drive to know or seek").
7. Freud, *Three Essays*, p. 31.
8. Ibid., p. 32 (emphasis mine).
9. Freud, *Three Essays*, p. 28.
10. See "Depression, Perversion, Sublimation" in Julia Kristeva, *Colette*, trans. Jane Marie Todd (New York: Columbia University Press, 2004).
11. Freud, *Three Essays*, p. 16.
12. Sigmund Freud, *Leonardo da Vinci and a Memory of His Childhood*, trans. Alan Tyson (New York: Norton, 1964), p. 67.
13. Page 66, in the Gallimard edition translated by Philippe Koeppel. It also appears in "Fragment of an Analysis of a Case of Hysteria" (1905), which was published after *Three Essays* but conceived earlier (1901).
14. Freud, *Three Essays*, p. 27.
15. Ibid., p. 44.

16. Sigmund Freud, *The Ego and the Id* (1923), trans. Joan Riviere (New York: Norton, 1962), p. 26.

17. Ibid., p. 37.

18. Sigmund Freud, "On the Grounds for Detaching a Particular Syndrome from Neurasthenia Under the Description 'Anxiety Neurosis'" (1895), in *Standard Edition* 3:87.

19. See McDougall, *The Many Faces of Eros*.

20. Cf. Julia Kristeva, "From Symbol to Flesh: The Polymorphous Destiny of Narration," trans. P. Barkay, *International Journal of Psycho-analysis* 81, no. 4 (August 2000).

21. Cf. Meltzer and Williams, *The Apprehension of Beauty*.

22. Cf. Lacan, *Le Triomphe de la religion*.

17. Atheism

1. He defines atheism as "a cruel and long-range affair." Sartre, *The Words*, p. 247. On Sartre's atheism, see also Julia Kristeva, *In the Beginning Was Love: Psychoanalysis and Faith*, trans. Arthur Goldhammer (New York: Columbia University Press, 1987).

2. Cf. Julia Kristeva, *Powers of Horror*, trans. Leon S. Roudiez (New York: Columbia University Press, 1982).

3. Cf. Julia Kristeva, *Tales of Love*, trans. Leon S. Roudiez (New York: Columbia University Press, 1987).

4. Freud, *The Ego and the Id*, p. 32.

5. Kristeva, *In the Beginning Was Love*.

19. What Is Left of Our Loves?

1. Origin of the text: preface for the Hebrew translation of Julia Kristeva's *In the Beginning Was Love: Psychoanalysis and Faith*, published by Restling Publishing, with an introduction by Dina Haruvi, in a translation by Amos Squeverer. See *In the Beginning Was Love: Psychoanalysis and Faith*, trans. Arthur Goldhammer (New York: Columbia University Press, 1988).

2. Cf. Julia Kristeva, *Colette*, trans. Jane Marie Todd (New York: Columbia University Press, 2004).

20. The Inevitable Form

1. Cf. "Hands Over Grapes," in Sarah Greenough, *Alfred Stieglitz: The Key Set*, vol. 1: *1886–1922* (New York: Abrams, 2002).

2. In Julia Kristeva, Jack Cowart, and Juan Hamilton, *Georgia O'Keeffe*, with letters selected and annotated by Sarah Greenough, trans. Martine Laroche (Paris: Adam Biro, 1989), p. 203.

Originally published in English as *Georgia O'Keeffe, Art and Letters* by the National Gallery of Art, Washington, 1987.—TRANS.

3. *Georgia O'Keeffe*, letter 29, 1923, p. 174.

4. Ibid., letter 90, 1945, p. 241.

5. Ibid., Jean Toomer, note to letter 68, p. 285.

6. Ibid., letter 6 to Anita Pollitzer, 1916, p. 148.

7. Kristeva, Cowart, Hamilton, *Georgia O'Keeffe*. References to the paintings, numbered by plate, correspond to the French edition of this work except for those reproduced here and referenced as such.

21. A Stranger

1. Cf. "The Malady of Grief: Duras" in Julia Kristeva, *Black Sun: Depression and Melancholia*, trans. Leon S. Roudiez (New York: Columbia University Press, 1989), pp. 219–259.

2. Duras, *The Lover*, p. 66.

3. Julia Kristeva, *The Old Man and the Wolves*, trans. Barbara Bray (New York: Columbia University Press, 1994); published in France in 1991. See the interview in *L'infini*, no. 37 (Spring 1992).

4. Duras, *The Vice-Consul*, p. 61.

5. Ibid., p. 158.

6. Ibid., p. 160.

7. Duras, *The Ravishing of Lol Stein*, p. 14.

8. Duras, *The Lover*, pp. 83–84 (emphasis mine).

9. Ibid., p. 21.

10. Ibid., p. 23.

11. Duras, *The Malady of Death*, p. 46.

12. Duras, *Destroy, She Said*, p. 27.

13. Ibid., p. 85.

14. Ibid.

15. Duras, *The Lover*, p. 84.

22. Writing as Strangeness and Jouissance

1. Silesius: "The rose is without why; it blossoms because it blossoms"—TRANS.

2. Barthes, *La Chambre claire*; Colette, *La Chambre éclairée* (Paris: Édouard Joseph, 1920). *La Chambre claire* was translated into English as *Camera Lucida*.—TRANS.

3. Roland Barthes, "L'étrangère," in *La Quinzaine littéraire*, June 1, 1970; cf. Barthes, *Oeuvres complètes*, 3:477–480.

4. Barthes, *Roland Barthes by Roland Barthes*, p. 86.

5. Barthes, "L'étrangère," p. 479.

6. Barthes, *The Pleasure of the Text* , p. 4.

Jouissance is translated here as "bliss."—TRANS.

7. Roland Barthes, "L'idée comme jouissance—Idea as delight" in *Roland Barthes by Roland Barthes*, p. 103.

Jouissance is translated here as "delight."—TRANS.

8. Ibid.

23. The "True-Lie," Our Unassailable Contemporary

1. Daniel Bougnoux, adviser to the conference organized at the BPI (Bibliothèque Publique d'information) in Paris, edited Aragon's complete works for the Bibliothèque de la Pléiade.

2. *Mentir-vrai* = Aragon's neologism for lying, fabrication, fiction. It is also the title of a collection of writings.—TRANS.

3. Aragon, *La Défense de l'infini, La Défense de l'infini: Romans, Blanche ou l'oubli.*

4. Aragon, "La Valse des adieux" (emphasis mine).

5. Aragon, *En étrange pays* (1942), in *La Diane française*, p. 135.

6. Andrieux, *Souvenirs d'un préfet de police*, edited by Jean-Paul Morel, who selected writings by the astonishing Louis Andrieux from two earlier volumes originally published in 1885.

7. *Jules* is slang for boyfriend, lover, or pimp and a metaphor for aggressive or stereotypically masculine behavior.

8. "Révélations sensationnelles," *Littérature,* no. 13, p. 22, reprinted in *Littérature, March 1919–August 1921* (Paris: Jean-Michel Place, 1978).

Louis Aragon, *The Adventures of Telemachus*, trans. R. R. Hubert and J. D. Hubert (Boston: Exact Change, 1987), p. 80—TRANS.

9. Cf. Aragon, "Lautréamont et nous."

10. Lecture given by Breton in Atenea, Barcelona, 1922.

Breton's lecture was reprinted in *Les Pas perdus* (The Lost Steps).—TRANS.

11. Preface to *Le Libertinage* (Paris: Gallimard, 1964), p. 13.

12. Aragon, *Treatise on Style*, p. 105.

13. Aragon, *La Défense de l'infini*, p. 55.

14. Louis Aragon, *Irene's Cunt*, trans. Alexis Lykiard (London: Creation, 1996), pp. 65–66.

15. Aragon, *Blanche ou l'oubli*, p. 133.

16. Ibid. p. 250.

17. Ibid. p. 474.

18. Ibid. p. 479. See also Julia Kristeva, *Intimate Revolt*, trans. Jeanine Herman (New York: Columbia University Press, 2002), p. 218.

19. Deleuze and Guattari, *L'Anti-Oedipe*; Gilles Deleuze and Félix Guattari, *Anti-Oedipus*, trans. Robert Hurley, Mark Seem, and Helen R. Lane (New York: Viking, 1977).

24. Murder in Byzantium

1. "Disposable publishing" refers to *poubellications* = publications that are rapidly con-sumed and end up in the *poubelle* (trash)—Trans.

2. In 2004 a girl in France claimed she was the victim of an anti-Semitic attack by six African and North African men on the RER (the rapid transit rail system). An-dré Techiné made a movie about it called *La Fille du RER* (*The Girl on the Train*) in 2009.—Trans.

3. Julia Kristeva, *Le Texte du roman* (The Hague: Mouton, 1970).

4. Lévy, "Bloc-notes."

5. Heidegger's *Holzwege*, published in English as *Off the Beaten Track* and in French as *Chemins qui mènent nulle part.*—Trans.

6. Julia Kristeva, *Colette*, trans. Jane Marie Todd (New York: Columbia, 2004), p. 194.

7. Delacroix = of the cross.—Trans.

8. Colette, *Break of Day*, trans. Enid McLeod (New York: Farrar, Straus and Giroux, 2002), p. 110.

9. Sigmund Freud and Lou Andréas-Salomé, *Letters* (New York: Norton, 1985), p. 45.

10. Samuel Beckett, *Nohow On: Three Novels by Samuel Beckett* (New York: Grove, 1980, 1981, 1983) p. 44.

NOTES ON THE ORIGINS OF THE TEXTS

"Secularism: 'Values' at the Limits of Life": talk presented before the Senate in June 2003, in the context of an "open door" conference on the theme of "Islams, Occidents: du monde ancien au monde de demain" (Islams, Occidents: from the ancient world to the world of tomorrow) for the first *Journée du livre d'histoire*, co-organized by the president of the Senate, the association Lire la politique (Reading Politics), and the City Hall of Paris.

"Liberty, Equality, Fraternity and . . . Vulnerability": a different version of this text was published in the review *Études*, no. 402–5 (May 2005). It borrows partially from the article "Avec le handicap: aux frontières du vivant," written in Chicago and first published in *Le Magazine littéraire*, October 2003.

"On Parity, Again, or, Women and the Sacred": first published in *Le Monde*, March 23, 1999; reprinted in *L'Infini*, no. 67 (Autumn 1999).

"From Madonnas to Nudes: A Representation of Female Beauty": prepared for a conference held in November 1999 at the Sorbonne on the topic of the current state of Christianity ("2000 ans après quoi?"). Published in *L'Infini*, no. 70 (Summer 2000), and reprinted in the conference proceedings, Cyrille Michon. ed., *Le Christianisme, héritages et destins* (Paris: Le Livre de Poche 2002).

"The Passion According to Motherhood": presented at the conference "La vie amoureuse," November 25 and 26, 2000, at La Maison de la Chimie, organized by the

Société psychanalytique de Paris (SPP). First published in Jean Cournut, Marie-Claire Durieux, and Michèle Emmanuelli, eds., *La Vie amoureuse* (Paris: PUF, 2001).

"The War of the Sexes Since Antiquity": preface written for François Charpin's *Le Féminin exclu: Essai sur le désir des hommes et des femmes dans la littérature grecque et latine*, (Paris: Librairie Calepinus/M. de Maule, 2001).

"Beauvoir, Presently": delivered at the conference "De Beauvoir à Sartre et de Sartre à Beauvoir," organized by the International Simone de Beauvoir Society (SDB) and Groupe d'études sartriennes at the Sorbonne, June 21, 2003. Published in 2004 in *Simone de Beauvoir Studies* 20 (2003–2004).

"Fatigue in the Feminine": talk presented at the conference "Vivre fatigué," January 17, 2004, at La Maison de la Chimie, organized by Presses universitaires de France and *Revue française de psychosomatique*. First published in the conference proceedings, *Vivre fatigué* (Paris: PUF, 2004).

"The Sobbing Girl; or, On Hysterical Time": talk presented at the Société psychanalytique de Paris (SPP), September 1995. A slightly altered written version appeared in *L'Infini*, no. 54 (Spring 1996).

"Healing, a Psychical Rebirth": presented at an international conference on cancer treatment, which gathered intellectuals, including Miguel Benasayag, Marie-José Imbault-Huart, David Khayat, Jean-Paul Moatti, and Antoine Spire, in a volume edited by Samy Abtrou, *Guérir* (Paris: Le Bord de l'eau, 2002).

"From Object Love to Objectless Love": presented at the conference "L'objet, des sciences aux arts"/"L'oggetto, tra le scienze e le arti" (The Object, from the Sciences to the Arts) in December 2003, organized by the Institut de la pensée contemporaine, Martin Rueff and Paolo Fabbri, conferencedirectors.

"Desire for Law": presented at the conference "Vive la loi," May 25, 2004, organized on the initiative of the Senate, presided over by Christian Poncelet, president of the Senate, in collaboration with the Centre d'études constitutionnelles et politiques of Université de Paris II. Published in the conference proceedings: *Vive la loi* (Paris: Éditions du Sénat and Université de Paris II, 2004).

"Language, Sublimation, Women": text presented in homage to the psychoanalyst André Green at the Centre culturel international in Cerisy, "Enjeux pour une psychanalyse contemporaine," September 11–15, 2004.

"Hatred and Forgiveness; or, From Abjection to Paranoia": presented at the conference "Haine de soi, haine de l'autre, haine dans la culture," organized by the Société psychanalytique de Paris (SPP), November 27–28, 2004, at La Maison de la Chimie. Published in *La Haine: Haine de soi, haine de l'autre, haine dans la culture* (Paris: PUF, 2005).

"*Three Essays*, or the Victory of Polymorphous Perversion": delivered at the national congress organized to mark the hundred-year anniversary of Sigmund Freud's *Three Essays on the Theory of Sexuality*, held in Paris on January 28 and 29, 2005, at l'espace

Pierre-Cardin, coordinated by Fabien Joly, presided over and copresented by René Roussillon.

"Atheism": first published in *Le Trait, revue de littérature* (Autumn 1999). Based on reflections started in *L'avenir d'une révolte* (The Future of Revolt), published in Paris in 1998 and translated into English as *Intimate Revolt*, part 2, trans. Jeanine Herman (New York: Columbia University Press, 2002).

"The Triple Uprooting of Israel": written for *La Bible, 2000 ans de lecture*, an anthology edited by Jean-Claude Eslin, Catherine Cornu, and Marc Leboucher (Paris: Desclée de Brouwer, 2003). Reprinted in *L'Infini*, no. 87 (Summer 2004).

"What Is Left of Our Loves?" preface for the translation into Hebrew of Julia Kristeva's *In the Beginning Was Love: Psychoanalysis and Faith*, published by Restling Publishing, with an introduction by Dina Haruvi, in a translation by Amos Squeverer.

"The Inevitable Form": published in a catalogue devoted to Georgia O'Keeffe in 1989: Julia Kristeva, Jack Cowart, and Juan Hamilton, *Georgia O'Keeffe*, with letters selected and annotated by Sarah Greenough, trans. Martine Laroche (Paris: Adam Biro, 1989). The catalogue was originally published in English as *Georgia O'Keeffe, Art and Letters* (Washington, DC: National Gallery of Art, 1987).

"A Stranger": published in a special issue of *NRF* devoted to Marguerite Duras (*La Nouvelle Revue française*), no. 542 (March 1998).

"On Writing as Strangeness and Jouissance": published in the exhibition catalogue "Roland Barthes" (November 27, 2002–March 10, 20003), coproduced by the Centre Pompidou and IMEC, Marianne Alphant and Nathalie Léger, eds., *R/B, Roland Barthes* (Paris: Centre Pompidou/Seuil, 2002).

"The 'True-Lie,' Our Unassailable Contemporary": a contribution to the conference "Aragon, la parole et l'énigme," held June 11–12, 2004, organized by the Bibliothèque publique d'information de Paris, based on *The Sense and Non-sense of Revolt* (Columbia), *Intimate Revolt* (Columbia), and a program broadcast on France Culture (Les Matins de France Culture) on June 26, 2002, published in Julia Kristeva, *Chronique du temps sensible* (Paris: de l'Aube, 2003).

On the topic of Aragon, see also Julia Kristeva, "Irène, Blanche ou l'oubli," pp. 11–30, in Carine Trevisan, ed., "Aragon: Le souci de soi," *Textuel*, no. 35 (1999); and "Aragon, *Blanche ou l'oubli* ou la quête bouffonne et farouche d'une conscience," in *Le Siècle d'Aragon* (Paris: Éd. Conseil général de la Seine-Saint-Denis, 1997). Published in English as "Aragon: *Blanche ou l'oubli*; or, "The Farcical and Ferocious Quest for a Consciousness" in Kristeva, *Intimate Revolt*.

"*Murder in Byzantium*, or Why I 'ship myself on a voyage' in a novel": interview conducted by Pierre Louis-Fort on the publication of *Meurtre à Byzance* (*Murder in Byzantium*) in Paris by Fayard in 2004. The first part of this interview was published in *L'Infini*, no. 91 (Summer 2005). The second part was published in issue no. 92 (Autumn 2005).

BIBLIOGRAPHY

All works published in Paris unless otherwise noted.

Albaret, Céleste. *Monsieur Proust.* Laffont, 1973.

Ameisen, Jean-Claude. *La Sculpture du vivant.* Seuil, 1999.

Andrieux, Louis. *Souvenirs d'un préfet de police.* Ed. Jean-Paul Morel. Mémoire du livre, 2002 [1885].

Aquinas, Saint Thomas. *Theological Summa.*

Aragon, Louis. *Le Paysan de Paris.* Gallimard, 1926.

—— *Le Traité du style.* Gallimard, 1928. *Treatise on Style.* Trans. Alyson Waters. Lincoln: University of Nebraska Press, 1991.

——"Madame Colette." In *Les Lettres françaises,* August 12–19, 1954.

—— *Blanche ou l'oubli.* Gallimard, 1967.

——"Lautréamont et nous." In *Les Lettres françaises,* no. 1185–1186, June 1967.

——*Je n'ai jamais appris à écrire,* ou *Les Incipit.* Geneva: Skira, 1969.

——"La Valse des adieux." In *Les Lettres françaises,* October 11, 1972.

—— *La Diane française,* suivi de *En étrange pays dans mon pays lui-même.* Seghers, 1975.

—— *Le Mentir-vrai.* Gallimard, 1980 [1964].

—— *La Défense de l'infini (fragments).* Ed. Édouard Ruiz. Gallimard, 1986.

—— *La Défense de l'infini: Romans.* Ed. Lionel Follet. Gallimard, 1997.

Arendt, Hannah. *Essays in Understanding: 1930–1954*. New York: Harcourt Brace, 1993.

—— "The Crisis in Culture." In *Between Past and Future*. New York: Penguin, 1993.

—— "The Jew as Pariah: A Hidden Tradition." In *Reflections on Literature and Culture*. Stanford: Stanford University Press, 2007.

Aulagnier, Piera. *La Violence de l'interprétation: du pictogramme à l'énoncé*. PUF, 1975.

Avila, St. Theresa of. *Oeuvres*. Trans. Mère Marie du Saint-Sacrement. 2 vols. Cerf, 1995.

Barande, Ilse. *Le Maternel singulier*. Aubier-Montaigne, 1977.

Barthes, Roland. *The Pleasure of the Text*. Trans. Richard Miller. New York: Farrar, Straus and Giroux, 1975.

—— *La Chambre claire*. Paris: Gallimard, 1980.

—— *Roland Barthes by Roland Barthes*. Trans. Richard Howard. Berkeley: University of California, 1994.

—— *Oeuvres complètes*. Ed. Éric Marty. 5 vols. Seuil, 2002.

Beauvoir, Simone de. *L'Invitée*. 1943.

—— *Le Deuxième Sexe*. 2 vols. Gallimard, 1986 [1949].

Bergson, Henri. *L'Évolution créatrice*. PUF, 2003.

—— *Matière et mémoire*. PUF, 2004 [1896].

Besançon, Alain. "La relation à Dieu dans le christianisme russe: Essai d'interprétation." *Cahiers du monde russe et soviétique* 7, no. 2 (1966).

Blanchard, Sandrine. "Julia Kristeva, intellectuelle de proximité." *Le Monde*, May 20, 2005.

Breuer, Josef, and Sigmund Freud. *Studies on Hysteria* (1895). Ed. and trans. James Strachey. Vol. 3. *The Standard Edition of the Complete Psychological Works of Sigmund Freud*. 22 vols. London: Hogarth and the Institute of Psychoanalysis, 1962.

Brusset, Bernard. "Métapsychologie des processus et psychologie." *Revue française de psychanalyse* 59 (March 1996): 1523–1528.

Céline, Louis-Ferdinand. *Voyage au bout de la nuit*. Denoël and Steele, 1932.

—— *Le Pont de Londres*. Gallimard, 1964.

Charcot, Jean Martin. *L'Hystérie*. Toulouse: Privat, 1971.

Charpin, François. *Le Féminin exclu: Essai sur le désir des hommes et des femmes*. Librairie Calepinus/Michel de Maule, 2001.

Chasseguet-Smirgel, Janine. *L'Idéal du Moi: Essai psychanalytique sur la maladie d'idéalité*. Tchou, 1975.

Chekhov, Anton. *En chemin*. Na puti, 1886.

Clément, Olivier. *L'Église orthodoxe*. 5th ed. PUF, 1995.

Colette, *Oeuvres complètes*. Vols. 1–4. Gallimard, 1984, 1986, 1991, 2001.

Deleuze, Gilles. *Proust et signes*. PUF, 1964.

Deleuze, Gilles, and Félix Guattari. *L'Anti-Oedipe*. Minuit, 1973.

Désert, Myriam, and Denis Paillard. "Les Eurasiens revisités." *Revue des études slaves* 56, no. 1 (1994).

Donnet, Jean-Luc. *Surmoi*, vol. 1: *Le Concept freudien et la règle fondamentale*. PUF, 1995.

Dostoyevsky, Fyodor. *A Writer's Diary, Dnevnik pisatelja* (1873). In *Complete Works*. Leningrad: Nauka, 1980.

—— *The Possessed*. 1872.

Duras, Marguerite. *Le Ravissement de Lol V. Stein*. Gallimard, 1964. *The Ravishing of Lol Stein*. Trans. Richard Seaver. New York: Pantheon, 1986.

—— *The Vice-Consul*. Trans. Eileen Ellenbogen. New York: Pantheon, 1968.

—— *Détruire, dit-elle*. Minuit, 1969. *Destroy, She Said*. Trans. Barbara Bray. New York: Random House, 1986.

—— *La Maladie de la mort*. Minuit, 1982. *The Malady of Death*. Trans. Barbara Bray. New York: Grove, 1994.

—— *L'Amant*. Minuit, 1984. *The Lover*. Trans. Barbara Bray. New York: Knopf, 1998.

Fleury, Danièle. "Simone de Beauvoir: De *L'Invitée* au *Sang des autres*, l'éveil à la solidarité." Ph.D. thesis, University of Paris 7—Denis Diderot, June 2004.

Freud, Sigmund. "On the Grounds for Detaching a Particular Syndrome from Neurasthenia Under the Description 'Anxiety Neurosis'" (1895).

—— *The Origins of Psycho-analysis: Letters to William Fliess, Drafts and Notes* (1887–1902).

—— *The Interpretation of Dreams* (1900).

—— *Cinq Psychoanalyses* (1905). Trans. M. Bonaparte and R. M. Loewenstein. PUF, 1954.

—— *Three Essays on the Theory of Sexuality* (1905). Trans. James Strachey. New York: Basic Books, 1962.

—— Notes Upon a Case of Obsessional Neurosis (1909).

—— "The Antithetical Sense of Primal Words" (1910).

—— *Leonardo da Vinci and a Memory of His Childhood* (1910).

—— "Metapsychology" (1917). Trans. Jean Laplanche and Jean-Bertrand Pontalis. Gallimard, 1968.

—— "A Phylogenetic Fantasy: Overview of Transference Neuroses" (1915).

—— *The Ego and the Id* (1923). New York: Norton, 1990.

—— "Group Psychology and the Analysis of the Ego" (1921).

—— "Negation" (1925).

—— *Civilization and Its Discontents* (1930).

—— "Female Sexuality" (1931).

—— *New Introductory Lectures on Psychoanalysis* (1933).

—— "Analysis Terminable and Interminable" (1937).

—— "Appendix C, Words and Things." In *Papers on Metapsychology* (1914–1916).

Freud, Sigmund, and Carl Jung. *Correspondance*. Gallimard, 1975.

Freud, Sigmund, and Sandor Ferenczi. *Correspondance 1908–1914*. Calmann-Lévy, 1992.

Green, André. *Le Discours vivant*, PUF. 1973. *The Fabric of Affect in the Psychoanalytic Discourse*. Trans. Alan Sheridan. London: Routledge, 1999.

—— *Narcissisme de vie et narcissisme de mort*. Minuit, 1983. *Life Narcissism, Death Narcissism*. Trans. Andrew Weller. London: Free Association, 2001.

———— *On Private Madness.* London: Hogarth, 1986.

———— *La Folie privée.* Gallimard, 1990.

———— "Cognitivisme, neurosciences, psychanalyse: Un dialogue difficile." In Catherine Couvreur, Agnès Oppenheimer, and Roger Perron, eds., *Psychanalyse, neurosciences, cognitivisme.* PUF, 1997.

Grosrichard, Alain. *Structure du sérail: La fiction du despotisme asiatique dans l'Occident classique.* Seuil, 1979. *The Sultan's Court: European Fantasies of the East.* Trans. Liz Heron. London: Verso, 1998.

Habermas, Jürgen, and Joseph Ratzinger. "Les fondements prépolitiques de l'État démocratique." *Esprit,* July 2004.

Hegel, Georg Wilhelm Friedrich. *La Phénoménologie de l'esprit.* Vol. 2. Trans. Jean Hyppolite. Aubier-Montaigne, 1941.

———— *Aesthetics: Lectures on Fine Art.* Trans. T. M. Knox. Oxford: Oxford University Press, 1998.

Heidegger, Martin. *Questions I.* Gallimard, 1968.

———— *Essais et conférences.* Gallimard, 1980.

———— *De l'essence de la liberté humaine.* Gallimard, 1987.

———— "Lettre sur l'humanisme." In *Questions III et IV.* Gallimard, 1990.

———— *Séjours (Aufenthalte).* Monaco: Rocher, 1992.

Huntington, Samuel P. "Religion and the Third Wave." *National Interest,* no. 24 (Summer 1991): 29–42.

Joseph, Gilbert. *Une si douce Occupation: Simone de Beauvoir et Jean-Paul Sartre, 1940–1941.* Albin Michel, 1991.

Joyce, James. *Ulysses.* 1922.

———— *Finnegans Wake.* 1939.

Kant, Immanuel. *Critique of Pure Reason.* 1781.

———— *Perpetual Peace.* 1795.

Klein, Melanie. *The Psychoanalysis of Children.* Trans. Alix Strachey. London: Hogarth, 1932.

———— *Contributions to Psychoanalysis, 1921–1945.* London: Hogarth, 1948.

Lacan, Jacques. *Le Triomphe de la religion.* Preceded by "Discours aux catholiques." Seuil, 2005.

Lévinas, Emmanuel. *Ethics and Infinity: Conversations with Philippe Nemo.* Trans. R. A. Cohen. Pittsburgh: Duquesne University Press, 1985.

Lévy, Bernard-Henri. "Bloc-notes: La Byzance de Julia Kristeva—Bondy et Reza—Libérez Battisti." *Le Point,* no. 1640, February 19, 2004, p. 114.

Lossky, Vladimir. *Théologie mystique de l'Église d'Orient.* Aubier-Montaigne, 1977.

McDougall, Joyce. *The Many Faces of Eros: A Psychoanalytical Exploration of Human Sexuality.* New York: Norton, 1995.

Mahéas, Christian. "Le rôle du pauvre au coeur de l'Église: L'expérience de l'Arche et le Mystère pascal." Thesis presented at the Toronto School of Theology, May 2003.

Mann, Thomas. *The Magic Mountain.* 1924.

Meltzer, Donald, and Meg Harris Williams. *The Apprehension of Beauty: The Role of Aesthetic Conflict in Development, Art, and Violence.* Worcester: Clunie, 1988.

Merleau-Ponty, Maurice. Preface to Hesnard, *L'Oeuvre de Freud et son importance dans le monde moderne.* Payot, 1960.

Milgram, Stanley. *Obedience to Authority.* New York: Harper and Row, 1974 [1963].

Moi, Toril. *The Making of an Intellectual Woman.* Cambridge: Blackwell, 1994. *Simone de Beauvoir: conflits d'une intellectuelle.* Trans. Guillemette Belleteste. Diderot, 1995.

Mondzain, Marie-José. *Image, icône, économie: Les sources byzantines de l'imaginaire contemporaine.* Seuil, 1996.

Moses, Stéphane. *L'Ange et l'histoire.* Seuil, 1992.

Nivat, Georges. "Aspects religieux de l'athée russe." In *Cahiers du monde russe et soviétique* 29, nos. 3–4 (July–December 1988).

——— *Eux et nous: L'Europe face à ses nouvelles déchirures.* Geneva: L'Âge d'Homme, 1998.

Painter, George Duncan. *Marcel Proust.* New York: Random House, 1989.

Parat, Catherine. "L'Organisation oedipienne du stade génital." XXVIIe Congrès des psychanalystes de langues romanes (1966). *Revue française de psychanalyse,* no. 31 (1967).

——— "À propos de la co-excitation libidinale." *Revue française de psychanalyse* 51, no. 3 (1987).

Pascal, Blaise. *Oeuvres complètes.* Vol. 1. Gallimard, 1998.

Proust, Marcel. *Correspondance.* Ed. Philip Kolb. 21 vols. Plon, 1976–1993.

——— *À la recherche du temps perdu.* Gallimard, 1987–1989.

Putnam, Frank W. "The Psychophysiologic Investigation of Multiple Personalities Disorder: A Review." *Psychiatric Clinics of North America* 7 (1984): 31–50.

Ricoeur, Paul. *De l'interprétation: Essai sur Freud.* Seuil, 1965.

——— *Temps et récit.* 3 vols. Seuil, 1983–1985.

Rimbaud, Arthur. *Illuminations.* 1873.

——— *A Season in Hell.* In *Complete Works.* Trans. Wallace Fowlie. Chicago: University of Chicago Press, 1966.

Rousseau, Jean-Jacques. *La Nouvelle Héloïse.* 1761.

——— *Émile.* 1762.

Sartre, Jean-Paul. *L'Être et le néant.* Gallimard, 1943.

——— *Les Mots.* Gallimard, 1963. *The Words,* trans. Bernard Frechtman. New York: Vintage, 1981.

——— *Being and Nothingness: An Essay on Phenomenological Ontology.* Trans. Hazel E. Barnes. London: Routledge, 1996.

——— *Lettres au Castor,* vol. 2. (1940–1963). Gallimard, 1983. *Quiet Moments in a War: The Letters of Jean-Paul Sartre to Simone de Beauvoir, 1940–1963.* New York: Scribner, 2002.

——— *Les Carnets de la drôle de guerre.* Gallimard, 1995.

Sollers, Philippe. "Le trou de la Vierge." Interview with Jacques Henric. *Art Press,* 1982.

—— *Femmes.* Gallimard, 1983.

—— *Théorie des exceptions.* Gallimard, 1985.

Stiker, Henri-Jacques. *Corps infirmes et sociétés.* Dunod, 1997. *A History of Disability.* Trans. William Sayers. Ann Arbor: University of Michigan Press, 2000.

Tadié, Jean-Yves. *Marcel Proust.* Gallimard, 1996.

Todorov, Tzvetan. *Théorie de la littérature.* Seuil, 1965.

Troisier, Hélène. "'La 'position féminine' chez la femme." *Revue française de psychanalyse* 57 (1993).

Victor, Barbara. *Army of Roses: Inside the World of Palestinian Women Suicide Bombers.* Emmaus, PA: Rodale, 2003.

Vincent, Jean-Didier, and Luc Ferry. *Qu'est-ce que l'homme?* Odile Jacob, 1998.

Voegelin, Eric. "The Origin of Totalitarianism." *Review of Politics* 15 (1953).

Warner, Marina. *Alone of All Her Sex: The Myth and Cult of the Virgin Mary.* London: Weidenfeld and Nicholson, 1976.

Winnicott, Donald Woods. "Birth Memories, Birth Trauma, and Anxiety" (1949). In *Collected Papers: Through Paediatrics to Psycho-analysis.* London: Hogarth, 1975.

—— "Souvenirs de la naissance, traumatisme de la naissance et angoisse" (1949). In *Psychologie* no. 3 (1988).

—— *Playing and Reality.* New York: Routledge, 2005.

Widlöcher, Daniel. "Hystérie, maladie de la mémoire." *Revue internationale de psychopathologie*, no. 5 (1995): 21–41.

INDEX

Abject, 160–61; as fragile/archaic sublimation, 187
Abjection: aversion to food as form of,
185; concept of, 12; imaginary, 13;
logic of, 186–87; paranoid hatred as
protecting objects from, 188–91; as
revolt of the being, 184
Abstraction, 256
Abu Ghraib Prison, 175
Academy of Paris, 13
Affect: language and, 177–78; as participating in drive-related introjection
dynamics, 178; primary symbolization
of, 178
Aggressiveness, 80; hatred v., 183
Ambitions: of feminism, 100; of humanity, 34
America: hatred of, 8; human liberty
and, 21

American Revolution, 51
Amnesias: hysterical, 130, 132; psycho-
genic, 130
Anality, 136–40
Analysis: dreams in, 138–39; homo-
sexual analyst in, 199; motherhood as
constructive, 88–89; psychosomatic
fatigue and, 124–25; as space of revolt,
154; *see also* Psychoanalysis
Anarchism, 10
Anger, 143
Anorexia, 161, 186
Antidepressants, 154
Antiquity, philosophers of, 52
Anxiety, 36
Aragon, Louis: background of, 260–61;
in Communist Party, 265; drama of,
271–72; essential themes of engage-
ment/work of, 259–60; feminine as

European Perspectives: A Series in Social Thought and Cultural Criticism

LAURENCE D. KRITZMAN, EDITOR